"This is a helpful introduction to theology, especially with its questions and suggestions for further study. Gregg Allison has done yeoman's labor helping us to understand why we came to the biblical convictions that we have throughout history. Here, he shows us why it is (and must be) grounded in the Scriptures."

Michael Horton, J. Gresham Machen Professor of Systematic Theology and Apologetics, Westminster Seminary California

"One of evangelicalism's finest theologians offers us this clear, handy, faithful, and insightful introduction to the major doctrines of the Christian faith. And he ably guides church leaders in organizing and teaching these truths. This is a wonderful handbook that church leaders will turn to time and time again."

Christopher W. Morgan, dean and professor of theology, School of Christian Ministries, California Baptist University

"This is a much-needed resource for the body of Christ, especially for new believers or those who have not as yet delved into the 'whole counsel of God.' Gregg Allison writes with insight on each issue and does a remarkable job of articulating multiple interpretations of each one. His presentation of the evidence and arguments for differing views is evenhanded and displays both the Christian charity and clarity that we have come to expect of everything he writes. For those who are put off by massive volumes on systematic theology, this is the book for you. And for those who want more than a surface, superficial treatment of critically important biblical and theological doctrines, this is the book for you. There is no one in whom I have more trust to write a book such as this than Gregg Allison. From this day forward, when I'm asked, What do Christians believe? How do I sort through the variety of positions? And why should I care? I will send them to Gregg's excellent volume."

Sam Storms, lead pastor for preaching and vision, Bridgeway Church

"This is a remarkably useful book for anyone who wants to teach biblically based Christian doctrine to God's people. It is refreshingly clear; it contains insightful questions that will encourage active discussion; it clearly explains and rejects the erroneous teachings that have sprung up to distort each biblical doctrine; and it continually makes application to life. Any church that works through this book will come out much stronger as a result!"

Wayne Grudem, research professor of theology
and biblical studies, Phoenix Seminary

"Systematic theologies are known as 'door stopper' texts. They both instruct the faithful and keep you from getting hit by solid wood. We need the longer books, but we also need shorter versions. Gregg Allison's new volume gives us a strong dose of sound doctrine, but in an easy-to-digest format. This is a great book for small groups, those in discipling relationships, and anyone who is tired of soft words and vague generalities. One of evangelicalism's top theologians has served Christ's body well."

Owen Strachan, associate professor of Christian theology,
Midwestern Baptist Theological Seminary;
coauthor, The Pastor as Public Theologian

50 CORE TRUTHS

—— OF THE ——

CHRISTIAN FAITH

50 CORE TRUTHS

—— OF THE ——

CHRISTIAN FAITH

A GUIDE TO UNDERSTANDING
AND TEACHING THEOLOGY

GREGG R. ALLISON

BakerBooks

a division of Baker Publishing Group
Grand Rapids, Michigan

Published by Baker Books
a division of Baker Publishing Group
PO Box 6287, Grand Rapids, MI 49516-6287
www.bakerbooks.com

Printed in the United States of America

Library of Congress Cataloging-in-Publication Data
Names: Allison, Gregg R., author.
Title: 50 core truths of the Christian faith : a guide to understanding and teaching theology / Gregg R. Allison.
Other titles: Fifty core truths of the Christian faith
Description: Grand Rapids : Baker Books, 2018. | Includes bibliographical references and index.
Identifiers: LCCN 2017035041 | ISBN 9780801019128 (pbk.)
Subjects: LCSH: Theology, Doctrinal. | Theology, Doctrinal—Study and teaching.
Classification: LCC BT77.3 .A45 2018 | DDC 230—dc23
LC record available at https://lccn.loc.gov/2017035041

18 19 20 21 22 23 24   7 6 5 4 3 2

I dedicate this book to the leadership, staff, and faculty of the Southern Baptist Theological Seminary. Through their constant encouragement to write, their valuing of publishing so their faculty can extend its influence throughout the world, and their provision of regular sabbaticals, they foster a creative environment that results in books like *50 Core Truths of the Christian Faith*.

My particular appreciation goes to the board of trustees; R. Albert Mohler, president; Randy Stinson, provost; Greg Wills and Adam Greenway, deans; Michael Wilder and Jonathan Pennington, directors of the PhD program; the administrative staff; and my faculty colleagues. We labor together to train, educate, and prepare ministers of the gospel for more faithful service to Jesus Christ our Lord and his church expanding throughout the world.

With thankfulness and profound respect, I dedicate this book to you.

CONTENTS

ix

Contents

Contents

PREFACE

In 2015 I was asked to write up a proposal for a book that would present the essential truths of Christian theology in a clear, user-friendly format. Fulfilling this request and writing the book consumed a large part of my time and energy for a year, and the result is *50 Core Truths of the Christian Faith*.

I am in my twenty-third year of teaching Christian theology, so this work flowed out of a lifetime of study and teaching experience. Currently, I am professor of Christian theology at The Southern Baptist Theological Seminary in Louisville, Kentucky. I am also a pastor of Sojourn Community Church.

This book is unique in its approach to Christian theology. Though Christian education books explain the theology, methodology, and techniques of teaching, and though Sunday School curricula provide the actual material for teaching, *50 Core Truths of the Christian Faith* is unique in that it provides guidance for how to teach each Christian doctrine. As far as I know, no book like it exists.

I explain how to teach Christian theology in the church. Specifically, the audience envisioned includes pastors who wish to preach doctrinal sermons; Sunday school teachers who are covering basic Christian doctrines in their classes; leaders of small groups who need to address doctrinal matters with group members; church members who are engaged in teaching the faith in catechism classes, leaders-in-training programs, and adult education courses; educators in Christian schools with classes on Christian doctrine; and the like.

The book is divided into fifty chapters. Each chapter begins with a concise summary of the primary content of what is believed, together with a list of the doctrine's "Main Themes." A list of "Key Scripture" is also provided, giving those biblical passages that ground the doctrine. When preaching and teaching these passages, one can refer to the doctrine and, if time permits, develop it. The first main heading is "Understanding the Doctrine," which explains the main themes as major affirmations that must be made in constructing sound doctrine. It also focuses on the biblical support for the doctrine and notes the major errors to be avoided. The teaching section also includes a list of perennial issues and problematic questions meant to alert teachers to matters that may be of pressing concern to participants; these are phrased from a participant's point of view. Each chapter also contains a teaching outline that can help structure your presentation of the material.

In addition to constructing the doctrine in the "Understanding the Doctrine" section, each chapter contains an "Enacting the Doctrine" section and a "Teaching the Doctrine" section. The application section connects the topic to daily living for both individual believers and churches. The teaching section offers guidance for communicating the doctrine to today's audiences.

To help you gain a more complete understanding of each core truth, I have included a "Resources" list in each chapter. These lists point to the relevant discussions (when applicable) in seven general books that cover the full range of topics treated in *50 Core Truths of the Christian Faith*. I selected these resources because they offer either deeper treatments of these themes, useful overviews that summarize key ideas, or broader evangelical perspectives that can complement my own. Many other resources could have been included in this list. Readers and teachers are encouraged to use their favorite theological resources—preferred authors, standard denominational works, in-depth treatments of specific subjects—as they study these doctrines or prepare to teach them. The resource lists include these seven works:

- Gregg R. Allison, *The Baker Compact Dictionary of Theological Terms* (Grand Rapids: Baker Books, 2016).
- Walter A. Elwell, ed., *Evangelical Dictionary of Theology*, 2nd ed. (Grand Rapids: Baker Academic, 2001).
- Millard J. Erickson, *Christian Theology*, 3rd ed. (Grand Rapids: Baker Academic, 2013).

- Stanley J. Grenz, *Theology for the Community of God* (Nashville: Broadman & Holman, 1994; paperback ed., Grand Rapids: Eerdmans, 2000).
- Wayne Grudem, *Systematic Theology: An Introduction to Biblical Doctrine* (Grand Rapids: Zondervan, 1994).
- Michael Horton, *Pilgrim Theology: Core Doctrines for Christian Disciples* (Grand Rapids: Zondervan, 2011).
- Erik Thoennes, *Life's Biggest Questions: What the Bible Says about the Things That Matter Most* (Wheaton: Crossway, 2011).

The format of this book arises from my conviction that doctrine is both true belief and true practice, and that it is to be confessed by the church and taught from generation to generation. Like Paul, I urge Christians to be "trained in the words of the faith and of the good doctrine that you have followed" (1 Tim. 4:6). My prayer is that this theological resource will help to form believers in sound doctrine and transform their lives for the glory of God.

ACKNOWLEDGMENTS

I am grateful to Baker Books, and especially to three people. Brian Vos is a friend and the editor who first approached me about this project. He was a great encouragement and resource as I conceptualized, designed, and wrote *50 Core Truths of the Christian Faith*. James Korsmo, whom I first met when he edited *The Baker Compact Dictionary of Theological Terms*, turned this current project into a publishable book through his meticulous editing and probing queries of my theological formulations and positions. Robert Banning, who did a yeoman's job in copyediting my massive *Historical Theology*, once again wielded his copyediting expertise to get *50 Core Truths* into good shape.

Portions of this material draw from and develop definitions in *The Baker Compact Dictionary of Theological Terms*.[1] For further study of the historical development of these fifty core truths, see my *Historical Theology: An Introduction to Christian Doctrine*.[2]

INTRODUCTION
TO CHRISTIAN DOCTRINE

In its most basic sense, Christian doctrine is Christian belief based on Scripture. Examples include that God is triune (God is three persons: Father, Son, and Holy Spirit), that Jesus is both fully God and fully man, and that salvation is by divine grace. Sound doctrine reflects in summary form what Scripture affirms and what the church is bound to believe.

Sound doctrine stands in contrast to false doctrine. Such heresy is false belief that misinterprets Scripture or overlooks some affirmations of Scripture. Examples include Unitarianism (God is only one person, not three), Arianism (Jesus is not fully God), and legalism (salvation is by human effort). The church is called to avoid heresy and correct its errors.

CHRISTIAN DOCTRINE IN ITS FOUR APPLICATIONS

Doctrine is believed. *Orthodoxy* is true belief, or sound doctrine.

Doctrine is practiced. *Orthopraxis* is right practice, or godly living.

Doctrine is confessed. *Confession* is the public profession of Christian belief.

Doctrine is taught. *Teaching* (the word "doctrine" comes from the Latin *docere*, "to teach") is the faithful transmission of Christian belief from generation to generation.

Accordingly, doctrine is believed, practiced, confessed, and taught. It is Christian belief that involves not just our head but our whole being: our mind, emotions, will, motivations, attitudes, intentions, behavior, words, and instruction.

CHRISTIAN DOCTRINE AS BELIEF AND PRACTICE

Christian doctrine as belief and practice is important for several reasons. Scripture associates sound doctrine with Christian maturity and leadership responsibilities. As for the first matter, Scripture's vision for mature believers in mature churches has this goal: "so that we may no longer be children, tossed to and fro by the waves and carried about by every wind of doctrine, by human cunning, by craftiness in deceitful schemes" (Eph. 4:14). Christian maturity aims at, and at least in part is measured by, the embrace of sound doctrine and the rejection of false doctrine.

Maturing Christians and maturing churches are characterized by good theology.

As for leadership responsibilities, Scripture describes good servants of Jesus Christ as disciples who are "trained in the words of the faith and of the good doctrine that [they] have followed" (1 Tim. 4:6). An elder/pastor/minister "must hold firm to the trustworthy word as taught, so that he may be able to give instruction in sound doctrine and also to rebuke those who contradict it" (Titus 1:9). Church leaders must embrace and live sound doctrine, as well as be able to refute those who oppose it.

Leaders of the church are characterized by good theology.

Negatively, an outsider to the Christian faith "teaches a different doctrine and does not agree with the sound words of our Lord Jesus Christ and the teaching that accords with godliness" (1 Tim. 6:3). Indeed, at the conclusion of a lengthy description of types of evil people—"the lawless and disobedient, . . . the ungodly and sinners, . . . the unholy and profane"—Paul indicates that the list could continue by adding a type of "etc.": "and whatever else is contrary to sound doctrine" (1:9–10). False doctrine, or heresy, stands opposed to sound doctrine. We are to reject the former and cling to the latter.

People outside of the faith are characterized by bad theology.

Thus, Christian doctrine as belief and practice is important.

CHRISTIAN DOCTRINE AS CONFESSION AND TEACHING

Christian doctrine as confession and teaching is important for several reasons. Several of the above biblical passages emphasize holding firmly to good theology and transmitting it. On many occasions and at many times, the church has publicly confessed what it believes. Here is a snippet of an early church creed about Jesus Christ, a confession found in the New Testament (1 Tim. 3:16):

> Great indeed, we confess, is the mystery of godliness:
>
> > He was manifested in the flesh,
> > > vindicated by the Spirit,
> > > > seen by angels,
> > > proclaimed among the nations,
> > > > believed on in the world,
> > > > > taken up in glory.

Early church creeds expressed in summary form the sound doctrine the church confessed. The Apostles' Creed, for instance, asserts, "I believe in God the Father almighty . . . and in Jesus Christ his only Son our Lord . . . [and] in the Holy Spirit."

The church publicly confesses good theology.

The church teaches sound doctrine. From its beginning, the church has the tradition of transmitting its faith—what it believes—to its new members. We sometimes refer to this as passing on a *tradition* (from the Latin *traditio*, "hand over"). Older Christians—in particular church leaders—instruct new believers in sound doctrine, which they in turn live out. Indeed, a disciple (from the Latin *discipulus*, "learner") is a student of good theology who grows in increasing conformity to the image of Jesus Christ. Without minimizing the important role that Christian schools, colleges, universities, and seminaries play in teaching theology, the church must never abdicate its position as the primary transmitter of sound doctrine.

The church transmits good theology from generation to generation.

Thus, Christian doctrine as confession and teaching is important.

CHRISTIAN DOCTRINE AS THE WISDOM OF THE AGES FOR THE CHURCH TODAY

For nearly two thousand years, the church has constructed sound theology based on Scripture. Because Scripture is the written Word of God and, as such, the ultimate authority for what the church is to believe and how it is to live, it is the foundation for good theology. Though challenged by false doctrine, and despite falling prey at times to heresy, the church has developed a theological consensus on many of its beliefs. Very broadly, and with significant disagreement on many details, these beliefs include the following:

- The inspiration, authority, truthfulness, power, and centrality of Scripture as divine revelation
- The existence, knowability, and nature/attributes of God
- The Trinity (God as Father, Son, and Holy Spirit)
- Divine creation and providence
- The reality and work of spiritual beings (angels, demons, Satan)
- The dignity of human beings as image bearers of God
- The depravity of human beings as fallen into sin (including original sin and actual sin)
- The deity and humanity of Jesus Christ (including his virgin birth)
- Jesus Christ's work of salvation (for example, incarnation, death, burial, resurrection, ascension)
- The person and work of the Holy Spirit
- The application of salvation (for example, the forgiveness of sins, regeneration, justification) as a gracious work of God appropriated by faith
- The church as the people of God, the body of Christ, the temple of the Holy Spirit
- The church as one, holy, catholic/universal, and apostolic
- Means of grace (for example, baptism and the Lord's Supper) through the church
- Personal eschatology in terms of death and the intermediate state
- Cosmic eschatology in terms of the return of Jesus Christ, the resurrection, the last judgment, and eternal punishment
- The new heaven and new earth as the ultimate hope[3]

Many factors contribute to this amazing theological consensus, not the least of which is the Word of God, upon which it is grounded, and the Spirit of God, who guides the church into sound doctrine. This heritage is a treasure of theological wisdom that helps the contemporary church construct its doctrine today.

In some churches, a popular motto is "No creed but the Bible." If this sentiment aims at underscoring the ultimate authority of Scripture, it is on target. If, however, it rejects the legacy of the above theological consensus, it cripples the church's embrace of sound theology. It is also naive, since the church has been, and continues to be, helped by factors outside of the Bible. For example, when the church affirms the doctrine of the Trinity and confesses that the Son is of "the same essence" as the Father, it is using nonbiblical terms (in these cases the Latin word *Trinitas* and the Greek word *homoousios*) to express its sound doctrine.

As the church believes, practices, confesses, and teaches sound theology, it is aided by theological wisdom from the past.

To summarize: Christian doctrine is Christian belief based on Scripture. The church bears the primary responsibility for constructing and transmitting good theology, with an essential assist from the theological wisdom of the ages. This sound doctrine is believed, practiced, confessed, and taught.

This is the vision of *50 Core Truths of the Christian Faith*.

PART 1

DOCTRINE

—— OF THE ——

WORD OF GOD

1

THE INSPIRATION
OF SCRIPTURE

SUMMARY

All Scripture is God-breathed, because the Holy Spirit super-intended the biblical authors as they composed their writings, the Word of God.

MAIN THEMES

- Scripture has God for its author.
- Scripture was also written by human authors under the direction of the Holy Spirit.
- All Scripture is God-breathed.
- Inspiration extends to the words of Scripture.
- The Spirit and the human authors wrote together.
- Various modes of inspiration were used.
- As a result of its inspiration, Scripture is authoritative and true.

KEY SCRIPTURE

Matthew 19:4–5; John 10:35; Acts 4:24–26; 1 Corinthians 2:10–12; 2 Timothy 3:16–17; 2 Peter 1:16–21

UNDERSTANDING THE DOCTRINE

Major Affirmations

As the Bible itself affirms, "All Scripture is God-breathed" (2 Tim. 3:16 NIV). The word "inspiration" has historically been used to describe this doctrine, referring to the divine guidance of the writers of Scripture through the movement of God's Spirit. But we should also think of the process as one of "expiration" (breathing out): Scripture is the product of the creative breath of God.

The Holy Spirit was particularly responsible for the Bible's inspiration: the biblical authors "spoke from God as they were carried along by the Holy Spirit" (2 Pet. 1:21). He superintended Moses, Isaiah, Luke, and the others as they composed their writings. While these authors employed their own personalities, theological perspectives, writing styles, and so forth, the Spirit ensured that what they wrote was what God wanted them to write: the Word of God, divinely authoritative and fully truthful.

At times, the church has tended to emphasize Scripture's divine authorship, even to the neglect of its human authorship. Indeed, the Holy Spirit's role in relation to the biblical authors was illustrated by a musician who strums his stringed instrument or a flautist playing her flute. At times the church embraced mechanical dictation. But the doctrine of the inspiration of Scripture affirms complete participation on the part of both its divine author—the Holy Spirit—and its human authors. Moses, Jeremiah, Matthew, Paul, and the others were fully engaged in the writing process. They consulted earlier writings, conducted interviews, selected the narratives to include, thought carefully, composed their writings, and more—all under the superintending work of the Holy Spirit.

Inspiration is *plenary*: *all* Scripture is God-breathed (2 Tim. 3:16). Inspiration is not confined to the "important" parts of Scripture, those passages that guide people to salvation or instruct about faith and obedience for pleasing God. Rather, its historical references (for example, Adam and Eve, Noah's ark, Jonah and the great fish), its affirmations about the world (for example, creation out of nothing, the sun and the moon appearing as two great lights), its genealogies, and more were inspired by the Spirit. The contemporary tendency to ascribe inspiration to some portions of Scripture but not to all is in part due to feelings of embarrassment about portions like the imprecatory psalms and God's decree to destroy Israel's enemies. But the difficulties encountered in Scripture are not a reason for dismissing its plenary inspiration. Readers of Scripture may find parts of it more or less inspiring at different times and different places, but *all* Scripture is God-breathed.

Inspiration is *verbal*: it extends to the *words* of Scripture. This is the sense of Paul's statement "all *Scripture* is God-breathed," as the term "Scripture" refers to the very words themselves. Because Scripture is verbally inspired, Jesus builds his argument for the resurrection of the dead on a present-tense verb, challenging its critics, "Have you not read what was said to you by God: 'I *am* the God of Abraham, and the God of Isaac, and the God of Jacob'? He is not God of the dead, but of the living" (Matt. 22:31–32, quoting Exod. 3:6; emphasis added). Likewise, Paul argues his case for a sole heir of the Abrahamic promises on a singular noun: "Now the promises were made to Abraham and to his offspring. It does not say, 'And to offsprings,' referring to many, but referring to one, 'And to your offspring,' who is Christ" (Gal. 3:16, quoting Gen. 12:7). Thus, while inspiration certainly applies to the biblical authors as they were being moved by the Holy Spirit as they wrote, it is true of the very words of Scripture themselves.

Inspiration is *concursive*: the Spirit and the human authors *wrote together*. The Spirit's work was not just the influence of providential care or guidance that all Christians experience as they walk with God. Nor did inspiration lead merely to a heightened religious consciousness, or extend only to the thoughts or ideas in the minds of the human authors. This particular work of the Holy Spirit was unique to the prophets and apostles, as he and they collaboratively wrote the Word of God. Thus, Jesus considered that what Moses said, God himself said (Matt. 19:4–5, quoting Moses's comment about marriage [Gen. 2:24] and ascribing it to "he who created them"—that is, God).

Though Scripture is inspired, the way that inspiration came about is largely mysterious. These modes include historical research (Luke 1:1–4), observation of life (Ecclesiastes), Spirit-assisted memory (John 14:26), miraculous revelation (2 Cor. 12:1–4), occasional dictation (Rev. 2–3), and sound counsel (1 Cor. 7:25–26, 39–40).

Because of its inspiration by God, Scripture is authoritative and true. It possesses the right to command what believers are to do and prohibit what they are not to do. Moreover, whatever it affirms corresponds to reality, and it never affirms anything that is contrary to fact.

Biblical Support

The doctrine of the inspiration of Scripture is evident in the Old Testament writings. "Moses spoke to the people of Israel according to all that the LORD had given him in commandment to them" (Deut. 1:3). The prophets affirmed of their instructions, "Thus says the LORD" (for example, Isa. 66:1). Still, the divine inspiration of those earlier writings is more fully presented in the New Testament. Paul highlighted plenary inspiration (2 Tim. 3:16–17). Peter underscored the collaboration between the Holy Spirit's superintending work and the human authors' writing of Scripture (2 Pet. 1:16–21). The early Christians attributed the words of a psalm of David to the "Sovereign Lord, . . . who through the mouth of our father David . . . said by the Holy Spirit . . ." (Acts 4:24–26, quoting Ps. 2:1–2). Jesus emphasized the unfailing authority of even casual clauses in the Old Testament: "Scripture cannot be broken" (John 10:35, referring to Ps. 82:6). Indeed, he warned people who thought that he had come to do away with Scripture. Rather, his intention was to fulfill its every word (Matt. 5:17–18).

As for the inspiration of the New Testament writings, Jesus himself promised the Holy Spirit as the guarantee that what the apostles taught and wrote would be a truthful, authoritative witness to him and his work (John 14:26; 16:13). The Holy Spirit, then, knowing completely the things of God, revealed them to the apostles and superintended their writing (1 Cor. 2:10–13). Paul wrote with the conviction that his instructions were given "through the Lord Jesus" (1 Thess. 4:2). Indeed, the gospel that he communicated was the very word of God (2:13). Even when he could not point to a specific teaching of Jesus on a particular topic, Paul sensed that he had the Spirit of God when presenting his sound judgment (1 Cor. 7:25–26, 39–40). Peter considered Paul's writings to be part of "the other Scriptures"—that is, together with the body of the inspired Old Testament writings (2 Pet. 3:15–16).

Major Errors

1. *The denial of the superintending work of the Holy Spirit.* This position dismisses all divine action in the writing of Scripture, reducing it to

a merely human book. This viewpoint refuses to listen to Scripture's own affirmation about itself, and demonstrates a very low view of divine action among human beings.

2. *The denial of the human authorship of Scripture.* The mechanical-dictation view considers the biblical authors to be passive secretaries without any significant and willful participation in the writing process. God simply dictated his Word, and they wrote it down. This position cannot explain the various personalities, theological perspectives, writing styles, and more that are clearly evidenced in the biblical writings. Some people deny the human role in writing Scripture out of fear that, if human beings actually wrote it, and if "to err is human," then Scripture must contain errors. This fear overlooks the superintending operation of the Holy Spirit that protected the Word of God from human error.

3. *The denial of plenary inspiration.* This view considers some parts of Scripture to be inspired, while others are not, dismissing what Scripture claims for its inspiration. A major problem with this view is the need for reliable criteria for deciding which parts are inspired and which parts are not.

4. *The denial of verbal inspiration.* This position claims that the Spirit guided the thoughts of the biblical authors as they wrote but that such inspiration did not extend to the words they used. This viewpoint rejects what Scripture claims for its inspiration.

ENACTING THE DOCTRINE

Because Scripture is God-breathed, it is divinely authoritative. The church is called to do what it commands, avoid doing what it prohibits, heed its warnings, believe its promises, and so forth. Also, inspired Scripture is completely truthful. The church is called to trust everything that it affirms. This is the case when Scripture addresses matters of salvation, faith and obedience, holy living, and worshiping God. It is likewise the case when it treats matters of history, creation and God's providence, genealogies, and more. All Scripture is God-breathed, inspired by the Holy Spirit!

Because non-Christians do not yet trust Jesus Christ for salvation, the church engages missionally by communicating the gospel to them. It believes that the Word of God, breathed out by him, is "the power of God for salvation to everyone who believes" (Rom. 1:16). As people become believers, the church disciples and cares for them by preaching and teaching inspired Scripture.

What's at stake in this doctrine? God's relationship to Scripture is. If the Bible is God-breathed, then God enjoys the closest possible relationship to it. Indeed, it means that he is fully invested in his Word, acting through it to save and transform the church. If this is not the case, then Scripture begins to resemble a human book. It is a book like all other books, filled with laws, proverbs, compelling stories, myths, and more. But being God-breathed, Scripture is the authoritative, truthful Word of God.

Perennial Questions and Problematic Issues

- Why is the doctrine of Scripture so foundational for the Christian faith?
- Some Scripture (for example, its genealogies, Paul's lists of people to greet) doesn't seem very inspiring, so why is inspiration important?
- It seems that the only way God could guarantee that the human authors got his Word right would be for him to dictate it to them.
- Did God really inspire the parts of Scripture that narrate Israel's destruction of the Canaanites and that present prayers for the destruction of enemies?
- If only parts of Scripture are God-breathed, what criteria enable us to identify those parts as inspired and other parts as not inspired?
- How can the church claim that only its holy book (Scripture) is from God? What about the Qur'an for Muslims, and the Vedas for Hindus?
- How does inspiration underscore the authority and truthfulness of the Bible?

TEACHING THE DOCTRINE

A good place to start teaching is with a Bible study focusing on Jesus's attitudes toward Scripture. The goal of this study is to understand what the Lord's view of Scripture was, establishing that he believed it to be the Word of God, fully inspired by the Holy Spirit, and thus truthful and authoritative. Once this point is demonstrated, the challenge becomes clear: If Jesus held this view of Scripture, and if we claim that Jesus is our Lord, then are we not obligated to hold the same view as he held? This point will challenge Christians who are struggling with the inspiration of Scripture and will encourage Christians who embrace its inspiration.

Teaching through the key biblical passages (2 Tim. 3:16; 2 Pet. 1:16–21; etc.) is next. As the major affirmations about divine authorship, human authorship, and more are made, they can be combined into a robust definition of inspiration. Making specifications about plenary, verbal, and concursive inspiration will help to clarify this doctrine and avoid misunderstandings. Major errors also need to be presented and discussed. Affirming this doctrine leads Christians to heed the authority of Scripture and to trust it as the truthful Word of God.

TEACHING OUTLINE

1. The word "God-breathed" and the summary
2. Bible study: Jesus's view of Scripture
3. Major affirmations (with biblical support)
   A. Divine authorship
   B. Human authorship (with rejection of mechanical dictation)
   C. Plenary inspiration
   D. Verbal inspiration
   E. Concursive inspiration
   F. Modes of inspiration
4. Major errors to avoid
   A. Denial of the superintending work of the Holy Spirit
   B. Denial of the human authorship of Scripture
   C. Denial of plenary inspiration
   D. Denial of verbal inspiration
5. Enacting the doctrine
   A. Authority and truthfulness of Scripture
   B. Sharing the gospel

RESOURCES

Allison, *Theological Terms*, s.v. "inspiration"
Elwell, *Evangelical Dictionary of Theology*, s.v. "Bible, Inspiration of"
Erickson, *Christian Theology*, chap. 8
Grenz, *Theology for the Community of God*, chap. 14
Grudem, *Systematic Theology*, chap. 4
Horton, *Pilgrim Theology*, chap. 2
Thoennes, *Life's Biggest Questions*, chap. 4

2

THE TRUTHFULNESS (INERRANCY) OF SCRIPTURE

SUMMARY

Truthfulness (inerrancy) is an attribute of Scripture by which whatever it affirms corresponds to reality, and it never affirms anything that is contrary to fact. It also means that Scripture never contradicts itself.

MAIN THEMES

- Truthfulness regards Scripture's correspondence with reality.
- Inerrancy concerns Scripture's absence of error.
- Inerrancy is consistent with the phenomena of Scripture.
- Infallibility means that Scripture is not liable to failure.
- As a result of its truthfulness, Scripture is trustworthy.

KEY SCRIPTURE

Numbers 23:19; Psalms 12:6; 18:30; 19:8; Proverbs 30:5; John 10:35; 14:26; 16:13; 17:17; Hebrews 6:18

UNDERSTANDING THE DOCTRINE

Major Affirmations

In prayer to his Father, Jesus affirmed, "Your word is truth" (John 17:17). *Truthfulness* has to do with correspondence to reality. For example, Scripture affirms that God created all that exists out of nothing. That affirmation corresponds to the reality that God brought the universe into existence not by combining already-existing materials but by creating the materials themselves. Additionally, Scripture's affirmation that Christ rose from the dead on the third day corresponds to the reality that on Easter Sunday, Christ's tomb was empty and the living Jesus appeared to people.

To frame this discussion differently, *inerrancy* means that Scripture never affirms anything contrary to fact. Inerrancy is characteristic of all of Scripture, not just the parts concerning salvation, faith, and doctrine. Inerrancy also means that Scripture never contradicts itself; it is self-consistent. For example, what it affirms about Jesus Christ being fully God does not contradict its affirmations about him being fully man. He is both God and man.

Reflecting the Chicago Statement on Biblical Inerrancy, Paul Feinberg offers a brief definition of inerrancy: "Inerrancy means that when all the facts are known, the Scriptures in their original autographs and properly interpreted will be shown to be wholly true in everything that they affirm, whether that has to do with doctrine or morality or with the social, physical, or life sciences."[4]

Critics of the Bible's inerrancy often misunderstand the concept. Inerrancy is consistent with the phenomena of Scripture—that is, the varied writing techniques employed by the human authors. Here are five examples:

1. *Ordinary speech*. Scripture does not use precise, technical language, but employs everyday language. When Moses narrates the creation of the two great lights in Genesis 1:16–18, he is not writing scientifically (technically, the sun is a light, but the moon merely reflects light). Rather, he is writing popularly, as we speak today, when, for example, we say the sun *rises* and *sets*. Inerrancy is consistent with Scripture's use of ordinary language.

2. *Loose quotations*. Sometimes the New Testament writers quote the Old Testament exactly, word for word (for example, Heb. 1:7 quotes Ps. 104:4). At other times they paraphrase, summarize, or allude to

it (for example, Heb. 3:2 alludes to Num. 12:7). Inerrancy does not preclude any of these writing conventions.

3. *Translations of Jesus's sayings.* Because Jesus taught in Aramaic, and the New Testament is written in Greek, it records very few of his exact words (exceptions: Mark 5:41; 7:34; 15:34). Instead, we have the exact voice of Jesus; that is, the Greek versions of his Aramaic sayings are faithful renditions of the words Jesus actually spoke. And Jesus did indeed speak those words. They were not invented by his disciples and placed in Jesus's mouth when the Gospels were written. Inerrancy is consistent with Scripture's translations of Jesus's words.

4. *Different ordering of events.* For example, Matthew presents the actual sequence of Jesus's temptations (Matt. 4:1–11), while Luke offers them without chronological ordering (Luke 4:1–13). These two ways of narrating the temptations are not contradictory because Matthew has one purpose as he writes (to recount the temptations in the order in which Jesus faced them), while Luke has a different purpose (to set forth three temptations without intending to narrate them sequentially). Inerrancy is consistent with Scripture's different ordering of events.

5. *Divergent parallel accounts.* Variant accounts relate the same event but present it with significant differences. In the Gospels, for example, the miracle of the feeding of the five thousand is narrated differently by the four authors. What can account for these differences? One version may present a summary of an event, while another provides more details. For example, Matt. 8:5–13 gives fewer details about Jesus's healing of the centurion's slave than Luke 7:1–10. Or one narrative may relate one part of an episode, while another narrates a different part. For example, Judas died by hanging (Matt. 27:1–10), and his body fell and burst open (Acts 1:15–19). Inerrancy is consistent with Scripture's use of variant accounts.

Importantly, the inerrancy of Scripture is consistent with these various writing conventions.

Augustine (354–430) made an important contribution to this doctrine when he dared to imagine what the presence of even one error in Scripture would lead to: it would not mean that all of Scripture is in error, but it would lead to the suspicion that any part could be in error. The church would be left to a hopelessly subjective evaluation of Scripture to discern which parts are true and which contain error.

Related to this discussion is *infallibility*, which means that Scripture is not liable to failure. It always accomplishes the purpose for which God intends it. Speaking of the word that goes out from his mouth, God assures us, "It shall not return to me empty, but it shall accomplish that which I purpose" (Isa. 55:11).

Through most of the church's history, infallibility and inerrancy meant the same thing and referred to Scripture's truthfulness. Sadly, last century witnessed the uncoupling of the two. Infallibility was narrowed to matters concerning salvation, faith, and holy living. But this idea leaves open the possibility—indeed, the actuality—of errors when Scripture addresses matters of history, genealogy, geography, and science. Also, error was redefined as *intentional* deception. Given this definition, critics could affirm Scripture's complete inerrancy—its authors never willfully mislead readers—while continuing to maintain the presence of actual errors in Scripture.

These developments must be rejected. Scripture itself never distinguishes between its "most important" parts, which are inspired and thus inerrant, and its "unimportant parts," which were not written under the Spirit's guidance and are thus errant. The Word of God is true (inerrant) and infallible, without error and not liable to fail.

Biblical Support

The doctrine of the truthfulness and inerrancy of Scripture is present in the Old Testament (Pss. 12:6; 18:30; 19:8; Prov. 30:5). In keeping with this high view of Scripture, Jesus affirmed that the Word of God "is truth" (John 17:17) that "cannot be broken" (10:35). He confidently appealed to Old Testament events, such as Adam and Eve (Matt. 19:3–6), the flood in Noah's time (24:36–39), Moses's writing of the Pentateuch (John 5:45–47), and Jonah and the great fish (Matt. 12:40). For Jesus, these narratives were true, corresponding to reality.

As for the truthfulness of the New Testament, Jesus promised to send the "Spirit of truth" to his disciples. Thus, he warranted them as his truth-telling witnesses: what they would preach, and what some of them would write, was guaranteed as an accurate testimony to Jesus's words and works (John 14:26; 16:13). As the Holy Spirit, the Spirit of truth, superintended their writing, he ensured the truthfulness of the New Testament (1 Cor. 2:10–13).

A theological consideration confirms the truthfulness of Scripture: God always speaks the truth; indeed, he does not and cannot speak lies (Num. 23:19; Heb. 6:18). Because Scripture is God-breathed (2 Tim. 3:16), it always relates the truth and never lies. Thus, inerrancy is a corollary of the inspiration of Scripture by the God who always tells the truth.

Major Errors

1. *The denial of the inspiration, and hence inerrancy, of Scripture.* This position dismisses the Holy Spirit's superintending action in the writing of Scripture, reducing it to a merely human book. As all human writings contain errors, so also does the Bible. This viewpoint refuses to listen to Scripture's own affirmation about its truthfulness and has a very low view of divine action among human beings.

2. *Pitting infallibility against inerrancy.* In addition to departing from the historical equivalency of these two terms, proponents redefine error as *intentional* deception. Given this definition, they affirm Scripture's complete inerrancy—its authors never willfully mislead readers—while maintaining the presence of actual errors. This position separates what the church has traditionally held together. Moreover, it is a deceitful way of giving lip service to biblical inerrancy while actually denying it.

3. *The claim that there are hundreds of errors in the Bible.* Actually, when all the alleged mistakes are listed, there are slightly over sixty of them. So, the claim is exaggerated, and while some of the problems are more severe than others, a resolution either can be offered or does not need to be offered. Why? In some cases, we live thousands of years too late to resolve the problems. Moreover, the biblical evidence is sometimes so limited that we don't have enough information to arrive at a solution. Furthermore, the same problems haunt all writings without causing a paralyzing suspicion of error. Thus, the church, without ignoring these problematic passages, can address them one by one from a posture of faith and not fall into despair or unbelief.

ENACTING THE DOCTRINE

Because Scripture is God-breathed, the revelation of the One who always tells the truth and cannot lie, it is truthful. The church is called to trust everything that it affirms: creation out of nothing, God's providential care, the miracles of Jesus Christ, instructions about human sexuality and marriage, salvation by faith alone, and more. Moreover, the infallibility of Scripture urges the church to be hopeful while patiently waiting for the divine promises to be fulfilled: a positive response by some to the gospel that we communicate, future release from suffering and death, the return of Christ, the new heaven and new earth, and more.

What about Christians who believe that Scripture contains error? Ask them to show you what these errors are. If they claim that Jesus is their Lord, and Jesus affirmed the inerrancy of Scripture, challenge them to be consistent and embrace their Lord's view of Scripture.

TEACHING THE DOCTRINE

A good place to start is with a Bible study focusing on Jesus's view of several Old Testament narratives that are the targets of fierce attack: Adam and Eve (Matt. 19:3–6), the flood in Noah's time (24:36–39), Moses's writing of the Pentateuch (John 5:45–47), and Jonah and the great fish (Matt. 12:40). The goal of this study is to understand what the Lord's view of Scripture was, establishing that he believed it to be the truthful and inerrant Word of God. This is particularly the case in regard to biblical stories that are considered to be in error by critics. Once this point is demonstrated, the challenge becomes clear: If Jesus the Lord held this view of Scripture's truthfulness, and if we claim that Jesus is our Lord, then are we not obligated to hold the same view that he held? This point will challenge Christians who are struggling with the truthfulness of Scripture and will encourage Christians who embrace its inerrancy.

Teaching through biblical affirmations of Scripture's truthfulness is next, followed by the traditional theological argument for its inerrancy. Underscore that the contemporary abandonment of this doctrine is out of step with the church's historic position. Working through Feinberg's definition, along with a careful explanation that inerrancy is consistent with the phenomena of Scripture, can be very helpful. As the points about

> ### *Perennial Questions and Problematic Issues*
>
> - Why is this doctrine of Scripture so foundational for the Christian faith?
> - How can we affirm the complete truthfulness of Scripture in the midst of a world that claims it is full of errors?
> - If to err is human, and human beings wrote the Bible, then how can it be free from error?
> - It seems that the only way God could guarantee that the human authors got his Word right would be for him to dictate it to them.

different ordering of events and divergent parallel accounts are discussed, invite participants to "fasten their seat belts," as the ride gets a bit rough. The goal is not to shake their confidence in Scripture's truthfulness but to prepare them to face attacks against biblical inerrancy when others challenge them with "Did you know that the Bible contains many errors?"

TEACHING OUTLINE

1. The summary
2. Bible study: Jesus's view of Scripture's truthfulness
3. Major affirmations (with biblical support)
   A. Truthfulness
   B. Inerrancy
   C. Consistency of inerrancy with the phenomena of Scripture
   D. Infallibility
   E. The problem of pitting inerrancy against infallibility
4. Major errors to avoid
   A. Denying the inspiration, and hence the inerrancy, of Scripture
   B. Pitting infallibility against inerrancy
   C. Claiming there are hundreds of errors in the Bible
5. Enacting the doctrine
   A. Trusting all Scripture
   B. Challenging the claims that Scripture contains errors

RESOURCES

Allison, *Theological Terms*, s.vv. "Chicago Statement on Biblical Inerrancy," "inerrancy," "infallibility of Scripture"

Elwell, *Evangelical Dictionary of Theology*, s.v. "Bible, Inerrancy and Infallibility of"

Erickson, *Christian Theology*, chap. 9

Grenz, *Theology for the Community of God*, chap. 14

Grudem, *Systematic Theology*, chap. 5

Horton, *Pilgrim Theology*, 57–58

Thoennes, *Life's Biggest Questions*, chap. 4

3

THE AUTHORITY
OF SCRIPTURE

SUMMARY

The authority of Scripture is the property by which it, as the inspired Word of the sovereign God, possesses the right to command what Christians are to believe, do, and be, and to prohibit what they are not to believe, do, and be.

MAIN THEMES

- Biblical authority has to do with the Bible's prerogative to command and to prohibit belief, actions, and character.
- The authority of Scripture is a corollary of its inspiration.
- Authority is an inherent property of Scripture.
- A key Reformation debate was over the authority of Scripture (*sola Scriptura*, Scripture alone).

KEY SCRIPTURE

Deuteronomy 30:15–18; Matthew 5:17–18; 1 Corinthians 2:10–13; 14:37; 1 Thessalonians 2:13; 4:2; 2 Thessalonians 2:15; 3:14; 2 Peter 3:15–16

UNDERSTANDING THE DOCTRINE

Major Affirmations

The authority of Scripture is its property whereby it possesses the prerogative to command what God's people are to believe, do, and be, and to prohibit what they are not to believe, do, and be. It is a subset of divine authority in general, the right that God possesses to establish laws, give orders, demand obedience, determine belief, and more.

Scripture reveals truth about God and his ways. Scripture, being authoritative, demands that Christians believe in sound doctrine and insists that they not believe in false doctrine. Moreover, Scripture establishes God's moral laws and requirements. Scripture, being authoritative, calls God's people to obey his commandments and forbids them to disobey them. Furthermore, Scripture proscribes certain matters. Scripture, being authoritative, prohibits Christians from engaging in sinful attitudes and evil actions. Finally, Scripture reveals what it means to be image bearers of God saved by his grace. Scripture, being authoritative, demands that God's people mirror his in their redeemed humanity.

Biblical authority is a corollary of its inspiration: because Scripture has God as its author, it possesses divine authority. This is represented in the diagram below.

divine author
_____

divine author-ity

As God-breathed, Scripture is itself authoritative. This affirmation differs from many contemporary views of the authority of Scripture:

1. The authority of Scripture is *functional*. Because the Bible functions in a certain way—Scripture leads to salvation, it equips believers

for godly living, it instructs Christians in sound doctrine—it is authoritative.

2. The authority of Scripture is *instrumental*. Because God uses the Bible as a means to reveal himself to his people—Scripture is a means of divine communication—it is authoritative.

3. The authority of Scripture is *conferred*. Because the church bestows authority on the Bible—the church acknowledges and proclaims that Scripture possesses authority—it is authoritative.

4. The authority of Scripture is *traditional*. Because the Bible has always held a high place of honor in Christianity—Scripture is its founding holy book and has always been at the heart of the church's liturgy—it is authoritative.

In one sense, these views contain some truth: biblical authority is functional, instrumental, conferred, and traditional. However, individually and together, these ideas are incomplete. Biblical authority is first and foremost an ontological matter: it has to do with the very nature of Scripture itself.

God sustains the closest possible relationship to his Word. Accordingly, to obey God's Word is to obey God himself. To disobey God's Word is to disobey God himself. To trust God's Word is to trust God himself. To mistrust God's Word is to mistrust God himself. "God has so *identified* himself with his words that whatever someone does to God's words . . . they do directly to God himself."[5] This affirmation does not equate God with his Word. But it does make clear that the God to whom all authority belongs to command what believers are to do and believe, and prohibit what they are not to do and believe, stands behind his authoritative Word.

The authority of Scripture was one of the most contested doctrines of the Reformation. Indeed, the formal principle of Protestantism was *sola Scriptura*: Scripture alone is the ultimate authority for the church. It is the ultimate judge of Christian doctrine and practice, standing above all human writings, traditions, church councils, and more. It is the touchstone against which all else is assessed. Moreover, anything that lacks biblical warrant cannot be authoritative for the church. No belief or practice lacking biblical support can bind the conscience of Christians. Scripture alone has the prerogative to determine doctrine and practice.

This principle stood opposed to the Roman Catholic view that authority consists of Scripture, Tradition, and the Catholic Church's Magisterium.

Tradition is Christ's unwritten teaching that he orally communicated to his apostles, who in turn communicated it to their successors, the bishops of the Catholic Church, which in turn nurtures this teaching. Being a mode of divine revelation, it is authoritative, on par with written Scripture. The Magisterium, or teaching office of the church, consisting of the pope and bishops, is the authoritative interpreter of Scripture and the authoritative determiner of Tradition. Thus, the Catholic Church denies *sola Scriptura*, as Scripture, Tradition, and the Magisterium make up its authority. Evangelical churches champion *sola Scriptura*, disagreeing with the alleged biblical support for Tradition and the Magisterium and dissenting from appeals to church history for an early development of these two authorities.

Biblical Support

As Moses puts the finishing touches on his writing of God's Word, his words underscore biblical authority: "If you obey the commandments of the LORD your God . . . , then you shall live and multiply, and the LORD your God will bless you. . . . But if your heart turns away, and you will not hear, but are drawn away to worship other gods and serve them, . . . you shall surely perish" (Deut. 30:16–18). The authority of Scripture is its prerogative to command what God's people are to believe, do, and be, and to prohibit what they are not to believe, do, and be.

This authority is inherent in Scripture itself, not merely an authority that is functional, instrumental, conferred, and traditional. Such inherent authority is due to the fact that the Trinity is at the heart of divine revelation. Four points are important:

1. Jesus affirmed that he did nothing on his own authority. As a corollary, Jesus denied that he spoke his words on his own authority (John 8:28; 14:10).
2. Jesus affirmed that the Father dwelt in him (Jesus) and did his work. In keeping with this, Jesus emphasized that his words were not his own, but those of the Father who sent him (John 7:16–18; 14:10, 24; 12:49). The authoritative words Jesus spoke were the Father's authoritative words.
3. Looking ahead, Jesus affirmed that the Holy Spirit would "not speak on his own authority, but whatever he [heard]" he would speak (John 16:13). As a corollary, Jesus promised that the Spirit would take his

(Jesus's) words and declare them to the disciples (v. 15). However, because Jesus's words were not his own, but those of the Father, the Spirit would actually take the Father's words through Jesus's words and disclose them.

4. This work of the Spirit was his inspiration of Scripture as he superintended the apostles as they wrote the New Testament. Their God-breathed words, then, are the Father's authoritative words through Jesus's authoritative words, taught by the Spirit (1 Cor. 2:10–13).

These four points underscore the trinitarian nature of divine revelation. Because such revelation is divinely authoritative, Scripture itself, as the Word of God, is authoritative.

Theological support for this doctrine comes from the fact that biblical authority is a corollary of the inspiration of Scripture. This doctrine, well supported biblically (2 Tim. 3:16; 2 Pet. 1:19–21), has already been covered (chap. 1, "The Inspiration of Scripture").

Scripture affirms its own authority. In the Old Testament, the prophets spoke and wrote with divine authority. For example, "Moses spoke to the people of Israel according to all that the LORD had given him in commandment to them" (Deut. 1:3). Nowhere is this more clearly seen than in the preface to many prophetic announcements: "Thus says the LORD" (for example, Isa. 66:1). The authority of Old Testament Scripture is attested to by Christ and the apostles. Jesus did not come "to abolish the Law or the Prophets . . . but to fulfill them" (Matt. 5:17–18), warning, "Scripture cannot be broken" (John 10:35). The apostles who wrote the New Testament constantly cited, paraphrased, summarized, and alluded to Old Testament Scripture because of its authority.

The authority of New Testament Scripture was anticipated by Jesus Christ and acknowledged by its apostolic authors. As already discussed, Jesus himself promised the Holy Spirit as the guarantee that what the apostles taught and wrote would be a truthful, authoritative witness to him and his work (John 14:26; 16:13).

The apostle Paul wrote with the conviction that his instructions were given "through the Lord Jesus" (1 Thess. 4:2), "a command of the Lord" (1 Cor. 14:37) to be obeyed (2 Thess. 2:15; 3:14). Indeed, the gospel that he communicated was the very word of God (1 Thess. 2:13). The apostle Peter considered Paul's writings to be part of "the other Scriptures"—that is, together with the body of the authoritative Old Testament writings (2 Pet. 3:15–16).

Major Errors

1. *The rejection of the inspiration of Scripture, leading to a denial of inherent biblical authority.* One author asserts, "The Bible's authority . . . rests in the very ingenuity and irresistibility of the experiences it describes, not in its having God as its author."[6] This viewpoint contradicts both Scripture's own affirmation and the church's historic position.

2. *The neglect or denial of* sola Scriptura. Proponents place some other authority alongside Scripture and consider it to be as authoritative as, or more authoritative than, Scripture. One example is the Roman Catholic Church with its Tradition and Magisterium. A second is the elevation of prophetic words and other personal revelations. A third example is personal experience. Sadly, when people embrace other authoritative sources on par with, or above, Scripture, those other authorities inevitably end up minimizing biblical authority. All multiauthority structures are inherently unstable.

ENACTING THE DOCTRINE

In an age and society that increasingly rejects authority, the church can no longer assume that unbelievers, and even some believers, will show deference toward Scripture. Neither is it the case that, once evidence for biblical authority is presented, people will respond with respect and acknowledgment. This reality underscores the importance of this doctrine.

More importantly, it emphasizes the need for the church to live out its confession of biblical authority. It will not do to simply say that we believe in the authority of Scripture. We must also demonstrate it by joyfully submitting to the Word personally, in our family, at our work, and among our friends and neighbors. The church must demonstrate joyful obedience by living out its profession of the gospel, which transforms its worship, relationships, discipline, care, mercy, and mission. A tragic charge registered far too commonly against the church is that it is hypocritical: it says it believes one thing but lives contrary to its belief. While concrete submission to biblical authority is not the only answer to that charge, it will go a long way toward its resolution.

TEACHING THE DOCTRINE

Engaging in a Bible study on Jesus's view of Scripture is a good place to start. The purpose is both to get participants into authoritative Scripture and to help them discover Jesus's high view of biblical authority. Examples of passages to study are his appeal to Scripture to defend his claim to deity (John 10:30–36), his rebuke "Have you not/never read?" directed at his critics (Matt. 12:1–8; 19:3–6; 21:14–16, 42–44; 22:21–33), his citation of Scripture when tempted (Luke 4:1–13), his reading of Scripture (4:16–21), and his fulfillment of Scripture (24:44–49). Make sure that participants grasp that Jesus believed the Word of God to be fully authoritative.

> ### *Perennial Questions and Problematic Issues*
>
> • Because authority can be abused, isn't it dangerous to talk about biblical authority?
>
> • I think Scripture is authoritative for Christians, but there are other holy books that are authoritative for other religions.
>
> • When God speaks to me directly, it seems much more authoritative than does the Bible.
>
> • I don't like the idea of submitting to any authority, Scripture or otherwise.

Work hard to establish the intimate connection between God and his Word. The authority of Scripture is not some mystical power that emanates from its pages. Rather, its divine author has invested it with divine authority. Make sure participants understand that when they read, study, memorize, and meditate on Scripture, they are dealing with God himself and his authority.

Because *sola Scriptura* is one of the foundations of Protestantism/evangelicalism, be sure to cover the debate. The debate also illustrates challenges to biblical authority. Engage the participants in discussing other challenges (prophecies, personal experiences), helping them to see the pitfalls of placing other sources on par with, or above, biblical authority.

TEACHING OUTLINE

1. The summary
2. Bible study: Jesus's view of the authority of Scripture
3. Major affirmations (with biblical support)
   A. Scripture's authority as a corollary of its inspiration
   B. The inherent authority of Scripture
   C. *Sola Scriptura* and detractors from biblical authority

4. Major errors to avoid
   A. Rejection of the inspiration of Scripture, leading to a denial of inherent biblical authority
   B. Neglect or denial of *sola Scriptura*
5. Enacting the doctrine
   A. Facing the rejection of biblical authority
   B. Living out biblical authority concretely

RESOURCES

Allison, *Theological Terms*, s.v. "authority of Scripture"

Elwell, *Evangelical Dictionary of Theology*, s.v. "Bible, Authority of"

Erickson, *Christian Theology*, chap. 10

Grenz, *Theology for the Community of God*, chap. 14

Grudem, *Systematic Theology*, chap. 4

Horton, *Pilgrim Theology*, chap. 2

Thoennes, *Life's Biggest Questions*, chap. 4

4

THE SUFFICIENCY
AND NECESSITY OF SCRIPTURE

SUMMARY

Sufficiency is an attribute of Scripture whereby it provides everything that people need to be saved and everything that Christians need to please God fully. Necessity is an attribute of Scripture whereby it is essential for knowing the way of salvation, for progressing in holiness, and for discerning God's will.

MAIN THEMES

- The doctrine of the sufficiency of Scripture regards God's provision of all the revelation that he wants his human creatures to have.

- Sufficiency and the Protestant principle of *sola Scriptura* (Scripture alone) are connected.

- The doctrine of the necessity of Scripture asserts that the people of God must know and live by Scripture, for without it, there can be no salvation, growth in holiness, or knowledge of God's will.

- Both of these doctrines stand against the Roman Catholic Church's insistence on its Tradition being part of divine revelation.
- As a result of its sufficiency and necessity, Scripture completely equips the people of God to please him fully.

KEY SCRIPTURE

Deuteronomy 4:2; Psalm 19:7–11; Proverbs 30:6; Matthew 4:4; Romans 10:13–17; 2 Timothy 3:15–17; 1 Peter 2:1–3; Revelation 22:18–19

UNDERSTANDING THE DOCTRINE

Major Affirmations

Scripture, both in its written form and as orally transmitted (for example, preached in church or read in oral cultures), is sufficient and necessary. Sufficiency is an attribute of Scripture whereby it provides everything that nonbelievers need to be saved. It is the revelation of the gospel of the death and resurrection of Christ for the forgiveness of sins, together with the explanation of how to appropriate that salvation. It is this gospel embraced by faith alone that saves. Furthermore, Scripture provides everything that Christians need to please God fully. For every task that God calls believers to do, he completely equips them to accomplish his will through his Word (and, certainly, empowered by his Spirit).

Scripture is not absolutely sufficient. Indeed, there is much about God and his ways that he has chosen not to reveal (Deut. 29:29). Rather, the sufficiency of Scripture is limited to its purpose, which is to instruct nonbelievers in the way of salvation and to prepare believers for every good work so as to fully please God.

The early church embraced the sufficiency of Scripture as the sole standard for Christian belief and practice. True belief must be established from it, and any belief that contradicts Scripture is heresy. Right practice must be based on it, and any practice that conflicts with Scripture is sin. The early church also developed a role for tradition (for example, its early creeds) in defense of its doctrines over against heresies like gnosticism.

32

But this tradition (small *t*) was not considered to be a supplement to Scripture.[7]

Tragically, the medieval Roman Catholic Church added Tradition (capital *T*) to Scripture and claimed that both are modes of the one divine revelation. Tradition includes Christ's unwritten teaching that he orally communicated to his apostles, who in turn communicated it to their successors, the bishops of the Catholic Church, which in turn nurtures this teaching. It also included the teaching of general church councils. Considering Tradition as a mode of divine revelation, the Catholic Church denied that Scripture is sufficient for salvation and godly living. There are doctrines to be believed, and behaviors and good works to be practiced, that are revealed in Tradition and not found in Scripture.

Against this insistence on the Catholic Church's Tradition, the Reformers formulated the Protestant principle of *sola Scriptura*: Scripture, and Scripture alone, completely equips people for knowing God and fully doing his will. This principle did not entail disregard for the wisdom from the church's past. But such tradition (small *t*), like the Apostles' Creed, is ministerial, serving but never supplementing Scripture, which is the church's ultimate authority.

Necessity is an attribute of Scripture whereby Scripture is essential for knowing the way of salvation. As the power of God to rescue sinful people, the gospel must be communicated—read, preached, broadcast, narrated, and more. Only by hearing the Word of God can people call upon Jesus Christ and be saved. Moreover, Scripture is necessary for progressing in holiness. It reveals all the commands and prohibitions, all the warnings and promises, all the narratives and songs, all the prophecies and proverbs by which the people of God can become increasingly Christlike. Furthermore, Scripture is essential for discerning God's will. In terms of content, nothing outside of Scripture is needed to formulate sound doctrine, communicate what is to be believed, prohibit what is forbidden, and command what is to be obeyed.

Scripture is not absolutely necessary. Indeed, before Scripture was written, people like Abraham, Isaac, and Jacob were in relationship with God, walked with him, and knew his will. Rather, the necessity of Scripture is conditioned on God's good pleasure to reveal himself and his ways through a written Word. As God wills to reveal his truth in that way, Scripture becomes necessary for salvation, sanctification, and knowledge of his will.

The early church affirmed the necessity of Scripture. Because of Scripture's necessity, Christians must daily read and meditate on the Bible. Its necessary revelation keeps them from heresy, sin, careless living, and aimless work.

Tragically, the medieval Roman Catholic Church believed that divine revelation consists of both Scripture and Tradition. This position meant that Scripture is not necessary for the church's existence but only for its well-being. Thus, Scripture could be lost or disappear, but the church would continue to exist on the basis of its Tradition. The Reformers insisted that Scripture is necessary: the church would lose its way, not just limp along, apart from the Word of God.

Additionally, the Reformers appealed to the necessity of Scripture against the fanatics. These mystics claimed that the Spirit of God speaks directly to believers apart from the Word of God. The Reformers rebuked this idea, insisting that the Spirit carries out his teaching ministry in believers only through Scripture, which can only be understood through the Spirit's aid.

Biblical Support

Commenting on the inspiration of Scripture, or "the sacred writings" (the church's Old Testament), Paul highlights the attribute of sufficiency: Scripture is sufficient to make people "wise for salvation through faith in Christ Jesus"—that is, to provide everything that nonbelievers need to know to be rescued from sin. Furthermore, for believers, Scripture is sufficient for "teaching," or the communication of sound doctrine; "reproof," or pointing out the wrong way people are headed; "correction," or directing people back to the right path; and "training in righteousness," or forming people in Christlikeness. Indeed, those who heed Scripture will be "complete, equipped for every [not some or much] good work" (2 Tim. 3:15–17). Scripture is sufficient.

This affirmation of the sufficiency of Scripture reflects the Old Testament's own perspective. Describing the profitability of the Word of God, the psalmist notes the benefits of reviving the soul, making wise the simple, rejoicing the heart, enlightening the eyes, warning about sin, and rewarding obedience (Ps. 19:7–11). Scripture is sufficient to accomplish all these good things.

At three junctures in Scripture, warnings are issued about adding to and taking away from the Word of God. One is in the last writing of the

Pentateuch (Deut. 4:2), the first installment in Scripture. A second warning is found in Proverbs (30:6): wise people do not add to God's words. A final warning is found in Revelation (22:18–19). Though it comes in reference to the book John wrote, providentially it comes in the last installment in Scripture: do not add to or subtract from this completed writing. At its beginning, at its end, and in its book on wisdom, Scripture emphasizes its completeness and strongly forbids changing it by addition or subtraction. It is sufficient.

The Bible also views itself as God's necessary revelation. Faced with fierce temptations, Jesus himself lived the reality that "man shall not live by bread alone, but by every word that comes from the mouth of God" (Matt. 4:4, quoting Deut. 8:3). Paul insisted that faith in Christ, the sole means by which people may be saved, comes from knowing the gospel (Rom. 10:13–17). Progress in the faith requires nourishing oneself on the Word of God (1 Pet. 2:1–3). As the church father Jerome rightly observed, "Ignorance of Scripture is ignorance of Christ." Scripture is necessary.

Major Errors

1. *An emphasis on the Spirit of God to the neglect or dismissal of the Word of God.* This extreme position results in subjectivism, zeal without knowledge, emotionalism, and chaos. It minimizes, or fails to heed, the call of Scripture and the historical church to be ruled by authoritative Scripture.

2. *An emphasis on the Word of God to the neglect or dismissal of the Spirit of God.* This extreme view results in spiritual deadness, knowledge without passion, and sterile intellectualism. It disregards the (biblically promised) guidance of the Spirit and the absolute need for the Spirit's illumination to understand Scripture in the first place.

3. *Some source other than Scripture usurping the supreme authority of Scripture.* This source could be the Catholic Church's Tradition, which includes belief in transubstantiation, the immaculate conception and bodily assumption of Mary, papal infallibility, purgatory, and more. It could be extrabiblical writings like the Book of Mormon or Mary Baker Eddy's *Science and Health with Key to the Scriptures*, which claim to supplement the closed canon of the Bible. This source could be a church's own tradition (small *t*) that stubbornly persists, drowning out Scripture. It could be a

prophecy or personal revelation that is allowed to trump biblical authority. All these sources diminish or destroy the sufficiency and necessity of Scripture.

ENACTING THE DOCTRINE

Because Scripture is sufficient, many practical applications arise. For example, we must not add anything to it, nor are we to consider any other writings of equal value to Scripture. Moreover, God does not require us to believe anything about himself or his work in saving and sanctifying us that is not found in Scripture. Furthermore, no prophecies or personal revelations from God are to be placed on a level equal to Scripture in authority. Additionally, nothing is sin that is not forbidden by Scripture. Finally, God does not require anything of us that is not commanded in Scripture.

From the necessity of Scripture flow other important applications. For example, we must nourish ourselves daily on the Word of God, reading, memorizing, praying, applying, and meditating on it. Moreover, Scripture must be at the heart of every ministry of the church: its worship, preaching, evangelism, discipleship, community groups, pastoral care, mercy, and more.

Perennial Questions and Problematic Issues

- Why are these doctrines of Scripture so foundational for the Christian faith?
- If Scripture contains everything Christians need to know to please God fully, what is the role of the following in discerning God's will: the counsel of others, sermons, our conscience, our feelings, the leading of the Holy Spirit, changes in circumstances, and prophecies?
- What does the sufficiency of Scripture have to say about my friends and/or my church (or even me) imposing some belief, rule, or prohibition on me that is not found in Scripture?
- What does the sufficiency of Scripture say about my friends and/or my church (or even me) emphasizing matters not given much attention in Scripture?
- It's hard for me to read, memorize, and study the Bible, and I seem to be doing all right without much attention to it as I just pray and ask God to guide and bless me.

Note: Some of these points have been adapted from Grudem, *Systematic Theology*, 135.

TEACHING THE DOCTRINE

After defining these two doctrines, teaching through the key biblical passages (2 Tim. 3:16; Ps. 19:7–11; Matt. 4:4; etc.) grounds them in Scripture itself and underscores its sufficiency and necessity. Challenges to both doctrines illuminate why they are so important. The Catholic Church's Tradition offers a clear foil for the sufficiency of Scripture and for the Protestant principle of *sola Scriptura*. Because participants are familiar with stories of prophetic activity, use these as an opportunity to emphasize how extreme cases do indeed contradict the sufficiency of Scripture. But use them also to discuss how a more balanced approach can affirm sufficiency while allowing for individual guidance from the Spirit.

Illustrations of people who rely on the Spirit of God while neglecting the Word of God provide a clear foil for the necessity of Scripture. Rather than a dismissive attitude toward these extreme cases, compassion and lament for the people whose lives are wrecked by such wrong ideas should be expressed. Use these cases as an opportunity to urge the participants to daily read and live Scripture.

TEACHING OUTLINE

1. The summary
2. Major affirmations (with biblical support)
   A. Sufficiency
   B. *Sola Scriptura*
   C. Necessity
   D. Challenges to, and detractors from, the sufficiency and necessity of Scripture
   E. The Protestant church's historical position
3. Major errors to avoid
   A. Emphasizing the Spirit of God to the neglect or dismissal of the Word of God
   B. Emphasizing the Word of God to the neglect or dismissal of the Spirit of God
   C. Permitting some source other than Scripture to usurp the supreme authority of Scripture
4. Enacting the doctrine
   A. Refusing to go beyond Scripture
   B. Featuring Scripture in our daily life and our church's ministries

RESOURCES

Allison, *Theological Terms*, s.vv. "necessity of Scripture," "sufficiency of Scripture"

Erickson, *Christian Theology*, chap. 7

Grudem, *Systematic Theology*, chaps. 7–8

Thoennes, *Life's Biggest Questions*, chap. 4

5

THE CLARITY OF SCRIPTURE

SUMMARY

Scripture is written in such a way that it can be understood by God's people.

MAIN THEMES

- The doctrine of the clarity (or perspicuity) of Scripture focuses on its intelligibility.
- What is needed to understand Scripture is the normal acquired ability to read texts or understand oral communication.
- Understanding Scripture does not depend on gender, age, experience, education, or cultural background.
- Scripture itself is characterized by the presumption of continued intelligibility.
- The clarity of Scripture goes hand in hand with the illumination of the Holy Spirit.
- A common mistake is to think that clarity means the Bible is easy to understand.
- This doctrine is affirmed in the context of the church.

- The clarity of Scripture demands concrete application of what is properly understood.
- Even unbelievers can achieve a general understanding of Scripture.

KEY SCRIPTURE

Deuteronomy 29:29; 30:11–14; 31:9–13; Nehemiah 8; Acts 17:10–12; Romans 4:22–24; 10:6–10; 15:4; 1 Corinthians 2:14–16; 10:6–11; 1 Timothy 4:13; 1 Peter 2:1–3

UNDERSTANDING THE DOCTRINE

Major Affirmations

"The secret things belong to the Lord our God, but the things that are revealed belong to us and to our children forever" (Deut. 29:29). While there is a great deal about God and his ways—"the secret things"—that his people cannot grasp, "the things that are revealed," which include Scripture, are accessible and intelligible to them.

The only prerequisite to understanding Scripture is the normal acquired ability to read texts (when a Bible is available to literate people) or to understand oral communication (when Scripture is read out loud or broadcast). This means that understanding Scripture does not depend on one's gender: both men and women can know it. It is not contingent on one's age: young, middle-aged, and old people can comprehend it. It does not depend on one's experience: new Christians as well as seasoned believers can comprehend it. Understanding the Bible is not contingent on one's education: unschooled people as well as scholars can grasp it. It does not depend on one's cultural background: different ethnicities, races, and language groups can comprehend it.

Scripture itself is characterized by the presumption of continued intelligibility: it assumes people will be able to understand it even when they are in contexts far removed from the original settings in which Scripture was written. This point is an important consideration when people claim that, because Scripture is such an ancient book, it cannot be grasped. Contemporary readers, they argue, are light-years removed from the times and experiences of people presented in Scripture. How is it possible for them to understand an outdated book?

As just noted, this supposedly outdated, "backward" book looks forward favorably to people being able to comprehend it in circumstances drastically different from when it was written. In part, this confidence is based on the fact that Scripture addresses realities common to all people at all times and in all places. Additionally, the clarity of Scripture dovetails with the illumination of the Holy Spirit, his ministry whereby he aids Christians in the proper understanding of clear Scripture.

Scripture's clarity should not be equated with "easy to understand." Whereas some Scripture is obvious, not all of it is. Its readers and hearers are well aware of the difference in comprehensibility between "God so loved the world that he gave his only Son" (John 3:16) and the discussion of Jesus's proclamation to "the spirits in prison, . . . [who] formerly did not obey . . . while the ark was being prepared" (1 Pet. 3:18–20). Clarity does not translate into ease of understanding.

God himself provides help in this task: this doctrine is affirmed in the context of the church, in which God has installed a teaching office (1 Tim. 5:17). Pastors and teachers have the responsibility to assist church members in better understanding and applying Scripture. These leaders can map the flow of a narrative, note the progression of an argument, clarify theological concepts, and offer other helps. And they model how to apply Scripture.

On this last point, the clarity of Scripture demands that what is rightly understood be applied concretely. Depending on the text of Scripture, this proper application may be obedience to its commands, trust in its promises, confession of sin, and the like. Clear Scripture grips its readers' hearts and demands a personal response.

Scripture's clarity is also beneficial to unbelievers. Certainly, those who are being aided by the Holy Spirit as he moves them toward salvation gain an understanding of the gospel. What previously appeared to them as foolishness now makes sense. Even unbelievers in general can grasp something of clear Scripture. Though they ultimately end up rejecting the truth of which they have some understanding, they do have intellectual knowledge of those matters.

Biblical Support

Scripture directly affirms its own clarity: "The secret things belong to the LORD our God, but the things that are revealed belong to us and to our children forever" (Deut. 29:29). Much about God and his ways is hidden from human understanding. We do not—indeed, cannot—comprehend those secret things. Though Scripture does not exhaust the category of "revealed things," Scripture is certainly within that category's scope. The revealed things belong to God's people in terms of being accessible and intelligible to them. If Scripture is part of the revealed things, then it too is accessible and intelligible to God's people.

As Moses was finishing the writing of the Pentateuch, he explained, "This commandment . . . is not too hard for you, neither is it far off" (Deut. 30:11). There is no need to go to heaven to bring the Word of God down, nor cross the sea to bring it near. "But the word is very near you. It is in your mouth and in your heart, so that you can do it" (vv. 12–14). Scripture is not an obscure book. When parents sit on the bed with their children and tell a Bible story, or when friends comfort one another with passages they have memorized, the clear Word of God is not "far off" but "very near."

The clarity of Scripture prompted Moses to give his writings to the leaders of Israel, along with this command: "At the end of every seven years, . . . you shall read this law before all Israel in their hearing. Assemble the people, men, women, and little ones, and the sojourner within your towns, that they may hear and learn to fear the LORD your God" (Deut. 31:9–12). Moses expected that his writings would continue to be intelligible to the people of Israel, even when read in contexts very different from that in which he wrote them. Where the people were going, Moses did not know. But he did know that his writings would continue to be clear in the future.

Paul, looking back on four stories that Moses narrated in those writings, had a similar perspective (1 Cor. 10:1–11). Paul referenced episodes of Israelite idolatry (Exod. 32), sexual immorality (Num. 25:6–9), testing the Lord (21:4–9), and grumbling (Num. 14), along with God's judgment of those sins. He expected the Corinthians—Greek-speaking, Gentile Christians—to learn from those stories and so avoid committing those same sins and incurring that same condemnation: "Now these things took place as examples *for us*, that we might not desire evil as they did" (1 Cor. 10:6; emphasis added). Similarly, Paul pointed to Abraham being counted as righteous (Gen. 15:6) as the stellar example of justification by faith (Rom. 4:22–25). Indeed, "whatever was written in former days was written for our instruction" (15:4). Earlier Scripture would continue to be clear in the present.

A common mistake people make is to equate clarity with "ease of understanding." Peter's reference to Paul's writings is instructive: "There are some things in them that are hard to understand" (2 Pet. 3:16); not all of Paul's letters, but some. Even those limited things are not impossible to understand, but hard. There is no discouragement or prohibition of reading Scripture here; only a caution that some Scripture requires great effort. Scripture provides illustrations of leaders helping God's people to grasp God's word. For example, Ezra and other priests "brought the Law before the assembly, both men and women and all who could understand what they heard. . . . They read from the book, from the Law of God, clearly, and they gave the sense, so that the people understood the reading" (Neh. 8:2, 8). Elders (1 Tim. 5:17) or pastor-teachers (Eph. 4:11) serve this role in the church, helping members to rightly understand and properly apply Scripture.

Major Errors

1. *The denial of the ability of contemporary readers to understand the Bible because it is an outdated book that presents an antiquated worldview.* This perspective ignores Scripture's own presumption of continued intelligibility and the fact that Scripture's particularity addresses realities common to all people at all times and in all places.

2. *The abdication of responsibility for the interpretation of Scripture to a certain caste of people—the Catholic clergy, Protestant pastors, Bible scholars, and the like.* This position overlooks the responsibility given to all church members to nourish themselves on the Word of God (1 Pet. 2:1–3) and to teach everyone with it (Col. 3:16).

3. *Laziness or discouragement in personally applying oneself to reading the Bible.* This spiritual discipline has nearly disappeared. Additionally, when people come to difficult parts of Scripture, they don't realize the hard work that is needed, or they feel ill-equipped to do careful study, and they become discouraged and quit. People who hold this viewpoint fail to ask for help from pastors and teachers in the church.

ENACTING THE DOCTRINE

Because Scripture is clear, we should read with the expectation of understanding it. This doctrine dispels laziness, discouragement, and lack of habit in reading the Bible. Similarly, we should encourage other Christians to approach the Bible with the same anticipation.

All reading of Scripture should begin with prayer for the illumination of the Holy Spirit, who aids in both understanding and application: obedience, trust, praise, and repentance. When difficult passages present a challenge, help from pastors and teachers should be sought. As we share the gospel with unbelievers and the Holy Spirit moves them toward salvation, we can expect that the good news will become intelligible for them.

At stake in this doctrine is God's ability to reveal himself and his ways to his people, who are in desperate need of that revelation to be saved and transformed. If the Bible is clear, then God has condescended adequately to the human level, and his people can expect that what he has said, they can understand.

Perennial Questions and Problematic Issues

- If this doctrine is true, why are there so many different interpretations of Scripture?

- It seems that if Scripture is truly clear, then it should be easy to understand.

- I find it easier to wait for God to speak to me directly than to consult the Bible to try to figure out what he wants me to do.

- When my pastor preaches, he often refers to Hebrew and Greek words and explains cultural information that forms the backdrop for a passage, so if that's what it takes to understand the Bible, I'll never understand it.

TEACHING THE DOCTRINE

A good place to start is leading a Bible study, thus demonstrating that Scripture can be understood. This exercise is not about teaching the Bible or giving principles of interpretation. Rather, it is about asking thoughtful questions that will get the participants to interpret the text.

An excellent text is the story of Philip and the Ethiopian eunuch (Acts 8:26–40). Diagram the narrative flow and ask questions about the characterization (Who are the characters and what do they do? vv. 26–28), rising action (What crisis occurs? vv. 29–34), climax (How is the crisis resolved? v. 35), falling action (What new tension occurs? vv. 36–39a), and resolution (How does the story end? vv. 39b–40). Self-discovery of Scripture will encourage Christians to embrace its clarity.

Teaching through the key biblical passages is next. Ask what implications and applications can be drawn from these texts for the doctrine of clarity. It is important to underscore Scripture's attitude toward itself: the presumption of continued intelligibility. While emphasizing the illumination of the Holy Spirit, avoid minimizing the careful study of the Bible. Encourage both going to the pastors and teachers of the church for help and personally applying what is understood. Affirming this doctrine leads Christians to read Scripture with the anticipation of understanding God's Word to them.

TEACHING OUTLINE

1. The word "clarity" (or perspicuity) and the summary
2. Bible study: Acts 8:26–40 (or some other text)
3. Major affirmations (with biblical support)
   A. Scripture is intended to be understood.
   B. Scripture itself presumes it will continue to be intelligible.
   C. The Holy Spirit illuminates the minds of Christians as they read.
   D. Clarity does not mean ease.
   E. Christians should seek help from pastors and teachers.
   F. Understanding Scripture demands application.
4. Major errors to avoid
   A. Denying the ability of contemporary readers to understand the Bible because it is an outdated book that presents an antiquated worldview
   B. Abdicating the responsibility for the interpretation of Scripture to a certain caste of people—the Catholic clergy, Protestant pastors, Bible scholars, and the like
   C. Becoming lazy or discouraged in personally applying oneself to reading the Bible
5. Enacting the doctrine
   A. Reading the Bible expectantly
   B. Praying for the Holy Spirit's illumination
   C. Asking for help from pastors and teachers

RESOURCES

Allison, *Theological Terms*, s.v. "perspicuity of Scripture"
Grudem, *Systematic Theology*, chap. 6
Horton, *Pilgrim Theology*, 61–62
Thoennes, *Life's Biggest Questions*, chap. 4

6

THE TRANSFORMATIVE POWER OF SCRIPTURE

SUMMARY

The transformative power of Scripture is the multifaceted effect that God, its author, brings about through his Word.

MAIN THEMES

- The doctrine of the power of Scripture focuses on its effect.

- This power is not the magical effect of the mere (written or spoken) words of Scripture but is the effect of God speaking through his Word.

- Scripture's transformative power may act unilaterally but often engages the readers/hearers of Scripture in trusting, obeying, and heeding Scripture in other appropriate ways.

- Because Scripture is inspired and illumined by the Holy Spirit, its transformative effect is particularly associated with him.

- The infallibility of Scripture means that it never fails to accomplish the purpose intended by God (though its immediate effect may not be seen).

KEY SCRIPTURE

Psalms 19:7–11; 107:20; Jeremiah 23:29; Romans 10:17; 1 Thessalonians 2:13; 2 Timothy 3:16; Hebrews 4:12; 1 Peter 1:23–25; 2:2

UNDERSTANDING THE DOCTRINE

Major Affirmations

God sustains the closest possible relationship to his Word; he is completely invested in it. Indeed, God acts in this world through his Word.

Scripture is something more than words written on a page or spoken/read out loud. It is more than speech. Indeed, it is speech-act, because God does things with his words. God does more than proclaim words through Scripture. He performs certain things through his words. He engages in speech-acts that produce an effect in this world. Indeed, "the words of the Bible are a significant aspect of *God's action* in the world."[8]

A speech-act is an utterance consisting of three parts: (1) the *locution*, the content that is communicated; (2) the *illocution*, the force or intention with which it is communicated; and (3) the *perlocution*, the (intended) response of the hearer of the speech-act.[9] For example, "I now pronounce you husband and wife" (locution) is a declaration (illocution) that legally joins a man and a woman in marriage (perlocution). That speech-act marries that man and woman. There are many types of speech-acts: declarations, commands, promises, affirmations, warnings, rebukes, corrections, and more.

Scripture consists of divine speech-acts, with God doing things with his words. For example, Paul's letter contains the locution "Do not be anxious about anything." Its illocutionary force is a command, and its intended response is obedience expressed in ceasing one's worry about a particular situation. As another example, John narrates Jesus's quieting his disciples with, "I will come again." Its illocutionary force is a promise, and its intended response is trust in the midst of much personal distress.

Seeing Scripture as divine speech-acts enables us to understand its transformative power. It is not the magical effect of the mere (written or spoken) words of Scripture. Rather, the power is the effect of the God of Scripture doing things with his words. Moreover, though God may act unilaterally, generally speaking his speech-acts engage their recipients in some type of appropriate response to him. He declares, and praise is voiced. God

48

commands, and obedience is prompted. He promises, and faith is ignited. God affirms, and sound doctrine is confessed. He warns, and danger is avoided. God rebukes, and repentance is enacted. He corrects, and plans are changed.

Closely associated with the transformative power of Scripture is the one who inspired it, moving in its authors as they wrote, and who illumines it, aiding its readers/hearers to understand it rightly. The Spirit of God and the Word of God are intimately linked in regeneration, justification, sanctification, and much more.

Closely related to the transformative power of Scripture is its infallibility: it never fails to accomplish the purpose intended by God. According to speech-act theory, the absence of a response or a wrong response (perlocution) does not negate the effectiveness of the content (locution) and force (illocution) of a speech-act. Though its immediate effect may not be seen, Scripture, when read or heard, always realizes the aim for which God gave it.

Biblical Support

In one sense, because the omnipotent God is the author of Scripture, it assumes his transformative power is operative through his Word. Still, Scripture provides many examples of this effect.

At the beginning of creation, "God said, 'Let there be light,' and there was light" (Gen. 1:3). This phrase "God said" occurs ten times in Genesis 1, narrating that God created the universe by his speech-acts (Ps. 33:6; Heb. 11:3). After the fall, God pronounced curses on the serpent, the woman, and the man. One specific curse was pronounced on the ground, which became rotten. So God cursed the earth and all that was in it by his speech-acts (Gen. 3:14–19).

As God spoke to Abram, he commanded him to leave country, kindred, and family, and to travel to an unknown land. Abram departed and journeyed. God commanded Abram by a speech-act, and Abram obeyed (Gen. 12:1–4). God also promised to make Abram great, the father of a mighty nation. This same word was later repeated when Abram wavered, thinking that Eliezer would be the divine provision of an heir. The word of God assured Abram that his very own son would instead be the heir. Again, God spoke: "Look toward heaven, and number the stars, if you are able to number them." The promise resounded, "So shall your offspring be." "And he [Abram] believed the LORD, and he counted it to him as righteousness." God promised Abram by a speech-act; Abram believed, and he was justified by faith (15:1–6).

These examples could be multiplied many times. Indeed, "God has *invested* himself in his words."[10] God not only proclaims but also performs his mighty acts of creating, promising, commanding, warning, and more, through his words. They are divine speech-acts.

Scripture presents the transformative power of God's words. Specifically, "the word of God is living and active, sharper than any two-edged sword" (Heb. 4:12). This power is at the heart of God's question, "Is not my word like fire, declares the LORD, and like a hammer that breaks the rock in pieces?" (Jer. 23:29).

Specific transformative effects of Scripture include reviving the soul, making the simple wise, rejoicing the heart, enlightening the eyes, warning against sin, rewarding for obedience (Ps. 19:7–11), healing, and deliverance from destruction (107:20). Still more, God-breathed Scripture is "profitable" as it communicates sound doctrine, flags the wrong path on which one is traveling, shows the right path on which one should travel, and effects growth in holiness (2 Tim. 3:16–17).

The close connection between the Spirit of God and the Word of God is affirmed by Scripture. For example, the gospel is "the word of God, which is at work in you believers" (1 Thess. 2:13) as it ignites faith, for "faith comes through hearing, and hearing through the word of Christ" (Rom. 10:17). Faith is also associated with the Spirit, apart from whom "no one can say 'Jesus is Lord'" (1 Cor. 12:3). A second example: unbelievers are "born again, not of perishable seed but of imperishable, through the living and abiding word of God. . . . And this word is the good news . . . preached" (1 Pet. 1:23, 25). Regeneration is also tied to "the renewal of the Holy Spirit" (Titus 3:5; see also John 3:1–8). A third example: justification, the divine speech-act declaring condemned people "not guilty" but "righteous instead" (Rom. 8:1; 4:1–6), comes by means of the Spirit of God (1 Cor. 6:11). Finally, sanctification, for which the Holy Spirit is particularly responsible (2 Thess. 2:13; 1 Pet. 1:1–2), has special reference also to the Word (1 Pet. 2:2). This Word of God, which powerfully transforms, is intimately linked with the Spirit of God, who powerfully transforms (2 Cor. 3:18).

The infallibility of Scripture is expressed by means of a parallel with the effectiveness of precipitation: "As the rain and the snow . . . water the earth, making it bring forth . . . seed to the sower and bread to the eater, so shall my word be that goes out from my mouth; it shall not return to me empty, but it shall accomplish that which I purpose, and shall succeed in the thing for which I sent it" (Isa. 55:10–11). Without failure, and even when its effect is not detectable, Scripture achieves the will of God.

Major Errors

1. *The rejection of the inspiration of Scripture, leading to a denial of divine power operating through it.* This viewpoint contradicts both Scripture's own affirmation and the church's historic position.

2. *The denial of the authority and sufficiency of Scripture, resulting in the elevation of other "speech-acts" that are thought to effect transformation.* Examples include the Tradition of the Roman Catholic Church and its Magisterium, prophetic words or revelations, and personal experience. When these other speech-acts ascend to a level of authority greater than Scripture, their "transformative power" is thought to eclipse that of Scripture. The question looms large, however, whether their effect corresponds with God's will and revelation.

3. *Any failure to respond correctly to the locution and illocution of God's speech-acts in Scripture.* If God commands and there is no response of obedience, or if the response is disobedience, he is displeased. If God promises and there is no response of trust, or if the response is mistrust, God is angered. Often, such failures result from misunderstanding Scripture as mere words on a page or sounds in the air. Rather, it consists of God's speech-acts.

ENACTING THE DOCTRINE

This doctrine reminds us that God is constantly engaging us with his Word, demanding a personal response. Indeed, he challenges us toward transformation. For example, if we fruitfully engage in some ministry activity and arrogantly conclude that we are God's gift to the world, his Word confronts us with our sinfulness and inadequacy apart from him. Oppositely, if we feel a sense of failure and worthlessness, God's Word comforts us with his delight in us as his redeemed children. In this sense, Scripture is our adversary, always challenging us with its speech-acts. We can never treat it as just another book, as an object to study, as some text to master.

With this attitude toward Scripture, we can approach it with eager expectation for God to transform us. We resonate with Jeremiah: "Your words were found, and I ate them, and your words became to me a joy and the delight of my heart" (Jer. 15:16).

TEACHING THE DOCTRINE

Because participants will have experienced the transformative power of Scripture, ask them to recount some specific changes God has brought about in them through it. In anticipation of explaining speech-acts, identify the type of speech-act—a command, a promise, a warning, a declaration, a correction—that effected that particular transformation. Living examples of Scripture's powerful effect on the participants will help them concretely grasp this doctrine.

Perennial Questions and Problematic Issues

- When I read the Bible, I never seem to get anything out of it.
- If Scripture is so important, should I focus on reading as much as I possibly can?
- When God speaks to me directly, I'm ready to trust and obey him, much more so than when I read or hear the Bible.
- I listen to so many sermons each week that I get dizzy just trying to count all the applications that I'm supposed to be making.

Though it may seem complicated, speech-act theory is quite simple and very practical. Don't shy away from teaching it. Use common examples such as the wedding illustration. Then show some biblical examples to demonstrate that Scripture consists of divine speech-acts.

Watch out for the far-too-common perspective that Scripture is a magical book whose words function like incantations that have mystical effects. An example of this is the Christian who reads his Bible for fifteen minutes every day, not to pay attention to God, but because he treats Scripture like a lucky charm, hoping to appease God and ward off evil. To correct this typical misconception, underscore the very close relationship between God and his Word. He is completely invested in it, and it is God with whom we must deal as we read and meditate upon it. This doesn't remove the mystery, but it rescues it from the realm of magic and puts it in the realm of God and his powerful work, where it rightly belongs.

In teaching about the close link between the Word and the Spirit, be sure to encourage the participants to pray for the Spirit's illumination as they read, study, memorize, and meditate on Scripture. His illuminating work will guide them into a sound understanding and will prepare them to respond rightly with praise, thanksgiving, repentance, trust, obedience, and more.

────────────── **TEACHING OUTLINE** ──────────────

1. The summary
2. Concrete examples of Scripture's transformative power
3. Introduction to speech-acts
4. Major affirmations (with biblical support)
   A. The close relationship between God and his Word
   B. Transformative power
   C. The intimate connection between the Word and the Holy Spirit
   D. Infallibility of Scripture
5. Major errors to avoid
   A. Rejecting the inspiration of Scripture, leading to a denial of divine power operating through it
   B. Denying the authority and sufficiency of Scripture, resulting in the elevation of other speech-acts that are thought to effect transformation
   C. Failing to respond correctly to the locution and illocution of God's speech-acts in Scripture
6. Enacting the doctrine
   A. Approaching Scripture as our adversary that challenges us
   B. Expecting Scripture to transform us

────────────── **RESOURCES** ──────────────

Allison, *Theological Terms*, s.vv. "infallibility of Scripture," "speech-act theory"
Grenz, *Theology for the Community of God*, chap. 14

7

THE CANONICITY
OF SCRIPTURE

SUMMARY

The canon of Scripture, or list of which writings belong in the inspired Word of God, consists of sixty-six books.

MAIN THEMES

- The doctrine of the canonicity of Scripture treats the list of books that belong in the inspired Word of God.
- The canon of the Protestant Bible consists of thirty-nine books in the Old Testament and twenty-seven in the New Testament.
- The canon of the Roman Catholic Bible contains additional material—the apocryphal writings—in the Old Testament; the New Testament is identical to that of the Protestant Bible.
- Generally speaking, the Eastern Orthodox Bible contains even more additional material in the Old Testament than does the Roman Catholic Bible; the New Testament is identical to that of the Roman Catholic Bible and Protestant Bible.

- The Hebrew Bible never contained the apocryphal writings, so the Bible of Jesus and the apostles was the same as the Protestant Old Testament.

- Until Augustine, the early church did not accept the apocryphal writings.

- The Protestant Reformers rejected the apocryphal writings, returning to the canon of the Bible of Jesus and the apostles and the canonical tradition of the early church.

- The Roman Catholic Council of Trent officially proclaimed the apocryphal writings as canonical and condemned the Protestant rejection of them.

- The apocryphal writings develop the idea of purgatory, praying for the dead, and merit.

KEY SCRIPTURE

Luke 24:44; 2 Timothy 3:14–17; 2 Peter 3:15–16; Revelation 22:18

UNDERSTANDING THE DOCTRINE

Major Affirmations

Which writings belong in the Bible? This question is at the heart of the canonicity of Scripture. The word "canon," used metaphorically, means "list." The biblical canon, then, is the list of the books that God wanted to be included in his inspired, authoritative Word.

One of the major points of difference between the Roman Catholic Church and Protestant churches is their canon of Scripture. This difference does not pertain to the New Testament; both traditions have the same twenty-seven books. The divergence arises with respect to the Old Testament canon: the Protestant Bible consists of thirty-nine writings, while the Roman Catholic Bible contains those thirty-nine books with additional materials. These are the apocryphal writings, or Apocrypha for short: seven extra books—Tobit, Judith, Wisdom, Ecclesiasticus (note the ending), Baruch, and 1 and 2 Maccabees—and additional sections to Esther and Daniel.

The church inherited its "sacred writings" (2 Tim. 3:15) from the Jews, and the Hebrew Bible consisted of the same books as found in the Protestant Old Testament. How those writings are grouped, and the order in which they are placed, is different in the Hebrew Bible than in the Protestant Old Testament, but the content is identical.

Before the time of Christ, the Hebrew Bible was translated into Greek— the Septuagint, or LXX for short—and contained writings not included in Hebrew Scripture. Thus, a longer version of the Old Testament eventually circulated among the largely Greek-speaking early church. Church leaders distinguished between canonical books and these additional books. Indeed, several early church lists of canonical Old Testament Scripture include only the writings found in the Hebrew Bible and explicitly deny that the Apocrypha belongs in the canon.

Commissioned in 382 to produce a new Latin translation of the Bible, Jerome (ca. 345–420) worked from the Hebrew Bible rather than the Septuagint. His list of canonical Old Testament Scripture included only the writings in the Hebrew Bible. He considered the apocryphal writings to be noncanonical. He advised that while the apocryphal writings could be read for the church's edification, they must not be used for doctrinal formulation.

The intervention of Augustine was decisive. He considered the Apocrypha to be canonical because the Holy Spirit had spoken through both the writers of the Hebrew Bible and the translators of the Septuagint. Thus both versions were divinely inspired and authoritative. Augustine prevailed upon Jerome to translate the apocryphal writings from the Septuagint and include those translations in Jerome's Latin Vulgate. This Old Testament, together with Jerome's Latin translation of the New Testament, circulated and became widely known. Thus, the apocryphal writings were included in the church's canon of Scripture. This expanded Latin Vulgate would be the church's Bible for the next one thousand years.

As the early Christians gathered to worship, they read not only the "sacred writings" of the Jews—the original Scriptures for the church—but also the writings of the apostles. Four accounts of the life and ministry of Jesus, a history of the apostolic church, letters, and an apocalypse (vision of the future) were held in high esteem during the first decades of the church. Eventually, twenty-seven of these were acknowledged to be the inspired, authoritative writings of the New Testament.

To recognize these rightful canonical writings, the church was aided by two criteria:

1. Apostolicity: Did this writing have an apostle (for example, Matthew, John) or someone associated with an apostle (for example, Luke in association with Paul, Mark in association with Peter) for its author?
2. Antiquity: Has the church historically recognized the voice of God speaking in this writing? Most of the writings in the developing New Testament were acknowledged as canonical from early on, and the first list of all twenty-seven writings appeared in 367.

Thus, through a relatively long historical process, the Old Testament and the New Testament became the Word of God for the church.

The issue of the canon of Scripture resurfaced in the Reformation. Protestants insisted that the church's Old Testament should correspond to the shorter Hebrew Bible, not the Septuagint with its additional apocryphal writings. Key to this position was the fact that the Bible of Jesus and the apostles was Jewish Scripture. Additionally, the Apocrypha had not been considered canonical by the early church. Moreover, following Jerome's distinction, the Reformers admonished the church to appeal to canonical Scripture alone to formulate its authoritative doctrines. Accordingly, Protestants rejected purgatory and the practice of praying for the dead, because they were based on an apocryphal writing (2 Maccabees). Furthermore, the Reformers modified or abolished certain church practices, like the sacrament of penance, because they were based on an inferior Latin Vulgate translation and not supported by the Greek New Testament.

The Roman Catholic Church denounced this Protestant challenge to its canonical Scripture. At the Council of Trent, it proclaimed the Latin Vulgate as its official version of the Bible, and it confirmed that the apocryphal writings belong to the canonical Old Testament.

Thus, one of the major points of division between Roman Catholics and Protestants is the canon of Scripture.

Biblical Support

As Moses was finishing his writing of the law, he "gave it to the priests, the sons of Levi, who carried the ark of the covenant of the LORD, and to all the elders of Israel" (Deut. 31:9). Thus began the process of collecting the "sacred writings" of Israel, a collection that was closed several centuries prior to Christ's coming. It was to this collection that Paul referred when describing Scripture as "God-breathed" (2 Tim. 3:14–17).

The canon of the Hebrew Bible consisted of twenty-two writings grouped into three divisions (note how some of the writings are joined together and counted as one book).

1. The Law: the five books of Moses
2. The Prophets: the thirteen prophetic books of Joshua, Judges (including Ruth), Samuel (one book), Kings (one book), Jeremiah (including Lamentations), Ezekiel, Isaiah, the Twelve Minor Prophets (one book), Job, Daniel, Ezra-Nehemiah (one book), Chronicles (one book), and Esther
3. The Writings: the four books of Psalms, Proverbs, Ecclesiastes, and Song of Songs

The New Testament refers to this threefold division as "the Law of Moses and the Prophets and the Psalms" (Luke 24:44); most commonly, the reference is to "the Law and the Prophets" (Matt. 7:12; Rom. 3:21). A comment by Jesus shows that the Hebrew Bible was ordered differently than the Old Testament is today, as it began with Genesis and concluded with Chronicles (Matt. 23:35). It was from this Jewish Scripture that Jesus taught in the synagogue (Luke 4:16–21). Indeed, Jesus frequently and definitively quoted from and alluded to Scripture throughout his three-year ministry: it was the inspired, authoritative Word of God.

Within decades of Jesus's death and resurrection, writings that are now part of the New Testament circulated among the early churches. Peter underscores the canonical status of Paul's writings, speaking of them in the context of "the other Scriptures"—that is, the Old Testament writings (2 Pet. 3:15–16). The closure of the canon of the New Testament is acknowledged with urgency at the end of its last book (Rev. 22:18).

Major Errors

1. *The denial of the canonicity of the Old Testament.* This perspective commits three mistakes: It ignores Jesus's view of Hebrew Scripture. It dismisses the early church's insistence on the unity of the Old and New Testaments and the necessity of both for understanding the identity and mission of Jesus Christ. And it scorns the two-thousand-year acknowledgment of the Old Testament as part of the canon of the Christian Bible.

2. *The suspicion that biblical books that include claims to authorship (for example, the Pastoral Letters claim Pauline authorship) were not written by those authors.* This suspicion can lead to the denial of the inspiration of Scripture. However, this view overlooks the solid internal and external evidence for the authorship of those biblical books, and rejects Scripture's own claim that it is inspired and thus the Word of God.

3. *The view that the process of the church's recognition of the biblical canon was a merely human activity, carried out without God's assistance.* This position denies God's providential action in the world. Not only did he guide the biblical authors as they were writing (2 Pet. 1:19–21), and not only did he breathe out the actual writings themselves (2 Tim. 3:14–17; 1 Cor. 2:10–16), but he also guided the early church to acknowledge which writings he wanted to be included in its Bible.

ENACTING THE DOCTRINE

While it is legitimate to read the apocryphal books for encouraging stories of wisdom, faith, courage, and hope, the church is not to consult them when formulating its doctrine. As for canonical Scripture, its rich variety of genre—narratives, prophecies, poems, laws, proverbs, apocalypses, letters, and gospels—brings a depth and breadth to divine revelation. The church should appreciate this wonderful diversity of biblical writing, which is intended to stir our mind, heart, emotions, motivations, and will—every aspect of our being. Still, amid this wide variety of genres, the Bible is one book with a unity: the good news of God's work through Christ in the Holy Spirit for the sake of his people's salvation and flourishing.

What's at stake in this doctrine? The key question is, Which writings belong in the Bible? Protestants reject the apocryphal writings that are included in the Roman Catholic Old Testament for several important reasons. Also at stake is what God requires of his people in order to be saved. Included in some of the apocryphal writings are the doctrines and practices of purgatory, praying for the dead, and achieving merit before God. But Protestants deny that souls need to go to purgatory after death in order to be cleansed of the taint of forgiven sin, a temporal process that can be shortened by their loved ones praying for their souls to be released from purgatory. And the idea that redeemed people can merit any favor from God contradicts the gospel of grace alone by faith alone in Christ alone.

- I've always been afraid to read the Apocrypha because it is Catholic and not Protestant.
- It seems that the recognition of the canon of the Christian Bible was largely the result of a historical process, but was the Holy Spirit active as well in helping the church to navigate this process?
- If God allowed the church from the fifth to the sixteenth century to consider the apocryphal writings to be part of the Bible, how do we Protestants know that we now have the correct Old Testament canon?

TEACHING THE DOCTRINE

A good place to start is to physically compare a copy of the Roman Catholic Bible (for example, the Jerusalem Bible) with a copy of a Protestant Bible (ESV, NIV, KJV). Attention should be drawn to the inclusion of the apocryphal writings in the former Bible and their absence in the latter Bible. Then, read a section of the Apocrypha (a good text is Bel and the Dragon, chapter 14 in the expanded Daniel) and ask for the participants' impressions. To underscore the key point that some of the apocryphal writings contain doctrines and practices with which Protestants disagree, read and discuss the section on purgatory and prayer for the dead in 2 Maccabees (12:38–46).

There is no getting around the fact that most of the teaching of this doctrine is a presentation of the historical development of the canon. Provide enough detail, but don't overwhelm or bore the participants. Additionally, emphasize the ongoing providence of God in directing this historical process, so that we can have confidence that we have the canon of Scripture that he wants us to possess.

TEACHING OUTLINE

1. The word "canonicity" and the summary
2. The difference between the Roman Catholic canon of Scripture, the Orthodox canon, and the Protestant canon
3. Reading(s) from the Apocrypha
4. Major affirmations (with biblical support)
   A. The Bible of Jesus and his apostles: Hebrew Bible without the Apocrypha
   B. Historical development of the Old Testament canon
   C. Historical development of the New Testament canon

5. Major errors to avoid
   A. Denying the canonicity of the Old Testament
   B. Doubting that biblical books that include claims to authorship were written by those authors
   C. Viewing the process of the church's recognition of the biblical canon as a merely human activity carried out without God's assistance
6. Enacting the doctrine
   A. Reading the apocryphal writings for encouragement
   B. Rejecting the apocryphal writings as grounds for church doctrines and practices

RESOURCES

Allison, *Theological Terms*, s.v. "canon of Scripture"
Elwell, *Evangelical Dictionary of Theology*, s.v. "Bible, Canon of"
Grudem, *Systematic Theology*, chap. 3

PART 2

DOCTRINE

—— OF ——

GOD

8

THE KNOWABILITY
AND INCOMPREHENSIBILITY
OF GOD

SUMMARY

Because of his self-revelation, God can be known, but never fully understood, by his human creatures.

MAIN THEMES

- Both general and special revelation are means by which God manifests himself.

- As divine-image bearers, human beings are able to obtain knowledge of God.

- This knowability is not exhaustive but real and sufficient, fitted to human capacity.

- Incomprehensibility means not that God is completely un-intelligible but that he can never be completely grasped.

KEY SCRIPTURE

Deuteronomy 29:29; Job 11:7–8; Psalm 19:1–4; Jeremiah 9:23–24; Matthew 11:27; John 17:3; Acts 14:8–18; 17:22–31; Romans 1:18–25; 2:12–16; 1 Corinthians 13:12; 1 John 5:20

UNDERSTANDING THE DOCTRINE

Major Affirmations

Because of his self-revelation, God can be known by his human creatures. This knowability is grounded on two facts: (1) God's free decision to make himself known through both general and special revelation, and (2) the God-given capacity of human beings, as image bearers of God, to know him. Knowing God personally is the greatest privilege and boast of believers. It is eternal life itself and comes only through the Son's revelation of God. Still, unbelievers possess some knowledge of God but suppress it to their own demise.

General revelation is God's disclosure of himself to all peoples at all times and in all places. It comes through the creation, conscience, God's providential care, and an innate sense of God with which all peoples are wired. The recipients of general revelation know that God exists, some of his divine attributes, and basic principles of his moral law.

Special revelation is God's disclosure of himself to particular peoples at particular times and in particular places. It comes through historical events, dreams and visions, direct divine speech, the incarnation, and Scripture. The recipients of special revelation know the way of salvation and how to walk with God so as to please him fully.

The knowledge of God that people possess is not exhaustive knowledge, but it is nonetheless real (it is bona fide knowledge of the Creator-Redeemer God) and sufficient, divinely tailored to finite human capacity. God is, in other words, incomprehensible. In one sense, incomprehensible means that something is completely unintelligible; nothing can be known about it. It is not in this sense that God is incomprehensible. Rather, it means that God can never be completely grasped: though knowable to the degree that, and in the manner in which, he reveals himself, God can never be fully comprehended. Indeed, not even one single aspect of God—his knowledge, power, ways, justice, and more—can be fully known. This limitation is due to two factors: finite creatures can never fully understand the infinite God, and human creatures suffer from the noetic (intellectual) effects of the fall such that their understanding of him is distorted.

Some Christians add to this discussion the traditional proofs for the existence of God. Ontological (from Greek *ontos*, "being") arguments have to do with the being of God. They are *a priori* arguments, meaning that they are prior to human experience. Thus, they focus on thinking about the concept of God and do not appeal to experiences of him. Cosmological (from Greek *kosmos*, "world") arguments have to do with this world. As *a posteriori* arguments, they are based on experience, specifically causation. For this world to exist, which it does, there must have been some cause, which is God. Teleological (from Greek *telos*, "purpose") arguments have to do with the design evident in this world. As *a posteriori* arguments, they are based on the experience of design and purpose. Moral arguments have to do with the human sense of right and wrong. As *a posteriori* arguments, they are based on human moral experience.

Christians are divided over the soundness and effectiveness of these rational arguments for God's existence.

Biblical Support

From its opening page, Scripture assumes that God is knowable. Indeed, Scripture is God's inspired written revelation of himself to his image bearers that they may know him. As Jeremiah underscores, "Thus says the LORD: 'Let not the wise man boast in his wisdom, let not the mighty man boast in his might, let not the rich man boast in his riches, but let him who boasts boast in this, that he understands and knows me, that I am the LORD who practices steadfast love, justice, and righteousness in the earth'" (Jer. 9:23–24). The only proper human boast is that one knows the living God.

The Bible witnesses to five modes of special revelation, which is God's communication to particular people whom he has chosen. (1) *Scripture* leads to faith in Christ for salvation and equips believers for every good work (2 Tim. 3:15–17). Other modes are (2) *historical events* (for example, the exodus), by which God manifested his power, righteousness, and wrath; (3) *dreams and visions* (for example, to Abraham and Joseph), internal communications by which God revealed his will; (4) *direct divine speech* (for example, God's communication with Moses), by which he expressed his commands and promises; and (5) the *incarnation*, by which the Son of God became a man and revealed the words, works, and nature of God. Particular people at particular times and in particular places are recipients of special revelation by which they personally know God, his ways, and his will.

Apart from, and affirmed by, Scripture, general revelation is the means by which God reveals himself universally. Such revelation comes through four modes: (1) the *creation*, which reveals God the Creator (Rom. 1:18–25; Ps. 19:1–4); (2) the *human conscience*, by which all people know something of God's standards of right and wrong, and which thereby reveals God the moral lawgiver (Rom. 2:12–16); (3) *divine providence*, the continuous work of God by which he sustains the creation in existence, thereby revealing his goodness and care (Acts 14:8–18); and (4) an *innate sense of God*, a divinely implanted awareness of God's existence and worthiness to be worshiped (17:22–31). All peoples at all times and in all places are recipients of general revelation, by which they know that he exists, some of his attributes, and something of his moral law.

General revelation, while truly manifesting God, is insufficient for people to have a personal knowledge of God that leads to heartfelt worship and dependence on him. The problem lies not with general revelation itself but with the sinful recipients who fail to see that revelation as they should. In their rejection of general revelation, they are without excuse (Rom. 1:20). They do not know God as they should; therefore, they "do not know God" (1 Cor. 1:21; Gal. 4:8; 1 Thess. 4:5).

Only by salvation through Christ can their sinful blindness be lifted. As Jesus explains, "No one knows the Son except the Father, and no one knows the Father except the Son and anyone to whom the Son chooses to reveal him" (Matt. 11:27). Knowledge of the Father is dependent on the Son's revelation of him, enabling sinful people to know God forever. As Jesus prayed, "And this is eternal life, that they know you, the only true God, and Jesus Christ whom you have sent" (John 17:3; cf. 1 John 5:20). This saving knowledge comes through the Holy Spirit, author of Scripture and applier of redemption (1 Cor. 2:10–13; 12:1–3). While waiting for face-to-face knowledge of God, believers now know him by faith in a partial, yet true, way (13:12).

Even when knowledge of God is face-to-face, he will forever remain incomprehensible. Certainly, God has manifested "the revealed things" to his people, but there is much about himself—"the secret things"—that

God has not revealed and will never reveal (Deut. 29:29). The divine incomprehensibility is highlighted in Job in a series of questions: "Can you find out the deep things of God? Can you find out the limit of the Almighty? It is higher than heaven—what can you do? Deeper than Sheol—what can you know?" (Job 11:7–8). The answers are "no" and "nothing."

This quandary is due to the Creator-creature distinction: God is infinite, and human beings are finite. Thus, they know finitely (Isa. 40:18). Indeed, they can never fully understand any single thing about God: his greatness (Ps. 145:3), his understanding (147:5), his knowledge (139:6), his ways and thoughts (Isa. 55:9), and his riches, wisdom, judgment, and ways (Rom. 11:33).

Accordingly, God is knowable in the way that, and to the degree to which, he makes himself known through both general and special revelation. Human knowledge of God is partial yet true and sufficient, while God remains incomprehensible.

Major Errors

1. *Agnosticism, the denial of God's knowability. Atheism is the denial of God's existence.* Both are contradicted by the biblical perspective on God's knowability and universal religious experience.

2. *Claims by certain people to know God more fully and intimately than other people can because of possessing some secret knowledge.* This gnostic or mystic view invents novel paths to access knowledge of God (for example, extreme asceticism leading to ecstatic experiences). It is refuted by the divinely ordained means, especially Scripture, by which such knowledge is to be obtained.

3. *The contemporary obsession with human experience as the ultimate source of the knowledge of God.* Eschewing divine revelation, especially Scripture, this approach formulates its view of God based on individual experience, personal revelations, and the like. This approach is nothing more than a human projection onto God.

ENACTING THE DOCTRINE

Scripture invites believers to boast in the highest privilege accorded to human beings—that they know God personally. Believers, then, should be forever grateful to God for revealing himself through his Son and Spirit and for granting them eternal life—not a reality that awaits death or the return of Christ, but the present possession of knowing God. This knowledge should be nurtured and lived every day through reading, praying, applying, and meditating on Scripture.

People's experience of general revelation is a good springboard for Christians to engage in conversations leading to the gospel. Questions such as "What do you sense when you observe the grandeur of mountain peaks or the vastness of the ocean?" "How do you deal with the hypocrisy in your heart when you fail to live up to the standards you set for yourself?" and "Why do you think you were spared in that devastating automobile accident?" can prompt self-reflection and may be steps along the path to embracing salvation through the gospel.

Perennial Questions and Problematic Issues

- We will never be able to know everything about God, so what does this indicate about our eternal relationship with him?

- If people suppress the knowledge of God that is available through general revelation, what good is it?

- I hear that many Muslims have dreams and visions of Christ, so what should we think about them?

TEACHING THE DOCTRINE

Jeremiah 9:23–24 is a wonderful jumping-off point for teaching this doctrine, as it calls for the participants to boast—something that Christians think they should avoid doing! Key to teaching, then, is to instill a sense of privilege and joy because the one, true, living God is knowable.

Teaching through the two modes of divine revelation helps participants to embrace both the universality of the knowledge of God, which is general revelation for all peoples, and the particularity of the personal knowledge of God, which is special revelation for particular peoples. While it is right to champion the exclusivity of salvation that comes through Christ alone, the church also insists on the inclusivity of the general knowledge of God through the creation, the human conscience, divine providence, and the innate sense of God. Leading a Bible study through the key passages (Rom. 1:18–25; 2:12–16; Acts 14:8–18; 17:22–31) is a great exercise to get participants into Scripture.

Teaching the incomprehensibility of God reminds participants of the difference between the infinite God and them as finite people. It also draws their attention to the errors in their thinking about God due to the noetic (intellectual) effects of the fall. Of course, the participants don't think they have incorrect thoughts about God, for surely if they had such errors, they would renounce them and start thinking rightly. Here's the key point: the participants are unaware of these incorrect thoughts. And that is one of the reasons why teaching theology is so important: to make people aware of errors in their understanding of God and his ways so they can correct those errors and know, love, and serve God more properly.

TEACHING OUTLINE

1. The summary
2. Major affirmations (with biblical support)
   A. Knowability
   B. General revelation
   C. Special revelation
   D. Incomprehensibility
3. Major errors to avoid
   A. Denying the knowability or existence of God
   B. Claiming to know God more fully and intimately than other people can because of possession of some secret knowledge
   C. Obsessing over human experience as the ultimate source of the knowledge of God
4. Enacting the doctrine
   A. Boasting in and cultivating the knowledge of God
   B. Turning others' experience of general revelation into opportunities to communicate the gospel

RESOURCES

Allison, *Theological Terms*, s.vv. "general revelation," "incomprehensibility," "knowability," "special revelation"

Elwell, *Evangelical Dictionary of Theology*, s.vv. "God, Arguments for the Existence of," "Revelation, General," "Revelation, Special"

Erickson, *Christian Theology*, chaps. 6–7
Grenz, *Theology for the Community of God*, chap. 1
Grudem, *Systematic Theology*, chap. 10
Horton, *Pilgrim Theology*, chap. 1
Thoennes, *Life's Biggest Questions*, chaps. 2, 5

9

THE INCOMMUNICABLE ATTRIBUTES OF GOD

SUMMARY

The incommunicable attributes are God's characteristics or perfections, as revealed by Scripture, that God does not communicate, or share, with human beings.

MAIN THEMES

- God's incommunicable attributes are those characteristics or perfections that he does not share with human beings.
- They are independence, immutability, eternity, omnipresence, simplicity, and spirituality.
- These attributes highlight the Creator-creature distinction and divine transcendence.
- God is to be praised for his incommunicable attributes.

KEY SCRIPTURE

Exodus 3:14; 1 Kings 8:27; Psalms 90:1–4; 102:25–27; 139:7–12; Malachi 3:1; John 4:24; 5:26; Acts 17:24–25; Romans 1:18–25; Ephesians 1:11; 1 Timothy 1:17; 6:15–16; James 1:17

UNDERSTANDING THE DOCTRINE

Major Affirmations

In the discussion of God's attributes, a common approach is to distinguish between his incommunicable attributes and his communicable attributes. This does not mean there are two distinct "bundles" of characteristics in God. Rather, the two headings are helpful in presenting a large amount of material. Moreover, they highlight important points—specifically, the Creator-creature distinction and God's transcendence (the incommunicable attributes), and the fact that human beings are created in God's image and thus mirror him in some ways (the communicable attributes).

The incommunicable attributes are God's characteristics or perfections that he does not communicate, or share, with human beings. As we are using the word here, "communicable" means "shareable." Certainly, God creates human beings in his image, meaning that they mirror him in some respect. However, the characteristics that human beings reflect are his communicable attributes, not his incommunicable attributes. The latter have no counterpoint in human beings.

Independence is the divine attribute of self-existence. God's very nature is to exist. He is not and cannot be dependent on anything or anyone. This attribute underscores the Creator-creature distinction: whereas the Creator is completely independent, creatures are completely dependent, contingent on his will for their existence. God is self-sufficient. Philosophically, God's existence is necessary: he must exist. By contrast, the existence of some things (for example, a square circle) is impossible, and the existence of other things (for example, angels and human beings) is possible. Unlike these things, God's existence—and his existence alone—is necessary. God must exist.

Immutability, or unchangeableness, is the divine characteristic signifying that God is unchanging yet consistently acting. He is immutable in terms of his essence: God eternally exists as Father, Son, and Holy Spirit.

He is unchanging with respect to his perfections: God is eternally omniscient, loving, holy, and so on. He is immutable in terms of his decree or plan: God has eternally established his purpose for creation, which he is sure to fulfill. He is unchanging with respect to his promises: God is completely committed to fulfilling his commitments, and he never reneges on his pledges. Immutability, like independence, underscores the Creator-creature distinction: whereas God is completely unchanging, human beings constantly change.

However, God's immutability does not mean that he is unmoving. Indeed, God responds to prayer and forgives people when they repent, acting consistently with his immutable being and purposes. Thus, there is no ultimate conflict between divine immutability and biblical statements that God relented or changed his mind.

Eternity is the divine attribute by which God is not bound by time but always exists. Eternity is God's infinity with respect to time. He has no beginning, end, or time-sequenced development in his being (he is not getting older). God is not bound by time. Indeed, he existed before he created the spatial-temporal universe. Still, he does act in time. For example, before time began, he chose believers (Eph. 1:4). Moreover, the Son became incarnate at the appropriate time (Gal. 4:4). This attribute underscores the divine transcendence: God is infinitely exalted over creation, which has a beginning and is temporal.

Omnipresence is the divine characteristic of being all-present. God is present everywhere with his entire being at the same time. He is not limited by space and should not be considered as being enormously big or located in one place rather than another. Though he is present everywhere, God manifests his presence in different ways in different situations, to bless, curse, warn, or comfort. This attribute underscores the divine transcendence: God is infinitely exalted over creation, which has spatial dimension and is located in one place.

Simplicity is the divine attribute signifying that God is his attributes. He is not composed of parts, with his characteristics like holiness, love, and power being ingredients of which he is made. Additionally, God is not a divine nature to which are added the perfections of knowledge, eternity, and justice. Rather, God is his nature, and he is his attributes. This attribute underscores the Creator-creature distinction: whereas God is simple, human beings are complex creatures, being both material (body) and immaterial aspect (soul/spirit).

Spirituality is the divine characteristic signifying that God is immaterial in nature. He has no physical aspect. This attribute underscores the Creator-creature distinction: human nature is complex, being both material and immaterial. God's nature, by contrast, is not material: he has no physical component, but is immaterial only. Divine spirituality does not mean that God cannot be present tangibly. Indeed, God can manifest his glory, yet his being can never be seen.

For his incommunicable attributes, God is to be worshiped and praised.

Biblical Support

God is "the One who is high and lifted up" (Isa. 57:15), "enthroned in the heavens" (Ps. 123:1). The Son is called the "firstborn of all creation," referring to his preeminence over all that was created "through him and for him" (Col. 1:15–16). This divine transcendence underscores the Creator-creature distinction, as seen particularly in God's incommunicable attributes.

God's *independence* is emphasized by the name by which he is known: YHWH, "I AM WHO I AM" (Exod. 3:14–15): God is, he is existent, and his very name underscores his self-existence. As the one who "has life in himself" (John 5:26), he "made the world and everything in it" and gives "life and breath and everything" to his creatures (Acts 17:24–25). He is independent, and all creation is dependent on him for its existence.

God declares his own *immutability*: "I the LORD do not change" (Mal. 3:6). With him "there is no variation or shadow due to change" (James 1:17). The divine immutability is contrasted with human change. Speaking of the heaven and the earth, the psalmist notes, "They will perish, but you will remain; they will all wear out like a garment. You will change them like a robe, and they will pass away, but you are the same, and your years have no end" (Ps. 102:26–27). Moreover, God does not vary his eternal plan. Rather, he "works all things according to the counsel of his will" (Eph. 1:11), which counsel "stands forever" (Ps. 33:11; Isa. 46:9–11). God's promises are unchanging as well: "God is not man, that he should lie, or a son of man, that he should change his mind. Has he said, and will he not do it? Or has he spoken, and will he not fulfill it?" (Num. 23:19).

God's *eternity* is affirmed by expressions like "from everlasting to everlasting" (Pss. 90:2; 106:48) and "before all time and now and forever" (Jude 25). Moreover, he is immortal (1 Tim. 1:17; Rom. 1:23); indeed, he "alone has immortality" (1 Tim. 6:16). His greatness and incomprehensibility are connected to his eternality: "Behold, God is great, and we know him not; the number of his years is unsearchable" (Job 36:26). God sustains a unique relationship to time, such that "with the Lord one day is as a thousand years, and a thousand years as one day" (2 Pet. 3:8; Ps. 90:4).

God's *omnipresence* is underscored in response to a question: "Where shall I go from your Spirit? Or where shall I flee from your presence?" Wrong answers include heaven, Sheol (the realm of the dead), the far reaches of the sea, and the cover of darkness (Ps. 139:7–12). There is no escaping God, for he "[fills] heaven and earth" (Jer. 23:24). Though his glorious presence dwells with his people, even the builder of the temple exclaims, "But will God indeed dwell on the earth? Behold, heaven and the highest heaven cannot contain you; how much less this house that I have built!" (1 Kings 8:27).

Divine *simplicity* is a theological conclusion drawn from such biblical affirmations as "God is love" (1 John 4:8), God is holy (1 Pet. 1:15–16), and "whose name is Jealous" (Exod. 34:14). God is not partly love, partly holy, and partly jealous. Rather, love, holiness, and jealousy are characteristic of the whole of God. Furthermore, God *is* love, he *is* holy, and he *is* jealousy, for God is his attributes.

The *spirituality* of God was affirmed by Jesus himself, who noted, "God is spirit" (John 4:24). It certainly is the proper theological conclusion drawn from biblical affirmations that God is invisible (Col. 1:15; 1 Tim. 1:17), such that "no one has ever seen or can see" him (1 Tim. 6:16). His nature is like that of no other, including human beings.

An example of worship directed to God for his incommunicable attributes is the following: "To the King of the ages [eternal], immortal, invisible, the only God, be honor and glory forever and ever. Amen" (1 Tim. 1:17).

Major Errors

1. *Any reduction of the Creator-creature distinction.* There is a tendency to define the divine attributes by beginning from a creaturely starting point and projecting creaturely notions onto those divine attributes. The starting point is wrong. We must begin instead with Scripture. And the projection approach is wrong. We must not impose our creaturely ideas on the divine attributes.

2. *Any overemphasis on the complete "otherness" of God such that biblical revelation of the divine attributes is minimized or discounted.*

Even with respect to his incommunicable attributes, God is not beyond definition. We have a measured sense of his independence, immutability, eternity, omnipresence, simplicity, and spirituality. And we are joyfully duty-bound to praise him as he has revealed himself in Scripture.

ENACTING THE DOCTRINE

God is great—that is, infinitely distinct from human beings, his image bearers. The incommunicable attributes emphasize this Creator-creature distinction and invite us to worship him. Certainly, God is immanent, dwelling with us, manifesting his presence to comfort, admonish, correct, and guide. But God is also transcendent, and meditating on his incommunicable attributes prompts us to acknowledge, and be humbled by, his greatness.

Perennial Questions and Problematic Issues

- If God is independent and self-sufficient, why did he create us?
- If God is immutable, how should we understand biblical passages that present God as changing his mind and relenting from his plan?
- If God creates human beings in his image, and human beings are physical/embodied, does that mean that God is physical as well?

TEACHING THE DOCTRINE

An excellent way to teach the attributes of God is to sing worship songs in which they are rehearsed. A good starting point (and ending point) of this teaching is to lead the participants in singing. Be sure to choose songs that accurately unfold the incommunicable attributes.

Because Scripture is the source of our knowledge of the incommunicable attributes, treating the biblical passages is key. Some attributes have many passages, so be sure to select a few so as not to overwhelm or bore the participants. Some of these attributes are theological conclusions drawn from biblical passages, which is a legitimate way of approaching those characteristics. Don't be afraid to deal with hard points.

Some people find some of these attributes troubling. For example, they are reluctant to affirm God's immutability in light of biblical passages that narrate a change in God's mind, such that he relents of the disaster he threatened. Teaching these passages (for example, Exod. 32:9–14; Jon.

3:1–10) involves highlighting the flow of the narratives: In one miserable situation, God threatens disaster against sinful people (the people of Israel, the people of Nineveh), just as we would expect him to do. In a second marvelous situation, God relents from the disaster and instead forgives the people (of Israel, of Nineveh). The key is the intervening narrative: someone steps forward (Moses, Jonah) and intervenes (for the Israelites, for the Ninevites), prompting God to be merciful in response to the intervention (of Moses's prayer, of Jonah's preaching of repentance), just as we would expect him to do.

Teaching the incommunicable attributes reminds participants of the Creator-creature distinction, so be sure to highlight the difference between the infinite God and them as finite people. This emphasis promotes a proper humility, as participants are reminded of how great, how beyond measure, God is. The right response is praise directed to the inscrutable God.

TEACHING OUTLINE

1. The summary
2. Singing songs praising God for his incommunicable attributes
3. Major affirmations (with biblical support)
   A. Independence
   B. Immutability
   C. Eternity
   D. Omnipresence
   E. Simplicity
   F. Spirituality
4. Major errors to avoid
   A. Reducing the Creator-creature distinction
   B. Overemphasizing the complete "otherness" of God such that biblical revelation of the divine attributes is minimized or discounted
5. Enacting the doctrine
   A. Worshiping God for his greatness
   B. Meditating on, and being humbled by, God's incommunicable attributes

RESOURCES

Allison, *Theological Terms*, s.vv. "eternity," "impassibility," "incommunicable attributes," "independence," "omnipresence"

Elwell, *Evangelical Dictionary of Theology*, s.v. "God, Attributes of"

Erickson, *Christian Theology*, chap. 11

Grenz, *Theology for the Community of God*, chap. 3

Grudem, *Systematic Theology*, chap. 11

Horton, *Pilgrim Theology*, chap. 3

Thoennes, *Life's Biggest Questions*, chap. 6

10

THE COMMUNICABLE ATTRIBUTES OF GOD

SUMMARY

The communicable attributes are God's characteristics or perfections, as revealed by Scripture, that God communicates, or shares, with human beings.

MAIN THEMES

- God's communicable attributes are those characteristics or perfections that he does share with human beings.
- God's communicable attributes are knowledge, wisdom, truthfulness, faithfulness, love, goodness, grace, mercy, patience, holiness, jealousy, wrath, righteousness/justice, and power.
- God calls his image bearers to mirror him by reflecting these attributes.
- God is to be praised for his communicable attributes.

KEY SCRIPTURE

Exodus 34:6–7; 2 Samuel 7:18–29; 1 Kings 8:22–30; 1 Chronicles 16:8–36; Psalms 89:1–8; 103:6–14; 139:1–6; Romans 11:33–36; Ephesians 1:11; 1 Timothy 1:17

UNDERSTANDING THE DOCTRINE

Major Affirmations

In the discussion of God's attributes, a common approach is to distinguish between his incommunicable attributes and his communicable attributes. This does not mean there are two distinct "bundles" of characteristics in God. Rather, the two headings are helpful in presenting a large amount of material, and they do highlight an important point about imitating God.

The communicable attributes are God's characteristics or perfections that he communicates, or shares, with human beings. As used here, the word *communicable* means *shareable*. God creates human beings in his image, meaning that they mirror him in some respect, specifically by reflecting his communicable attributes. These characteristics have a counterpoint in human beings.

Knowledge refers to the divine attribute of being all-knowing (omniscience): God knows all things. He fully knows (1) himself, his infinite knowledge encompassing his infinite being; (2) the past, which is as vivid to him as the present; (3) the present, even the most minute details of life; (4) the future, even the freewill decisions and actions of his creatures; (5) all actual things—that is, people and events that exist and happen; and (6) all possible things—that is, people and events that could possibly exist and happen, but never do.

Wisdom is the divine attribute signifying that God always wills the greatest goals and the best means to achieve those goals for his own glory and his people's blessing. Yet wisdom is not mere efficiency, a calculated and streamlined process designed solely for greater productivity. Instead, wisdom is sound judgment expressed in God's activities of creation, redemption, guidance, and the like.

Truthfulness is the divine attribute signifying that God, who is the only true God, never lies but always tells the truth. This means that Scripture, which is the Word of the truth-telling God, is inerrant and always affirms the truth.

Faithfulness is the divine attribute signifying that God never goes back on his word but always fulfills his promises. Even when his people deny him, God always remains faithful.

Love is the divine attribute signifying that God gives of himself. The Godhead is an eternally loving community as the Father, Son, and Holy Spirit love one another. From this fullness of self-giving, God created image bearers, whom he loves even when they fall into sin. Again, in his infinite love, God gave his Son to rescue his fallen people. Jesus demonstrated the highest self-sacrificial love for his enemies, who are united to God and to one another by the love of the Holy Spirit.

Goodness is the benevolent kindness that characterizes God and his ways. God, who alone is good, is good in himself, and all he does is good. The varieties of the divine goodness are grace, mercy, and patience.

Grace is God's goodness expressed to those who deserve condemnation. It is God's unmerited favor. This gift is not owed to people derelict in person and duty who engage in good works. Rather, God's gracious salvation is appropriated by faith.

Mercy is God's goodness expressed to those who are afflicted. Like grace, mercy cannot be merited. This attribute is seen in God's fatherly compassion for his children, whose weakness and failings he knows well. It is seen in Jesus's pity toward the miserable who cry, "Have mercy on us" (Matt. 9:27).

Patience is God's goodness in withholding punishment. It is God's slowness to anger. While he is ready to express his displeasure, he holds off. This temporary stay of punishment should not be construed as God clearing the guilty. Rather, it should prompt people toward repentance.

Holiness is the divine attribute signifying that God is exalted above creation and is absolutely morally pure. The holy God, as transcendent, is completely separated from his creation. Being incomparably exalted, he is worthy of worship. Moreover, he is proclaimed to be "Holy, holy, holy" (Isa. 6:3), utterly pure and uncorrupted by sin. Still, he engages with a sinful world and acts to render sinful people holy.

Jealousy is the divine attribute by which God is protective of his honor. Because God alone is worthy of ultimate allegiance, when his people give themselves to something or someone else, God is provoked to jealousy. This divine attribute is not like the sinful form of jealousy, which is akin to covetousness or envy. God rightly protects his own honor and thus is not jealous in a covetous sense.

Wrath is the divine attribute by which God intensely hates sin and is poised to punish it fully. For forgiveness leading to salvation from God's wrath to occur, his anger must be assuaged. Christ's death, as a propitiation for human sinfulness, appeases God's wrath. Accordingly, Christians will never face the divine wrath, but unbelievers will experience God's fury in eternal punishment.

Righteousness/justice is God's uprightness of person, ways, standards, and judgments. God himself is perfectly righteous, as are his ways in creation, providence, and salvation. As righteous, God himself establishes moral standards that reflect his nature, and he requires conformity to those standards. His judgments of his creature are righteous: he always and justly rewards obedience to his standards and punishes disobedience to them.

Power refers to the divine attribute of being all-powerful (omnipotence). God can do everything that is proper for him as God to do. Examples include the creation out of nothing, the exodus, and the incarnation of the Son of God. Importantly, God cannot do certain things, such as sin, lie, do the logically absurd, die, break a promise, or be thwarted in his plans. Such "inabilities" are part of the perfection of God. Also, God is not constrained to act but does as he pleases.

In creating human beings in his image, God intends them to mirror him in some respect, specifically by reflecting his communicable attributes.

For his communicable attributes, God is to be worshiped and praised.

Biblical Support

Scripture often rehearses the communicable attributes together, as when God proclaimed his name: "The LORD, the LORD, a God merciful and gracious, slow to anger, and abounding in steadfast love and faithfulness" (Exod. 34:6). Scripture also presents these attributes individually.

In terms of divine *knowledge*, or *omniscience*, Scripture affirms, "God knows everything" (1 John 3:20; poetically, Ps. 139:1–6). God fully knows himself (1 Cor. 2:10–11), the past (Ps. 90:4), the present (Heb. 4:13), the future (Isa. 42:8–9; 46:9–10), all actual things (Job 28:24), and all possible things (1 Sam. 23:11–13; Matt. 11:21–23).

God, who is "the only wise God" (Rom. 16:27), employed *wisdom* in creating the world (Ps. 104:24; Prov. 8:12, 22–32) and in designing salvation, though his wisdom appears as foolishness to sinful people (1 Cor.

1:18–31). Through the church God reveals his wisdom to heavenly beings (Eph. 3:7–11), and he acts wisely for the good of his people (Rom. 8:28).

The *truthfulness* of God extends from him being the only true God (Jer. 10:10–11; John 17:3). He does not and cannot lie (Rom. 3:3–4; Titus 1:2; Heb. 6:18). Thus, Scripture is wholly true (John 17:17; Prov. 30:5). In telling the truth, God's people imitate his truthfulness (Eph. 4:25; Col. 3:9–10).

God's *faithfulness* is underscored by two questions: "Has he said, and will he not do it? Or has he spoken, and will he not fulfill it?" (Num. 23:19). The answer is no, because God is faithful. God's faithfulness does not depend on his people being faithful to him. Even when they are faithless, God remains faithful (2 Tim. 2:13).

Love exists eternally in the Godhead (John 17:23–26). In his infinite love, God sent his Son (3:16), whose death was an act of sacrificial love for his enemies (Rom. 5:8). The Spirit now unites God's people in love (5:5), and they respond by loving God and loving others (Matt. 22:37–40).

God, who alone is *good* (Mark 10:17–18), is good in himself (Ps. 34:8) and in all he does (119:68). As the good God, he is the source of all good things (James 1:17; Ps. 84:11).

Divine *grace* is most commonly associated with his work of salvation: justification is by grace and not works (Rom. 3:23–24; 4:16; 11:6), as is sanctification (5:2; 1 Cor. 15:10).

God grants *mercy* to those to whom he wills to grant mercy (Rom. 9:14–18). Like a father, he has compassion on his weak and failing children (Ps. 103:13–14). God's mercy is seen in Jesus's pity toward the blind men who begged him, "Have mercy on us" (Matt. 9:27). Because God is merciful, his people are to be merciful (Luke 6:35–36).

God extends his *patience* toward unbelievers to prompt them toward repentance (Rom. 2:4), and he is patient toward believers to give them time to communicate the gospel (2 Pet. 3:9). Because God is patient, Christians are to master their life (Prov. 16:32), endure suffering (1 Pet. 2:20), and bear with the idle, the fainthearted, and the weak (1 Thess. 5:14).

God's *holiness* (Isa. 6:1–7) is both his exaltedness over creation (Exod. 15:11) and his incorruptibility from sin (Hab. 1:13). The holy God calls his children to progress in holiness (1 Pet. 1:13–16; 2 Cor. 6:14–7:1).

God, "whose name is Jealous" (Exod. 34:14), forbids his people from engaging in idolatry because of his *jealousy* for them (20:5). Such divine jealousy means that God seeks to prevent his people from chasing after anything or anyone seeking to usurp his rightful place (2 Cor. 11:1–4).

Human sinfulness provokes the divine *wrath* (Exod. 32:9–14; Deut. 9:7–8). Christ came to rescue "children of wrath" (Eph. 2:3) from the divine wrath (1 Thess. 1:10; Rom. 5:9–10), but this pertains only to his disciples (John 3:36). God's people imitate him when they express righteous anger (Eph. 4:26), modeling themselves after Jesus (Mark 3:1–6; John 2:13–17).

God is "just and upright" and "all his ways are justice" (Deut. 32:4; cf. Gen. 18:25). This divine *righteousness/justice* is reflected in his righteous declarations, standards, and judgments (Isa. 45:19; Ps. 19:8). He rewards obedience (Rom. 2:7) and punishes disobedience (2 Thess. 1:8).

The divine *power*, or *omnipotence*, is manifested in creation (Jer. 32:17), the outworking of the divine purpose (Isa. 14:27), the incarnation (Luke 1:26–38), and salvation (Mark 10:23–27). God "does all that he pleases" (Pss. 115:3; 135:6).

God directs his people to imitate him (Eph. 5:1), living out his communicable attributes such as his holiness (1 Pet. 1:15–16), mercy (Luke 6:36), love (1 John 4:11, 19), and bearing up under unjust suffering (1 Pet. 2:21–25). Such imitation is not an external conformity carried out in one's own strength, but must be the fruit of walking in the Spirit (Gal. 5:22–23) in accordance with Scripture.

Besides imitating these characteristics, God's people are to worship him for his communicable attributes. For example, "Oh, the depth of the riches and wisdom and knowledge of God! How unsearchable are his judgments and how inscrutable his ways! . . . To him be glory forever. Amen" (Rom. 11:33, 36).

Major Errors

1. *Defining the divine attributes according to human concepts.* While there is a human counterpoint for the communicable attributes, it is wrong to begin with the fallen expressions of human love (sentimentality), jealousy (covetousness, envy), mercy (pity without action), and so on, and then to draw conclusions about God's attributes. Rather, Scripture must reveal the nature of these divine attributes.

2. *Any neglect or dismissal of (some of) the divine attributes because they chafe against human sensitivities or preferences.* Two examples are rejection of divine wrath and rejection of retributive justice, which people discard because these attributes do not present God in the way people want

him to be. This approach to Scripture is dangerous because it sets people's fallen desires or perspectives over God.

3. *Pitting one divine attribute against another.* An example is an alleged conflict between the love of God and his justice. It is seen in the misunderstanding that the Old Testament presents one view of God—just and wrathful, not loving and gracious—while the New Testament presents a gentler, kinder God. This approach to Scripture is dangerous because it is unjustified.

ENACTING THE DOCTRINE

God created us in his image so that we would reflect him in some way, particularly by mirroring his communicable attributes.

> ### *Perennial Questions and Problematic Issues*
>
> • If God is all-knowing and all-powerful, how can we imitate these attributes, because we are not infinite people?
> • God's jealousy and wrath seem to be very difficult to imitate.
> • What's the difference between mercy and grace?
> • Some people I know are impossible to love.

Concrete character transformations, new attitudes, edifying words, sanctified imaginations, and godly actions enact this doctrine. Meditating on his communicable attributes and mirroring them in our lives prompt us to be dependent on him as we represent him.

TEACHING THE DOCTRINE

Singing worship songs in which the communicable attributes are rehearsed is an excellent way to teach them. Start (and end) the teaching time with singing, making sure to choose songs that accurately present the communicable attributes.

With Scripture as the source of our knowledge of the communicable attributes, treating the biblical passages is key. Some attributes have many passages, so be sure to select a few so as not to overwhelm or bore the participants.

Teaching the communicable attributes reminds participants of their responsibility to mirror these characteristics. For each attribute, ask, "How can you imitate this attribute in your life, work, schooling, friendships, marriage, family, and ministry?" Encourage the participants to be very specific in responding. Answers like "I need to pray about being more holy" are fine, but a response such as "Anytime I hear the Lord's name being taken in vain, I'm going to challenge that person to speak in another way" is far better.

TEACHING OUTLINE

1. The summary
2. Singing songs praising God for his communicable attributes
3. Major affirmations (with biblical support)
   A. Imitating God
   B. Presentation of each of the attributes: knowledge, wisdom, truthfulness, faithfulness, love, goodness, grace, mercy, patience, holiness, jealousy, wrath, righteousness/justice, power
4. Major errors to avoid
   A. Defining the divine attributes according to human concepts
   B. Neglecting or dismissing (some of) the divine attributes because they chafe against human sensitivities or preferences
   C. Pitting one divine attribute against another
5. Enacting the doctrine
   A. Mirroring the communicable attributes of God
   B. Meditating on God's communicable attributes

RESOURCES

Allison, *Theological Terms*, s.vv. "communicable attributes" and each of the individual attributes

Elwell, *Evangelical Dictionary of Theology*, s.v. "God, Attributes of"

Erickson, *Christian Theology*, chap. 12

Grenz, *Theology for the Community of God*, chap. 3

Grudem, *Systematic Theology*, chaps. 12–13

Horton, *Pilgrim Theology*, chap. 3

Thoennes, *Life's Biggest Questions*, chap. 6

11

THE TRINITY

SUMMARY

The one true God is triune, or three-in-one, eternally existing as the three persons of Father, Son, and Holy Spirit.

MAIN THEMES

- There is only one God.
- This God eternally exists as three persons: Father, Son, and Holy Spirit.
- Each of these three persons is fully God.
- The three persons share in the one divine nature and thus are equal in essence, glory, and power.
- The three persons are distinct in terms of their roles and relations.
- As for the distinctions in roles, the Father creates, the Son saves, and the Holy Spirit sanctifies (yet the three operate inseparably in all divine works).

- As for the distinctions in relationships, each of the three persons has a unique eternal characteristic not shared by the others.

KEY SCRIPTURE

Genesis 1:26; Deuteronomy 6:4; Psalms 45:6–7; 110:1; Matthew 3:16–17; 28:19; 1 Corinthians 12:4–6; 2 Corinthians 13:14; 1 Peter 1:2

UNDERSTANDING THE DOCTRINE

Major Affirmations

The doctrine of the Trinity affirms that the one true God eternally exists as three persons: Father, Son, and Holy Spirit. Each of these three persons is fully God: The Father is fully God. The Son is fully God. The Holy Spirit is fully God. The three persons are equal in nature, glory, and power, sharing in the one Godhead. None of the three persons is dependent on the other for his deity. Rather, each is God of himself: The Father is God of himself. The Son is God of himself. The Holy Spirit is God of himself. Yet there are not three gods, but one God in three persons.

The three persons are different in terms of their roles and relations. As for the distinctions in roles (the economic Trinity), the Father exercises the primary role in creation (working with the Son and the Spirit to create). The Son exercises the primary role in salvation (working with the Father and the Spirit to save). The Holy Spirit exercises the primary role in sanctification (working with the Father and the Son to bring transformation). Indeed, the three distinct persons in their different activities inseparably work together in creation, salvation, and sanctification. Still, these particular divine works are appropriated by—are the specific responsibility of—one of the three persons.

As for the distinctions in relations (the ontological, or immanent, Trinity), each of the three persons has a unique eternal characteristic not shared by the others. The eternal characteristic of the First Person is paternity: He is the Father of the Son. He is not generated or begotten (which is true of the Son), and he does not proceed (which is true of the Spirit). The eternal characteristic of the Second Person is sonship or filiation: He is the Son of the Father, eternally generated or begotten of the Father (though not created by him or dependent on him for his deity). The eternal characteristic of the Third Person is procession: the Holy Spirit eternally proceeds from both the Father and the Son (though not created by them or dependent on them for his deity). By paternity, generation (begottenness), and procession, the three are distinct persons.

Biblical Support

The doctrine of the Trinity is progressively revealed in Scripture. The Old Testament provides a partial revelation. When God deliberates, "Let *us* make man in *our* image, after *our* likeness" (Gen. 1:26; emphasis added), the plural words imply more than one person. At least God and the Spirit of God (1:1–2) are included in the Godhead. Yet there is only one God (Deut. 6:4).

In Psalm 45, one person called "God" addresses another person called "God": "Your throne, O God, is forever and ever. The scepter of your kingdom is a scepter of uprightness; you have loved righteousness and hated wickedness. Therefore God, your God, has anointed you with the oil of gladness beyond your companions" (vv. 6–7). The Son is called God, and, because of his righteous rule, he is addressed and rewarded by another one called "your God," the Father (Heb. 1:8). In Psalm 110, one person called "Lord" addresses another person called "Lord": "The Lord says to my Lord: 'Sit at my right hand, until I make your enemies your footstool'" (v. 1). God the Father addresses God the Son (Matt. 22:43–44).

The New Testament offers a fuller revelation of the Trinity. At the beginning of Jesus's ministry, God the Father speaks words of commendation concerning Jesus (God the Son) while God the Holy Spirit descends upon the baptized one (Matt. 3:16–17). At the conclusion of his ministry, Jesus instructs his disciples concerning making disciples of the nations' peoples, which includes "baptizing them in the name of the Father and of the Son and of the Holy Spirit" (28:19). The oneness of God is also emphasized (Rom. 3:30; Gal. 3:20).

The three persons are diversely engaged in the salvation of these new disciples: the Father elects them, the Spirit sanctifies them, and Christ, whom they are to obey, cleanses them (1 Pet. 1:2). Upon these disciples, the apostle pronounces a trinitarian blessing: "The grace of the Lord Jesus Christ and the love of God and the fellowship of the Holy Spirit be with you all" (2 Cor. 13:14). The three also engage in the church's mission: "Now

91

there are varieties of gifts, but the same Spirit; and there are varieties of service, but the same Lord; and there are varieties of activities, but it is the same God who empowers them all in everyone" (1 Cor. 12:4–6).

Such cooperation in divine activity supports the doctrine of the inseparable operations of the Trinity. Other passages similarly show the three divine persons acting in common. For example, the divine mission is presented as the Father sending his Son so that people alienated from him might become adopted sons. "And because you are sons, God has sent the Spirit of his Son into our hearts, crying, 'Abba! Father!'" (Gal. 4:4–6). The three persons engage indivisibly in the divine mission.

Theologically, the doctrine of inseparable trinitarian operations flows from three other doctrines: (1) The unity of the three persons in the one divine nature indicates that the one God creates, saves, and sanctifies. (2) The mutual indwelling of the three persons (perichoresis) means that as the Father works, the Son and the Spirit, who together dwell in him, work together with him. (3) Sharing in the one divine nature, the three persons possess one will, knowledge, and power. As Augustine expressed it, "The Father, and the Son, and the Holy Spirit, as they are indivisible, so work indivisibly."[11]

The development of this doctrine took place over the church's first few centuries. The church developed and expressed a trinitarian consciousness. For example, prayer was trinitarian, addressed to the Father in the name of Jesus and through the Holy Spirit. So, too, the church's worship was directed at God the Father, God the Son, and God the Spirit. Tertullian (160–240) was the first to use the term "Trinity" to refer to the three-in-oneness.

Fighting against heresy that denied the deity of the Son and of the Holy Spirit, the church convened councils. One of the fruits of these general assemblies was the formulation of creeds, which have a trinitarian structure: "I believe in one God the Father almighty . . . and in one Lord Jesus Christ . . . and in the Holy Spirit." Thus, the church confessed its faith in the Triune God. Its doctrine became one substance (the divine nature shared equally) and three persons (Father, Son, and Holy Spirit), oneness in threeness. As Gregory of Nazianzus (ca. 330–ca. 390) affirmed: "No sooner do I conceive of the One than I am illumined by the Splendor of the Three; no sooner do I distinguish Them than I am carried back to the One."[12]

A church council in 589 inserted one word into the Nicene Creed (which had stated that the Holy Spirit "proceeds from the Father"), affirming that the Holy Spirit proceeds "from the Father *and the Son*" (*filioque*; emphasis added). This double procession of the Spirit is embraced by the Roman

Catholic Church and Protestant churches but rejected by the Eastern Orthodox churches.

Major Errors

1. *The affirmation that God is only one person.* Unitarianism rejects the deity of the Son and the Spirit.

2. *The affirmation that there are three gods.* Tritheism fails to embrace the biblical teaching that God is one.

3. *The denial of the distinctions between the three persons.* For modalism, "Father," "Son," and "Holy Spirit" are different names of the same person. This viewpoint cannot account for the passages in which the three persons are active at the same time (for example, Jesus's baptism).

4. *The denial of the deity of the Son.* Arianism cannot explain the passages that affirm that Jesus is God.

5. *The denial of the deity of the Holy Spirit (Pneumatomachianism).* This position cannot explain the passages that affirm that the Spirit is God.

ENACTING THE DOCTRINE

Christians exist, trust, obey, hope, and love because God is triune. Becoming conscious of the Trinity for our creation, salvation, and sanctification is the first step in living this doctrine.

This doctrine distinguishes the Christian faith from all other religions. No other religion—Islam, Buddhism, Hinduism, Mormonism, and more—comes close to embracing the God who is Father, Son, and Spirit. This means that these other religions worship false gods, prompting Christians to communicate the gospel of the true Triune God.

Worship is distinctively trinitarian. The church's liturgy, songs, prayers, sermons, and ordinances should reflect God's triune reality. For example, gospel-centered preaching, while focusing on the Son, should also make much of the Father and the Spirit.

This doctrine banishes misunderstandings of God: (1) God was lonely and thus created people for companionship. Rather, the Triune God is an eternal, perfect fellowship. (2) God needed to love and be loved and thus created people to fill that deficit. Rather, Father, Son, and Spirit eternally love one another. (3) God craved glory and thus created people to spread his fame. Rather, the three persons eternally honor one another.

What's at stake in this doctrine? In one word: everything! Christianity does not exist if God is not triune. But because God eternally exists as three persons in one divine essence, the church knows the one true God, experiences salvation, engages in prayer, undergoes transformation, and participates in mission to help others know the Trinity.

TEACHING THE DOCTRINE

When this doctrine is taught, an initial obstacle is the feeling that the Trinity is impossible to understand. In one sense, this idea is correct: the Trinity is a mystery, and even the best explanations fall short of reality. In another sense, its difficulty cannot deter the church from affirming what God reveals about his triune essence. Teachers should also take heart: when presented well, this doctrine is life changing, as might be expected from the fact that the Trinity concerns the very essence of God!

Perennial Questions and Problematic Issues

- The Trinity is too hard to understand.
- How is it that Christians do not believe in three gods?
- Doesn't eternal generation make the Son inferior to the Father?
- Doesn't eternal procession make the Holy Spirit inferior to the Father and the Son?
- How can the church claim that it alone worships the true God?
- How does this doctrine protect the church from false ideas about God?

To help with this dismay, a good place to start teaching is to affirm that the church experientially knows the Trinity. Indeed, the Trinity is the foundation for the gospel, sound doctrine, Christian community, worship, and more. For example: (1) Salvation is from and leads to the Trinity: The Father purposed and directed the Son to become incarnate. The Son willingly obeyed the Father and accomplished salvation. The Spirit applies salvation to people's lives. Believers then worship God, who is triune. (2) Prayer is trinitarian: it is addressed to the Father, in the name of the Son, in step with the Spirit. The church knows the Trinity!

Once this familiarity with the Trinity is established, the doctrine can be taught. Because the church knows that God is triune by his revelation, Scripture must be central. Although analogies have been used to explain the Trinity, even their inventors emphasize that they fail. So avoid analogies or examples of the Trinity like the three states of H_2O, the analogy of a

94

father–son–husband, and the analogy of a lover–the one loved–love itself. Using such devices usually backfires, as what is taught is wrong!

TEACHING OUTLINE

1. The word "Trinity" and the summary
2. You know the Trinity (examples: salvation, prayer)
3. Major affirmations (with biblical support)
    A. There is only one God.
    B. This God eternally exists as Father, Son, and Holy Spirit.
    C. Each of the three persons is fully God.
    D. The three are distinct in roles yet engage inseparably in divine works.
    E. The three are distinct in eternal relations.
4. Major errors to avoid
    A. Affirming that God is only one person
    B. Affirming that there are three gods
    C. Denying the distinctions of the three persons
    D. Denying the deity of the Son
    E. Denying the deity of the Holy Spirit
5. Enacting the doctrine
    A. Acknowledging that this doctrine distinguishes Christianity from all other religions
    B. Worshiping God as triune
    C. Banishing misunderstandings of God's triune nature

RESOURCES

Allison, *Theological Terms*, s.v. "Trinity"
Elwell, *Evangelical Dictionary of Theology*, s.v. "God, Doctrine of"
Erickson, *Christian Theology*, chap. 14
Grenz, *Theology for the Community of God*, chap. 2
Grudem, *Systematic Theology*, chap. 14
Horton, *Pilgrim Theology*, chap. 4
Thoennes, *Life's Biggest Questions*, chap. 7

12

CREATION

SUMMARY

Creation is the mighty act of God to bring into existence the universe and all it contains, including this world and human beings, for his glory.

MAIN THEMES

- God is the Creator of everything that exists.
- He created everything *ex nihilo,* out of nothing.
- God created everything for his glory—that is, to manifest his goodness and greatness.
- The Father spoke the universe into existence through his Word, the Son, with the activity of the Holy Spirit.
- The original creation was created very good.
- As a result of the fall, the original creation was subjected to decay and death, but one day it will be completely renewed as the new heaven and new earth.

KEY SCRIPTURE

Genesis 1; Nehemiah 9:5–6; Psalm 33:6, 9; John 1:1–3; Acts 17:24–25; Romans 8:18–25; Colossians 1:16; Hebrews 11:3; Revelation 4:11; 21:1–22:21

UNDERSTANDING THE DOCTRINE

Major Affirmations

The doctrine of creation affirms that one of the mighty acts of God was to bring into existence the universe and everything that exists within it. This creation includes "the heavens," or the realm of God and immaterial, angelic beings, and "the earth," or the world consisting of oceans and mountains, plants and animals, and human beings. God created all these things *ex nihilo*, or out of nothing. That is, God did not use already-existing materials to form the creation. Rather, he brought those materials into existence and formed them into what now exists. For example, God did not take already-existing hydrogen and oxygen atoms and rearrange them to make H_2O, or water, but created the hydrogen and oxygen atoms in the first place and then combined them to make water.

Of course, God did not create himself; he is eternal, existing without beginning. So why did God create? Several answers are surely wrong: God created the universe because he needed something to glorify him. Or God created human beings because he was lonely and required loving relationships to be fulfilled. On the contrary, God eternally exists as Father, Son, and Holy Spirit, who eternally love and glorify one another. So God did not create because he had to or because he needed something that only a creation could supply.

Rather, God created everything out of the superabundance of his love to display his glory—that is, to manifest his goodness and greatness. Indeed, the creation displays some of the attributes of God, including his power, knowledge, wisdom, independence, and sovereignty. For this reason, Christians praise and thank God for his creative work.

Creation was an act of the Father, Son, and Holy Spirit working together inseparably (as they do in all divine works). The Father spoke the universe into existence. He spoke through his Word, the Son, through whom everything was created. The Holy Spirit engaged in this work as well, preparing and protecting the original materials for their fashioning into a world that would be hospitable for human beings created in the image of God.

This original creation was very good. As God assessed each stage of his creative work, he determined it to be good. Then, when he had completed creating everything, he appraised it as very good. This affirmation was not one of moral goodness, for evil had not yet entered the world. Rather, it was one of fittedness: the creation, as coming from the hand of God, corresponded perfectly to the divine design.

As a result of Adam and Eve's fall into sin, this creation is no longer the way it is supposed to be. Rather than being a hospitable place in which humanity flourishes, the creation is marked by fallenness: human relationships, marriage, sexuality, family, vocation, and even life itself are tainted with sin and suffer fracturing in a wasteland. One day, however, the curse on the creation will be reversed: God will renew the creation so that, once again, it will be very good. Then, the new heaven and new earth will be filled with the glory of God.

Biblical Support

From the opening page of Scripture, God is introduced as the Creator of "the heavens and the earth" (Gen. 1:1), an expression indicating everything that exists. Of course, God did not create himself; rather, "he himself gives to all mankind life and breath and everything" (Acts 17:24–25). The universe and everything in it was created by God (Neh. 9:5–6).

God created *ex nihilo*. Because no one was present to observe the original creation out of nothing, this truth is to be believed: "By faith we understand that the universe was created by the word of God, so that what is seen was not made out of things that are visible" (Heb. 11:3; cf. Rom. 4:17). His purpose was to display his goodness and greatness: "The heavens declare the glory of God" (Ps. 19:1). Specific divine attributes manifested by the creation include power, wisdom, and understanding (Jer. 10:12; Rom. 1:20); sovereignty (Rev. 4:11); and independence (Acts 17:24–25).

Working together inseparably, the Father, Son, and Holy Spirit did not divide up this mighty act into three parts, with each of the three persons responsible for a third of creation. Still, Scripture indicates that the three persons were each active in creation: (1) The Father spoke the universe into existence. Ten times in Genesis 1, the affirmation "and God said" appears (vv. 3, 6, 9, 11, 14, 20, 24, 26, 28, 29). Simply put, "By the word of the LORD the heavens were made. . . . For he spoke, and it came to be; he commanded, and it stood firm" (Ps. 33:6, 9). Creation is a speech-act of God the Father.

(2) God spoke creation into existence through his Word, who is the Son: "In the beginning was the Word. . . . All things were made through him, and without him was not any thing made that was made" (John 1:1, 3). Thus, the Father created everything through the agency of the Son and for his honor: "For by him [the Son] all things were created, in heaven and on earth, visible and invisible, whether thrones or dominions or rulers or authorities—all things were created through him and for him" (Col. 1:16).

(3) At the beginning of creation, "the earth was without form and void, and darkness was over the face of the deep. And the Spirit of God was hovering over the face of the waters" (Gen. 1:2). The hovering Spirit was preparing and protecting the chaotic core of creation for God's future work of fashioning it into a place that would be hospitable for the apex of creation—the divine-image bearers, human beings.

The goodness of the original creation emerged progressively: six times, God assessed his handiwork as being "good" (Gen. 1:4, 10, 12, 18, 21, 25). Then, for the seventh time, after his creation was complete, he assessed it as being "very good" (v. 31). Tragically, the fall wrecked this pristine condition of the original creation (3:17–19). As punishment, God subjected the creation to "bondage to corruption" (Rom. 8:18–25). This state of enslavement will be reversed through the renewal of all that exists in the new heaven and new earth (Rev. 21–22).

This doctrine of creation means that the universe is not eternal (Aristotle's belief) but has a beginning. Furthermore, the doctrine refutes the proposal of atomism that life originated from the random collision of atoms. On the contrary, the creation was purposeful, according to the divine plan. The doctrine also stands against the gnostic idea that creation occurred through a demiurge (an emanation from God). Rather, God himself is the Creator.

As to when creation occurred, the church has historically believed that God created everything in six days fairly recently. This last determination of the recent origin of the world depended on a fanciful application of the phrase "with the Lord one day is as a thousand years" (2 Pet. 3:8). Irenaeus (ca. 130–ca. 200) calculated, "In as many days as this world was made, in so many thousand years it shall be concluded."[13] Accordingly, the church's historical position is that the world was created fairly recently and will exist for six thousand years. Bishop James Ussher (1581–1656) sought to pinpoint the precise date of creation: Sunday, October 23, 4004 BC.

Attacks against the church's doctrine began in the seventeenth century. The most noted and hostile challenge continues to be Charles Darwin's theory of evolution (*Origin of Species*, 1859): what exists now has evolved according to natural selection as mutations randomly produced changes without purpose or design over a long time. How anything came into existence in the first place is often explained by the big bang theory. The church has responded in various ways, including (1) young earth creationism: creation was fairly recent, perhaps several thousand years ago; (2) old earth (progressive) creationism, such as the day-age theory and the intermittent day theory, with the universe perhaps fourteen billion years old; (3) the gap theory; (4) the framework hypothesis; and (5) theistic evolution.

Major Errors

1. *God is not the Creator because he does not exist.* Atheism dismisses biblical revelation of God's existence and divine creation.

2. *Evolution can fully account for the existence of all living things.* Naturalistic evolution fails to consider the many difficulties with the theory of evolution, and it contradicts the biblical worldview of God's involvement in the entirety of creation.

3. *When combined with some divine activity, evolution can be regarded as the mechanism that God employed in the development of all that exists.* Numerous assertions of theistic evolution are challenged by the biblical account of creation, the problems of evolutionary theory, the historical consensus of the church, and the rejection of any appeal to divine activity in the evolutionary process by many in the scientific community.[14]

ENACTING THE DOCTRINE

Christians worship God as both the Creator and the Redeemer, as underscored by Isaiah 42: God provides his Spirit-anointed servant to accomplish salvation (vv. 1–4, 6–7), and God "created the heavens and stretched them out" (v. 5). Praise to the Creator-Redeemer is the proper way of living this doctrine. In face of intense attack by evolution, the church should continue to confess, "I believe in God, the Father almighty, maker of heaven and earth" (Apostles' Creed).

What's at stake in this doctrine? The existence of everything other than God: the universe, planet earth, human beings, the church! God did not have to create anything. The reality of creation prompts us to understand our place and role in God's design and to depend on and give thanks to him as our Creator.

TEACHING THE DOCTRINE

In the teaching of this doctrine, the debate between the various theories of origins (young earth creationism, old earth [progressive] creationism, theistic evolution, and naturalistic evolution) can become a distraction. It is key, therefore, to prevent the discussion from being hijacked by controversy. A kind but firm statement that this doctrine is much more than the current debate should (re)focus the teaching on what it should emphasize.

Because the church worships God as Creator (rather than debates the doctrine), a good place to start teaching is to sing about God's mighty work of creation. Many hymns and songs that praise God for his creative work are available and rehearse the divine attributes displayed by the creation: "I Sing the Mighty Power of God," "Our Great God," "Let All Things Now Living," "God of All Creation," "The Earth Is Yours," "How Great Thou Art," "All Creatures of Our God and King," and many more.

Because the church knows about creation *ex nihilo* by God's revelation, Scripture must be central. Be careful not to ground this doctrine on something outside of the Bible—scientific considerations, archaeological evidence, historical consensus, and more. Though these matters confirm divine creation, to substitute something other than biblical truth

Perennial Questions and Problematic Issues

- This doctrine is so hotly debated that it is better not to discuss it to avoid dividing the church.

- Are you a young earth creationist, an old earth creationist, a theistic evolutionist, or a naturalistic evolutionist?

- Though the original creation was very good, ever since the fall it has been marked by decay and death, so how should we handle the problem of evil?

- Can Christians enjoy the creation (for example, taking hikes, appreciating the beauty of rainbows and sunsets), or should they avoid becoming attached to this world because it is temporal and will cease to exist?

- Can Christians be involved in care for creation (for example, recycling, working to protect the environment, and developing renewable fuels), or should they not be concerned because the world is here today and gone tomorrow?

and authority as the foundation of this doctrine undermines the biblical perspective that it is a matter of faith. Additionally, in arguing against evolution, don't present yourself as an expert—unless you are a professional who is skilled in the field. At the same time, an emphasis on how inimical evolution is to the doctrine of creation is needed.

TEACHING OUTLINE

1. The expression "creation *ex nihilo*" and the summary
2. Praising God as Creator by singing
3. Major affirmations (with biblical support)
   A. God created everything out of nothing and for his glory.
   B. The act of creation was trinitarian.
   C. The original creation was very good but is now spoiled.
   D. God will renew the creation as the new heaven and new earth.
4. Major errors to avoid
   A. Denying God is Creator because he does not exist
   B. Believing that evolution can fully account for the existence of all living things
   C. Regarding evolution, by combining it with some divine activity, as the mechanism that God employed in the development of all that exists
5. Enacting the doctrine
   A. Praising God the Creator of all things
   B. Depending on God as our Creator

RESOURCES

Allison, *Theological Terms*, s.v. "creation *ex nihilo*"
Elwell, *Evangelical Dictionary of Theology*, s.v. "Creation, Doctrine of"
Erickson, *Christian Theology*, chap. 16
Grenz, *Theology for the Community of God*, chap. 4
Grudem, *Systematic Theology*, chap. 15
Horton, *Pilgrim Theology*, chap. 5

13

PROVIDENCE

SUMMARY

Providence is the continuing work of God to sustain in existence the created universe and all it contains, directing it toward its divinely designed end.

MAIN THEMES

- Providence is God's ongoing activity to care (or *provide*) for what he has created.

- Preservation is God's work to maintain the creation in existence and functioning as he designed it.

- Concurrence is God's work of collaborating with all created realities as they act and occur.

- Government is God's work of directing the creation toward its divinely purposed end.

- The position of meticulous providence asserts that God ordains and controls everything that happens.

- The position of general providence is the view that God attends broadly but not exhaustively to what occurs.

KEY SCRIPTURE

Genesis 45–50; Nehemiah 9:6; Esther; Psalm 139:13–16; Proverbs 16:4, 33; 19:21; Isaiah 14:24–27; 37:26; 41:22–23; 44:7–8; 46:9–11; Jeremiah 10:23; Matthew 10:29–30; Acts 2:23; 4:27–28; Romans 8:28; Colossians 1:17; Hebrews 1:3

UNDERSTANDING THE DOCTRINE

Major Affirmations

The doctrine of providence affirms that one of the continuous mighty acts of God is to maintain in existence, and provide for, the universe he created. This doctrine concerns God's ongoing relationship to his creation. Providence encompasses three aspects: preservation, concurrence, and government.

Preservation is God's work to sustain the creation in existence and functioning as he designed it. Chemical bonds retain their properties, the laws of physics (gravity, aerodynamic lift) continue to operate, lions capture and eat their prey, and human beings endure for eighty-some years until death overtakes them. Trees don't morph into stars, and human beings don't become angels, because God keeps created realities functioning as he designed them. And God does not simply consign the creation to be sustained by natural laws, genetic code replication, and physiological development, though he does use these means. He is not the god of deism.

Concurrence is God's all-encompassing cooperation with his creation in its every action and development. He cooperates with (1) plants and animals, to promote their flourishing or terminate their existence; (2) angelic beings, to engage holy angels in his service and to permit Satan and demons to wreak limited havoc; and (3) human beings, to responsibly will and work for the accomplishment of his plan, or to culpably reject his goodness out of hardness of heart. Thus, created realities never work apart from God: while the universe and its inner dynamics (for example, the collapse of black holes and the replication of DNA in cells) can be explained scientifically, God is always and fully cooperating with every action and development.

Government is God's work of directing the creation toward its divinely planned end. When God brought the universe into existence, his creative activity was purposeful: he created a world that was initially good, with his image bearers as upright people. God permitted human beings to fall, wreaking havoc throughout the entire created order. He is redeeming his people from their sin and condemnation. God will one day intervene decisively to consummate this present existence and renew all things. Government is God's guidance of the creation according to his plan to accomplish his purpose.

The extent of divine providence is a matter of debate. The position of *meticulous providence* holds that God has ordained and is in complete control of everything that occurs. Divine providence is exhaustive, but it never functions in such a way that human freedom and responsibility are minimized. And human beings decide and act as morally responsible creatures, but never in a way that renders God dependent on their decisions and actions.

The position of *general providence* holds that God broadly attends to what occurs, but his control is not exhaustive. Whereas God determines and acts unilaterally in some matters, his activity often incorporates human freedom in decisions and actions so that these matters are not completely determined.

Biblical Support

From the opening page of Scripture, divine creation and divine providence go hand in hand. In terms of creation, God said, "Let there be . . . ," and his word brought something into existence ("and it was so"). In terms of providence, "the earth brought forth vegetation, plants yielding seed according to their own kinds, and trees bearing fruit in which is their seed, each according to its kind" (Gen. 1:11–12). Moreover, God commanded his creatures to be fruitful and multiply. God has endowed his creation with the power of replication.

But divine providence does not mean that God is removed from the process of ongoing existence. He is not the god of deism, who designed and built everything, then, with hands off, consigned the creation to run by itself. Rather, God actively sustains all that he has created.

His providence extends to the nonrational world. Physical phenomena—wind, fire, rain, and snow—occur according to God's plan (Ps. 148:8). Providence covers the plant world and the animal kingdom (vv. 14–30). Indeed, all creatures look to God "to give them their food in due season" (v. 27). Their existence depends on God's preservation of them. Sparrows have little value, yet "not one of them will fall to the ground apart from your Father" (Matt. 10:29).

Divine providence encompasses the beginning and end of each human life: God is active in the development of a fetus *in utero*, and every day of that new human being's life has been established: day of birth, family of origin or nurture, body type, marriage or singleness, family, career, and the time and circumstances of death (Ps. 139:13–16).

As we might expect, providence includes the good deeds of good people (Eph. 2:10), but it extends to the evil deeds of evil people as well (Prov. 16:4). For example, Sennacherib, king of Assyria, brought destruction on Israel according to the eternal plan of God (Isa. 37:26). And in regard to his evil brothers, Joseph affirmed, "As for you, you meant evil against me, but God meant it for good" (Gen. 50:20).

Indeed, Scripture does not give abstract discussions of divine providence. Rather, God's plan and its effective outworking are presented as part of the very fabric of the biblical narrative. For example, the story of Zacchaeus underscores that Jesus, on the Father's mission, *had* to go to the little man's house (Luke 19:1–10). Even the crucifixion of Jesus took place "according to the definite plan and foreknowledge of God" (Acts 2:23) as Herod, Pontius Pilate, the Roman executioners, and the religious leaders conspired "to do whatever [God's] hand and [God's] plan had predestined to take place" (4:27–28).

The three aspects of divine providence are well supported. In terms of preservation, God conserves all that he has created (Neh. 9:6), specifically in Christ, who holds all things together (Col. 1:17). Regarding concurrence, the Joseph narrative affirms that Joseph's evil brothers sold him into slavery in Egypt and, at the same time, that God was responsible for sending him to Egypt (Gen. 45:5–8): "So it was not you who sent me here, but God" (v. 8). Even powerful human rulers experience divine concurrence: "The king's heart is a stream of water in the hand of the LORD; he turns it wherever he will" (Prov. 21:1). As for government, God the Son "upholds the universe by the word of his power" (Heb. 1:3). He rules as king over his kingdom (Isa. 40:17), "and none can stay his hand or say to him, 'What have you done?'" (Dan. 4:34–35).

The position of meticulous providence points to biblical passages that emphasize God's exhaustive control over everything that occurs. Paul affirms that predestination is "according to the purpose of him [God] who works all things according to the counsel of his will" (Eph. 1:11). This plan and its outworking are all-inclusive, extending to seemingly random events (Prov. 16:33) and mundane facts (Matt. 10:30). While human decisions and actions are certainly weighty matters, wisdom acknowledges, "Many are the plans in the mind of a man, but it is the purpose of the LORD that will stand" (Prov. 19:21). Human beings rightfully and responsibly decide and act, yet wisely know "that the way of man is not in himself, that it is not in man who walks to direct his steps" (Jer. 10:23).

The position of general providence emphasizes biblical passages that underscore human responsibility. For example, Joshua challenged the people of Israel: "Choose this day whom you will serve, whether the gods your fathers served . . . or the gods of the Amorites. . . . But as for me and my house, we will serve the LORD" (Josh. 24:15). Paul urges people to embrace the gospel "because, if you confess with your mouth that Jesus is Lord and believe in your heart that God raised him from the dead, you will be saved" (Rom. 10:9). Human beings choose, obey, rebel, believe, defy, and more. For this view, human freedom and moral responsibility seem incompatible with meticulous providence.

Major Errors

1. *By overemphasizing divine providence, one minimizes human responsibility.* People so underscore trusting God that they become passive in terms of working, planning, saving for the future, buying insurance, and more. This view dismisses the many biblical passages on the importance of human decisions and actions.

2. *One specific view that overemphasizes providence is fatalism, or hard determinism.* Fatalism believes that everything that occurs is inevitable. Not even God can intervene to change what is so determined, so nothing could be different from what it is. Fatalism misunderstands the biblical presentation of God's personal and caring providential activity, and makes him dependent on fate.

3. *By overemphasizing human responsibility, one minimizes divine providence.* People so underscore working for God that the success of his kingdom becomes dependent on their effort and energy. This view dismisses the many biblical passages calling for trust in God and reliance on his providential activity as the foundation for human cooperation.

4. *Some denials of divine providence make God contingent on human decisions and actions.* Process theology and open theism dismiss the many

biblical affirmations that God's purpose stands forever and his will cannot be thwarted.

ENACTING THE DOCTRINE

For Christians, this doctrine is a source of great comfort and assurance. God's purpose cannot be frustrated. His good pleasure will be accomplished. As God works all things for his people's good (Rom. 8:28), they can rely upon him in every circumstance, whether that is pleasant or sorrowful. Thus, with Job, Christians can say, "The LORD gave, and the LORD has taken away; blessed be the name of the LORD" (Job 1:21).

The right perspective is also reflected in how Christians plan for the future. Rather than purpose according to their own agenda, they "ought to say, 'If the Lord wills, we will live and do this or that'" (James 4:15). The proper approach eschews both extremes of irresponsibility and hyperresponsibility: trust in divine providence goes hand in hand with decision making and activity in line with God's purpose. And Scripture reminds and comforts Christians: "For the LORD of hosts has purposed, and who will annul it? His hand is stretched out, and who will turn it back?" (Isa. 14:27).

What's at stake in this doctrine? The comfort and certainty that God actively preserves his creation, cooperates with every action and happening, and brings about his good pleasure in everything. He is the God who is providentially with us.

Perennial Questions and Problematic Issues

- It is very hard to strike a proper balance between divine providence and human responsibility.
- What am I supposed to do when I'm seeking to trust God's providence but he isn't providing for me (for example, with regard to a job, money, a spouse, children)?
- If what we've said about providence is true, how should we handle the problem of evil?
- I'm afraid to trust God's providence because of what he might ask me to do.

TEACHING THE DOCTRINE

A good place to start is with a rehearsal of how the participants have experienced God's providence. Encourage people to reflect on and testify

108

about God's preservation, concurrence, and government in their life, their family, their career, and more. Expect them to share both joys and heartaches. Encourage them to recognize God's providential hand in all their circumstances when such acknowledgment is not forthcoming.

In teaching the doctrine, make sure to communicate the comfort and assurance that flow from it. Personal illustrations of God's providential activity are very helpful. Because providence is often hidden from sight, emphasize biblical teaching and urge people to trust that God is providentially working even when it is not evident. Be careful not to ground this doctrine on positive thinking or a stoic attitude toward difficulties. And be sure to avoid, and correct when needed, the extremes presented above.

TEACHING OUTLINE

1. The word "providence" and the summary
2. Sharing evidences of God's providence
3. Major affirmations (with biblical support)
   A. Preservation
   B. Concurrence
   C. Government
   D. Meticulous or general providence
4. Major errors to avoid
   A. Overemphasizing divine providence and minimizing human responsibility
   B. Embracing fatalism, or hard determinism
   C. Overemphasizing human responsibility and minimizing divine providence
   D. Denying divine providence and making God contingent on human decisions and actions
5. Enacting the doctrine
   A. Finding comfort and assurance in divine providence
   B. Avoiding both extremes of irresponsibility and hyperresponsibility by trusting in divine providence along with making decisions and acting in line with God's purpose

RESOURCES

Allison, *Theological Terms*, s.vv. "compatibilism," "determinism," "incompatibilism," "providence"

Elwell, *Evangelical Dictionary of Theology*, s.v. "Providence of God"

Erickson, *Christian Theology*, chaps. 17–18

Grenz, *Theology for the Community of God*, chap. 4

Grudem, *Systematic Theology*, chap. 16

Horton, *Pilgrim Theology*, 110–13

Thoennes, *Life's Biggest Questions*, chap. 12

PART 3

DOCTRINE

—— OF ——

GOD'S CREATURES

14

ANGELS, SATAN, AND DEMONS

SUMMARY

Angels are highly intelligent, morally good, spiritual beings created by God. Some angels rebelled against God, lost their original goodness, and now as demons (with Satan as their head) attempt to combat God and his work.

MAIN THEMES

- Angels are created beings whose nature is simple, being immaterial only (though they can take on the appearance of human beings).
- Angels are highly intelligent, holy, and powerful creatures.
- There seem to be several categories of angelic beings: archangels, angels, cherubim, and seraphim.
- As for their activities, angels mediate God's revelation, carry out his will, and worship him.
- Tragically, one angel, leading a significant number of other angels, rebelled against God and, as punishment, was banished from heaven to earth, where he seeks to wreak havoc.

- Demons are Satan's minions, who likewise oppose God and attempt to disrupt his work.
- Christians counter Satan and demons by engaging in spiritual warfare.

KEY SCRIPTURE

Genesis 3:1–7; Job 1–2; Isaiah 14:13–14; Daniel; Matthew 12:22–32; Acts 10:1–31; 2 Corinthians 12:7; Revelation

UNDERSTANDING THE DOCTRINE

Major Affirmations

One of the most fascinating parts of Scripture is its revelation of a category of beings that are different from human beings. Like us, angels are created by God. Unlike us, angels are simple in nature, being immaterial only. Still, when Scripture presents angels, they often appear as human beings, in many ways like us. These angelic appearances are accommodations enabling angels to reveal themselves to, speak to, rescue, and guide human beings.

In terms of their capacities, angels are highly intelligent, but not all-knowing like God. Indeed, they cannot know about salvation that God provides for sinful human beings (1 Pet. 1:10–12), and they learn about grace through God's wisdom displayed in the church (Eph. 3:10). Furthermore, angels are morally good. Such holiness means that they live in the presence of the holy God, whom they worship, and always do his holy will. Moreover, angels are powerful, but not all-powerful like God. Still, they are able to carry out God's tasks for them.

As for an angelic classification, there appear to be several categories: Archangels (for example, Michael; Jude 9) are rulers of the other angels, even leading an angelic army (Dan. 10:13). Angels are the immaterial beings we are describing. Cherubim prevented the return of Adam and Eve into the garden of Eden (Gen. 3:24) and accompanied God and his glory (Ezek. 10; Ps. 18:10). Seraphim are six-winged creatures who worship God by praising his holiness (Isa. 6:2–3; Rev. 4:8). It may be that descriptions

114

of angelic beings as thrones, dominions, rulers, and authorities (Col. 1:16; cf. Eph. 1:20–21) indicate other ranks of angels.

The angelic job description includes being mediators of God's revelation. For example, angels played a role in delivering the Mosaic law (Gal. 3:19; Acts 7:53; Heb. 2:2), and they are often portrayed as conveying messages from God to people (for example, Gabriel's announcement to Mary; Luke 1:26–38). They serve God in other ways, such as ministering to believers, even rescuing some from impending death (for example, the imprisoned Peter; Acts 12:6–17). Even more, they surround the throne of God, constantly worshiping him.

Tragically, this presentation of angels takes an evil turn. Though all angels were created upright, one of them, joined by a large number of other good angels, rebelled against God. Puffed up with pride, Satan and his followers overstepped the boundaries with which they were created and, for their treason, were punished by God. Indeed, God banished the evil army from heaven and confined them to earth, where they oppose God and seek to thwart his work. Satan is referred to as "the ruler of this world" (John 12:31), "the god of this world" (2 Cor. 4:4), and "the prince of the power of the air" (Eph. 2:2).

The name "Satan" means "adversary"; he stands against God and his people. Other names that reveal his nature include devil (accuser, slanderer), Abaddon or Apollyon (destroyer), Beelzebul (dung god), and the "ancient serpent" (the tempter in Eden). As the "evil one," he engages in wicked activities through temptation, accusation, deception, lying, blinding, destruction, and torment. Satan's minions, the demons, oppose God and attempt to disrupt his work by engaging in evil activities like disseminating false doctrine, spreading sickness, fomenting self-destructiveness, and even possessing people.

Because Satan is a defeated foe and demons are in subjection to Christ (Eph. 1:21–23; Col. 2:15), Christians never need to fear (Heb. 2:14) but should instead resist by engaging in spiritual warfare, especially communicating the gospel (Eph. 6:10–20).

From its outset, the church has added a great deal of speculation to its biblically based knowledge about this doctrine. The church conjectured about the wings and speed of angels, their immense number, and their functions. The early church father Origen (ca. 185–254) believed that human beings will eventually become like angels. The church denied that angels should be worshiped and that prayer should be directed to

115

them. But it did develop the belief in guardian angels who guide people to do the good, prompt them to repent when they do evil, and help them when they pray.

Augustine (354–430) imagined that, to restore harmony to the universe, God will replace the number of fallen angels with the same number of redeemed human beings. Dionysius the Pseudo-Areopagite, writing about a century after Augustine, speculated that there are nine orders in the hierarchy of angelic beings. Thomas Aquinas (1225–74), nicknamed the "Angelic Doctor," believed that God created angels in his image by his intellect. Angels, therefore, are completely intellectual beings and most like God of any creatures—including human beings.

As for Satan and demons, some Christian leaders believed that the fall of angels was due to Satan's jealousy of human beings because they were created in the image of God. Others attributed the fall to angels having sexual intercourse with human women. While Origen speculated that even Satan and demons would ultimately be saved, the church condemned his idea. Guardian angels were deemed necessary to counteract the temptations and attacks of demons. When demonic influence turned into possession, exorcism was considered the solution. Of great help in warding off evil beings, it was thought, was asceticism, the severe treatment of the body by denying it legitimate pleasures like food and sleep.

Such speculation goes far beyond the biblical presentation of angels, Satan, and demons.

Biblical Support

Biblical narratives reveal important details about the nature, types, capacities, and roles of angels. Some of the Old Testament narratives are Abraham's hospitality to angels (Gen. 18:1–22), Lot's rescue by angels (19:1–22), and Balaam's donkey and the angel of the Lord (Num. 22:22–35). In relation to Jesus, the New Testament narrates angelic activity at his birth (Luke 2:8–15), temptation (Matt. 4:11), resurrection (John 20:11–13), and future return (Matt. 16:27; 25:31). Other New Testament stories include angelic deliverance of the persecuted apostles (Acts 5:17–26; 12:6–11) and angelic messages for Philip (8:26), Cornelius (10:1–33), and Paul (27:21–26). Apocalyptic literature is replete with references to angelic activity (Daniel; Revelation). Job 38:4–7 implies that angels were created before God created the earth and human beings.

Similarly, biblical narratives about Satan and demons present their evil nature and activities. The fall of Satan may be recounted in Isaiah (14:12–14) and Ezekiel (28:12–18), and other passages provide glimpses into the demise of Satan and his minions (Luke 10:17–20; 1 Tim. 3:6; 2 Pet. 2:4; Jude 6). Specific satanic and demonic encounters with human beings include Satan's temptation of Eve (Gen. 3:1–7; 2 Cor. 11:1–3), his attempted destruction of Job (Job 1–2), his temptation of Jesus (Matt. 4:1–11), his eighteen-year torment of a woman (Luke 13:16), his role in Judas's betrayal of Jesus (22:3), and the ongoing ordeal that Paul experienced at Satan's bidding (2 Cor. 12:7). Biblical narratives of demonic possession include the man tormented by "Legion" (Mark 5:1–20), the mute man (Matt. 9:32–33), a young boy (17:14–21), and the Syrophoenician woman's daughter (Mark 7:26–30). Jesus's enemies accused him of being in cahoots with Satan and therefore demon possessed (Matt. 12:22–32; John 8:48–52; 10:20).

Major Errors

1. *In terms of belief, the church embraces this doctrine but engages in significant speculation about angels and demons.* When it departs from the limited biblical material and joins theology with philosophy or allows popular conceptions to exert a strong influence, the church errs. Examples include belief in guardian angels, praying to angels, overstressing the influence of Satan and demons, blaming personal sin on demonic activity, and more. This is the error of exaggeration.

2. *As for unbelief, the church either treats this doctrine with benign neglect, almost being embarrassed by it, or dismisses it outright.* Three problems result from such unbelief. One is difficulty in understanding biblical narratives in which angels and/or Satan and demons play a role. A second is living in ignorance of the real spiritual world that is part of earthly reality. This neglect results in being poorly prepared for demonic temptation and attack and dismissing much-needed angelic aid. A third is belittling Christians throughout the world who daily live the reality of angels and demons.

ENACTING THE DOCTRINE

God created a realm of beings that are immaterial in nature: the angels. We are not angels. But they play important roles for us, including being

117

examples of perfect obedience to God and being his servants in helping us through protection, rescue, guidance, and more. Fallen angels—Satan and demons—oppose God and attempt to disrupt his work. Accordingly, with a proper awareness of their strategies of temptation, accusation, deception, torment, dissemination of false doctrine, spread of sickness, and even possession, we are to engage in spiritual warfare by resisting their evil through the authority of Christ.

Perennial Questions and Problematic Issues

- Though the Bible is full of stories about angels and demons, I've never had an encounter with them and thus find it hard to believe they really exist.

- Isn't it dangerous to talk about Satan and demons because, if we give them too much attention, we might fall under their influence?

- How should I counsel my friend who blames his sins of anger, worry, lust, and greed on demonic temptations and attacks ("the devil made me do it")?

TEACHING THE DOCTRINE

Christians are rarely ambivalent about this doctrine, but often tend toward one of the two extremes just noted. On the one hand, because of fascination with angels and demons (for example, many popular-level books treat the subject) and the scarcity of biblical material devoted to them, watch for an excessive curiosity for this topic. Correction of common conceptions that have little or no biblical support (for example, guardian angels) or even contradict Scripture (for example, the view that believers become angels after death) will be necessary.

On the other hand, because science and theological liberalism belittle the notion of spiritual realities and immaterial creatures, watch for a rationalistic dismissal of angels and demons. Often what is rejected is the popular conception of these beings—greeting cards present angels as blond-haired, blue-eyed, harp-playing, plump little boys, and films portray demons as otherworldly, naive, confounded meanies clearly recognizable by their horns, tails, and pitchforks. These common ideas are to be rejected. The existence of Satan and demons is not.

A good place to start is to ask people about their experience with angels and demons. Caution should be exercised so as not to allow this sharing to get out of hand. A possible question to ask after people have explained their encounters is, "Does your experience correspond to anything presented in Scripture?" This question isn't intended to cast doubt on their experience, but it can establish the pattern of relying on the biblical material and avoiding rampant speculation about angels and demons, a perennial problem. You can easily point out the contemporary fascination with this topic by referencing books, TV shows, and movies on angels and demons.

In terms of teaching, focus first on a few narrative passages in which angels and demons are featured, discussing what can be learned about them. Then present the rest of the biblical material systematically, teaching about the nature, attributes, categories, and roles of angels, and the evil nature and activities of Satan and demons.

Encourage open discussion about doubts, problems, and possible abuses that may arise from this doctrine.

--------------------- TEACHING OUTLINE ---------------------

1. The question "What is your experience with angels, Satan, and demons?" and the summary

2. References to books, TV shows, and movies that feature angels and demons

3. Major affirmations (with biblical support)

   A. The status of angels as creatures

   B. Their attributes: intelligence, holiness, and power

   C. Their categories: archangels, angels, cherubim, and seraphim

   D. Their activities: revelation, service, and worship

   E. The fall of angels

   F. The evil nature and activities of Satan and demons

   G. Spiritual warfare

4. Major errors to avoid

   A. Embracing this doctrine but engaging in significant speculation about angels and demons

   B. Treating this doctrine with benign neglect, almost being embarrassed by it, or dismissing it outright

5. Enacting the doctrine

   A. Embracing the important roles of angels

   B. Standing firm against the evil one and demons

RESOURCES

Allison, *Theological Terms*, s.vv. "angels," "demons," "Satan"

Elwell, *Evangelical Dictionary of Theology*, s.vv. "Angel," "Demon, Demonization," "Satan"

Erickson, *Christian Theology*, chap. 19

Grenz, *Theology for the Community of God*, chap. 8

Grudem, *Systematic Theology*, chaps. 19–20

15

HUMAN BEINGS
IN THE IMAGE OF GOD

SUMMARY

God created human beings in his image, making them of all created things the most like him, and endowing them with dignity and significance.

MAIN THEMES

- God created human beings in his image; thus, they are the *imago Dei* (image of God).
- The church has various understandings of the image of God.
- Jesus Christ is the perfect image of God.
- Christians are being progressively renewed into the image of Christ.
- Full restoration is a future blessing and reality.

KEY SCRIPTURE

Genesis 1:26-28; 5:1-3; 9:6; John 14:8-9; Romans 8:29-30; 1 Corinthians 15:49; 2 Corinthians 3:18; Colossians 1:15; 3:9-10; James 3:9; 1 John 3:2

UNDERSTANDING THE DOCTRINE

Major Affirmations

Creation in the image of God is the foundation of the doctrine of humanity. When God purposed to create a being more like him than any other creature, he created human beings. The *imago Dei* (the image of God) is our essential reality: we exist as either male image-bearers or female image-bearers. Everything else—for example, height, eye color, and body type—is a secondary characteristic. Creation in the divine image means that all people have dignity and significance.

Throughout its history, the church has developed various understandings of the image of God. The *substantive view* considers the image of God to be some characteristic such as rationality, free will, or moral consciousness. A particular method is often used: by examining the rest of creation and focusing on the attribute that distinguishes human beings from other creatures, the church can identify the image of God. It is some quality or attribute of human nature.

The *relational view* considers the image of God to be the experience of community that men and women enjoy among themselves and, derivatively, that human beings and God enjoy. The key idea is that God experiences a relationship within himself ("Let *us* make man in *our* image"), and humanity reflects this experience on two levels: people in relationship with people, and people in relationship with God. The key support is Genesis 1:27, which emphasizes that God created humanity in his image as "male and female." Appealing to this passage, and relying on the idea that God experiences an "I-Thou" relationship within himself, Karl Barth developed this view. Relationality is the image of God.

The *functional view* considers the image of God to be some human activity. In creating human beings in his image, God designed them to exercise dominion over the other creatures (Gen. 1:26). When he actualized his plan, God commanded them to "have dominion . . . over every living thing that moves on the earth" (1:28). This exercise of dominion—being stewards of the creation—is the image of God.

Old Testament scholars appeal to the concept of the image of god(s) in ancient Near Eastern literature: the image is a king or a statue of a king representing the god(s), whereby the god(s) exercise(s) dominion over its/their territory.[15] Assuming that Genesis reflects this background, the functional view takes shape: the image of God is humanity's exercise of dominion over the creation.

The *holistic view* finds the other views to be reductionistic and considers the image of God to be people themselves in the totality of their being, relationships, and activities. Again, the key support is Genesis 1: having deliberated about the creation of image bearers (v. 26), and having actualized that plan (v. 27), God created human beings—not just a part of them (as in reason or free will), not just in terms of relationships (though maleness and femaleness are essential to the image), not just for purposeful activity (though they exercise dominion), but in their wholeness. Developments in neuroscience, demonstrating the intimate interconnectedness of all aspects of human existence, provide additional support. Human beings as individuals, and humanity as a whole, are created in the image of God.

Biblical Support

The biblical concept of the image of God is developed in a handful of passages. Genesis 1:26–28 is the foundational text. It begins with the divine intention: "Let us create man in our image, after our likeness." This deliberation is then actualized: God creates man in his image, specifically as male and female. To his newly created image bearers, God gives the mandate to build society through extending humanity (procreation: "Be fruitful and multiply and fill the earth") and ruling the creation (vocation: "and subdue it, and have dominion . . .").

Two issues arise. First, Roman Catholic theology makes a distinction between the "image," consisting of the natural gifts of rationality and free will, and the "likeness," consisting of the supernatural gifts of original holiness and immortality. This distinction, however, has been overturned; there is little difference between "image" and "likeness." Indeed, Genesis 5:3 indicates that the two words are nearly interchangeable.

Second, as discussed above, the various views appeal to Genesis 1:26–28 in support. Is the image some human attribute, the experience of relationships, engagement in activity, or humanity in its wholeness? A holistic view considers what an image is—namely, a reflection of something—and what it does—that is, it represents something. Accordingly, the image of God means that human beings reflect God: his attributes of knowledge, power, goodness, faithfulness, truthfulness, and more. And they represent God: as coregents, they are stewards of the rest of creation as they build civilization through procreation and vocation.

Two other passages highlight the importance of people being created in the divine image: it is the reason for the prohibition of homicide (Gen. 9:6) and for the prohibition of cursing human beings, "who are made in the likeness of God" (James 3:9). Because all human beings are created in the divine image, they are to be treated with dignity and respect.

Jesus Christ is the perfect image of God (2 Cor. 4:4–6; Col. 1:15). The incarnate Son makes visible the invisible God, as Jesus himself affirms: "Whoever has seen me has seen the Father" (John 14:8–9). Indeed, the Son is "the radiance of the glory of God and the exact imprint of his nature" (Heb. 1:3).

With their Savior being the perfect image of God, believers are being restored into his image. Full conformity to the Son's image is the divine design for believers (Rom. 8:29–30), and they experience this progressive renewal through the Holy Spirit (2 Cor. 3:18; Col. 3:9–10). Still, this renewal is incomplete in this lifetime. Rather, full restoration into the image of God is ultimately a future blessing and reality (1 Cor. 15:48–49). Though we are already children of God, "what we will be has not yet appeared; but we know that when he appears we shall be like him, because we shall see him as he is" (1 John 3:2).

Major Errors

1. *The image is reduced to some human characteristic* or *the experience of relationships* or *the activity of exercising dominion (reductionism).* This oversimplification neglects the biblical presentation of human beings as holistic image-bearers.

2. *The image of God is only spiritual in nature.* This gnostic heresy believes that the physical is inherently evil and the spiritual is inherently good. Thus, the divine image cannot include something material; the human body is not part of the image of God. But Scripture does not denigrate the physical as does gnosticism. Indeed, God created humanity as embodied beings.

3. *Evolution can fully account for the existence of human beings, who do not hold a special position over other creatures from which they have evolved.* Naturalistic evolution overlooks the many difficulties with the theory of evolution, and it contradicts the biblical worldview of God's creation of human beings as distinct from the rest of creation.

4. *While generally employing the mechanism of evolution to develop the world, God intervened to form the first human being in his image.* Theistic evolution maintains that prehuman beings (hominids like *homo erectus*) evolved according to natural processes, and at a certain point God instilled a soul or spirit into them, thereby creating human beings in his image. Theistic evolution is challenged by the biblical account of creation and the problems of evolutionary theory (see chap. 12, "Creation").

Perennial Questions and Problematic Issues

- This doctrine has so many views that it is difficult to know which one is correct.

- Why do we highlight the wonder of the image of God when people are so thoroughly sinful?

- If the image refers particularly to human intellect or rationality, are mentally handicapped people created less in the image of God?

- Likewise, if the image refers particularly to the exercise of dominion, are physically handicapped people inferior image bearers?

- Are unbelievers still in the image of God, or has sin annihilated the image?

ENACTING THE DOCTRINE

All human beings are created in the image of God, consequently possessing dignity and significance. Accordingly, all people should be treated with respect, with appreciation for God's excellent design. Racism, sexism, classism, and ageism are categorically excluded. Additionally, according to God's mandate for his image bearers, the vast majority of human beings will be married, the vast majority of those will have children, and all able-bodied people will work in their vocation. Though still sinful, Christians should rejoice that they are being restored into the divine image, and they should look forward with hope to the future blessing and reality of being fully conformed to the image of Christ at his return.

What's at stake in this doctrine? The fundamental identity, dignity, and significance of human beings. Through his creation of humanity in his image, God has designed people to reflect and represent him. This reality prompts us to understand our identity and purpose in this world as image bearers of God.

TEACHING THE DOCTRINE

John Calvin closely tied the knowledge of God with the knowledge of oneself: "Nearly all the wisdom we possess, that is to say, true and sound wisdom, consists of two parts: the knowledge of God and of ourselves."[16] Accordingly, a good place to start teaching is to underscore the wonder of human beings, with a discussion of Psalm 139:13–16 being a springboard. By considering ourselves, we marvel at God's amazing creation and grasp our fundamental identity: we are image bearers of God, more like him than any other created being.

This emphasis may provoke a negative response, as some people are prone to focus on human sinfulness. They should be reminded of our original state of integrity: by origin, human nature is good. Our fallen condition is not the way we are supposed to be. Indeed, our fundamental identity is not that of sinfulness but that of divine-image bearing.

Work hard at helping participants to embrace the whole story line of Scripture, whose first act is creation. This theme starts the biblical story and narrates our essential identity as divine-image bearers. Yes, the second act is the fall. But as the word emphasizes, this crisis is movement away from the original state of creation. Fallenness is neither God's design for human beings nor our primary identity. Indeed, the third act of the story line (redemption) and its fourth act (consummation) narrate what God has done and will do to rectify our fallenness and restore us to the original design. Thus, salvation is not merely the overcoming of human sinfulness (though that is certainly true) but a gracious restoration to being image bearers of God. This is good news!

Because of the variety of views on the identity of the image of God, a significant discussion of Genesis 1:26–28 should start the biblical teaching. The passage should be read, followed by the interpretation it is given by the different views. If the church sides with one of the views, that position should be advocated.

Other important points should be made: Jesus is the perfect image of God, so we can know both who God is and what God's design is for us by knowing Jesus's character, relationships, and activities from Scripture. We are progressively becoming renewed in that image. It is also the blessing and reality for which we hope: to be fully conformed to his image.

The ethical implications of creation in the divine image provide other practical applications of this doctrine. It certainly rules out abortion, euthanasia, cloning, and more. Moreover, the purpose of humanity—always of interest to people—is revealed by this doctrine: to reflect God and represent him through building society and caring for the world of nature.

TEACHING OUTLINE

1. The expression *"imago Dei"* and the summary
2. The call to be full of wonder at God's marvelous creation of human beings in his image
3. Major affirmations (with biblical support)
   A. God created human beings in his image.
   B. Christians hold various views of the image of God.
   C. Jesus Christ is the perfect image of God.
   D. Christians are being progressively restored to Christ's image.
   E. Full restoration into the divine image awaits the future return of Christ.
4. Major errors to avoid
   A. Reducing the image of God to some human characteristic or the experience of relationships or the activity of exercising dominion
   B. Believing the image is only spiritual in nature
   C. Maintaining that evolution can fully account for the existence of human beings, who do not hold a special position over other creatures from which they have evolved
   D. Believing that while he generally employed the mechanism of evolution to develop the world, God intervened to form the first human being in his image
5. Enacting the doctrine
   A. Treating all people with respect and denouncing all forms of racism, sexism, classism, and ageism
   B. Reflecting God as his image bearers in the world in which we live

RESOURCES

Allison, *Theological Terms*, s.v. "image of God"

Elwell, *Evangelical Dictionary of Theology*, s.v. "Image of God"

Erickson, *Christian Theology*, chap. 22

Grenz, *Theology for the Community of God*, chap. 5

Grudem, *Systematic Theology*, chap. 21

Horton, *Pilgrim Theology*, chap. 5

Thoennes, *Life's Biggest Questions*, chap. 11

16

HUMAN NATURE

SUMMARY

The nature of human beings consists of a material aspect (the body) and an immaterial aspect (soul, spirit) united into one person.

MAIN THEMES

- Human nature is complex, consisting of two elements: material and immaterial.

- Being complex, human nature is unlike the simple nature of God and of angels.

- There are two major views of the complexity of human nature: trichotomy and dichotomy.

- Both views are opposed to monism, the belief that human nature is simple, being material only.

- During this earthly existence, the material and immaterial aspects are inseparably united; after death, the material element (the body) is sloughed off while the immaterial person continues to exist; after the resurrection, the aspects are rejoined and the person exists forever as a material-immaterial unity.

- A minor dispute occurs over the origin of the immaterial element, with creationism and traducianism being the opposing positions.

- The proper state of human beings is embodiment.

KEY SCRIPTURE

Matthew 10:28; Luke 1:46–47; 1 Corinthians 15; 2 Corinthians 5:1–9; 1 Thessalonians 5:23

UNDERSTANDING THE DOCTRINE

Major Affirmations

One of the perennial questions people ask is, what is a person? Scripture indicates that a human being is a complex reality consisting of two different yet intimately related aspects: a material element, which is the physical aspect, or body, and an immaterial element, which is the spiritual aspect, called the soul or spirit (these are sometimes differentiated; see below). This complexity of nature means that human beings are different in essence from God, whose nature is simple and immaterial only, and who is everywhere present. It also means that human beings are different in essence from angels, whose nature is simple and immaterial only, yet who are unlike God by not being everywhere present but located in space in time.

While all Christians agree about the material component of human nature (the body), there is disagreement over the immaterial component. This disagreement leads to two major views of the complexity of human nature: trichotomy and dichotomy. *Trichotomy* (literally, "cut into three parts") believes human nature consists of three aspects: one material element, the body, and two immaterial elements, soul and spirit. The soul is the intellect, emotions, and will. The spirit is the capacity to relate to God, who is spiritual in nature. *Dichotomy* (literally, "cut into two parts") believes human nature consists of two aspects: one material element, the body, and one immaterial element, which is the soul or the spirit (these are interchangeable terms for the one immaterial component).

130

Both views, which are versions of dualism, reject monism, the position that human nature is simple rather than complex. If human nature is material only, then a person is completely identified with her body, such that after death, she no longer exists—indeed, she can no longer exist. Materialistic monism believes that the properties that used to be considered the realm of the soul—consciousness, rationality, morality, faith—are ultimately explained by physical processes in the brain and central nervous system. Monism is contradicted by the biblical affirmation that believers continue to exist in a disembodied state in heaven after their death.

This last statement prompts a consideration of human nature in its different phases. During this earthly existence, the material and immaterial aspects are inseparably united. Indeed, what exactly of the various capacities—consciousness, mind, emotions, will, conscience, motivations, activities—are due to the immaterial element(s) and what are due to the material element is a mystery. After death, the material element is sloughed off, and the body is usually buried or cremated. The immaterial person continues to exist in the intermediate state: the disembodied believer in heaven, and the disembodied unbeliever in torment. After the resurrection of the body, the aspects are reunited: the reembodied believer, restored to her material-immaterial unity, in the new heaven and earth, and the similarly reconstituted unbeliever in the lake of fire.

Though disagreement over the origin of the immaterial element of human nature was strong for most of the church's history, it continues as a minor dispute today. To be dismissed immediately is Origen's theory of the *preexistence* of the soul: before God created this visible, material world in which we live, he created an invisible, spiritual world populated by good souls that, after falling into sin, are joined to bodies to become human beings. It has no biblical support. *Creationism* is the view that God creates a soul and then unites it to a body that is generated through procreation by parents. *Traducianism* is the view that both the soul and the body are generated through procreation by parents.

According to God's design, and demonstrated above, the proper state of human beings is embodiment. In this earthly existence, and in the eternal state, human beings are embodied. People are disembodied only during the intermediate state, a condition due to sin and therefore an abnormal state.

The position that embodiment is the normal state of human existence has faced numerous challenges throughout the church's history. On the one hand, the church was deeply influenced by Plato's philosophy, expressed in gnosticism, that pitted the inherently evil material aspect, the body, against the inherently good immaterial aspect, the soul or spirit. This view resulted in a denigration of the body. This belittlement expressed itself in monasticism and in the promotion of asceticism, severe treatment of the body denying it legitimate physical pleasures like food, drink, sleep, and sexual intercourse. Moreover, the church's appreciation for the humanity of Jesus suffered, the honor of marriage suffered, and the clergy, who were sworn to celibacy, suffered as sexual immorality became rampant.

On the other hand, the church pointed to the goodness of God's creation of the physical world, which included his formation of human beings as embodied creatures. Moreover, the incarnation of the Son as the embodied God-man, together with his resurrection, underscores the importance of embodiment. So also do the future resurrection of the body and the new creation, which will be a physically restored world. All this contradicted the gnostic notion of the inherent evilness of material existence. And it emphasized that embodiment is the divinely designed, proper state of human existence.

Biblical Support

The Bible has no direct statement on human nature, so inferences about it are drawn from several texts. Support for the complexity of human nature is drawn from Paul's affirmation about the intermediate state (2 Cor. 5:1–9). He notes that it is a place of physical dissolution following death ("the tent that is our earthly home is destroyed"; v. 1); thus, believers are disembodied ("naked," "unclothed"; vv. 3, 4). Yet they are present with Christ ("away from the body and at home with the Lord"; v. 8; cf. Phil. 1:23). Only some form of dualism—trichotomy or dichotomy—that includes some idea of the complexity of human nature can account for continued existence after death in a disembodied state in heaven.

In support of trichotomy, proponents appeal to Paul's mention of three elements in his prayer: "May your whole spirit and soul and body be kept blameless at the coming of our Lord Jesus Christ" (1 Thess. 5:23). Similarly, a distinction is made elsewhere between soul and spirit (Heb. 4:12). Add the body to these two elements, and trichotomy is supported. Proponents of dichotomy point to Jesus's warning that mentions two elements: "Do not fear those who kill the body but cannot kill the soul. Rather fear him who can destroy both soul and body in hell" (Matt. 10:28). Paul similarly focuses on two components—spirit and body (1 Cor. 5:3, 5). Dichotomists also make a case for the interchangeability of "soul" and "spirit" (Luke 1:46–47; compare John 12:27 with 13:21). These two terms, being synonyms, refer to one component of human nature—the immaterial aspect.

Major Errors

1. *The elevation of the immaterial aspect of human nature above the material aspect, resulting in a neglect of or even hatred for the human body.* The church has resources, mentioned above, to counteract this gnostic error, so it needs to recover the goodness of creation and human embodiment and to cultivate hope in the resurrection of the body and the future restoration of the physical world.

2. *The denial of the immaterial element of human nature, resulting in a dismissal of the traditional doctrine of life after death in the intermediate state.* Of course, if a human person is identical to his body, he cannot continue to exist after death, the cessation of the functioning of his physical organism. Materialistic monism is contradicted by the biblical affirmation of the intermediate state and the doctrine of the resurrection.

3. *Contemporary confusion over gender identity leading to surgical reconstruction as the opposite sex.* The psychological disorder of gender dysphoria is a feeling of confusion or distress due to a disconnect between a person's biological sex and their emotional identity as the opposite gender: a person whose biological sex is male but who feels himself to be a female, or vice versa. Gender dysphoria may lead to transgenderism, or the physical switch to the opposite sex. This disorder and its consequences run counter to God's creation of human nature. Since it is a complex problem, people who experience it need compassionate care from the church, which must point to the hope of the gospel.

ENACTING THE DOCTRINE

God created a realm of beings that are immaterial in nature: the angels. We are not angels. Indeed, God created another realm of beings who are both immaterial and material in nature—human beings. By divine design, human beings are embodied beings—in this earthly life and in the new heaven and the new earth. In consequence, we should embrace our embodiment, refusing to see our body as inherently evil or as an obstacle to

God's work in our life. Moreover, because God has created human nature as either male or female, our genderedness is a fundamental given of life that cannot be rejected but should be welcomed with thanksgiving.

What's at stake in this doctrine? The proper perspective on what constitutes a human person. We are a material-immaterial unity, unlike God, unlike angels. We are wisely designed to flourish as God's people in the integrity of our body and soul—now, and in the age to come.

Perennial Questions and Problematic Issues

- It feels strange to talk about human beings and our nature, because our focus is usually on God and rarely on us.

- What practical difference does one's view of human nature—trichotomy or dichotomy—make?

- If the greatest minds in the church have not been able to decide between trichotomy and dichotomy, or creationism and traducianism, how can we expect to figure it out?

- I have always hated my body and viewed it as the ultimate source of sin and the major hindrance to my walk with God, but now you are saying something different.

- Should men who are women and women who are men have a place in our church?

TEACHING THE DOCTRINE

Because the church is (rightly) dedicated to God and his attributes, it rarely gives attention to human nature. A good place to start, then, is to discuss the question, what is a human person? Answers will likely include key terms such as "soul," "spirit," "body," "male," and "female." Be sure everyone knows what these words mean.

An important attitude to watch for is a belittling of the body. Sentiments like "If I could just get rid of this sinful body of mine," "I feel hindered in my relationship with God by my flesh," and "I can't wait to get to heaven and be truly me" should prompt a discussion of the error of gnosticism and the biblical affirmation of the goodness of material reality in general and human embodiment in particular. Be ready for significant pushback on this issue, as many Christians disparage their body.

Because of the two views of human nature, a presentation of trichotomy and dichotomy is needed. This disagreement is not a major one, so avoid an exaggerated division. As both views are forms of dualism, that position should be advocated over against monism, which is contradicted by Scripture. If time remains, a brief presentation on the origin of the soul can be included, but don't let this issue dominate and become a major point of disagreement. Furthermore, by tracing the three phases of human nature—earthly existence, the intermediate state, and after the resurrection—you can emphasize the propriety of human embodiment.

The ethical implications of this doctrine should be presented, with particular attention given to gender confusion and transgenderism. This topic should be approached with sensitivity and compassion, along with firmness.

TEACHING OUTLINE

1. The question "What is a human person?" and the summary
2. Major affirmations (with biblical support)
   A. The complexity of human nature: material and immaterial
   B. The complexity of human nature: different from the simplicity of divine nature and angelic nature
   C. Two positions on the complexity of human nature: trichotomy and dichotomy
   D. A warning against materialistic monism
   E. The different stages of human nature
   F. The origin of the soul: creationism and traducianism
   G. The importance of human embodiment
3. Major errors to avoid
   A. Elevating the immaterial aspect of human nature above the material aspect, resulting in a neglect of or even hatred for the human body
   B. Denying the existence of the immaterial element of human nature, resulting in a dismissal of the traditional doctrine of life after death in the intermediate state
   C. Yielding to confusion over gender identity, leading to surgical reconstruction as the opposite sex
4. Enacting the doctrine
   A. Embracing embodiment as the divinely designed state of human beings
   B. Embracing our genderedness as male or female

RESOURCES

Allison, *Theological Terms*, s.vv. "dichotomy," "human nature," "monism," "trichotomy"

Elwell, *Evangelical Dictionary of Theology*, s.vv. "Dichotomy," "Mankind, Doctrine of," "Trichotomy"

Erickson, *Christian Theology*, chap. 23

Grenz, *Theology for the Community of God*, chap. 6

Grudem, *Systematic Theology*, chap. 23

Horton, *Pilgrim Theology*, chap. 5

Thoennes, *Life's Biggest Questions*, chap. 11

17

SIN

SUMMARY

Sin is any lack of conformity to the moral law of God. Original sin is the state of all human beings at birth, and it includes their sin nature, which is the root of all actual sins that violate God's law.

MAIN THEMES

- Sin, as the lack of conformity to the moral law of God, applies to one's nature, actions, attitudes, words, and motivations.
- Though created in a state of goodness, Adam and Eve rebelled against God and fell into sin.
- Original sin is the state of all people at birth and derives from Adam's originating sin.
- The sin nature is the corrupt essence that characterizes all human beings and from which flow all actual sins.
- Temptation is not sin, and acts of sin vary in nature.
- The consequences of sin impact various relationships.

- The church has historically viewed the relationship between Adam's sin and the human race in three different ways.

KEY SCRIPTURE

Genesis 3; 2 Samuel 11–12; Psalm 51; Isaiah 1; Ezekiel 8; Hosea; Matthew 12:22–23; 23:1–39; Romans 3:10–18, 23; 5:12–21; 7:7–25; 1 Corinthians 5; James 1:13–15

UNDERSTANDING THE DOCTRINE

Major Affirmations

The doctrine of sin is presented in Scripture from Genesis 3 through Revelation 19 and is experienced in every realm of the creation—human, angelic, and natural. The pervasiveness and perversity of sin manifest themselves in various ways: *disobedience*, any noncompliance with God's will; *faithlessness*, the lack of trust in God and his provision; *abomination*, any heinous crime that is particularly reprehensible to God; *transgression*, a violation of a divine commandment or prohibition; *autonomy*, or setting up oneself rather than God as the ultimate authority; *missing the mark* (the most common notion of sin in the New Testament), or intentionally aiming away from the target so as to miss it; *pride*, or thinking more highly of oneself than one ought to think; *rebellion*, a revolt against God's design; *indifference*, or apathy toward God; *injustice*, any unfairness or discrimination by which others are not given the respect and treatment they are due; *hopelessness*, the premature abandonment of trust in God and his promises.

Generally speaking, sin is any lack of conformity to the moral law of God. Such nonconformity applies to one's (1) being: the sin nature, or tendency to sin; (2) actions: evil deeds like idolatry and murder; (3) attitudes: wrong mind-sets like envy and pride; (4) words: inappropriate communications like gossip and slander; and (5) motivations: disoriented purposes like self-glorification and people-pleasing. As sovereign and holy, God establishes the moral law as a reflection of his righteous nature, and sin is any violation of this law. For example, God always speaks the truth, so lying, which is against his nature, is prohibited, yet people lie and thus sin.

Sin did not originate with God. On the contrary, he created Adam and Eve in a state of integrity in which they obeyed and were faithful to him. Still, God ordained that sin would enter the world through the (wrong) moral choices of his creatures. The angelic beings were created good, but Satan and many others fell before human beings did. In the garden of Eden, Satan appeared as a serpent and tempted Eve through deception, and Adam joined her in rebelling against the divine prohibition not to eat from the tree of the knowledge of good and evil. This originating sin had horrific consequences for the rest of creation.

The consequence for humanity is original sin, the state of all people at birth. This condition consists of (1) original guilt, the liability to suffer eternal condemnation (some churches deny this element); and (2) original corruption, the sinful nature or tendency toward evil. This sin nature characterizes all human beings from the moment of their conception and is the fountainhead of all actual sins. Some churches further detail this corruption as consisting of (2a) total depravity, meaning that every aspect of human nature is infected with sin; and (2b) total inability, referring to the absence of spiritual goodness and the incapacity to reorient oneself from self-centeredness to God. Original sin derives from Adam's originating sin because of all people's solidarity with Adam and his disobedience.

As for temptation and actual sins, temptation is any enticement to sin that arises from one's fallen nature. Temptation itself is not sin, but it will lead to sin if not checked. For example, a proper desire for achievement, tainted by sin, lures the overachiever to slander his colleagues and exaggerate his accomplishments so he will be promoted at work. Actual sin can be characterized as (1) sins of presumption (intentional, high-handed sins) or sins of ignorance (unintentional), and as (2) sins of omission (failure to do what one should have done) or sins of commission (doing what one should not have done).

The consequences of sin impact all relationships and realities. As all sin is ultimately against God, it alienates from him, produces enmity with him, and brings guilt before him. Its impact on oneself is seen in self-centeredness, self-deception, and enslavement to sin. In regard to others, sin breaks relationships, brings shame, fosters competition rather than cooperation, and destroys empathy for others. Sin's impact on the creation is seen in hardship in work, natural disasters like hurricanes and tsunamis, human sickness, and genetic problems. Sin is a very serious matter, with devastating consequences.

Historically, the church has viewed the solidarity between Adam's sin and that of all humanity that comes from him in three ways: (1) Pelagianism, named after the British monk Pelagius (354–420/440), denies any relationship whatsoever between the two. Adam's sin affected him and him only: no guilt or corruption is transmitted to his descendants. At worst, Adam's sin provides a bad example for people, each of whom is responsible for their own sin.

(2) Augustinianism and its later counterpart, Lutheran and Reformed theology, strongly opposes Pelagianism. There exists a solidarity between Adam and humanity such that his sin affects every one of his progeny. Each person is born with original sin, which consists of both guilt before God and corruption of their nature. All people, therefore, stand condemned and are liable to eternal punishment, first and foremost because Adam's sin is imputed to them.

(3) Semi-Pelagianism maintains that people are not so much dead in sin as weakened by it. Possessing a free will, they are not so sinful that they are incapable of cooperating with divine grace for salvation. In its later development, (3a) Arminianism affirms the doctrine of original sin but also believes that the negative effects of original sin are suspended for all people by God's prevenient grace. In still a later development, (3b) Wesleyan Arminianism holds that original sin affects all people because of their solidarity with Adam, and this includes liability to eternal death, total depravity, and total inability. Yet it denies that people are condemned for Adam's sin alone; something more is needed. Actual sins are punished by God. Additionally, Wesleyan Arminianism appeals to prevenient grace that removes the disabilities due to corrupt human nature.

Biblical Support

Though Scripture begins with the creation of a good world and upright image-bearers, a turn for the worse happens soon afterward. The narrative of the fall of Adam and Eve presents Satan's temptation and the act of disobedience to God's prohibition. The now-broken story continues with the meting out of divine punishment on Satan, the woman, and the man, as well as the banishment of the fallen couple from the garden (Gen. 3).

From Genesis 3 through Revelation 19, the reign and ruination of sin is narrated, prophesied, confessed, legislated against, and ultimately, through Christ, defeated. Key presentations include the flood as God's judgment against a sin-saturated world (Gen. 6–9), the tower of Babel as disobedience to the divine mandate (Gen. 11), David's sin with Bathsheba and his confession (2 Sam. 11–12; Ps. 51), the constant waywardness of Israel in breaking the Mosaic law and failing to enact justice for the oppressed (Isa. 1; Hosea), Israel's abominations (Ezek. 8), Jesus's confrontation of the self-righteous religious leaders (Matt. 23), the battle to overcome indwelling sin (Rom. 7), and the incestuous man in Corinth (1 Cor. 5).

Particular aspects of the doctrine are treated: the universality of sin (1 Kings 8:46; Eccles. 7:20; Rom. 3:10–18, 23), the nature of temptation (James 1:13–15), the unpardonable sin (Matt. 12:22–32), and the solidarity between Adam's sin and all humanity (Rom. 5:12–21).

Major Errors

1. *The denial of any relationship between Adam's sin and humanity.* Pelagianism has been countered by leaders such as Augustine (who was a contemporary of Pelagius) and denounced by the church as heresy.

2. *The modern minimization or dismissal of personal sin, with an accompanying blame placed on systemic, social sin.* An example is the social gospel movement. While acknowledging and combatting systemic sin—expressed as racism, ageism, classism, sexism, and more—is both right and necessary, such battle cannot be waged apart from the recognition of and salvation from personal sin.

3. *The many views that salvation from sin can occur through something other than the gospel.* Examples abound and include legalism, moralism, behaviorism, therapeutic approaches, and social/economic/political liberation. These methods fail to grasp the pervasive and devastating nature of sin, people's impotence to resolve the problem, and the exclusivity of the gospel, as God's power, to effect such rescue.

ENACTING THE DOCTRINE

Christians are fundamentally image bearers of God. Because of their association with Adam and his sin, however, that ultimate identity is deeply marred—they are sinful. Emerging from this corrupt nature are all sorts of actual sins: words, attitudes, actions, motivations, and more. The perversity and pervasiveness of sin are a somber, tragic reality.

What's at stake in this doctrine? Coming to grips with the reality of human guilt and fallenness to such a profound degree that the gospel shines brighter than sin and thus becomes the only hope of salvation from it—both for us and for others.

TEACHING THE DOCTRINE

When teaching this doctrine, expect a good bit of discomfort; sin is not a pleasant matter. Still, it is good to encourage people to express their own struggles with sin and their concerns about the church's sins. Importantly, check the tendency to move on quickly from the doctrine, rushing to get to the gospel. In order to encourage deep confession and repentance from sin, we need to grasp and confront its profound entrenchment.

At the same time, avoid overemphasizing this doctrine to the point that people become sin centered rather than gospel centered. Though we are fallen into sin, guilty before God, and corrupt in essence, our sin nature is not our fundamental identity. That primary reality is being image bearers of God. Salvation from sin, therefore, does not involve becoming sin centered but gospel centered, as Christ alone can rescue from sin and restore us into his image.

The issue of the relationship between Adam's sin and us as his descendants can be quite controversial (Rom. 5:12–21). Fairly representing the various positions is important, as is advocating for our church's view. If that view is the Augustinian/Reformed position, an important matter with which to wrestle is the fairness of being considered guilty, and hence condemned, not because of our own actual sins (though that is another

Perennial Questions and Problematic Issues

- What is our church's view on original sin—Pelagianism, semi-Pelagianism, Augustinian-Reformed, Arminianism, Wesleyan Arminianism, or other—and why do we hold it?

- What do the different views of original sin mean for miscarriages, stillborn babies, and infants who die?

- If our view is the Augustinian-Reformed view, how does the fact that we are guilty before God and liable to suffer condemnation because of our solidarity with Adam's sin make us feel?

- I sense that our church doesn't adequately address the social dimensions of sin.

- I sense that our church overly addresses the social dimensions of sin.

reason) but first and foremost because of our solidarity with Adam and his sinful disobedience.

Not to be overlooked, nor overemphasized, is the social dimension of sin. Sin is indeed a personal matter, affecting all aspects of human nature. But fallen human nature expresses itself through the construction of political, educational, economic, legal, and social systems that function sinfully, even to the point of engulfing people who want to escape them.

Finally, participants will tend to try to figure out sin. They will speculate why Adam and Eve abandoned everything and sinned. Be sure to underscore this truth: sin is irrational. We dare not think that we have answered the riddle, or that we can solve the mystery, of sin. We do not, and cannot, figure out sin.

TEACHING OUTLINE

1. Encouragement to face sin honestly, and the summary
2. Major affirmations (with biblical support)
   A. Definition of sin
   B. Origin of sin
   C. Original sin and the various views of it
   D. The sin nature, temptation, and actual sins
   E. Consequences of sin
3. Major errors to avoid
   A. Denying any relationship between Adam's sin and humanity
   B. Minimizing or dismissing personal sin, with an accompanying blame placed on systemic, social sin
   C. Holding that salvation from sin can occur through something other than the gospel
4. Enacting the doctrine
   A. Coming to grips with the reality of human guilt and fallenness
   B. Embracing the gospel as our only hope of salvation from sin

RESOURCES

Allison, *Theological Terms*, s.vv. "original sin," "sin," "sin nature"
Elwell, *Evangelical Dictionary of Theology*, s.v. "Sin"

Erickson, *Christian Theology*, chaps. 25–29
Grenz, *Theology for the Community of God*, chap. 7
Grudem, *Systematic Theology*, chap. 24
Horton, *Pilgrim Theology*, chap. 6
Thoennes, *Life's Biggest Questions*, chap. 13

PART 4

DOCTRINE

—— OF ——

GOD THE SON

18

THE PERSON OF THE SON OF GOD

SUMMARY

The Son of God is the Second Person of the Trinity, equal with the Father and the Holy Spirit. In the incarnation, he took on human nature and became the God-man, one person with two natures.

MAIN THEMES

- The Son of God is the Second Person of the Trinity, sharing in the one divine nature.
- Being fully God, the Son is equal with the Father and the Holy Spirit in nature, power, and glory, but he is distinct from them in terms of his eternal relation and roles.
- Two thousand years ago, the eternal Son of God became incarnate, taking on a full human nature, and became the God-man, Jesus Christ.
- By the hypostatic union, he is both fully God and fully man, two natures united in one person.

- This classical Christology stands opposed to various heresies, both early and modern.
- The Son is worthy of worship, obedience, trust, and service.

KEY SCRIPTURE

Philippians 2:5–11; Colossians 1:15–20; 1 Timothy 3:16; Titus 2:13; 1 John 4:1–3

UNDERSTANDING THE DOCTRINE

Major Affirmations

The Son of God is the Second Person of the Trinity, eternally existing together with the Father and the Holy Spirit in the one Godhead. He is fully God, as are the Father and the Spirit, possessing the same attributes of independence, immutability, omnipresence, omnipotence, omniscience, holiness, love, and more. The three share in the one divine essence. Thus, the Son is fully God, coequal with the Father and the Holy Spirit.

The Son is a distinct person from the Father and the Spirit, distinguished from them by his particular eternal relation and his particular roles. In terms of relation, the Son is eternally generated, or begotten, of the Father. Eternal generation does not mean that the Father created the Son. Nor does it mean that the Father gives him his deity, as the Son is God-of-himself. Rather, eternal generation means the Father grants him his sonship life, or person-of-the-Son. In this way, he is distinct from the Father. He is also distinct from the Spirit, who eternally proceeds from both the Father and the Son.

Another distinction between the three has to do with their roles. Though the Father, Son, and Spirit operate together inseparably, the Son engages in particular ministries. This theme is treated in chapter 20, "The Work of the Son of God."

Two thousand years ago, the eternally existing and fully divine Son of God took on a fully human nature. This incarnation was a hypostatic union, the joining together (the union) of the two natures in the one person (Gk. *hypostasis*), Jesus Christ.

Specifically, the preexistent Son became incarnate by taking on a complete human nature—both a material aspect (body) and an immaterial aspect (soul). The man Jesus had no existence prior to the incarnation. He was *anhypostatic*: without personal existence. The Son did not unite himself to an already-existing human being. Rather, the human nature exists in the divine person. It is *enhypostatic*: it exists in the Son of God. The Son took on a fully human nature: body and soul. In the incarnation, the Son became, and remains forever, the God-man.

The early church developed this classical Christology. It had to address numerous departures from both Christ's full divinity and his full humanity. Classical Christology's highest expression is the Chalcedonian Creed:

> Our Lord Jesus Christ is both complete in divinity and complete in humanity, truly God and truly man, consisting also of a rational soul and body. He is of one substance [*homoousios*] with the Father as regards his Godhead, and at the same time of one substance with us [human beings] as regards his humanity; like us in all respects, apart from sin. As regards his Godhead, he is begotten of the Father before the ages. But as regards his humanity he was begotten [born], for us and for our salvation, of Mary the virgin, the God-bearer [*theotokos*]. He is at the same time Christ, Son, Lord, only begotten, recognized in two natures, without confusion, without change, without division, without separation. The distinction of natures was in no way annulled by the union. Rather, the characteristics of each nature were preserved and came together to form one person and subsistence [*hypostasis*], not as parted or separated into two persons, but one and the same Son and only begotten God the Word, the Lord Jesus Christ.[17]

The Chalcedonian Creed stands opposed to several errors, both early and modern.

Docetism denied the humanity of the Son in the incarnation. It has two major tenets: (1) Jesus Christ only seemed (Gk. *dokeō*) to be a man; (2) instead, he was a spirit being appearing as a human being.

Arianism denied the deity of the Son. Its major tenets are as follows: (1) God created a Son as the first and highest of all created beings. (2) Through him, God created everything else, yet the Son is a created being. (3) The Son is not eternal, meaning that he is *heteroousios*, of a different nature, not *homoousios*, of the same nature, as the Father.

Apollinarianism denied the full humanity of the incarnate Son. It has two main tenets: (1) in taking on human nature, the Word of God only became united with "flesh" (John 1:14); and (2) Christ's human nature consisted of only a human body, but not a human soul, which was replaced by the divine Word.

Nestorianism denied the hypostatic union, that the incarnate Christ had two natures united in one person. It has two major tenets: (1) in the incarnation, two distinct persons—one divine, one human—worked in conjunction with each other; (2) this is true because a union of divine and human would have involved God in change, which is impossible.

Eutychianism also denied the hypostatic union; it has two forms. The major tenet of one form is that the divine nature nearly absorbed the human nature of Christ, meaning that his one nature is DIVINEhuman. In its second form, Eutychianism holds that the divine and human natures fused together, meaning that Christ's one nature is d^h i^u v^m i^a n^n e.

Kenoticism, a modern heresy, denied the full deity of the Son in the incarnation. The term is derived from the Greek verb *kenoō* in Philippians 2:7: the Son "emptied himself." The major tenets of kenoticism are as follows: (1) In the incarnation, the Son of God divested himself not of his essential divine attributes but of those attributes that are relative to his activity in the world: omniscience, omnipresence, and omnipotence. (2) After his exaltation, the Son again took up those attributes.

Biblical Support

The Son of God eternally exists. Thus, the incarnation is not the beginning of his existence. Rather, he is the Son of God, eternally generated (begotten) of the Father. Jesus affirmed his eternal generation: "For as the Father has life in himself, so he has granted the Son also to have life in himself" (John 5:26). The Father eternally generates the Second Person, to whom he grants his person-of-the-Son, or sonship life (cf. 1 John 5:18).

The Son's preexistence (before his incarnation) is affirmed: "In the beginning was the Word, and the Word was with God, and the Word was God" (John 1:1). At the time God created the universe ("in the beginning," reminiscent of Gen. 1:1), the Word was already in existence, both distinct from, and in relationship with, God. Furthermore, this Word was himself God. Indeed, through him the world was created (John 1:3; cf. Col. 1:15–20). It was this preexisting Word that became flesh—took on human nature—in the incarnation (John 1:14).

150

Accordingly, the incarnation involved the eternal Son, who existed "in the form of God," refusing to selfishly hold on to his "equality with God" status. Rather, he "emptied himself," not by yielding or muffling divine attributes such as omnipotence, omnipresence, and omniscience, but by "taking the form of a servant," becoming a real and fully human being (Phil. 2:5–7). As Gregory of Nazianzus explained, while remaining what he was (that is, fully God), the Son became what he was not (that is, a fully human being).[18]

Scripture supports the Son's full deity: (1) His divine titles demonstrate that he is God. He is the *Son of God* (Mark 1:9–11; John 3:16) and *Lord* (Acts 2:36). (2) The divine references support his deity, as he is referred to as "our great God and Savior Jesus Christ" (Titus 2:13; 2 Pet. 1:1; cf. Heb. 1:8). (3) His nature is divine: "He is the radiance of the glory of God and the exact imprint of his nature" (Heb. 1:3; cf. Phil. 2:6). Indeed, Jesus claims, "I and the Father are one" (John 10:30), such that "whoever has seen me has seen the Father" (14:8–9).

(4) He exhibits divine attributes such as omnipresence (Matt. 28:20), omniscience (Matt. 26:20–25, 30–35; John 2:25; 18:4), and authority (Matt. 28:18). (5) He engages in divine activities such as creating (John 1:3; Col. 1:16), sustaining (Col. 1:17), judging (John 5:22, 27; Acts 17:31), forgiving sins (Mark 2:10), and granting eternal life (John 5:21; 10:28). (6) His miracles demonstrated that he was the divine Son of God (20:30–31 and the seven "signs" in John: changing water into wine, 2:1–11; healing the official's son, 4:46–54; healing the invalid, 5:1–15; feeding the five thousand, 6:5–14; walking on water, 6:16–24; healing the blind man, 9:1–7; and raising Lazarus from the dead, 11:1–45).

These points underscore the full deity of the Son of God (John 20:28).

Scripture supports the incarnate Son's full humanity: (1) Jesus was born like any other human being (Luke 2:1–7). (2) He grew and matured like others (2:40, 51–52). (3) Christ had normal physical needs such as food, drink, rest, and sleep. (4) He expressed common human emotions like love, wonder, joy, compassion, and anger. (5) He enjoyed the kind of relationships that are characteristic of human beings. For example, John was "the disciple whom Jesus loved" (John 21:7, 20), one of Jesus's three closest friends (Peter, James, and John; Mark 5:37; 9:2; 14:33). Jesus spent three years of ministry with the Twelve (Matt. 10:1–4), and had close friendships with women (Luke 8:1–2), including Mary and Martha (John 11:1–41). And Jesus was "a friend of tax collectors and sinners"

(Matt. 11:19; cf. 9:10–11). (6) He suffered and died like any other human being (John 19:34).

These points underscore the full humanity of the Son of God incarnate (1 Tim. 3:16).

The hypostatic union finds biblical support as well. (1) The virgin birth (or conception) united the eternal Son with a human nature (Luke 1:26–35; Matt. 1:18–25). (2) His genealogies are traced back to both Abraham (Matt. 1:1) and God (Luke 3:38). (3) As the incarnate Son, he faced temptations (4:1–12) and learned obedience to become the perfect source of salvation (Heb. 5:8–9). (4) To be orthodox, one must confess that the Son of God has become incarnate in Jesus Christ (1 John 4:1–3).

Perennial Questions and Problematic Issues

- Some people say that Jesus Christ never existed.
- How can Jesus be fully God yet say that he doesn't know the time of his own return (Mark 13:32)?
- Does Jesus deny that he is God because he is less than God (John 14:28)?
- Does eternal generation make the Son inferior to the Father?
- Why is it important that Jesus Christ be both fully God and fully man?

Major Errors

1. *The denial of the (full) deity of the Son (Arianism, kenoticism).* This position cannot explain the passages that affirm that the Son is God.

2. *The denial of the (full) humanity of the Son (Docetism, Apollinarianism).* This position cannot explain the passages that affirm that the Son took on a fully human nature.

3. *The denial of the hypostatic union (Nestorianism, Eutychianism).* This position fails to hold together the biblical affirmations of Christ's deity and humanity.

ENACTING THE DOCTRINE

Because the Son of God is the fully divine Second Person of the Trinity, he is worshiped together with the Father and the Holy Spirit. As they are, so the Son is worthy of honor, thanksgiving, obedience, trust, and service.

What's at stake in this doctrine? Our salvation! The God-man, sent by the Father to accomplish salvation, is the unique mediator between God and his fallen image-bearers. Only he as the fully divine Son could pay the infinite penalty for sin. Only he as the fully human Son incarnate could be the perfect substitute for sinful human beings. He and he alone is the Savior in whom God's people trust for their salvation. And through the Son we enjoy a personal relationship with the living God!

TEACHING THE DOCTRINE

A good place to start is with Jesus's question to his disciples: "Who do people say that the Son of Man is?" (Matt. 16:13). Press the participants to think of answers that might be given by an atheist, a Jew, a Muslim, a liberal Christian, and more. Follow up with Jesus's second question to his disciples: "But who do you say that I am?" (16:15). Ask responders to explain their answers.

Though the eternal generation of the Son from the Father can be difficult to teach, it is important that the basic idea be presented, since this eternal relation distinguishes the two persons. Biblical support for both the full deity and the full humanity of the God-man, along with the hypostatic union, is crucial for both understanding the nature of the incarnation and preparing participants to answer questions about the person of the Son from critics and seekers alike.

———— TEACHING OUTLINE ————

1. The summary of the person of the Son of God
2. Who do people/you say that Jesus Christ is?
3. Major affirmations (with biblical support)
    A. The eternal generation of the Son
    B. The deity of the Son
    C. The humanity of the Son
    D. The hypostatic union
    E. The proper reverence that is to be shown to the Son
4. Major errors to avoid
    A. Denying the (full) deity of the Son
    B. Denying the (full) humanity of the Son
    C. Denying the hypostatic union

5. Enacting the doctrine
   A. Worshiping the Son of God
   B. Trusting in the fully divine and fully human Son of God for our
      salvation

RESOURCES

Allison, *Theological Terms*, s.vv. "hypostatic union," "Jesus Christ, deity of,"
"Jesus Christ, humanity of"

Elwell, *Evangelical Dictionary of Theology*, s.vv. "Jesus Christ," "States of Jesus
Christ"

Erickson, *Christian Theology*, chaps. 30–34

Grenz, *Theology for the Community of God*, chaps. 9–11

Grudem, *Systematic Theology*, chap. 26

Horton, *Pilgrim Theology*, chap. 7

Thoennes, *Life's Biggest Questions*, chap. 8

19

THE OFFICES OF THE SON OF GOD

SUMMARY

The offices of the Son of God are his threefold work of salvation as Prophet, Priest, and King.

MAIN THEMES

- The technical term for this doctrine is *munus triplex*, the threefold office of Christ.
- God established three offices in Israel: prophet, priest, and king.
- Held by different people, these three offices featured three different types of work.
- The Old Testament projected the coming of One who would be Prophet, Priest, and King, uniting the three offices.
- The Son of God fulfills this Old Testament expectation.
- As Prophet, he reveals God and his ways.
- As Priest, he mediates between God and his people.
- As King, he rules over creation, including humanity.

KEY SCRIPTURE

Deuteronomy 17:14–20; 18:15–18; Psalms 89:28–35; 110:1–4; Luke 1:32, 35; Acts 3:22–24; 13:22–23, 33; Romans 1:3–4; Ephesians 1:19–23; Hebrews 7–10

UNDERSTANDING THE DOCTRINE

Major Affirmations

Most commonly, people view the saving work of Jesus Christ in terms of his sacrifice on the cross and his resurrection. While these were certainly the focus of his mission, Christ's work cannot be limited to them. The *munus triplex*, or threefold office of Christ, underscores the multifaceted nature of his work of salvation.

God established three offices in Israel: prophet, priest, and king. These were distinct offices held by different people and featured different roles. By speaking God's words through the Holy Spirit, the prophets gave divine revelation, making known God and his ways to his people. As mediators between God and his people, the priests offered sacrifices to atone for the people's sins and interceded for them before God. As God's representatives, the kings ruled over the people of God.

The three distinct roles of prophet, priest, and king were carried out by three distinct types of people. Importantly, the Old Testament prophesied the coming of One who would join the three offices together. He would be Prophet, Priest, and King, engaging in the work of all three offices.

The Son of God fulfilled this prophecy. Uniting the three offices together and doing the work of all three, Jesus is Prophet, Priest, and King.

Biblical Support

The Old Testament background is extensive. The office of prophet is seen with respect to Isaiah, Jeremiah, and the other prophets (2 Pet. 1:19–21). Prophetic messages exposed the sinfulness of God's people (Isa. 1), portrayed future judgment (Isa. 3), revealed specific direction (6:8–13), announced the coming Messiah (9:1–7), and more.

The office of priest is most clearly associated with the high priest, who once a year on the Day of Atonement would offer sacrifices for the forgiveness of the people's sins (Lev. 16). There were many other priests who likewise offered sacrifices for sins. These sacrifices, though prescribed by God, could not ultimately save those for whom they were offered. Rather, "in these sacrifices there is a reminder of sins every year. For it is impossible for the blood of bulls and goats to take away sins" (Heb. 10:3–4; cf. v. 11). An additional priestly responsibility was the offering of prayers on behalf of God's people. In particular, priestly prayers were blessings in the name of the Lord (Num. 6:24–26; Deut. 21:5; 1 Chron. 23:13).

The office of king began with Saul, continued with David and Solomon, and split between two kingdoms. Before its inauguration, however, God had made provision for a king for his people. The king's key responsibility would be to copy, daily read, and obey Scripture (Deut. 17:14–20). Each of Israel's kings failed to live up to these expectations.

The Old Testament predicted the coming of One who would be Prophet, Priest, and King, uniting the three offices. Moses, the first prophet, anticipated a future prophet like him: "The LORD your God will raise up for you a prophet like me. . . . And the LORD said to me, '. . . I will put my words in his mouth, and he shall speak to them all that I command him'" (Deut. 18:15–18).

The Old Testament also provided hints of a priest unlike those before him: "And I will raise up for myself a faithful priest, who shall do according to what is in my heart and in my mind" (1 Sam. 2:35). This one to come would be both king—sitting at the Lord's right hand, ruling over his enemies (Ps. 110:1–2)—and "a priest forever after the order of Melchizedek" (v. 4).

The Old Testament offered an expectation of a "Davidic" king, coming from the line of David, Solomon, and the kings following them. His kingdom would be forever. Significantly, he would be a faithful son of God (2 Sam. 7; Ps. 89:28–35). Other prophecies presented him as "a righteous Branch" of David (Jer. 23:5–6; cf. 30:9) whose birthplace would be humble (Mic. 5:2) and whose entry in Jerusalem would be triumphant (Zech. 9:9).

The New Testament affirms Jesus as this One to come. He was Prophet, acknowledged as such by people like the Samaritan woman (John 4:19) and the blind man (9:17). Indeed, there was a vague sense that Jesus was "one of the prophets" (Matt. 16:14). Citing Deuteronomy 18:15, Peter identified Jesus as the expected Moses-like prophet (Acts 3:22–24).

Like the prophets of old, Jesus spoke the words of God to his people: "You have heard that it was said, . . . but I say to you . . ." (Matt. 5:21–22, 27–28, 31–32, 33–34, 38–39, 43–44). Accordingly, he established himself as the authoritative interpreter of Old Testament revelation and the giver of new revelation. As the main focus of his ministry, Jesus preached the gospel (4:17, 23; Mark 1:15–17; Luke 4:43).

In addition to revealing the words of God, Jesus as Prophet revealed the works of God: "The works that the Father has given me to accomplish [are] the very works that I am doing" (John 5:36). Jesus's works revealed the Father's works.

Beyond the revelation of God's words and God's works, Jesus as Prophet revealed God himself. To his friend Philip, Jesus explained, "Whoever has seen me has seen the Father" (John 14:9). Indeed, the Son incarnate is "the exact imprint of his [God's] nature" (Heb. 1:3).

Accordingly, Jesus is Prophet, speaking the words of God, manifesting the works of God, and, being God himself, revealing God to his people.

The New Testament presents Jesus as Priest. He is "a priest forever, after the order of Melchizedek" (Heb. 5:6; 6:20; 7:3, 17, 21) in fulfillment of prophecy (Ps. 110:4). In particular, Jesus is High Priest, though significantly unlike the high priests before him. One contrast was his sinlessness. As High Priest he was "holy, innocent, unstained, separated from sinners. . . . He has no need, like those high priests, to offer sacrifices daily, first for his own sins, and then for those of the people" (Heb. 7:26–27).

A second contrast is with the nature of his offering. "But when Christ appeared as a high priest, . . . he entered once for all into the holy places, not by means of the blood of goats and calves but by means of his own blood" (Heb. 9:11–12). Uniquely, as the sacrificer, he sacrificed himself. Third, Christ and his once-for-all sacrifice on the cross contrast with the priests and their repetitive sacrifices: "But when Christ had offered for all time a single sacrifice for sins, he sat down at the right hand of God" (10:12–14).

Jesus also was a Priest who prayed for God's people. His High Priestly prayer is one example (John 17). Jesus as the eternal High Priest continues in his ministry of prayer (Heb. 7:24–25; cf. Rom. 8:34). In his priestly praying, Jesus also blesses his people, particularly the poor, the meek, the merciful, and more (Matt. 5:1–12).

Accordingly, Jesus is Priest, offering the ultimate sacrifice and praying for God's people.

The New Testament affirms Jesus as King. Herod worried that the recently born Jesus was "king of the Jews" (Matt. 2:1–8), born in Bethlehem in accordance with Micah's prophecy (2:5–6; Mic. 5:2). Jesus's triumphal entry as King was also the fulfillment of prophecy (Matt. 21:1–11; Zech.

9:9). At Jesus's death, the charge against him was "This is Jesus, the King of the Jews" (Matt. 27:37).

Moreover, Jesus was the "Davidic" King whose coming was long anticipated. He was the son of David (Matt. 1:1; 9:27; John 7:42; Acts 13:22–23). He was the Son of God (Mark 1:1; Luke 3:38; Matt. 16:16). The New Testament joins these two identities together (Luke 1:32, 35; Acts 13:22–23, 33; Rom. 1:3–4).

Jesus's kingly rule is especially associated with his exalted heavenly position. As the cosmic head, Christ is king over all creation in general and over the church in particular (Eph. 1:19–23). At his return, the conquering Lamb will appear in glory as "Lord of lords and King of kings" (Rev. 17:14).

Accordingly, Jesus is King, ruling over all creation and particularly over God's people.

Major Errors

1. *A complete neglect of the threefold office.* Though it is not a major doctrine or even the gospel's focal point (which is Christ's death and resurrection), it does have strong biblical support and deserves treatment.

2. *Confusing it with how other religions view Christ.* For example, Muslims maintain that Jesus is a great prophet. But the Christian doctrine of Christ as Prophet is far removed from the Islamic view and should not be confused with it.

3. *The view that this doctrine detracts from the deity of Christ.* Because prophets, priests, and kings were human beings, to affirm that Christ is Prophet, Priest, and King seems to some people to so emphasize his work as a human being that it eclipses his deity. But this doctrine does not pretend to exhaust discussion about Christ. Rather, it focuses on a few aspects of his work, which he carried out not as a mere human being but as the God-man.

ENACTING THE DOCTRINE

This doctrine highlights important aspects of the person and work of the Son of God. Scripture, which is our ultimate authority, points us to him, the ultimate Word by whom the Father spoke (Heb. 1:1–2). The Son reveals the words, the works, and the very being of God. We rejoice in knowing him, and we make it our daily work to give heed to the One who is Prophet.

The Son eternally intercedes for us. He prays that our faith remains strong (Luke 22:31–32). He prays against the attacks and accusations of the evil one (Rev. 12:10). His constant praying means that our salvation is sure (Heb. 7:25). We are thankful for his ministry of prayer, and we draw near with confidence to the One who is Priest.

The Son is King, ruler over all creation and head of the church. We long for the entire world to submit to him, praying, "Your kingdom come, your will be done, on earth as it is in heaven" (Matt. 6:10). Until his kingdom comes, we as the church joyfully obey the One who is King.

A common way of presenting this doctrine is to encourage Christians to imitate Christ in his three offices. How can believers be prophets, priests, and kings today? Or, thinking more individually, am I more prophetic, priestly, or kingly in terms of my gifts, passions, and abilities? Generally speaking, a "prophetic" person is concerned about communicating the gospel and leading through casting vision. A "priestly" person focuses on caring for and counseling people and engaging in ministries of mercy. A "kingly" person gives attention to concrete tasks and leading through strategizing and implementing vision. Prior to engaging in these applications, be sure to ask the church to discern how appropriate they are.

Perennial Questions and Problematic Issues

- I've never heard of Christ's three-fold work of Prophet, Priest, and King.
- If human beings were prophets, priests, and kings, are we saying that Christ was a mere human being acting as prophet, priest, and king?
- Someone told me that I have a prophetic ministry (or priestly ministry or kingly ministry).

TEACHING THE DOCTRINE

Much teaching is concentrated on Christ's death and resurrection, and rightly so. Teaching on his offices is a good reminder that Christ's work was and is far more extensive than the apex of it. Participants will appreciate the great breadth of what Christ accomplished on their behalf.

Because it is a much-neglected discussion, be prepared to deal with participants who are completely unfamiliar with it. Put their minds at ease that what is being taught is not a new idea. Indeed, the church historian Eusebius (263–340) pioneered the discussion,[19] and John Calvin (1509–64) treated the doctrine in his *Institutes of the Christian Religion*.[20]

TEACHING OUTLINE

1. The *munus triplex* and the summary of the offices of the Son of God
2. Major affirmations (with biblical support)
   A. The three offices in Israel were prophet, priest, and king.
   B. The Old Testament anticipated the coming of One who would unite these three offices.
   C. Jesus fulfills this expectation.
   D. Christ fulfills the office of Prophet.
   E. Christ fulfills the office of Priest.
   F. Christ fulfills the office of King.
3. Major errors to avoid
   A. Neglecting the threefold office
   B. Confusing the doctrine with how other religions view Christ
   C. Holding that this doctrine detracts from the deity of Christ
4. Enacting the doctrine
   A. Giving heed to the Son who is Prophet
   B. Being thankful for his ministry of prayer, and drawing near with confidence to the Son who is Priest
   C. Obeying the Son who is King

RESOURCES

Allison, *Theological Terms*, s.v. "priesthood"
Elwell, *Evangelical Dictionary of Theology*, s.v. "Offices of Christ"
Erickson, *Christian Theology*, chap. 35
Grudem, *Systematic Theology*, chap. 29
Horton, *Pilgrim Theology*, 183–89
Thoennes, *Life's Biggest Questions*, chap. 10

20

THE WORK OF THE SON OF GOD

SUMMARY

The atonement is the death of the incarnate Son on the cross and what it accomplished.

MAIN THEMES

- Atonement is what Christ's death achieved.
- It consists of five aspects: propitiation, expiation, redemption, reconciliation, and cosmic victory.
- A debated issue is the extent of the atonement.
- The church has developed several models of the atonement.

KEY SCRIPTURE

Leviticus 16; Mark 10:45; Romans 3:25–26; 5:8; 8:32; 1 Corinthians 5:7; 2 Corinthians 5:14–21; 8:9; Ephesians 1:7, 10; 5:2, 25; Colossians 1:19–20; 1 Timothy 2:4–5; Hebrews 2:14–15; 9:1–10:39; 1 Peter 1:18–19; 3:18; 1 John 2:2

UNDERSTANDING THE DOCTRINE

Major Affirmations

The preceding chapter, "The Offices of the Son of God," rehearsed Christ's works as Prophet, Priest, and King. This chapter focuses on his atonement, his work on the cross. As the long-expected Prophet, Priest, and King, Jesus offered himself as the atonement for sin.

The atonement is the death of the God-man, Jesus Christ, on the cross and what it accomplished. Because of human sinfulness, a sacrifice for sin is necessary to avert condemnation and restore people to God. Old covenant sacrifices made provisional atonement, looking forward to the work of Christ to accomplish atonement fully and forever.

At the heart of the death of Christ is *penal substitution*, explained in seven affirmations: (1) The atonement is grounded in the holiness of God, who, being perfectly holy, hates and punishes sin. Thus, the sin of humanity against a holy God necessitates the atonement. (2) It is an objective, not a subjective, work. The atonement is what Christ accomplished by his death, not its application (which is another divine work). (3) A penalty for sin must be paid, and paid in full. (4) No sinful person can pay for her own sin and be saved. Rather, the penalty is death. (5) Only God can pay the penalty for sin and rescue sinful people, but he must partake of human nature to save them. (6) The God-man Jesus Christ paid the penalty for sin. (7) The atonement had to be accomplished in this way.

The atonement may be viewed from five perspectives: (1) *Propitiation*: Christ's death appeased the wrath of God against sinful people. At the heart of propitiation is retributive justice: because God is just, he must punish sin fully. God mercifully meted out that punishment by pouring out his wrath on his Son.

(2) *Expiation*: Christ's death removed the liability to suffer eternal punishment because of sin and guilt. Some people object to the idea of propitiation, maintaining instead that Christ's death was an expiatory sacrifice. Scripture affirms both. As expiation, Christ's death cleanses sinful people through the removal and forgiveness of sins.

(3) *Redemption*: This aspect of Christ's death is set against the backdrop of enslavement: human beings are captive to sin. The need is for someone to pay a ransom and set slaves free from such bondage. Christ's blood is the ransom price paid. Redemption as freedom from enslavement begins in this life and ultimately includes the resurrection of the body.

(4) *Reconciliation*: This aspect of Christ's death is set against the backdrop of enmity: because of human sin, there is hostility between God and his image bearers. The need is for someone to remove that antagonism and restore peace between these two warring parties. Christ is the mediator, and his death is the means of mediation for reconciliation.

(5) *Cosmic victory*: Christ's death defeated or overcame sin, death, the curse of the law, and Satan and demons.

The debate on the extent of the atonement has historically been between two perspectives. Limited atonement is the position that Christ died with the intent of actually and certainly saving only the elect. Unlimited atonement is the position that Christ died with the intent that his death be the payment for sin for everyone, making it possible for any and all to be saved. A recent version, the multiple-intentions view, is the position that God had multiple intentions that he accomplished through Christ's death: Christ died for the purpose of (1) securing the sure salvation of the elect; (2) paying the penalty for the sins of everyone, making it possible for all who believe to be saved; and (3) reconciling all things to God.

In addition to penal substitution, the church has developed various models or theories of what Christ's death accomplished.

1. *Recapitulation theory*. As the second Adam, Jesus recapitulated, or summed up, all the life events of fallen humanity. Instead of repeating Adam's sin and living out these events in disobedience to God, however, Christ lived them obediently. Thus, he reversed the sinful direction in which people were headed.

2. *Ransom to Satan theory*. Satan usurped God's rightful ownership of human beings; thus, they illegitimately belong to Satan. Christ's death was the ransom that was paid to free people from this bogus enslavement, and it was paid to Satan.

3. *Satisfaction theory*. Sin is robbing God of his honor. People must render satisfaction for their sin: they must repay—actually, pay back more than—the honor they have stolen from God. People cannot pay their debt, for whatever they could pay is owed already to God. Only the God-man can offer satisfaction. By dying, Jesus gave something that he did not owe to God—the obligation to die—and thus obtained a reward. Christ gave this reward to provide satisfaction for people's sin.

4. *Moral influence theory*. People need their love for God to be stimulated. A persuasive exhibition of God's love is necessary to stimulate

such love for God. Christ's death provided that demonstration of divine love, which in turn stimulates people to love God.

5. *Governmental theory*. God is the governor of the universe, whose love for sinful human beings is his highest attribute. In his mercy, God relaxed the demands of his law while remaining holy by still upholding it to some degree. Christ's death emphasized that the law must be respected, but it did not meet the exact requirements of the law (which had been relaxed). Thus, Christ died, not as a full satisfaction for the law's exact penalty, but as a token of God's concern to uphold his law.

6. Christus Victor *model*. It has elements of cosmic victory (noted above) and bears some resemblance to the ransom to Satan theory.

Biblical Support

Biblical support for Christ's death as a penal substitution is two-fold. First, Christ is a substitute as demonstrated by the many affirmations that his death was "for us" and "for our sake": "God shows his love for us in that while we were still sinners, Christ died for us" (Rom. 5:8; cf. 8:32; 2 Cor. 5:21; 8:9; 1 Pet. 3:18). Second, Christ bears the penalty of sin as a sacrifice. Old Testament imagery conveys this point: "Christ, our Passover lamb, has been sacrificed" (1 Cor. 5:7). Indeed, he sacrificed himself once for all, unlike the many repeated sacrifices under the old covenant (Heb. 9:26; 10:12).

These two aspects of sacrificial penalty paying and substitution are presented together: "Christ loved us and gave himself up for us, a fragrant offering and sacrifice to God" (Eph. 5:2). Thus, Christ's death was a penal substitution for the sins of fallen humanity.

Biblical support for the various facets of the atonement is rich. (1) Christ's death is presented as a *propitiation* against the Old Testament background: the blood of sacrifices was sprinkled on the mercy seat, thereby assuaging God's wrath and ensuring mercy instead (Lev. 16:11–17). The New Testament presents Christ's death as "the propitiation . . . for the sins of the world" (1 John 2:2) and "as a propitiation by his blood" (Rom. 3:25–26).

(2) Christ's death was an *expiation*, again against the Old Testament backdrop of the blood of sacrifices that covered the sins of God's people and cleansed them to avoid impending judgment (Lev. 16). The New Testament highlights Christ's once-and-for-all expiatory sacrifice purifying people through the forgiveness of their sins (Heb. 9:6–15; 10:5–18).

(3) Christ's death is presented in terms of *redemption* using the imagery of enslaved people being held captive in the slave market of sin. The only way of release is by means of a ransom paid. As Jesus himself affirmed, "The Son of Man came . . . to give his life as a ransom for many" (Mark 10:45). Specifically, the ransom price was "the precious blood of Christ, like that of a lamb without blemish or spot" (1 Pet. 1:19; cf. Eph. 1:7).

(4) Christ's death enacted *reconciliation* against the background of enmity between God and sinful people. This hostility or separation must be overcome for the two to be in relationship. God acted "through him [Christ] to reconcile to himself all things, . . . making peace by the blood of his cross" (Col. 1:20; cf. 1 Tim. 2:5).

(5) Christ's death effected a *cosmic victory* over the enemies of God and his people: sin, which enslaves humanity (Rom. 6:16; 8:2); death, which is humanity's "last enemy" (1 Cor. 15:26); the law (Rom. 4:15; 5:20), which brings death (7:8–11); and Satan and demons (Heb. 2:14–15). Christ triumphed over these enemies through his death on the cross.

As for the debate on the extent of the atonement, each position marshals biblical and theological support. Biblical support for limited atonement includes affirmations that Christ died for the elect (Rom. 8:32–33; 2 Cor. 5:14–15), a particular group of people—his sheep (John 10:11) and church (Eph. 5:25). Theological support appeals to agreement within the Trinity: those whom the Father purposed to save are the same people for whom Christ came to die and the same people to whom the Spirit applies salvation. The elect alone are in view.

Biblical support for unlimited atonement includes affirmations that Christ died for "the whole world" (1 John 2:2; cf. 2 Cor. 5:17–21). Theological support includes the following: (1) an argument from God's universal love and desire that everyone be saved (2 Pet. 3:9), which makes it impossible that Christ died only for some; (2) an argument from prevenient grace, which restores to everyone the ability to embrace salvation.

Biblical and theological support for multiple intentions combines the strongest arguments for limited atonement and the strongest arguments for unlimited atonement.

Major Errors

1. *Understanding the atonement as a subjective influence (for example, kindling one's love for God or prompting obedience) rather than as an*

166

objective reality (what Christ's death did). This position confuses the accomplishment of salvation and the application of salvation.

2. *Understanding the atonement as a ransom to Satan.* This theory has no biblical basis. Ransom was not paid to Satan but to God.

3. *The denial of God's retributive justice and the consequent need for propitiation.* This position detaches the atonement from its Old Testament background and interprets it in terms of contemporary cultural values (for example, an elevation of God's love above all his other attributes, a fear that the Father's punishment of his Son is a form of [divine] child abuse, and a concern that Jesus's submission to beating and crucifixion encourages passivity in the face of violence).

ENACTING THE DOCTRINE

Few doctrines are more important to rehearse and understand than what the death of Christ on the cross accomplished for us. Because of his propitiation, we are justified by faith. Because of his expiatory sacrifice, we never have to face judgment leading to condemnation. Because of his redemptive work, we are free from our enslavement to sin. Because of his mediation, we who were once enemies are now reconciled in friendship to God. Because of his cosmic victory, all our enemies—sin, death, the law, and Satan—are defeated. Accordingly, we enact this doctrine by being full of thanksgiving, faith, a sense of freedom, and appreciation for our new standing before God because of what Christ did on our behalf.

> ### Perennial Questions and Problematic Issues
>
> - Why did Christ have to die?
> - Did Christ die for the elect only or for all people, and what difference does it make?
> - I know people today who are turned off to Christianity because of the violence of Christ's death on the cross.
> - Which of the theories of the atonement does our church hold?

TEACHING THE DOCTRINE

This doctrine lends itself to a rich discussion. Of course, covering the biblical material is foundational. Because Scripture presents the multifaceted nature of the atonement, a thorough presentation of propitiation, expiation, redemption, reconciliation, and cosmic victory is key. Also, a discussion of the various theories helps to highlight the different understandings of what Christ's death accomplished. Be sure to emphasize the church's position while fairly presenting and critiquing the other views. While there is great interest (and properly so) in the extent of the atonement, be careful not to let this topic dominate the time.

TEACHING OUTLINE

1. The summary of the work of the Son of God
2. Major affirmations (with biblical support)
   A. The nature of the atonement
   B. Five perspectives on the atonement
   C. The extent of the atonement
   D. Theories of the atonement
3. Major errors to avoid
   A. Understanding the atonement as a subjective influence rather than as an objective reality
   B. Denying God's retributive justice and the consequent need for propitiation
4. Enacting the doctrine
   A. Giving this doctrine the importance it is due
   B. Being thankful for what the death of Christ accomplished for us

RESOURCES

Allison, *Theological Terms*, s.vv. "atonement," "*Christus Victor*," "expiation," "governmental theory," "moral influence theory," "penal substitution theory," "propitiation," "ransom to Satan theory," "reconciliation," "redemption"

Elwell, *Evangelical Dictionary of Theology*, s.vv. "Atonement," "Atonement, Extent of," "Atonement, Theories of," "Propitiation," "Reconciliation," "Redeemer, Redemption"

Erickson, *Christian Theology*, chaps. 35–38

Grenz, *Theology for the Community of God*, chap. 12

Grudem, *Systematic Theology*, chap. 27

Horton, *Pilgrim Theology*, chap. 8

Thoennes, *Life's Biggest Questions*, chap. 10

21

RESURRECTION, ASCENSION, AND EXALTATION

SUMMARY

After his crucifixion, the last stage of his humiliation, Jesus Christ entered the stage of exaltation: his resurrection from the dead; his ascension, or return to heaven; and his session, or enthronement at the right hand of the Father.

MAIN THEMES

- The three stages of Jesus Christ are his preexistence, state of humiliation, and state of exaltation.
- The first part of his exaltation was the resurrection from the dead, three days after his crucifixion.
- The next part was his ascension, or return to glorification in heaven, forty days after his resurrection.
- As the ascended Lord, he was elevated to the right hand of the Father, the position of authority.
- The next part of his exaltation, still to come, is his future return to earth.

KEY SCRIPTURE

Psalms 16:8–11; 110:1; Isaiah 53:10–12; Matthew 16:21; 28:1–15; Mark 16:1–8; Luke 24:1–51; John 20:1–29; Acts 1:6–11; 2:4–36; Romans 6:1–11; 1 Corinthians 15; Ephesians 1:20–23; 2:6–7; 4:7–16; Philippians 2:5–11; 1 Peter 1:3

UNDERSTANDING THE DOCTRINE

Major Affirmations

Prior to his incarnation, the Second Person of the Trinity preexisted, being the eternal Son of God. For the sake of human salvation, he entered into a state of humiliation. He became incarnate, taking on the fullness of human nature while remaining fully divine: the God-man. He lived in obedience to the law, resisted all temptations, never sinned, and accomplished the will of the Father. As the last part of his humiliation, Jesus was crucified on a cross, died, and was buried. Some add another aspect of Jesus's humiliation: his descent into hell.

Humiliation did not have the last word, however. After three days, Jesus rose from the grave, thus entering into his state of exaltation. Jesus's death, like all human death, involved a separation of his soul and body. His body was laid in a tomb, while he, as disembodied Jesus, continued to exist. Three days later, he rose from the dead, being reembodied: he returned to earthly existence with a glorified body, which shared some features with his preresurrected body (it bore the marks of his crucifixion) and yet was different (it could pass through unopened doors).

The resurrection was a work of the Triune God. The Father, the Son himself, and the Holy Spirit operated together to raise the crucified one from the dead. The resurrection openly manifested the deity of the powerful Son of God. His resurrection marked the Father's satisfaction with the Son's completed work of salvation; nothing more remained to be accomplished. Indeed, the justification of the ungodly is directly tied to Christ's resurrection. His resurrection was the first of many: all who follow the Son as their Savior will follow him in his resurrection at his return. His resurrection fulfilled the promise that the Holy One would not see corruption but would be vindicated for his obedience to the Father's will.

Critics of Christianity have invented wild theories to dismiss Jesus's resurrection:

1. The disciples stole Jesus's entombed body and then claimed he had risen. What was the motive for their deception? The disciples were power-hungry and greedy men who would not allow Jesus's death to interrupt their grab for fame and fortune.
2. Jesus did not die but faked his death and then proclaimed his resurrection, deceiving his apostles. Is this picture of Jesus in any way consistent with what we know of him from the Gospels?
3. The disciples concocted the idea of Jesus's resurrection, which thus is a myth. They could not accept Jesus's death, so they sought to honor him as Lord by inventing the resurrection.
4. The women went to the wrong tomb and, finding it open, viewed their visit to the tomb as proof of Jesus's resurrection. How his actual body escaped eventual discovery is a mystery.
5. With Jesus as part of their plot, some outsiders conspired to fake his death, and when he died anyway, they removed his body from the tomb and one of them appeared as the risen Jesus. Again, the portrait of Jesus that this theory paints clashes strongly with the way the Gospels present him.
6. Jesus's disciples hallucinated or imagined that he had risen from the dead. But how could a hallucinated or imagined resurrection actually sustain the disciples for the rest of their lives?

Thankfully, Christian apologists have exposed the absurdity of these theories and defended the traditional belief in the resurrection.

For forty days, the resurrected Jesus appeared to his apostles and hundreds of other followers. Then, he was lifted from their sight, ascending into heaven. The one who descended through incarnation and humiliation now ascended, returning to his state of exaltation and the realm of glory with the Father and the Holy Spirit.

Ascending back into heaven, Jesus sat down at the right hand of the Father, the position of exaltation. The Father granted him all authority to rule over the entire creation as the now-exalted God-man. He reigns as the cosmic head, having defeated all his enemies and is waiting until their ultimate, public defeat in the future. Together with the Father, the ascended

Christ poured out the Holy Spirit, giving birth to the church. Indeed, as cosmic head, he is also head of the church, which is his body. Together with the outpoured Holy Spirit, Christ gave gifted people and spiritual gifts to his church, for whom he prays. He will descend once again, returning one day to save his people fully.

Thus, the church confesses, "I believe . . . in one Lord Jesus Christ, . . . who suffered and was buried; and the third day he rose again, according to the Scriptures, and ascended into heaven and is seated at the right hand of the Father" (Nicene-Constantinopolitan Creed).

Biblical Support

The Old Testament prophesied of the Suffering Servant/Messiah who would come in humiliation to save his people from their sins. Hints of the Servant's exaltation are woven into this hope. Psalm 16:8–11 speaks of the resurrection (referenced in Acts 2:24–32), and Psalm 110:1 addresses the ascension and session (referenced in the Synoptic Gospels and Acts 2:33–36). Isaiah 53, the most noted prophecy of the Suffering Servant, contains clues about his vindication (Isa. 53:10–12).

Jesus himself predicted not only his crucifixion and burial but his resurrection as well. At a crucial juncture in his ministry, "Jesus began to show his disciples that he must go to Jerusalem and suffer many things from the elders and chief priests and scribes, and be killed, and on the third day be raised" (Matt. 16:21). All four Gospels narrate the resurrection (28:1–15; Mark 16:1–8; Luke 24:1–49; John 20:1–29). The narratives feature the women's discovery of Jesus's empty tomb, angelic statements about Jesus not being in the tomb but resurrected, his appearance to the women, the amazement of the apostles at the news, and his appearances to the twelve.

The rest of the New Testament presents the doctrinal and ethical implications of Jesus's resurrection: it is linked with regeneration (1 Pet. 1:3), justification (Rom. 4:25), and believers' resurrection from the dead (1 Cor. 15:12–17). Moreover, baptism vividly portrays believers' identification with the death, burial, and resurrection of Jesus, like whom they walk in newness of life (Rom. 6:1–11).

New Testament narratives of Jesus's ascension recount his being lifted up from his disciples and, as he was departing, taken from their sight by means of a cloud (Luke 24:50–51; Acts 1:6–11). Through Jesus's resurrection and ascension, "God has made him both Lord and Christ" (Acts 2:36). Because Jesus is resurrected and ascended, his followers are already raised up and seated with him (Eph. 2:6–7).

Returning to the realm of glory, the ascended Lord was seated at the right hand of the Father, the position of universal authority, which Christ holds over all angels, rulers, authorities, and powers (Eph. 1:20–21; 1 Pet. 3:22). As exalted head over all things, he is given to be head of his body, the church (Eph. 1:22–23), for which he constantly prays (Rom. 8:34), thereby guaranteeing his followers' salvation (Heb. 7:25). Together with the Father, Christ poured out the Holy Spirit (Acts 2:33), thus inaugurating the age of the Spirit and the new covenant church (2:1–21). In conquering his enemies and pouring out the Spirit, Christ gave gifted people and spiritual gifts to his church for its progressive maturity (Eph. 4:7–16). He also commissioned his church to engage in multiplication through Spirit-empowered evangelism, discipleship, and global church-planting (Matt. 28:18–20).

The once-humiliated, now-resurrected-and-ascended Lord "will appear a second time, not to deal with sin but to save those who are eagerly waiting for him" (Heb. 9:28).

Major Errors

1. *Dismissal of the historicity of the resurrection (demythologization).* This position wrongly holds that miracles cannot occur, and it cannot explain the amazing expansion of Christianity in the face of persecution, an expansion fueled by the hope of resurrection based on Christ's resurrection.

2. *Absurd theories that deny the resurrection (noted above).* Many of these view Jesus as a charlatan or madman and/or view the disciples as power-grabbing opportunists and deceivers, none of which reflect the historical record we have of them (the Gospels). If the resurrection was a product of their vivid imagination, how can their martyrdom for the Christian faith be explained?

3. *In communicating the gospel, an overemphasis on Jesus's death to the neglect of what followed.* Without downplaying his humiliation through crucifixion, the good news must also emphasize Jesus's exaltation through resurrection, ascension, and session at the Father's right hand.

ENACTING THE DOCTRINE

Though less known and less emphasized than his state of humiliation, Christ's state of exaltation is equally important. Christ has risen. Christ has ascended. Christ is seated at the right hand of the Father. As the exalted God-man, the Lord engages in ministries in which he never before participated. And because Christ is exalted, we may walk in resurrection power, may live a new identity as citizens of heaven, may experience the new covenant work of the Holy Spirit, are assured of salvation through Christ's intercessory ministry, and employ our gifts for the maturity and multiplication of the church.

Furthermore, we await the return of our exalted Lord. No longer hidden from our sight, his lordship will be publicly displayed in triumphant glory!

Perennial Questions and Problematic Issues

- It seems like our church always preaches about Christ's death but rarely mentions his resurrection and even less his ascension and session at the Father's right hand.

- Why didn't Jesus just resurrect and then immediately ascend back into heaven?

- I always thought that Jesus's resurrection was just a spiritual resurrection.

- Practically, what does it mean that I am raised up, ascended, and seated in heaven with Christ?

- Why and for what is Christ praying for me?

TEACHING THE DOCTRINE

One way of teaching this doctrine is to study attentively the four narratives of Jesus's resurrection. Then present the various theories denying it and discuss how, just based on those narratives, the participants would counter these attacks. This exercise will underscore how far removed these theories are from Scripture itself and will emphasize the importance of paying close attention to what the Bible actually affirms.

Another approach is to ask the question, "If there is anything that would cause you to abandon your faith in Christ, what would it be?" Most participants either will not know (because they have never thought about it) or will deny that anything could ever shake their faith. Next, discuss Paul's point in 1 Corinthians 15:12–19, summarized in verse 17: "And if Christ has not been raised, your faith is futile and you are still in your sins." If the resurrection is not true, then the Christian faith is not true, and Christians should abandon it. This point is called a *defeater* of Christianity: if

Christ died and did not rise again, then Christianity is false and should be abandoned. This exercise emphasizes the often-underappreciated yet utter importance of the doctrine of the resurrection!

Because few question the reality of the resurrection, ascension, and exaltation of Christ, the majority of the time should focus on their implications for Christians and the church. We walk in newness of resurrected life, thus experiencing empowered living. We are seated with Christ in heaven, giving us our true citizenship and identity. Christ's headship over his body means that the church submits to his authority. Christ's unceasing ministry of intercession provides assurance of salvation. His giving of gifted leaders and spiritual gifts to the church demands and fosters every-member participation. His Great Commission launches the church on its missions. These implications should be practically applied.

TEACHING OUTLINE

1. The summary of the resurrection, ascension, and exaltation
2. Attacks against the resurrection, and the defeater of Christianity
3. Major affirmations (with biblical support)
    A. From preexistence to humiliation to exaltation
    B. The resurrection and its implications
    C. The ascension and its implications
    D. The session and its implications
4. Major errors to avoid
    A. Dismissing the historicity of the resurrection
    B. Holding to absurd theories that deny the resurrection
    C. Communicating the gospel with an overemphasis on Jesus's death to the neglect of what followed
5. Enacting the doctrine
    A. Living in light of the ministries of the exalted God-man
    B. Awaiting the return of our exalted Lord

RESOURCES

Allison, *Theological Terms*, s.vv. "ascension," "exaltation of Christ," "resurrection of Christ," "session of Christ"

Elwell, *Evangelical Dictionary of Theology*, s.vv. "Ascension of Christ," "Resurrection of Christ," "Session"

Erickson, *Christian Theology*, 709–12

Grenz, *Theology for the Community of God*, chap. 12

Grudem, *Systematic Theology*, chap. 28

Horton, *Pilgrim Theology*, chap. 8

Thoennes, *Life's Biggest Questions*, chap. 10

PART 5

DOCTRINE
—— OF ——
GOD THE HOLY SPIRIT

22

THE PERSON
OF THE HOLY SPIRIT

SUMMARY

The Holy Spirit is the Third Person of the Trinity, equal in terms of nature, power, and glory with the Father and the Son and to be worshiped together with them.

MAIN THEMES

- The Holy Spirit is the Third Person of the Trinity, sharing in the one divine nature.
- He is a divine person, not a power, force, or influence.
- Being fully God, the Spirit is equal with the Father and the Son in nature, power, and glory, but he is distinct from them in terms of his relation and roles.
- As the fully divine Third Person of the Trinity, the Holy Spirit is worthy of worship, obedience, trust, and service.

KEY SCRIPTURE

Genesis 1:2; Isaiah 11:2; 42:1; 61:1–2; Jeremiah 31:31–34; Ezekiel 36:25–27; Joel 2:28–32; Luke 3:15–17; 24:49; John 1:33; 7:37–39; 14:1–16:33; Acts 1:4–5; 2:1–47; 5:3–4, 9; Romans 8:9

UNDERSTANDING THE DOCTRINE

Major Affirmations

The Holy Spirit is the Third Person of the Trinity, eternally existing together with the Father and the Son in the one Godhead. He is fully God, as are the Father and the Son, possessing the same attributes of independence, immutability, omnipresence, omnipotence, omniscience, holiness, love, and more. The three share in the one divine essence. Thus, the Holy Spirit is fully God, coequal with the Father and the Son.

He is a divine person, not a power, force, or influence. Some difficulties arise when we consider the personality of the Spirit. It is fairly easy to think of the first and second members of the Trinity as persons because of their names: "Father" and "Son." But the name "Holy Spirit" is not as transparent as those names in terms of personality. Indeed, the word "spirit" is associated with what is immaterial: wind and breath. Thus, it is more difficult to embrace the personality of the Holy Spirit.

But he is closely associated with the Father and the Son, and his relationship with the First *Person* and the Second *Person* underscores his reality as the Third *Person* of the Trinity. Moreover, he possesses personal characteristics: intelligence, emotions, and will are properties of persons (both human and divine). Furthermore, he engages in personal activities: speaking, teaching, praying, and bearing witness are activities of persons (both human and divine). Additionally, Jesus refers to the Holy Spirit as "another Helper/Comforter," who will take Jesus's place. Because Jesus, the original Comforter, is a person, it makes sense the Holy Spirit, the other Comforter, is a person too.

The Spirit is a distinct person from the Father and the Son, distinguished from them by his particular eternal relation and his particular roles. In terms of eternal relation, the Spirit eternally proceeds from both the Father and the Son. This eternal double procession does not mean that the Father and the Son created the Holy Spirit. Nor does it mean that the Father and the Son give him his deity, as the Spirit is God-of-himself. Rather, the Father and the Son together grant him his person-of-the-Spirit. In this way, he is distinct from them: the Third Person of the Triune God.

Another distinction between the three has to do with their roles. Though the Father, Son, and Spirit operate together inseparably, the Spirit engages in particular ministries. This theme will be presented in the next chapter, "The Work of the Holy Spirit."

Biblical Support

The doctrine of the Holy Spirit is progressively revealed in Scripture. The Old Testament presents the Spirit as active in creation (Gen. 1:2), being the presence of God in the world and particularly for the people of Israel. A major theme was the expectation of a fresh, unprecedented outpouring of the Holy Spirit associated with his empowerment of the Suffering Servant/Messiah (Isa. 11:2; 42:1; 61:1–2) and the expectation of a new covenant to replace the old covenant (Jer. 31:31–34; Ezek. 36:25–27; Joel 2:28–32).

In the New Testament, John the Baptist continues and heightens this anticipation of a new, unprecedented outpouring when he describes the Messiah as the one who will baptize with the Holy Spirit (Luke 3:15–17; John 1:33). The Son of God incarnate, who was conceived by the Holy Spirit, is Jesus the Messiah (Luke 1:30–35). He is characterized by the fullness of the Spirit; indeed, the Father gives the Spirit without measure to his Son (John 3:34).

Jesus also continues and heightens the expectation of a fresh, unprecedented outpouring of the Spirit. Jesus promises to send "another Helper/Comforter" in his place (John 14:16, 26; 15:26; 16:7, 13–14). Moreover, he anticipates a future day in which "rivers of living water" will flow out of his followers (7:37–39). By this promise, Jesus heightened the expectation of a new work of the Spirit. Before this fresh outpouring could take place, however, Jesus first had to die, rise, and ascend back to heaven. Appropriately, then, after his crucifixion and resurrection he tells his disciples to wait in Jerusalem until he sends the promised Holy Spirit to clothe them with power from on high (Luke 24:49; Acts 1:4; 2:33).

The day of Pentecost marks the sending of the Spirit in a fresh, unprecedented way, an outpouring in fulfillment of the earlier promises. As the Spirit descends upon the waiting disciples, he inaugurates his new covenant ministry and gives birth to the church as the body of Christ and the temple of the Spirit (Acts 2:1–21). From that time onward, the same promised Holy Spirit is poured out on every disciple of Jesus (Rom. 8:9).

This Holy Spirit is fully God. The parallels in Peter's rebuke of Ananias underscore the deity of the Spirit: "Ananias, why has Satan filled your heart to *lie to the Holy Spirit*? . . . You have not *lied* to man but *to God*" (Acts 5:3–4; emphasis added). Peter's question to Sapphira is equally revealing: "How is it that you have agreed together to test the Spirit of the Lord?" (Acts 5:9). In the Old Testament, the expression "the Spirit of the LORD" is a reference to God. Moreover, Paul's description of the church highlights the Spirit's deity: "Do you not know that you are God's temple and that God's Spirit dwells in you?" (1 Cor. 3:16). In the Old Testament, the temple was the place in which God dwelt. Now, the church as God's temple is the place in which the Spirit of God dwells. Thus, the Spirit of God is God himself.

The Holy Spirit eternally proceeds from both the Father and the Son. Jesus affirms this double procession in several of his statements about the coming of the Spirit:

- "The Holy Spirit, whom the Father will send in my name . . ." (John 14:26)
- "When the Helper comes, whom I will send to you from the Father, the Spirit of truth, who proceeds from the Father . . ." (John 15:26)
- "If I do not go away, the Helper will not come to you. But if I go, I will send him to you." (John 16:7)

Combining these statements (which look forward to the sending of the Spirit and his descent on Pentecost), we see that Jesus affirms that (1) the Father will send the Spirit in Jesus's name, (2) Jesus will send the Spirit from the Father, and (3) the Spirit proceeds from the Father (without limiting this procession to the Father *alone*). Moreover, on the day of Pentecost, Peter affirms of the exalted Jesus, "Having received from the Father the promise of the Holy Spirit, he has poured out this that you yourselves are seeing and hearing" (Acts 2:33).

A question properly arises, Why is it that the Father and the Son send the Holy Spirit *temporally* on Pentecost? The church has historically answered, "Because the Holy Spirit *eternally* proceeds from the Father and the Son." Indeed, he is both "the Spirit of God [the Father]" and "the Spirit of Christ [the Son]" (Rom. 8:9). Thus, the Father and the Son, who together grant him his person-of-the-Spirit, sent him into the world on the day of Pentecost on his new covenant ministry. The eternal procession of the Holy Spirit is the ground for, and is properly expressed in, the Spirit's temporal mission.

Accordingly, the church confesses, "I believe in the Holy Spirit, the Lord and Giver of Life, who proceeds from the Father and the Son, who with the Father and the Son together is worshipped and glorified, who spoke by the Prophets" (Nicene-Constantinopolitan Creed, with the *filioque* clause, "proceeds from the Father *and the Son*").

As the next two chapters underscore, the beginning of the twentieth century marked the rise of divisions among churches regarding the work of the Holy Spirit and the gifts of the Holy Spirit. As Pentecostal and charismatic theology has flourished, much attention and energy has been focused on the Holy Spirit. However, churches remain largely united in terms of the historic doctrine of the Spirit's deity, personhood, and (except for the Eastern Orthodox Church) double procession.

Major Errors

1. *The denial of the deity of the Holy Spirit.* Opponents like the Pneumatomachians (Spirit-fighters) point to the fact that he is the Third Person of the Trinity, thus behind the Father (First Person) and the Son (Second Person). They understand this "behind" to mean "less divine," inferior to them. This position cannot explain the passages that affirm that the Spirit is God.

2. *The denial that he is a person distinct from the Father and the Son.* Modalism holds that "Holy Spirit" is just a different name, as are "Father" and "Son," for the same person. Thus, the church knows God as "Holy Spirit," but he is not a different person from the other two. This viewpoint cannot account for the passages in which the three persons are active at the same time (for example, Jesus's baptism).

3. *The denial that the Spirit is a divine person.* This view holds that the Spirit is only a powerful force or divine influence; thus the Spirit is referred to with the pronoun "it." This position, held by Jehovah's Witnesses and some extreme Pentecostals/charismatics, fails to distinguish between divine personhood and divine power.

ENACTING THE DOCTRINE

Because the Holy Spirit is the fully divine Third Person of the Trinity, "with the Father and the Son together he is worshiped and glorified" (Nicene-Constantinopolitan Creed). He is worthy of honor, obedience, trust, and service. While all-powerful as are the Father and the Son, the Spirit is distinct from his power. Thus, the church must not belittle him by imagining him to be some force field and thus energy to be dispensed upon others. Reverence is due him.

Accordingly, when the church gathers for worship, songs of praise, prayers of thanksgiving, expressions of faith, and acts of obedience should be directed toward the Holy Spirit.

What's at stake in this doctrine? If the Holy Spirit is not a divine person, he cannot engage in the works that are presented in the following chapter.

Perennial Questions and Problematic Issues

- It seems like Christianity affirms that the Holy Spirit is a third god along with the Father and the Son.

- Doesn't the title "Holy Spirit" (or, still worse, "Holy Ghost") make it seem like he/it is a mere power or energy?

- Eternal procession makes the Holy Spirit inferior to the Father and the Son.

- I've always had trouble worshiping the Holy Spirit, so what can you say to help me?

TEACHING THE DOCTRINE

Unlike God the Father and God the Son, God the Holy Spirit seems amorphous and hard to relate to. He seems more like a force than a person. To counter this misconception, a good place to start teaching is to affirm that the church experientially knows him. Indeed, no one would be a Christian if not for the Holy Spirit! Given that salvation comes through the Spirit, it only makes sense that he is God. The biblical affirmations of the deity of the Holy Spirit should be explored thoroughly and thoughtfully.

Though the double procession of the Holy Spirit from the Father and the Son can be difficult to teach, it is important that the basic idea be presented. It does help explain the several statements of Jesus discussed above. Moreover, the eternal relations distinguish the three persons: The Father is unbegotten and does not proceed. The Son is eternally begotten or generated from the Father. The Holy Spirit eternally proceeds from the Father and the Son. Thus, the double procession of the Spirit is important for clearly understanding the distinctions between the three fully divine persons.

TEACHING OUTLINE

1. The summary of the person of the Holy Spirit
2. Knowing the Holy Spirit
3. Major affirmations (with biblical support)
   A. The deity of the Holy Spirit
   B. The person of the Spirit
   C. The Holy Spirit and his trinitarian relations with the Father and the Son
   D. The proper reverence that is to be shown to the Holy Spirit
4. Major errors to avoid
   A. Denying the deity of the Holy Spirit
   B. Denying that the Holy Spirit is a person distinct from the Father and the Son
   C. Denying that the Holy Spirit is a divine person
5. Enacting the doctrine
   A. Honoring, obeying, trusting, and serving the Holy Spirit
   B. The church's gathered worship directed toward the Holy Spirit

---

RESOURCES

Allison, *Theological Terms*, s.v. "Holy Spirit, person"
Elwell, *Evangelical Dictionary of Theology*, s.vv. "God, Doctrine of," "Holy Spirit"
Erickson, *Christian Theology*, chap. 39
Grenz, *Theology for the Community of God*, chap. 13
Grudem, *Systematic Theology*, chap. 14
Horton, *Pilgrim Theology*, chap. 9
Thoennes, *Life's Biggest Questions*, chap. 9

23

THE WORK
OF THE HOLY SPIRIT

SUMMARY

While the Father, Son, and Holy Spirit work together inseparably, their roles in creation, redemption, and consummation are also distinct. The Spirit's work is particularly associated with speaking, the application of salvation (re-creating and perfecting), and indwelling the people of God (the divine presence).

MAIN THEMES

- The inseparable operations of the Triune God mean that the three persons always work together in creation, redemption, and consummation.
- Still, their roles can be distinguished, which means that the Holy Spirit is particularly associated with certain divine works.
- The Spirit carries out the divine will in the world and brings it to completion, with special reference to speaking, applying

salvation through re-creating and perfecting, and indwelling God's people so they are filled with his presence.

KEY SCRIPTURE

John 3:1–8; 7:37–39; 16:7–11; Acts 2:1–47; Romans 8; 1 Corinthians 12:13; 2 Corinthians 3:18; Galatians 4:4–6; 5:16–25; Ephesians 1:13–14; 4:30; 5:18–21; Titus 3:4–7; 2 Peter 1:19–21

UNDERSTANDING THE DOCTRINE

Major Affirmations

Before attention can be given to the specific works of the Holy Spirit, it is appropriate to underscore the inseparable operations of the Trinity. This doctrine affirms that the Father, the Son, and the Holy Spirit act as one agent in all the divine works of creation, redemption, and consummation.

Biblically, this doctrine arises from passages that show the three divine persons acting in common. For example, the divine mission is presented as the Father sending his Son so that sinful people alienated from the Father might become adopted sons. "And because you are sons, God has sent the Spirit of his Son into our hearts, crying, 'Abba! Father!'" (Gal. 4:4–6). The three also engage in the church's mission: "Now there are varieties of gifts, but the same Spirit; and there are varieties of service, but the same Lord; and there are varieties of activities, but it is the same God who empowers them all in everyone" (1 Cor. 12:4–6).

The three persons engage indivisibly in the divine mission and the church's mission. Such cooperation in divine activity supports the doctrine of the inseparable operations of the Trinity.

Theologically, the doctrine of inseparable trinitarian operations flows from three other doctrines: (1) The unity of the three persons in the one divine nature indicates that the one God creates, saves, and sanctifies. (2) The mutual indwelling of the three persons (perichoresis) means that as the Father works, the Son and the Spirit, who together dwell in him, work together with him. (3) Sharing in the one divine nature, the three persons possess one will, knowledge, and power. As Augustine expressed it, "The Father and Son and Holy Spirit, as they are indivisible, so work indivisibly."[21]

Though all the works of the Triune God are common to all three persons, certain activities are appropriated to, or particularly associated with, one of them. So, in no divine work does the Holy Spirit act independently from the Father and the Son. Yet some divine works are the particular responsibility of the Spirit, without excluding the other two persons. These works are speaking, re-creating and perfecting, and indwelling.

It is quite common in Scripture to find that when the Spirit comes upon someone, that person engages in some kind of speaking (for example, prophecy, blessing, praise, and speaking in tongues). For instance, when God "took some of the Spirit that was on [Moses] and put it on the seventy elders," they prophesied (Num. 11:16–17, 25). Again, when the Spirit of God came upon (the non-Israelite) Balaam (24:2–4), he prophesied as one "who hears the words of God," thereby blessing rather than cursing Israel (Num. 22–24). According to the Gospel of Luke, Elizabeth was filled with the Holy Spirit and pronounced a blessing on Mary (1:41–42). Similarly, Zechariah was filled with the Holy Spirit and prophesied (1:67). And "the Holy Spirit was upon" Simeon, who "came in the Spirit into the temple" and blessed God (2:25–32).

In terms of authoritative written revelation, divine speaking takes place through the inspiration of Scripture. This work is particularly ascribed to the Holy Spirit (2 Pet. 1:19–21). Indeed, the Nicene-Constantinopolitan Creed confesses belief in "the Holy Spirit, the Lord and Giver of life, . . . *who spoke by the prophets*" (emphasis added). Thus, speaking is a work of the Triune God that is particularly associated with the Holy Spirit.

The second work is the Spirit's role in redemption. All the benefits that God provides in Jesus Christ come to Christians through the Holy Spirit, who unites them to Christ and his saving work. While he was certainly engaged in creating the world (Gen. 1:2), the Spirit's particular role in salvation features him re-creating fallen human beings and perfecting them by bringing about their full conformity to the image of Jesus Christ. This is another work of the Triune God that is specifically linked to the Holy Spirit.

As Christians believe in the gospel, Christ baptizes them with the Holy Spirit, they are incorporated into Christ's body, and they are filled with the Holy Spirit. Thus, they are temples of the Holy Spirit, meaning that the Triune God dwells in believers through the Spirit.

This particular work of indwelling is the fulfillment of divine promises made long ago. In the garden of Eden, God dwelt with his image bearers. Because of their sin, the garden in which Adam and Eve were placed and in which God dwelt with them became shuttered to them. They were banished from God's presence. Still, the theme of hope sounded forth, as God promised, "I will make my dwelling among you, and my soul shall not abhor you. And I will walk among you and will be your God, and you shall be my people" (Lev. 26:11–13; cf. Exod. 29:45–46).

To fulfill this promise, the Son of God became flesh (a work of the Holy Spirit) and dwelt among the people whom he came to save. Then, pointing to the church, Paul notes, "For we are the temple of the living God; as God said, 'I will make my dwelling among them and walk among them, and I will be their God, and they shall be my people'" (2 Cor. 6:16). Paul's appeal is to the Old Testament expectation, which is now fulfilled in the church: God dwells in his people, just as he promised long ago. Thus, the Holy Spirit fills the church (Eph. 5:18–21), and its leaders are characterized by the fullness of the Spirit (for example, Acts 6:1–7). Accordingly, indwelling is another work of the Triune God that is specifically associated with the Holy Spirit.

Biblical Support

As discussion of the Spirit's works of speaking and indwelling has already been supported, attention now turns to biblical support for his role in salvation (re-creating and perfecting).

Even before people embrace the gospel, the Holy Spirit is at work to "convict the world [people hostile to God] concerning sin and righteousness and judgment" (John 16:8). That is, the Spirit exposes their failure to believe in Christ as their only hope of salvation (John 16:9). Moreover, he reveals the futility of their self-righteousness to merit favor with God (John 16:10). Furthermore, the Spirit unmasks the worldly judgment by which nonbelievers seek to justify themselves by comparing themselves favorably to those who are "worse sinners" (John 16:11; see also, for example, Luke 18:9–14). Through the Spirit's conviction, nonbelievers sense their guilt and shame, readying them for the only hope of rescue.

This hope is the application of the mighty acts of God in salvation. Regeneration is the removal of the old sinful nature and the implanting of a new nature. This new birth comes by the Holy Spirit (John 3:3–8; Titus 3:5–7). As for the human response to the Spirit's activity, conversion is prompted by the Spirit. Indeed, "No one can say 'Jesus is Lord' except in the Holy Spirit" (1 Cor. 12:3). Because the Spirit ignites faith, the mighty divine act of justification, which comes through faith, occurs. Indeed, "You were justified in the name of the Lord Jesus Christ and by the Spirit of our God" (1 Cor. 6:11; cf. Titus 3:5–7).

Another mighty work of salvation, this one initiated by Christ, is his baptizing of new believers with the Holy Spirit to incorporate them into Christ's body (1 Cor. 12:13; John 1:33). This divine Spirit seals these believers, guaranteeing their salvation (Eph. 1:14; 4:30). Moreover, he grants them, through his inner witness, assurance of salvation (Rom. 8:16; 1 John 4:13). He is also "the Spirit of adoption" (Rom. 8:15) by which believers are brought into the new family of the one to whom they cry out "Abba! Father!" (Gal. 4:4–6). To the church, the Holy Spirit grants unity (Eph. 4:3), leaders (Acts 20:28), power to engage nonbelievers with the gospel (1:8), and spiritual gifts (1 Cor. 12–14; treated in the next chapter, "The Gifts of the Holy Spirit").

As Christians are continually filled with the Holy Spirit (Eph. 5:18–21), they are guided by him to fulfill all of God's moral requirements (Rom. 8:1–8). Indeed, walking in the Spirit prevents them from engaging in the works of their sinful nature, producing instead the fruit of Christlikeness in their life (Gal. 5:16–25). This sanctification, attributed to the Holy Spirit (1 Pet. 1:2), is a progressive movement from sinfulness to holiness (2 Cor. 3:18). And it is fueled by Scripture—with believers aided by the illumination of the Spirit (1 Cor. 2:10–16)—and by prayer, which is also helped by the Spirit (Rom. 8:26–27). At the end of this pilgrimage, when Christ returns, is glorification, with the resurrection of the body being the work of the Spirit (8:11).

This, then, is the specific work of the Triune God in re-creating and perfecting, and it is particularly associated with the Holy Spirit.

Major Errors

1. *The denial of, or apathy toward, the ongoing work of the Holy Spirit in his many ministries.* This view fails to grasp that salvation, sanctification, understanding Scripture, overcoming temptation, assurance of salvation, and much more are dependent on the work of the Spirit.

2. *An excessive attention paid to the Holy Spirit, leading to ignorance or neglect of the Father and the Son, Scripture, a mindful faith, wisdom from others, and more.* This position overlooks much of what is essential for robust Christianity through a narrow focus on the Spirit.

ENACTING THE DOCTRINE

People become and mature as Christians, and the church exists and expands, because of the Holy Spirit. Becoming conscious of the Spirit for our salvation and sanctification, and for the church's growth and witness, is the first step in living this doctrine.

Paul commands us to "be filled with the Spirit" (Eph. 5:18–21). This continuous imperative demands a moment-by-moment posture of submitting to the Spirit's gracious control. Such "life in the Spirit" yields genuine community with others, heartfelt worship of God, a constant attitude of thanksgiving, preferring others above ourselves, resistance to sin, and much other "fruit of the Spirit" (Gal. 5:16–24).

What's at stake in this doctrine? The entire application of the salvation that Christ accomplished for us, the possibility of becoming more and more conformed to his image, and the perfection of his work in our life!

TEACHING THE DOCTRINE

As the work of the Holy Spirit is presented, participants should be encouraged to share their stories of his many acts in their life. Remembering their conversion—sensing guilt and shame because of sin, experiencing the new birth, calling Jesus "Lord," understanding the gospel, sensing the Spirit's inner witness for assurance of salvation, breaking with their former life—should help them to recognize the Spirit as particularly responsible for their salvation. And rehearsing all that the Spirit does in sanctification should prompt them to become ever more conscious of the desperate need for him to guide, fill, empower, and transform everything. Pointing out the Spirit's roles in the church should stimulate them to rely less on programs and traditions and more on the life-giving power of the Spirit.

> ### *Perennial Questions and Problematic Issues*
>
> - It seems like our church emphasizes the Father and the Son to the neglect of the Holy Spirit and his many works.
> - When I hear stories of the Holy Spirit's powerful works of convicting of sin, regenerating, guiding, sanctifying, and the like, it makes my story seem rather tame, even lacking something.
> - If the Holy Spirit's role is to glorify Christ (John 16:14), isn't it better for Christians not to talk much about the Holy Spirit?
> - The Word of God, as written divine revelation, is more important than the Spirit of God.

TEACHING OUTLINE

1. The summary of the work of the Holy Spirit
2. Stories of the Holy Spirit's mighty acts
3. Major affirmations (with biblical support)
   A. Inseparable operations of the Triune God
   B. The specific works of the Holy Spirit
      i. Speaking
      ii. Re-creating and perfecting
      iii. Indwelling
4. Major errors to avoid
   A. Denying, or being apathetic toward, the ongoing work of the Holy Spirit in his many ministries
   B. Paying excessive attention to the Holy Spirit, leading to ignorance or neglect of the Father and the Son, Scripture, a mindful faith, wisdom from others, and more
5. Enacting the doctrine
   A. Becoming conscious of the Holy Spirit and his ministries
   B. Being filled with the Holy Spirit

RESOURCES

Allison, *Theological Terms*, s.v. "Holy Spirit, work"
Elwell, *Evangelical Dictionary of Theology*, s.vv. "God, Doctrine of," "Holy Spirit"
Erickson, *Christian Theology*, chap. 40
Grenz, *Theology for the Community of God*, chap. 13
Grudem, *Systematic Theology*, chap. 30
Horton, *Pilgrim Theology*, chap. 9
Thoennes, *Life's Biggest Questions*, chap. 9

24

THE GIFTS OF THE HOLY SPIRIT

SUMMARY

One particular aspect of the work of the Holy Spirit is his giving gifts to the church. The purpose of these endowments is to foster the church's growth, especially by equipping its members for ministry.

MAIN THEMES

- In keeping with his particular works, the Holy Spirit endows the church with gifts.
- The main purpose of spiritual gifts is to nurture the maturity and mission of the church by equipping each and every member to engage in ministry.
- Other purposes are the confirmation of the gospel message and its messengers; provision of a foretaste of the fuller, future work of the Spirit; and the manifestation of Christ's victory over his enemies.
- It is important that believers identify their gift(s), learn how to use their gift(s), and serve in ministries in accordance with their gift(s).

- Disagreement exists between cessationism, which believes that some spiritual gifts have ceased, and continuationism, which maintains that all the gifts continue today.

KEY SCRIPTURE

Romans 12:4–8; 1 Corinthians 12–14; Ephesians 4:7–16; 1 Peter 4:10–11

UNDERSTANDING THE DOCTRINE

Major Affirmations

The Holy Spirit is specifically associated with the divine works of speaking, re-creating and perfecting, and indwelling the people of God. Therefore, the gifts that the Spirit grants to the church reflect these three particular operations: his gifts to the church express and promote the works of the Triune God for which the Spirit is particularly responsible.

The purpose of spiritual gifts is to foster the church's growth in two principal areas: (1) its maturity, by deepening the church's Christlikeness, ensuring its doctrinal fidelity, intensifying and purifying its community life, and more; and (2) its mission, by multiplying the church's proclamation of the gospel and discipleship throughout the entire world.

Beyond advancing the church's maturity and mission, spiritual gifts have served other purposes. Together with signs, miracles, and wonders, spiritual gifts attested to the truthfulness of the gospel message and authenticated its messengers. How could people who came into contact with the early church be assured that its "new" message about salvation through Christ's death and resurrection was true? How could they recognize that Peter, John, Stephen, Philip, Paul, and a host of others were bona fide messengers of the gospel? God bore witness to his message and his messengers through spiritual gifts given to them (Heb. 2:1–4).

Moreover, spiritual gifts provide a foretaste of the fuller, future work of the Spirit in the age to come. Just as the work of the Spirit is more extensive and more intensive in the new covenant era—the age of the Spirit—than in the old covenant period, so there is an expectation of a more extensive and intensive work of the Spirit after Christ returns, in the age to come.

Furthermore, spiritual gifts are the manifestation of Christ's victory over his enemies. Christ ascended into heaven as the exalted head of all creation, having conquered his enemies. Then he sent the Holy Spirit, whose descent inaugurated the new age of the Spirit. By his triumph and exaltation, and through his Spirit, Christ gave gifts to his people (Eph. 4:7–11). Thus, spiritual gifts display his victory.

Until the rise of Pentecostalism and the charismatic movement, spiritual gifts were not much emphasized and practiced in the church. These developments, however, touched off an important debate: Does the Holy Spirit continue to distribute all the spiritual gifts to the church, including the "sign gifts" of prophecy, speaking in tongues, interpretation of tongues, word of knowledge, word of wisdom, miracles, and healings? This view is called continuationism. Or has the Holy Spirit ceased to distribute these sign gifts while still giving the other gifts such as teaching, leading, serving, giving, and more? This view is called cessationism.

Pentecostal and charismatic theology holds to continuationism, and its churches are characterized by regular expression of all the gifts, including the sign gifts. Continuationism was picked up by some evangelicals, resulting in "third wave evangelicalism" with its belief that the Spirit continues to distribute all the spiritual gifts to the church today.

Biblical Support

Four sections of Scripture treat the gifts of the Spirit. Ephesians 4:7–16 underscores that gifts, which come from Christ to his church, manifest his triumph over his enemies (vv. 7–10). Gifted leaders—apostles, prophets, evangelists, and pastors and teachers (v. 11)—equip the rest of the church for ministry, with the result that the church matures (vv. 12–14). At the heart of this growth is a dual dimensionality. First and as a foundation for the second dimension, a divine dimension is at work: Christ "makes the body grow." Second and derivatively, from this divine foundation, a human dimension is at work: the church is "to grow up in every way into him who is the head, into Christ, . . . so that it builds itself up in love" (vv. 15–16). This dual dimensional synergy produces the growth of the church.

First Corinthians 12–14 emphasizes that each believer is given at least one gift, which they are to use "for the common good" (12:7). Additionally, it is the Spirit "who apportions to each one individually as he wills" and empowers believers as they exercise their gifts (12:11). Here, again, the dual dimensionality of spiritual gifts comes into focus. The Spirit sovereignly distributes and empowers spiritual gifts. This is the divine dimension.

Correspondingly, there is a human dimension: spiritual gifts are endowments for believers. As the gospel is communicated, it is the evangelist who shares it. As a meeting is directed, it is by one who has the gift of leadership. As a revelation is given, it is spoken by a prophet. Moreover, the church is to "earnestly desire the higher gifts" (1 Cor. 12:31), those that, like prophecy, have the greatest potential to build up the greatest number of people (14:1–5). Thus, the exercise of the gifts is a fully human activity "for the common good." But it is not a merely human activity, because of the Spirit's work.

This discussion also dispels all notions of inferiority and superiority in the matter of spiritual gifts. Believers with "just" the behind-the-scenes gifts of helping and administration should not be disappointed. Neither should those with the public gifts of teaching and leading be proud (1 Cor. 12:12–26). Indeed, the atmosphere in which the exercise of spiritual gifts thrives is that of love (1 Cor. 13).

Romans 12:4–8 addresses several specific gifts and how they should be employed in the church. The assumption is that believers know what gift(s) they have, so they can pay attention to and benefit from these instructions. First Peter 4:10–11 presents similar instruction. When Christians properly use their spiritual gift(s), they "serve one another" and bring glory to God.

Does the Holy Spirit continue today to distribute to the church all the gifts? Or has he ceased to give the sign gifts? In favor of continuationism are the following points: (1) Because the primary purpose for spiritual gifts is to foster the church's maturity and mission, the church, which is still maturing and has not completed its mission, continues to need all of the gifts. (2) First Corinthians 13:8–13 (also 1:7–8) places the cessation of spiritual gifts at the return of Christ, not before that event. (3) Over against cessationism, which specifically links sign gifts with the apostles, continuationism notes that many nonapostles exercised the gifts of prophecy, speaking in tongues, miracles, and healing (1:7; Gal. 3:5; Acts 8:4–8; 10:44–48). Thus, it is wrong to argue that because there are no more apostles, there can be no more sign gifts. (4) Historical evidence points to the continuation of sign gifts in the post-first-century church.

In favor of cessationism are the following points: (1) First Corinthians 13:8–13 associates the cessation of sign gifts such as prophecy and speaking in tongues with the completion of the New Testament canon. It is this fullness of revelation to which the phrase "when the perfect comes" refers (13:10). Sign gifts were the means God used to provide his revelation to the early church. When the perfect came—when God's provision of revelation was finished with the completion of the New Testament—these revelatory gifts no longer had a function and have ceased. (2) A modification of point 1 is that 1 Corinthians 13:8–13 does not specify the time of the cessation of these spiritual gifts. Thus, the determination of this issue must be made on the basis of other passages. (3) Sign gifts were specifically associated with the apostles (2 Cor. 12:12). Because apostles no longer exist, the sign gifts associated with them are no longer being given to the church. (4) Because the sign gifts have to do with the giving of revelation, their continuation would challenge the sufficiency of Scripture. (5) Historical evidence points to the cessation of sign gifts in the post-first-century church.

Major Errors

1. *The church neglects instruction about and use of spiritual gifts, emphasizing instead theology, the Bible, and/or the officers of the church as those who are gifted and responsible for its growth.* This practice robs church members of important biblical teaching and the exercise of their gift(s). And it handicaps churches from maturing and multiplying by means of all of the resources God grants to them.

2. *The church overemphasizes spiritual gifts and/or they are expressed in ways contrary to biblical instruction.* Prophecy and speaking in tongues are often abused. Claims of healings and miracles, when unsubstantiated, lead to skepticism about sign gifts. Often, this position overlooks the teaching of Scripture regarding the purpose and use of spiritual gifts.

ENACTING THE DOCTRINE

Love is the atmosphere in which the use of the gifts must be undertaken. Thus, the church does well not to measure its level of spirituality or maturity by the mere presence of teaching, mercy, giving, service, prophecy, tongues, and the like taking place in its assemblies. Rather, it insists that its spiritually gifted members—all of the church—evangelize with concern for the lost, heal not for show but out of compassion for those who suffer, give not to get back in return but to care for others, lead not with complaining but out of devotion for the church, and the like.

TEACHING THE DOCTRINE

Because several major passages of Scripture address this topic, a Bible study on spiritual gifts is a good place to start. Be sure to highlight the purpose(s) of spiritual gifts, their dual dimensionality, and the proper atmosphere of love.

Perennial Questions and Problematic Issues

- How can I know what gift(s) the Holy Spirit has given to me?
- I'm frustrated because I've filled out a spiritual gifts inventory before, but I've not been put into a ministry in which I can exercise my gift(s).
- I feel like I have the gift of prophecy (or speaking in tongues), but there's no room to exercise this gift in our church.
- Don't the many excesses of Pentecostal and charismatic theology warn against paying too much attention to the Holy Spirit and his gifts?

Teaching should include helping participants identify which gift(s) the Spirit has sovereignly given to them. There are several ways to approach this part. One popular method is to have participants work through a spiritual gifts inventory. Another way is to encourage participants to express to one another how they have been blessed by the others' encouragement, their teaching, their leading, their prophetic words, and so forth. Such fruitfulness in ministry points to the spiritual gift(s) at the heart of it.

As participants identify their gift(s), they should be instructed in the proper exercise of their gift(s). Such instruction includes exercising them in love, seeking to build the church and not using their gift(s) for self-glorification, and relying on the Spirit's empowerment. Teaching must ultimately lead to the participants concretely implementing their gift(s) in the service of the church.

Care should be taken not to fall into several excesses: (1) A fascination with spiritual gifts. While Christians should be encouraged to know and use their gift(s), this topic should not be allowed to dominate the doctrine of the Holy Spirit. (2) A captivation with the sign gifts of speaking in tongues, prophecy, healings, and more. While a frank discussion of cessationism and continuationism is needed (with the church's position being advocated with firmness yet charity), the church shouldn't be allowed to get caught up in the controversy and miss the many other ministries of the Spirit. (3) A fear of talking about the Spirit because of the many excesses associated with his gifts.

198

TEACHING OUTLINE

1. The summary
2. Bible study on the major passages
3. Spiritual gifts inventory or some other way to identify participants' spiritual gift(s)
4. Major affirmations (with biblical support)
   A. Spiritual gifts as reflections of the works particularly associated with the Holy Spirit
   B. The purpose(s) for spiritual gifts
   C. The debate between cessationism and continuationism
5. Major errors to avoid
   A. Neglecting instruction about and use of spiritual gifts, emphasizing instead theology, the Bible, and/or the officers of the church as those who are gifted and responsible for its growth
   B. Overemphasizing spiritual gifts and/or expressing them in ways contrary to biblical instruction
6. Enacting the doctrine
   A. Exercising spiritual gifts in an atmosphere of love
   B. Refusing to measure spirituality or maturity by reference to the use of spiritual gifts

RESOURCES

Allison, *Theological Terms*, s.vv. "cessationism," "continuationism," "miraculous gifts," "spiritual gifts"

Elwell, *Evangelical Dictionary of Theology*, s.v. "Spiritual Gifts"

Erickson, *Christian Theology*, 790–810

Grudem, *Systematic Theology*, chaps. 52–53

Horton, *Pilgrim Theology*, 413–19

PART 6

DOCTRINE

—— OF ——

SALVATION

25

COMMON GRACE

SUMMARY

Common grace is the universal favor that God grants to all people, both believers and unbelievers.

MAIN THEMES

- Though the grace of God is usually associated with his mighty acts of salvation, God shows his favor to all people through his common grace.

- As God's universal favor, common grace is different from saving grace, the specific favor he grants only to believers for salvation.

- Common grace is also different from prevenient grace, the universal favor God grants to prepare all people to meet the conditions of salvation.

- God created human beings in his image and grants his favor to them all.

- Common grace is seen in various realms.

- Though common in the sense that it is given to everyone, this grace is not experienced in the same measure by everyone.

- Common grace is intended to prompt unbelievers to embrace the gospel through saving grace, and it evokes thanksgiving from believers.

KEY SCRIPTURE

Genesis 4; Matthew 5:45; Acts 14:17; Romans 2:4, 14–15; 13:1–7; 1 Timothy 4:3–4

UNDERSTANDING THE DOCTRINE

Major Affirmations

A discussion of the grace of God appropriately inaugurates this section on the doctrine of salvation. In the following nine chapters, the grace of God in his mighty acts of redemption (for example, regeneration and justification) will be the focus. Before we rehearse this aspect of divine grace, another aspect—common grace—deserves treatment.

Common grace is the favor that God grants to all people, both believers and unbelievers. It is God's universal, gracious blessings that are not directly related to salvation. This common grace, therefore, is different from saving grace, which is God's particular favor granted only to believers for the purpose of their salvation.

Common grace is also distinguished from Arminian theology's prevenient grace. It, too, is God's universal favor, but it is directly related to salvation by its effect of restoring the ability to repent of sin and believe in Christ to all people. Reformed theology holds not to prevenient grace but to common grace and saving grace instead.

Common grace is the favor that God grants to all people because he has created them in his image. As the Father of his children by way of creation, he loves and blesses his image bearers in innumerable ways and in various realms.

One realm of common grace is God's physical provisions to sustain human life. It is manifested in his provision of food, water, shelter, and other basic needs for human existence.

Another arena is human abilities to fulfill the cultural mandate. To his image bearers God gave the responsibility to build civilization through procreation and vocation. Through his common grace, human beings possess the gifts and talents to fulfill this mandate. This common grace is manifested in intellectual capacities (for example, the ability to make scientific discoveries and technological advances), artistic abilities (musical talent and a flair for writing), athletic endowments (gymnastic skills and sprinting capabilities), vocational expertise (judicial discernment and political savvy), and more.

The human conscience is another area of common grace. God has hard-wired every human being with an innate sense of ethical duty. This moral arbiter enables people to know the basic principles of right and wrong and to distinguish what is right and wrong in different situations. Moreover, the conscience applauds obedience and rebukes disobedience while pointing to the moral Lawgiver who stands behind right and wrong. This common grace is manifested when people do what is good and avoid what is evil, promote a culture of life, and fight against social injustice.

Yet another arena is societal structures such as the family and government. Most adult human beings are married, and most of those couples have children. Procreation is part of the responsibility for divine-image bearers to build society through the expansion of the human race. Common grace is manifested in relational, parental, and filial abilities by which loving, caring, and nourishing families flourish.

Human government is another structure that promotes societal prosperity. Every nation, tribe, clan, and community has some type of government, which is divinely established. Common grace is manifested in just laws, fair treatment, protection against harm, restraint of evil, punishment of wrong, and promotion of good.

God's common grace is everywhere displayed but not necessarily in the same measure. Though every human being is the recipient of divine care, some experience greater provision than others. This difference is due to both the measure of common grace bestowed and other factors (for example, devastation caused by an earthquake). Though every human being is gifted with some abilities, some are more gifted than others. This difference is due to both the measure of common grace bestowed and other factors (for example, access to education to develop those abilities). Though every human being originates through sexual intercourse between a man and a woman, some experience greater familial relationships than others. This difference is due to both the measure of common grace bestowed and other factors (for example, the willingness of an unwed couple to be a family and to raise their child). Though every human being is under some government, some are governed better than others. This difference is due to both the measure of common grace bestowed and other factors (for example, a corrupt government that favors the elites and fails to protect other citizens).

Accordingly, common grace does not mean "in the same measure for all" but "universal," extended to everyone. Neither does it mean "mundane," though common grace is often taken for granted and detached from its source, who is God. It is anything but dull and ordinary, as seen in bountiful fields, medical advancements, artistic genius, loving families, global initiatives against human trafficking, and much more.

Common grace is intended to stimulate two responses: Unbelievers, experiencing God's favor though undeserving of it, should be moved to seek the Provider of common grace and then embrace the gospel through saving grace. Believers, experiencing both saving grace and common grace, though undeserving of both, should give thanks to God for his immeasurable blessings.

Biblical Support

Creation in the divine image is set forth in Genesis 1. God purposed to create a being more like him than any other created being, then he uniquely created human beings in his image (1:26–27). To his image bearers, both male and female, God gave the mandate to build civilization through procreation ("Be fruitful and multiply and fill the earth") and vocation ("and subdue it, and have dominion over" the rest of the creation; 1:28). His common grace assists human beings in fulfilling their responsibility.

Common grace is manifested in God's physical provisions to sustain human life: "He makes his sun rise on the evil and on the good, and sends rain on the just and on the unjust" (Matt. 5:45). Indeed, God does "good by giving [people] rains from heaven and fruitful seasons, satisfying [their] hearts with food and gladness" (Acts 14:17).

God's common grace blesses human beings with abilities to carry out their responsibilities to build civilization. Genesis rehearses the beginning of the fulfillment of both aspects of the cultural mandate. Procreation is underscored by the oft-repeated expression "and he fathered so-and-so."

Adam and Eve produce the first children, Cain and Abel (4:1–2), and the human race expands (Gen. 5; 10; 11). Vocational engagement is specified in the work of shepherding and farming (4:2), building cities (4:16–17), tending livestock, playing music, and forging tools (4:20–22). Human abilities for procreation and vocation are the fruit of common grace.

The human conscience is another manifestation of common grace. Paul affirmed that the Gentiles "show that the work of the law is written on their hearts, while their conscience also bears witness, and their conflicting thoughts accuse or even excuse them" (Rom. 2:14–15). By common grace, all people know the basic principles of right and wrong and are held morally accountable to follow the dictates of their conscience.

The structures of the family and government are other manifestations of common grace. God is "the Father, from whom every family in heaven and on earth is named" (Eph. 3:14–15). To be without a family is a tragedy, as seen in God proclaiming himself "Father of the fatherless and protector of widows" (Ps. 68:5). Common grace is seen in the structure of human family.

A second structure is government. After underscoring the fact that every authority has been "instituted by God," Paul demands submission to those authorities. Resistance to authority is resistance to "what God has appointed, and those who resist will incur judgment." Government exists to curb wrongdoing, punish evil, and contain the spread of sin. Paul summarizes: "The authorities are ministers of God" (Rom. 13:1–7), fruit of common grace.

The proper response to common grace is twofold. Addressing unbelievers, Paul wonders, "Do you presume on the riches of his kindness and forbearance and patience, not knowing that God's kindness is meant to lead you to repentance?" (Rom. 2:4). The experience of common grace should prompt unbelievers to acknowledge God's favor, certainly undeserved because of their rebellion against him, and then turn from their sin and seek salvation. For believers conscience, societal structures, physical provisions, and gifts and abilities to fulfill their divinely given responsibilities are more reasons for giving thanks to God (1 Tim. 4:3–4).

Major Errors

Because this doctrine is infrequently taught, major errors are not associated with it. Still, its neglect is an error, as is the confusion of common grace with saving grace.

1. *Neglect or dismissal of common grace.* This underdeveloped view fails to appreciate the innumerable blessings of God's favor for both believers and unbelievers.

2. *Confusion between common grace and saving grace.* The doctrine of common grace does not affirm or even imply that this divine favor is somehow salvific. It does not hold or even suggest that unbelievers, as recipients of common grace, can cooperate with this grace (or do anything else, for that matter) to be saved. The good that unbelievers do as the fruit of common grace—obedience to their conscience, vocational excellence, being exemplary parents—does not merit saving grace.

Perennial Questions and Problematic Issues

- I feel ill at ease with this doctrine because it sounds like unbelievers are able to do good and even save themselves.

- Why are there different measures of common grace?

- Why does God often give greater intellectual, artistic, athletic, and vocational abilities to non-Christians than he gives to Christians?

ENACTING THE DOCTRINE

Being mindful of common grace extended to both believers and unbelievers alike helps us live with a greater awareness of God's innumerable blessings and with greater thankfulness for those gifts to the human race. A response of approbation in various forms is proper: Admiration for well-engineered and -constructed skyscrapers. Appreciation for acre after acre of apple trees and soybeans. Feelings of despair and laughter when watching a tragicomedy. Wonder at Olympic swimmers and sprinters setting new world records in their sports. Acknowledgment of correct judicial decisions. Exhilaration when painting a picture, carving a sculpture, writing a book, or composing a song. As common grace is manifested, its fruit stimulates these responses and, behind them all, greater thanksgiving to God.

TEACHING THE DOCTRINE

A good place to start is to have participants share stories of the divine blessings that they experience or that unbelieving family members, friends, and colleagues experience. Highlighting actual manifestations of common grace will help to render this doctrine concrete. Pay attention to participants who feel uncomfortable with this discussion, and make sure to correct any misunderstandings they may have.

A key misunderstanding is that this doctrine seems to elevate unbelievers in an inappropriate way. Some participants may disregard non-Christians or view them with contempt—as sinners hated by God and ready for eternal condemnation. These participants struggle to think or say anything good about unbelievers for fear of minimizing their dire straits. Remind them that all human beings are created in the image of God and are loved by him as their Father in the sense of creation. God's common grace is his favor rightfully bestowed on his children.

The desired outcome of this teaching is for the participants to give thanks to God for his innumerable blessings. Most are accustomed to offering thanks for saving grace in its many manifestations in their life. Help them to also acknowledge the blessings of common grace that they experience every day. These manifestations provide more reason to constantly be thankful to God.

TEACHING OUTLINE

1. The summary of common grace, and its difference from saving grace
2. Stories of the blessings of common grace
3. Major affirmations (with biblical support)
    A. Creation in the divine image
    B. Physical provisions to sustain human life
    C. Human abilities to obey the cultural mandate
    D. The conscience
    E. Structures of the family and government
    F. Common grace given in different measure
4. Major errors to avoid
    A. Neglecting or dismissing common grace
    B. Confusing common grace and saving grace
5. Enacting the doctrine
    A. Being thankful for God's innumerable blessings
    B. Responding with approbation for God's gifts to both believers and unbelievers alike

RESOURCES

Allison, *Theological Terms*, s.vv. "common grace," "prevenient grace," "saving grace"

Elwell, *Evangelical Dictionary of Theology*, s.v. "Grace"

Grudem, *Systematic Theology*, chap. 31

Horton, *Pilgrim Theology*, 113–15

26

ELECTION AND REPROBATION

SUMMARY

Election is God's purpose regarding the redemption of people. Reprobation is God's purpose not to save certain people.

MAIN THEMES

- Election and reprobation are usually linked with predestination, which includes God's purpose regarding people's eternal destinies.
- For some, God's purpose in salvation consists of two aspects: election and reprobation.
- For others, God's purpose is limited to election only.
- Those who hold to unconditional election assert that God's choice of people for salvation is based on his sovereign will and good pleasure to save them.
- Reprobation is God's sovereign, eternal purpose not to save certain people but to give them over to their sins, for which he justly punishes them.

- Those who hold to conditional election assert that God's choice of people for salvation is dependent on their faith in the gospel and continuation in Christ, which God foreknows.

KEY SCRIPTURE

Acts 13:48; Romans 9:14–24; 11:5–7; Ephesians 1:3–14; 1 Thessalonians 1:4–5; 2 Thessalonians 2:13–14; 1 Timothy 2:4; 2 Timothy 1:9; 1 Peter 2:4–8; 2 Peter 3:9

UNDERSTANDING THE DOCTRINE

Major Affirmations

Predestination is God's sovereign determination of everything that comes to pass, including his purpose regarding people's eternal destinies. It involves two elements. The first element is election, which is God's eternal purpose regarding the salvation of certain people. More specifically, the issue is the nature of election: whether it is unconditional or conditional. The second element is reprobation, which is God's eternal purpose not to save certain people. More specifically, the issue is whether reprobation is part of divine predestination or not.

Election concerns God's choice of certain people to experience salvation. Those who affirm unconditional election maintain that this divine choice is based on God's sovereign will and good pleasure to save them. Key tenets are as follows: (1) God is sovereign, and his election is sovereign. (2) In eternity past, and from his grace in Christ, God chose certain people to be saved. (3) In time, God grants saving grace and faith to the elect alone. (4) Election precedes and results in the mighty acts of God in salvation (like regeneration and justification).

For those who embrace both aspects of predestination, reprobation is God's sovereign, eternal purpose not to save certain people but to give them over to their sins, for which he justly punishes them. This divine decision is not based on foreknowledge of people's unbelief and evil deeds. Still, though the divine decision is not favorable for the reprobate, they willingly sin and are held accountable for it, and they are rightly punished.

Those who affirm conditional election maintain that God's choice of people for salvation depends on their faith in the gospel and continuation in Christ, which God foreknows. The key tenets of this position are as follows: (1) God desires all people to be saved. (2) Although all people are hopelessly sinful, prevenient grace restores the ability to repent of sin and believe the gospel. (3) In his perfect foreknowledge, God foresees those who will embrace salvation and continue in it, and elects them accordingly.

There is a major divide between Reformed and Arminian theologies on this doctrine. Reformed theology holds to election and reprobation, both of which are unconditional. Arminian theology holds to election, which is conditional. Some varieties do not address reprobation, but those that do reject unconditional reprobation.

Biblical Support

Biblical support for divine predestination includes the affirmation that such foreordination is "according to the purpose of him [God] who works all things according to the counsel of his will" (Eph. 1:11). Without minimizing the important role of human decisions and actions, wisdom acknowledges, "Many are the plans in the mind of a man, but it is the purpose of the LORD that will stand" (Prov. 19:21). Human beings rightfully and responsibly decide and act, yet wisely know "that the way of man is not in himself, that it is not in man who walks to direct his steps" (Jer. 10:23).

Reformed theology holds that divine predestination encompasses both election and reprobation. Both are unconditional, grounded on God's sovereign will and gracious pleasure to save or not to save.

Biblical support includes the following: God chose people "in Christ." He predestined them for adoption "according to the purpose of his will." And God predestined them "according to the purpose of him who works all things according to the counsel of his will" (Eph. 1:4, 5, 11). As many as are appointed to eternal life believe (Acts 13:48). Divine election, which is in Christ, is based on God's purpose and will.

Election is also by grace. Historically, the remnant of Israel was "chosen by grace." It was true in Paul's day: "So too at the present time there is a remnant, chosen by grace." The lesson he draws regards election: "But if it is by grace, it is no longer on the basis of works; otherwise grace would no longer be grace" (Rom. 11:5–6). So, combining both above points, we see that divine election is based on God's "own purpose and grace" (2 Tim. 1:9).

God's purpose is that the elect "should be holy and blameless before him" (Eph. 1:4) and live "to the praise of his glorious grace" (Eph. 1:6, 12, 14). Election is not based on good deeds and a life of praise, but it will certainly result in such things. Indeed, though a divine decision, God's choice becomes known as believers embrace Christ and live for him (1 Thess. 1:4–5).

As for its timing, election took place "before the foundation of the world" (Eph. 1:4). The elect, chosen in Christ "before the ages began" (2 Tim. 1:9), according to God's purpose and grace, experience the powerful work of the Holy Spirit, respond to the divine call, and embrace the gospel by faith so as to be saved (2 Tim. 1:9).

Proponents of reprobation point to three biblical passages. In Romans 9:15–18, Paul cites God's words to Moses, "I will have mercy on whom I have mercy." Thus, salvation "depends not on human will or exertion, but on God, who has mercy." The opposite is true as well, as illustrated by God's treatment of Pharaoh: "So then he [God] has mercy on whomever he wills, and he hardens whomever he wills." God is responsible for both mercy and hardening.

For those who balk at such divine determination, Paul emphasizes God's right to do as he pleases. He speaks of "vessels of wrath prepared for destruction" and "vessels of mercy, which he [God] has prepared beforehand for glory." The latter group—the elect—receive that which they could never obtain by themselves: salvation is all of God. The former group—the reprobate—are prepared for destruction. Should this affirmation be understood in the sense that they prepare themselves for their ultimate demise by their faithlessness and evil deeds? Again, the context underscores divine sovereignty over both election, resulting in God's mercy, and reprobation, resulting in hardening and destruction (Rom. 9:14–24). Divine predestination stands behind both destinies.

Paul rehearses a similar theme in Romans 11. The ground of election is God's gracious choice of sinful people. Thus, "the elect obtained it [salvation], but the rest were hardened" (v. 7). There are two categories of people: the elect and the reprobate. As to this latter group, Peter explains that they trip over the cornerstone, Christ. Specifically, "they stumble because they disobey the word, as they were destined to do" (1 Pet. 2:4–8). That is, the stumbling of unbelievers due to their disobedience to God's word is their destiny. God has appointed the reprobate to be unbelievers, taking offense at Christ, tripping over him.

214

Arminian theology holds that divine predestination encompasses election but not, according to some of its forms, reprobation, and certainly not unconditional reprobation. Moreover, election is conditional, grounded on a response to the gospel of repentance and faith, and continuation in salvation, which God perfectly knows. Thus, on the basis of God's foreknowledge of those who will respond with repentance and faith and continue in salvation, he elects them.

Proponents of conditional election make the following argument: God "desires all people to be saved and to come to the knowledge of the truth" (1 Tim. 2:4; cf. 2 Pet. 3:9). If this is the divine wish, then it makes no sense that God elects only some for salvation. In light of this divine desire, the basis of election must be some reason other than divine choice selecting some for salvation and excluding others from it.

In keeping with his divine wish, God grants prevenient grace to all sinful people, restoring to everyone the ability to meet the conditions of salvation. This only makes sense, as demonstrated by Scripture's universal appeals for people to be saved: "Come to me, all who labor and are heavy laden, and I will give you rest" (Matt. 11:28; cf. Isa. 45:22). Such appeals to all people would be nonsensical if the ability to embrace salvation was granted only to some people, the elect. Through prevenient grace, when people hear the gospel, they offer the proper human response to it of repentance and faith. Moreover, because of his perfect foreknowledge, God foresees those who will embrace salvation and continue in it. He elects them for salvation. Thus, election is conditional.

Major Errors

1. *Any overemphasis on divine predestination that results in a complete denial of human responsibility for repentance and faith leading to salvation, and for faithlessness and disobedience leading to condemnation.* Hard determinism overlooks the biblical teaching that human beings are morally responsible agents, accountable for their choices.

2. *Oppositely, any overemphasis on human responsibility that results in a complete denial of the divine role in salvation. Both Reformed theology (underscoring saving grace) and Arminian theology (stressing prevenient grace) emphasize the necessity of grace for salvation.* To minimize or negate the importance of the divine role in salvation overlooks the biblical teaching that human sinfulness can only be overcome by God's grace.

'3. *Any dismissal of the Reformed doctrine of election on the basis that it contradicts God's stated wish for all people to embrace salvation, or that it is a deterrent to evangelism, or that it is unfair.* The Reformed view distinguishes between God's wish and God's will. Because the two are different matters, God's desire that everyone be saved (a wish that he does not actualize) is not the same as his decision to elect some people and pass over others. Moreover, election cannot be a deterrent to evangelism because for the elect to be saved, they must hear the gospel and believe it. As to the charge that election is unfair, the Reformed position points out that if God were to be fair, no one would be saved. If God wishes to elect some, leading to their salvation, that is an act of his grace, which goes beyond judgment to grant favor instead.

4. *Any dismissal of the Arminian doctrine of election on the basis that it doesn't require divine grace or that it amounts to salvation by works.* As noted in major error 2, Arminian theology emphasizes the necessity of prevenient grace that enables unbelievers to respond rightly to the gospel and continue in salvation as the elect of God.

5. *Any casual, flippant attitude toward the doctrine of reprobation.* As Calvin underscored, it is a "horrific doctrine." It addresses the eternal destiny of our ancestors, parents, siblings, spouses, children, friends, co-workers, and multitudes of others. The sobering nature of this difficult doctrine should prompt eternal thanksgiving in the elect for their salvation. Oppositely, God should not be pictured as a mad tyrant sadistically consigning the reprobate to an eternity in hell. They are, after all, his image bearers whom he loves.

ENACTING THE DOCTRINE

According to Paul, the proper response to divine election is to be "holy and blameless before him" (Eph. 1:4) and to live "to the praise of his glorious grace / glory" (1:6, 12, 14). There is not one element in us that distinguished us from everyone else and prompted God in eternity past to choose us. We are all equal with respect to being image bearers of God. We are all equal with respect to our fallenness into sin. We are all equal with respect to our inability to rescue ourselves or merit salvation.

From an Arminian viewpoint, people are saved and continue in that salvation as they cooperate with prevenient grace. Their election is conditioned on this cooperation, which God perfectly foreknows. They rejoice in God's provision. From a Reformed position, the elect receive divine grace that enables them to embrace salvation and continue in that salvation. Their election is unconditional, based on God's good pleasure and sovereign will to grant them his grace. They rejoice in God's provision.

From both perspectives, a sense of arrogance, favoritism, and entitlement is banished. How unthinkable it would be for humans to boast in themselves! Election levels everyone, putting all who are saved in debt to their Savior and his work on their behalf.

TEACHING THE DOCTRINE

Because of the debate that rages around these doctrines, wrestling with biblical texts provides an excellent starting point. Discuss a passage like Ephesians 1:3–14. The purpose of this exercise is to get the participants into Scripture, show them that it calmly addresses predestination, and help them link election with redemption, adoption, knowledge of God's ultimate will, and more.

Clearly set forth both views, advocating the church's position while helping the participants see the coherence of the other perspective. What are the points held in common (for example, the necessity of divine grace)? What are the points of difference (for example, election is unconditional or conditional)? Make sure to clarify misconceptions of both positions, of which there will be many.

Perennial Questions and Problematic Issues

- Why did God choose me for salvation?
- Election seems so unfair.
- Why didn't God choose everyone to be saved?
- If the elect are going to be saved, why should we engage in evangelism?
- Is there a conflict in God between his wish for everyone to be saved and his choice of only some to be saved?
- I believe in election, but I just can't believe in reprobation.

TEACHING OUTLINE

1. The summary
2. Bible study: Ephesians 1:3–14
3. Major affirmations (with biblical support)
   A. Predestination
   B. Predestination: election and reprobation

    C. Predestination: election only

    D. Election: unconditional

    E. Reprobation

    F. Election: conditional

    G. Contrast between Reformed theology and Arminian theology

4. Major errors to avoid

    A. Overemphasizing divine predestination, thereby completely denying human responsibility for repentance and faith leading to salvation, and for faithlessness and disobedience leading to condemnation

    B. Overemphasizing human responsibility, thereby completely denying the divine role in salvation

    C. Dismissing the Reformed doctrine of election on the basis that it contradicts God's stated wish for all people to embrace salvation, that it is a deterrent to evangelism, or that it is unfair

    D. Dismissing the Arminian doctrine of election on the basis that it doesn't require divine grace or that it amounts to salvation by works.

    E. Expressing a casual, flippant attitude toward the doctrine of reprobation

5. Enacting the doctrine

    A. Rejoicing in God's provision of grace

    B. Banishing any sense of arrogance, favoritism, or entitlement

RESOURCES

Allison, *Theological Terms*, s.vv. "conditional election," "decree," "predestination," "reprobation," "unconditional election"

Elwell, *Evangelical Dictionary of Theology*, s.vv. "Decrees of God," "Elect, Election," "Predestination," "Reprobation"

Erickson, *Christian Theology*, chap. 43

Grenz, *Theology for the Community of God*, chaps. 15–16

Grudem, *Systematic Theology*, chap. 32

Horton, *Pilgrim Theology*, chap. 10

27

UNION WITH CHRIST

SUMMARY

Union with Christ is the mighty work of God to join his people in eternal covenant with the Son, who accomplished their salvation, through the Holy Spirit, who applies their salvation.

MAIN THEMES

- This mighty work by which God unites his people in covenant relationship with his Son through the Holy Spirit involves them in every aspect of salvation.
- Believers are identified with the death, burial, resurrection, and ascension of Christ.
- God communicates all his blessings of salvation through this union.
- The Triune God personally dwells with believers by means of the Holy Spirit.
- Believers are united in community with one another.

KEY SCRIPTURE

John 14:23; 15:1–5; 17:20–23; Romans 6:1–11; 12:4–5; 1 Corinthians 12:12–27; Galatians 2:20; 3:28; Ephesians 1:3–14; 2:4–7; 3:14–17; Colossians 2:12–13; 3:1–5

UNDERSTANDING THE DOCTRINE

Major Affirmations

According to John Murray, union with Christ is "the central truth of the whole doctrine of salvation."[22] This mighty work of God joins his people in eternal covenant with the Son, who accomplished their salvation, through the Holy Spirit, who applies their salvation. Accordingly, though it is focused on Christ, union with him places his disciples in relationship with the Triune God.

Believers are united with Christ in his death, burial, resurrection, and ascension. Through union with Christ's death and burial, their sinful nature is rendered powerless so that they are no longer enslaved to sin. They die to sin and are set free from its dominion. Through union with Christ's resurrection and ascension, believers are raised with him and seated with him in heaven. They presently live a new life of faithfulness and obedience to God, and they look forward to a future life of God's eternal goodness and blessing. They are no longer identified with their old Adamic self, but are identified with Christ instead.

Baptism vividly portrays union with Christ, and the Lord's Supper celebrates and fosters this relationship. As the new believer is lowered under the water, her identification with the death and burial of Christ is pictured. As she is brought up out of the water, her identification with the resurrection and ascension of Christ is depicted. She is done with her old way of life. She now walks in newness of life. Furthermore, the Lord's Supper celebrates and nurtures this relationship. As believers share in the one loaf and the one cup, their participation with Christ in his death and their unity as members of his one body are portrayed.

God communicates all his blessings of salvation through union with Christ: In Christ, God grants his grace leading to salvation. In Christ, believers are given redemption through his blood. God gives eternal life in Christ. Regeneration occurs as believers become a new creation in Christ.

220

Justification is in Christ, as is sanctification. God gives spiritual gifts through his grace in Christ. Resurrection will take place in Christ.

Moreover, through union with Christ, the Triune God personally dwells with believers by means of the Holy Spirit. Christ is in believers, living in them. Because of his intimate union with the Father, as Christ the Son dwells in believers, so too does the Father. The Holy Spirit effects this indwelling as he fills believers. Through Christ's baptism of believers with the Spirit and the Spirit's indwelling, the Triune God dwells in believers. More than an individual blessing, the presence of God is promised to the church generally and specifically when it engages in its mission, discipline, and administration of the Lord's Supper.

The flip side is also true: believers dwell in the Triune God through union with Christ.

All those who are in union with Christ are united with one another. Without destroying the many differences that characterize humanity (for example, gender, race, ethnicity, culture, and socioeconomic status), all believers are one in Christ. Thus, while remaining what they were, believers are now more importantly characterized by their membership in the body of Christ, with profound implications for loving, serving, and honoring one another.

Biblical Support

At the heart of God's mighty work of salvation is the oft-recurring expression "in Christ." Indeed, union with Christ encompasses the whole of redemption.

Paul presents union with Christ in his discussion of baptism. Those who "have been baptized into Christ Jesus were baptized into his death . . . [and] were buried . . . with him by baptism into death." Believers are identified with Christ's death and burial. Furthermore, "if we have been united with him in a death like his, we shall certainly be united with him in a resurrection like his" (Rom. 6:3–5). Believers are identified with Christ's resurrection. The implications of this identification are death to sin, crucifixion of the old self, release from the dominion of sin, freedom to walk in newness of life, and ultimate victory over death (6:1–11; cf. Col. 2:12–13).

A further identification is with Christ's ascension, as God "raised us up with him and seated us with him in the heavenly places in Christ Jesus." The future and eternal effect of this identification is that God will "show the immeasurable riches of his grace in kindness toward us in Christ Jesus" (Eph. 2:4–7). The implications are that believers should "seek the things that are above, where Christ is, seated at the right hand of God" and "put to death what is earthly" (Col. 3:1–5).

Accordingly, union with Christ brings a new identity. Believers are no longer branded with their old Adamic self, which has died, but have a new identity in Christ: "I have been crucified with Christ. It is no longer I who live, but Christ who lives in me" (Gal. 2:20). Again, this new identity has strong ethical implications, as Christ's followers should "no longer live for themselves but for him who for their sake died and was raised" (2 Cor. 5:15).

Through union with Christ, God grants the many blessings of salvation: grace leading to salvation (Eph. 1:6; 2 Tim. 2:10), redemption (Eph. 1:7), eternal life (1 John 5:11), regeneration (2 Cor. 5:17), justification (Rom. 8:1), sanctification (1 Cor. 1:30; Eph. 2:10), spiritual gifts (1 Cor. 1:4–5), and resurrection (15:21–22). Indeed, God "has blessed us in Christ with every spiritual blessing in the heavenly places" (Eph. 1:3).

Moreover, through union with Christ, the Triune God dwells in believers, and they dwell in the Triune God. As noted above, Christ dwells in believers (Gal. 2:20; cf. Col. 1:27). But the Father and the Son mutually dwell in each other. Thus, Christ's dwelling in believers means the Father dwells in them as well (John 14:23). Indeed, Jesus prays for believers "that they may all be one, just as you, Father, are in me, and I in you, that they also may be in us" (17:20–23). The Father is in the Son, and the Son is in the Father. Through union with Christ, the Son dwells in believers (15:4–5); therefore, the Father dwells in believers.

The Holy Spirit is the one who effects this mutual indwelling. Christ baptizes believers with the Holy Spirit, incorporating them into his body (1 Cor. 12:13). Moreover, the Spirit indwells believers, joining them with the Father and the Son. Specifically, Paul prays that the Father would strengthen believers through the Holy Spirit, "so that Christ may dwell in [their] hearts through faith" (Eph. 3:14–17). The Triune God dwells in believers, and they dwell in the Triune God.

Certainly, because of union with Christ, his presence is with the church generally. Still, Christ promises his particular presence to the church in specific circumstances: as it labors to fulfill the Great Commission (Matt. 28:18–20), as it exercises discipline (18:15–20), and as it celebrates the Lord's Supper (1 Cor. 10:16).

Through union with Christ, all believers are united with one another. The metaphor of the body of Christ underscores the unity of Christians: "For as in one body we have many members, . . . so we, though many, are one body in Christ, and individually members one of another" (Rom. 12:4–5; cf. 1 Cor. 12:12–27). The unity of the members in union with Christ also means that "there is neither Jew nor Greek, there is neither slave nor free, there is no male and female, for you are all one in Christ Jesus" (Gal. 3:28).

Major Errors

1. *Neglect of the intimate union that believers enjoy with the Triune God through union with Christ.* At times the other mighty works of God like regeneration and justification are so emphasized that the personal indwelling of God in Christians is overlooked. His transcendence is certainly to be magnified, but so is his immanence: God the Creator and Redeemer dwells with his people (Isa. 57:15).

2. *An overemphasis on union with Christ as a mystical intimacy.* Throughout church history, various leaders have encouraged Christians to seek detachment from self and from the world so as to mystically unite their soul with Christ. This path to intimacy has often bypassed the normal means of knowing and loving God. This position fails to appreciate that God has given believers everything they need for life and godliness, and mystical additions may compromise or even contradict those means.

ENACTING THE DOCTRINE

Several years ago the motto "WWJD?" was very popular. The initials stand for "What Would Jesus Do?" Though a fad, this call to imitate Christ is actually a good application of our union with Christ. His mimetic role (1 Cor. 11:1) is the pattern that Christ has established, the model after which we are to walk (1 John 2:6). It means that we are to imitate him in specific ways: forgiving one another (Col. 3:13), loving one another (John 13:34; 15:12; 1 John 4:11), welcoming one another (Rom. 15:7), sacrificing ourselves for one another (1 John 3:16), suffering unjust treatment (1 Pet. 2:18–23), and more.

Personally, because of our union with Christ, our lives must be different from what they were before experiencing salvation in Christ. We are not to continue in sin. We must consider ourselves dead to sin. We are not to allow sin to reign over us. Rather, we are to walk in newness of life (Rom. 6:1–11).

As a church, we should deeply appreciate the special presence of Christ as we engage in making disciples, rebuking and correcting sinful members, and celebrating him in the Lord's Supper. This is not to deny his presence with the church at other times. But it is to mark out for particular thanksgiving his manifest presence in these ministries.

Finally, we are to live out our whole life *coram Deo*, in God's presence (2 Cor. 2:10; 1 Tim. 5:21; 6:13–14; 2 Tim. 4:1). This challenge does not mean we are to neglect the counsel and commands of others. But it does mean that at the end of the day, at the end of our life, there is ultimately only an audience of one whom we hope to have pleased, and it is from him that we hope to hear, "Well done, good and faithful servant" (Matt. 25:21, 23). We live out every thought, attitude, word, and action in the presence of Christ, with whom we are united.

Perennial Questions and Problematic Issues

- I never realized how important this doctrine is, but now I see that everything God does on our behalf is "in Christ."

- How does our church's practice of baptism portray union with Christ?

- How does our church's administration of the Lord's Supper picture union with Christ?

- I'm struggling with consistently living out my new identity with Christ and often fall into my old patterns of life.

- Some of my friends have read Theresa of Ávila and John of the Cross, and I feel uncomfortable with how mystical they have become.

TEACHING THE DOCTRINE

A key to teaching union with Christ is to communicate how central to salvation and how extensive it is in Scripture. Emphasize that every blessing that God gives us is always in Christ. Because it is often overlooked, underscore the intimacy that this union brings: we are indwelt by the Triune God, and we dwell in him. This relationship is now ours by faith, and we look forward to a face-to-face encounter with God in the future.

Two divinely given "visual aids" help us understand union with Christ. The first is baptism. Highlight how this sacrament/ordinance vividly portrays our identification with Christ's death, burial, resurrection, and ascension. The second is the Lord's Supper. Underscore how this sacrament/

ordinance celebrates and fosters our participation with Christ in his death and our union with one another.

Union with Christ has many ethical implications for us. Be sure to challenge the participants to live the reality of this doctrine.

TEACHING OUTLINE

1. The summary
2. Major affirmations (with biblical support)
   A. Identification with Christ
   B. Communication of the blessings of salvation
   C. The presence of the Triune God
   D. Community and unity with other believers
3. Major errors to avoid
   A. Neglecting the intimate union that believers enjoy with the Triune God through union with Christ
   B. Overemphasizing our union with Christ as a mystical intimacy
4. Enacting the doctrine
   A. Imitating Jesus Christ, our example
   B. Embracing the special presence of Christ to bless
   C. Living our whole life *coram Deo*, in the presence of God

RESOURCES

Allison, *Theological Terms*, s.v. "union with Christ"
Elwell, *Evangelical Dictionary of Theology*, s.v. "Identification with Christ"
Erickson, *Christian Theology*, 877–82
Grudem, *Systematic Theology*, chap. 43
Horton, *Pilgrim Theology*, 271–77

28

REGENERATION

SUMMARY

Regeneration is the mighty work of God by which unbelievers are given a new nature, being born again.

MAIN THEMES

- The sinful condition of human nature is the reason why regeneration is necessary.

- Regeneration, which is completely a work of God, is particularly ascribed to the Holy Spirit working through the gospel.

- Regeneration consists of both the removal of one's old, sinful nature and the imparting of a new nature that is responsive to God.

- As to the timing of this mighty work, Reformed/Calvinist theology holds that regeneration precedes conversion, while Arminian theology maintains that conversion precedes regeneration.

KEY SCRIPTURE

John 1:9–13; 3:1–8; Ephesians 2:5; Colossians 2:13; Titus 3:5; James 1:18; 1 Peter 1:23–25; 1 John 2:29; 3:9; 4:7; 5:1, 3–4, 18

UNDERSTANDING THE DOCTRINE

Major Affirmations

In conversation with Nicodemus, Jesus insisted, "Unless one is born again he cannot see the kingdom of God" (John 3:3). This new birth, or regeneration, is necessary because of sinful human nature. As justification answers the problem of guilt before God, regeneration resolves the problem of corruption of nature.

Regeneration is completely a divine work to which human beings contribute nothing. This stands in contrast with conversion, which is the human response to the gospel involving repentance from sin and faith in Christ. Apart from all human engagement, God unilaterally brings about the new birth. The Holy Spirit is the divine person particularly responsible for the new birth. Moreover, the instrument by which regeneration takes place is the gospel.

Regeneration is an instantaneous event, taking place in a moment. This stands in contrast with sanctification, which is the ongoing transformation into greater Christlikeness. And to return to the earlier point, regeneration is wholly the work of God, whereas sanctification is a cooperative activity between God and believers.

Regeneration consists of two aspects: the removal of one's old, sinful nature and the imparting of a new nature. Gone is the former nature that was disobedient to God, the former identity of thoroughgoing sinfulness, the former life of darkness and lostness. In its place is the new nature that is responsive to God, the new identity as redeemed child, the new life of light and salvation.

Still, this divine work remains largely mysterious. No one can see the divine act take place, but what becomes evident is the fruit of regeneration: thinking rightly about God, embracing and walking in God's ways, a lessening of anxiety and worry, making decisions in accordance with God's will, being motivated by the love of God, and purposing to give glory to God.

Regeneration is often associated with the effective call. This is the divine summons to embrace salvation that is extended to the elect through the proclamation of the gospel. It guarantees a response of repentance and faith.

An important debate centers on the relationship of regeneration to conversion, another event in the order of salvation. Though no biblical passage directly addresses this matter, theological considerations lead to different positions. Also, in terms of sequence, these two events occur simultaneously. So the order is a logical one, not a temporal one.

Reformed/Calvinist theology holds that regeneration precedes conversion. Theologically, appeal is made to the intractability of sinful corruption to permit any kind of human response—conversion, including repentance and faith—before the change of human nature through regeneration. Corruption of nature includes both total depravity (no aspect escapes the devastating effect of sin) and total inability (corrupt human nature is incapable of responding positively to God). Given this obstinacy of sin, the new birth must precede the human response of conversion.

Arminian theology maintains that conversion precedes regeneration. Theologically, appeal is made to prevenient grace, divine favor that goes before all people to prepare their will to embrace salvation. This prevenient grace is universal and preconscious, prompting people's initial desire to seek God, arousing a sense of sin, awakening a longing for salvation, and enabling them to repent of sin and believe in Christ. Responding to this grace as the gospel is proclaimed, people respond rightly to it, and as a consequence, regeneration occurs.

An important development in the early church was the belief that baptism brings the new birth. This baptismal regeneration became closely linked with infant baptism, and it became the official doctrine and practice of the church by the fifth century. Indeed, the Roman Catholic Church believes that when the sacrament of baptism is administered to an infant, she is cleansed from original sin and regenerated.

Though his concept of baptismal regeneration was significantly different from the Catholic Church's view, Martin Luther continued to link regeneration with (infant) baptism. The key differences were his emphases on the Word of God and faith. John Calvin rejected baptismal regeneration but carefully linked three elements: (1) faith wrought by the Holy Spirit; (2) repentance that follows, and is born of, faith; and (3) regeneration, which is the death of the sinful nature and the giving of new spiritual life. Still, he held to some type of unusual work of God to cause regeneration in infants, and he continued to practice infant baptism as a sign of future repentance and faith.

Biblical Support

Jesus underscored the necessity of the new birth in his conversation with Nicodemus: "Truly, truly, I say to you, unless one is born again he cannot see the kingdom of God. . . . Truly, truly, I say to you, unless one is born of water and the Spirit, he cannot enter the kingdom of God. That which is born of the flesh is flesh, and that which is born of the Spirit is spirit" (John 3:3–6).

Set against Nicodemus's misunderstanding that Jesus was referring to some type of second physical birth, Jesus's demand was for a spiritual rebirth. Such transformation is essential for inclusion in God's kingdom, to be under the divine rule and reign. Only a divine intervention can change a person's identity as "flesh"—characterized by one's sinful nature—to that of "spirit," characterized by the reality that is also true of God ("God is spirit"; John 4:24). That new birth is the mighty work of the Holy Spirit to cleanse from sin, bring internal renewal, and give the indwelling Spirit to cause obedience. Specifically, Jesus's challenge reflects the prophecy of Ezekiel (36:25–27).

The presupposition for the necessity of this new birth is people's sinful state. Scripture describes unbelievers as being "dead in the trespasses and sins, . . . following the course of this world, . . . [living] in the passions of [the] flesh, carrying out the desires of the body and the mind, and . . . by nature children of wrath" (Eph. 2:1–3; cf. 4:18). Given this dreadful state, regeneration is essential.

As Jesus noted, regeneration is especially associated with the Holy Spirit. Indeed, Scripture presents this spiritual transformation as "the washing of regeneration and renewal of the Holy Spirit" (Titus 3:5). God the Father is also mentioned as agent in this work: unbelievers are "born" or "brought forth" of the Father (John 1:13; James 1:18) and "made alive" by him (Eph. 2:5; Col. 2:13).

The Word of God—the gospel—is the instrument by which regeneration comes about: "You have been born again, not of perishable seed but of imperishable, through the living and abiding word of God. . . . And this word is the good news that was preached to you" (1 Pet. 1:23, 25). Accordingly, God sovereignly works without human assistance to effect regeneration through the gospel: "Of his own will he brought us forth by the word of truth" (James 1:18).

This divine transformation of human beings involves the removal of their old nature and the impartation of a new nature. That is, they are no longer characterized by "the flesh"—the sinful nature—but by "the spirit," the new nature. By means of regeneration, their old habitual patterns of sin and worldly behavior are overcome. Love for God and for others abounds. And protection from Satan guards against ultimate falling into his clutches (1 John 2:29; 3:9; 4:7; 5:3–4, 18).

As for the debate on the order of regeneration and conversion, both sides marshal biblical support. The Reformed/Calvinist position points to the following: "Everyone who believes that Jesus is the Christ has been born of God, and everyone who loves the Father loves whoever has been born of him" (1 John 5:1). That is, the new birth (marked by the past tense, "has been born") precedes and is the ground for belief in Christ (marked by the present tense, "believes") and love for the Father (marked by the present tense, "loves").

The Arminian position points to this affirmation about Christ: "The true light, which gives light to everyone, was coming into the world" (John 1:9). That is, all people have a measure of this light of Christ, which is prevenient grace restoring to all people the ability to meet the conditions of salvation.

Still, this divine work remains largely mysterious, as Jesus noted: "The wind blows where it wishes, and you hear its sound, but you do not know where it comes from or where it goes. So it is with everyone who is born of the Spirit" (John 3:8). We should be cautious in attempting to delineate this divine work of salvation and robbing it of its proper mystery.

Major Errors

1. *A disrespect for, or neglect of, Jesus's emphasis on the mystery of regeneration.* This leads to an inappropriate detailing of this divine work. Caution is urged to guard against overreaching the biblical affirmations and engaging in theological speculation about regeneration.

2. *A confusion between regeneration and conversion (the topic of the next chapter)*. Regeneration is completely a work of God in which human engagement plays no part. Accordingly, Billy Graham's *How to Be Born Again*, while a fine book, is mistitled.

ENACTING THE DOCTRINE

As born-again disciples of Jesus Christ, we should be thankful to God for his mighty work of regeneration. In bringing about our new birth, he did for us something that we could not do for ourselves: He removed our sinful nature, our old identity, our life of futility and desperation. He gave us a new nature that is responsive to him, a new identity, and a life that is abundant and eternal.

While properly wary not to trespass the boundary of the mystery of regeneration, we must consider all the biblical affirmations as we develop and practice this doctrine. Specifically, the church's idea of the results of regeneration should be drawn from Scripture, with care taken to examine the church's tradition on this matter. For example, some churches point to certain overt behavior patterns that the newly regenerated need to stop: smoking, drinking, swearing, playing cards, watching movies, and more. The results of regeneration as outlined in Scripture focus on other matters and envision the expected transformation as a lifelong process. The church should bring its expectations in line with Scripture's presentation of the new birth.

> ### Perennial Questions and Problematic Issues
>
> - Did God regenerate me because, when I heard the gospel, I repented of my sins and believed in Christ?
> - Did I respond to the gospel with repentance from sin and trust in Christ because God had regenerated me?
> - Why do some people refer to themselves as "born-again believers"?
> - What impact do various understandings of the order of regeneration and conversion have on our evangelism?

Addressing the topic of regeneration reminds us to be concerned about people who have not yet experienced the new birth. As regeneration comes through the instrumentality of the gospel, we should be eager to engage in communicating the good news.

TEACHING THE DOCTRINE

Given the debate over this doctrine, a key aspect of teaching is to compare and contrast the opposing view. While advocating the church's position, be careful to fairly represent the other side. Of particular importance is the assessment of the different theological arguments for the proper order of (1) regeneration, then conversion, or (2) conversion, then regeneration. Challenge participants to judge which position is most persuasive theologically.

Because the new birth is completely a divine work and, as Jesus explained, largely mysterious, be careful of overanalysis. It is most proper to praise God for his powerful work to remove one's sinful nature and implant in its place a new nature. All sides agree that such regenerative work is according to divine grace, which removes human boasting and a sense of superiority.

TEACHING OUTLINE

1. The summary
2. The two divergent positions
3. Major affirmations (with biblical support)
   A. The sinful condition as presupposition of regeneration
   B. Regeneration as a divine work, and its relationship to the gospel
   C. Regeneration as consisting of both removal and implanting
   D. The relationship between regeneration and conversion
4. Major errors to avoid
   A. Disrespecting or neglecting Jesus's emphasis on the mystery of regeneration
   B. Confusing regeneration and conversion
5. Enacting the doctrine
   A. Being thankful to God for his mighty work of regeneration
   B. Developing the right expectations for the results of regeneration
   C. Communicating the gospel by which unbelievers may be born again

RESOURCES

Allison, *Theological Terms*, s.v. "regeneration"
Elwell, *Evangelical Dictionary of Theology*, s.v. "Regeneration"
Erickson, *Christian Theology*, chap. 44
Grenz, *Theology for the Community of God*, chap. 16
Grudem, *Systematic Theology*, chap. 34
Horton, *Pilgrim Theology*, 258–61
Thoennes, *Life's Biggest Questions*, chap. 14

29

CONVERSION

SUMMARY

Conversion is the human response to the gospel, consisting of repentance from sin and faith in Jesus Christ.

MAIN THEMES

- If regeneration and conversion are like two sides of a coin, regeneration is a divine work and conversion is a human response.
- Conversion is a response to the gospel and consists of two aspects: repentance from sin and faith in Christ for salvation.
- Though it is a human response, it is not merely human, being divinely aided.
- As to the order of this human response, Reformed/Calvinist theology holds that regeneration precedes conversion, while Arminian theology maintains that conversion precedes regeneration.

KEY SCRIPTURE

Genesis 15:6; Jonah 3:1–10; Matthew 3:2; 4:17; Luke 24:47; John 3:16; Acts 2:38; 17:30–31; Romans 3:1–4:25; 10:9; 2 Corinthians 7:9–11; Ephesians 2:8–9; 1 John 5:1

UNDERSTANDING THE DOCTRINE

Major Affirmations

As the church engages in its mission of communicating the gospel, an important element of its message is to call hearers of the good news to repent of their sins and believe in Jesus Christ in order to be saved. This human response to the gospel is conversion.

Its two aspects are repentance and faith. Repentance is changing one's mind and life. It involves acknowledging that one's thoughts, words, and actions are sinful and thus grievous to God. Furthermore, it includes a sorrow for one's sin, as well as a decision to break with sin. Repentance is different from feeling sorry for one's situation or regret that one's mistakes have been exposed. Rather, it involves an intellectual component, an emotional component, and a volitional component.

Faith is belief and personal trust. It involves an understanding of the person and work of Christ to provide salvation. Moreover, it includes an assent to one's need for forgiveness, as well as a decision to trust Christ to personally save. Faith that saves stands in contrast with bogus faith, which is mere intellectual understanding or assent. It also differs from temporary faith and apparent faith. Like repentance, faith involves intellectual, emotional, and volitional components.

Though a fully human response, conversion is not merely human, because it is ignited by the gospel and prompted by the grace of the Holy Spirit. Arminian theology holds to prevenient grace, a type of divine enabling that goes before all people to prepare their will, which is unresponsive to God because of sin, to embrace salvation. This grace is universal and preconscious, enabling sinful people to repent of sin and believe in Christ.

Reformed theology does not hold to prevenient grace. Rather, it embraces saving grace, God's favor that is given to the elect only. It secures their proper response to the gospel for salvation.

235

These two theological positions disagree as to the order of this human response to the gospel. Reformed/Calvinist theology holds that regeneration precedes conversion, while Arminian theology maintains that conversion precedes regeneration. This order is not a temporal one, because both occur at the same time. Rather, the order is a logical one.

The Reformed view maintains that because of human depravity and inability, and because there is no such thing as prevenient grace, sinful people must be born again before (logically, not temporally) they can convert. Having a new nature through regeneration, they are able to offer the proper human response to the gospel of repentance and faith. The divine work of regeneration logically precedes the human response of conversion.

The Arminian view may also embrace human depravity and inability, but believes that prevenient grace restores to all sinful people the ability to meet the conditions of salvation. Accordingly, when people hear the gospel, they offer the proper human response of repentance and faith. Aided by prevenient grace, the human response of conversion logically precedes the divine work of regeneration.

Biblical Support

Throughout Scripture, the call for sinful people to convert is heard in the appeal for them to repent of their sin and trust in the Lord. In the Old Testament, repentance appears as the call to Israel (2 Chron. 7:14) and the call to the pagans of Nineveh (Jon. 3:1–10) to "turn from their wicked ways." In the New Testament, both John the Baptist and Jesus preached, "Repent, for the kingdom of God is at hand" (Matt. 3:2; 4:17). After his resurrection, Jesus told his disciples "that repentance for the forgiveness of sins should be proclaimed in his name to all nations, beginning from Jerusalem" (Luke 24:47).

Accordingly, Peter announced the gospel in Jerusalem on the day of Pentecost and urged his listeners, "Repent and be baptized every one of you in the name of Jesus Christ for the forgiveness of your sins" (Acts 2:38). Salvation was not reserved for repentant Jews, however, as demonstrated by the conversion of Cornelius and his family. In fact, the Jewish onlookers concluded, "Then to the Gentiles also God has granted repentance that leads to life" (11:18). Indeed, God "commands all people everywhere to repent, because he has fixed a day on which he will judge the world in righteousness by a man whom he has appointed" (17:30–31).

Repentance involves a remorse for sin that is different from worldly sorrow. Paul contrasts "a godly grief" with a "worldly grief." In the latter case, the grief remains at the level of feeling sorry for one's situation or regret that one's mistakes have been exposed. By contrast, "godly grief produces a repentance that leads to salvation without regret, whereas worldly grief produces death" (2 Cor. 7:9–11). True repentance manifests itself in concrete acts and attitudes, "fruits in keeping with repentance" (Luke 3:8).

Accompanying this call to repentance is the call to believe or have faith. The quintessential example of salvation is Abraham, who "believed the Lord, and he counted it to him as righteousness" (Gen. 15:6; Rom. 4:9, 22). The contrast between appropriating salvation by faith rather than works appears often: "For by grace you have been saved through faith. And this is not your own doing; it is the gift of God, not a result of works, so that no one may boast" (Eph. 2:8–9).

The object of saving faith is Jesus himself, sent by the Father to the world that he loved, "that whoever believes in him should not perish but have eternal life" (John 3:16). Indeed, justification is by faith in Christ (Rom. 10:9).

Saving faith contrasts with bogus faith, which is mere intellectual understanding or assent. "Even the demons believe [that God is one]—and shudder!" (James 2:19). Moreover, it differs from temporary faith, as with "the one who hears the word and immediately receives it with joy, yet he has no root in himself, but endures for a while, and when tribulation or persecution arises on account of the word, immediately he falls away" (Matt. 13:20–21). Furthermore, saving faith differs from apparent faith (Heb. 6:4–10; 1 John 2:18–19).

As for the logical order of regeneration and conversion, both positions claim the support of Scripture. The Reformed position points to the following: "Everyone who believes that Jesus is the Christ has been born of God, and everyone who loves the Father loves whoever has been born of him" (1 John 5:1). That is, the new birth (marked by the past tense, "has been born") precedes and is the ground for belief in Christ (marked by the present tense, "believes") and love for the Father (marked by the present tense, "loves"). Regeneration precedes conversion.

The Arminian position points to this affirmation about Christ: "The true light, which gives light to everyone, was coming into the world" (John 1:9). That is, all people have a measure of this light of Christ, which is prevenient grace restoring to all people the ability to meet the conditions of salvation. Additionally, support for this type of grace has historically been found in the Latin version of Psalm 59:10: "God's mercy 'shall meet me' [*praevenient*]. . . . It goes before the unwilling to make him willing."[23] Thus, aided by prevenient grace, people willingly respond to the gospel with repentance and faith, as they are called to do. Then they experience the new birth. Conversion precedes regeneration.

Major Errors

1. *Taking credit for one's conversion, or making the decisive factor one's own repentance and faith for salvation.* Whether approached from a Reformed position or an Arminian perspective, conversion must redound to the glory of God for his overcoming work of grace. Accordingly, Reformed criticism of the Arminian view must not overlook the Arminian insistence on prevenient grace as the divine initiative for conversion.

2. *Oppositely, minimizing the importance of the human role in conversion.* Whether approached from a Reformed position or an Arminian perspective, conversion must leave room for human responsibility. Accordingly, Arminian criticism of the Reformed position must not misunderstand it as denying the role of human response—repentance and faith—in conversion.

3. *An insistence that the conversion of others must be similar to one's own conversion.* Within revivalist traditions, for example, a radical conversion accompanied by strong emotions (weeping over sin), physical sensations ("I felt as if the weight of the world came off my shoulders"), immediate cessation of addictive behaviors (excessive drinking, sexual immorality), and more is held out as the norm. Tragically, this insistence on a particular experience of conversion denigrates the milder conversions of others. It may also raise doubts as to the salvation of the children of parents who experienced radical conversions. Their children are protected from many of the sins into which the parents fell. Thus, the conversion of the children cannot be as radical as that of the parents, leading to doubts about the genuineness of the children's salvation.

4. *Defining conversion as involving faith only, without repentance.* A contemporary movement links repentance with discipleship and following Christ as Lord, while insisting on faith alone for salvation and embracing Christ as Savior. The Free Grace Society position fails to put together Scripture's two emphases on repentance and faith. For example, the first hearers of the gospel were told to repent, and they were referred to as believers (Acts 2:38, 44).

ENACTING THE DOCTRINE

As we look back on our conversion, we should be thankful to God for his grace that enabled us to repent of our sins and believe in Christ for salvation. We take no credit for it, acknowledging that our response was divinely aided. At the same time, we do not minimize the importance of our turning from sin and embracing Christ by faith.

If someone else's conversion story was helpful in leading us to Christ, we should also be thankful that God brought that person into our life at the right moment. The gospel is passed down from one converted Christian to others, who, as they experience conversion, pass it down to still others. Accordingly, teaching on this doctrine encourages us to be burdened for people who have not yet repented and trusted Christ. It should prompt us to ask, "With whom can I share the gospel and my story?"

TEACHING THE DOCTRINE

A good place to start is to have several of the participants share their stories of conversion. It would be most helpful to have several different stories narrated, to make the important point that conversion is an individual experience. Watch for people whose conversion was not radical. They may feel inferior to those whose experience was dramatic. Remind the participants not to disparage their own conversion, nor that of others.

This is also a good point at which to help people work on their stories of salvation. Along with knowing how to communicate the gospel, being able to share one's testimony is a powerful element in leading others to Christ. A simple worksheet—my life before coming to Christ, how I came to know Christ, my life after coming to Christ—provides good direction. Ask participants to write out their stories, then share them with friends for help in editing, clarifying, and simplifying their stories. In the weeks

> ### *Perennial Questions and Problematic Issues*
>
> - Did I respond to the gospel with repentance from sin and trust in Christ because God had regenerated me?
> - Did God regenerate me because, when I heard the gospel, I repented of my sins and believed in Christ?
> - Sometimes I wrestle with the fact that nothing dramatic happened to me when I converted, so maybe I'm not a Christian.
> - The Reformation insistence on "faith alone" has me worried about this talk about repentance.

to come, carve out a few minutes for the participants to share their testimonies. This "practice" will help them overcome the fear of telling their stories to others. It will also help the participants to know one another's story, with praise to God for his mighty work!

As always, biblical teaching is key, so make sure that both elements in conversion receive adequate treatment.

TEACHING OUTLINE

1. The summary
2. Stories of conversion
3. Major affirmations (with biblical support)
   A. Conversion as a human response to the gospel
   B. Conversion as consisting of both repentance and faith
      i. Repentance
      ii. Faith
   C. The relationship between conversion and regeneration
4. Major errors to avoid
   A. Taking credit for one's conversion, or making the decisive factor one's own repentance and faith for salvation
   B. Minimizing the importance of the human role in conversion
   C. Insisting that the conversion of others must be similar to one's own conversion
   D. Defining conversion as involving faith only, without repentance
5. Enacting the doctrine
   A. Thanking God for his grace that enabled us to repent of our sins and believe in Christ for salvation
   B. Sharing the gospel and our story of conversion with others

---

RESOURCES

Allison, *Theological Terms*, s.vv. "conversion," "faith," "prevenient grace," "repentance," "saving faith"

Elwell, *Evangelical Dictionary of Theology*, s.vv. "Conversion," "Faith," "Grace," "Repentance"

Erickson, *Christian Theology*, chap. 44

Grenz, *Theology for the Community of God*, chaps. 15–16

Grudem, *Systematic Theology*, chap. 35

Horton, *Pilgrim Theology*, 262–69

Thoennes, *Life's Biggest Questions*, chap. 14

30

JUSTIFICATION

SUMMARY

Justification is the mighty act of God by which he declares sinful people not guilty but righteous instead by imputing the perfect righteousness of Christ to them.

MAIN THEMES

- The guilt of sinful people before God, and their liability to suffer condemnation, is the reason why justification is necessary.

- Justification is a legal declaration by which God pronounces sinful people not guilty but righteous instead.

- Justification consists of two aspects: the forgiveness of sins (the declaration "not guilty") and the imputation of the perfect righteousness of Christ (the declaration "righteous instead").

- Justification by God's grace alone through faith alone by the merits of Christ alone was the material principle (the main doctrinal content) of the Reformation.

- This Protestant doctrine stands in stark contrast with the Catholic doctrine of justification.

KEY SCRIPTURE

Genesis 15:1–6; Romans 3–8; Galatians 2:15–3:29; Ephesians 2:8–9; 1 Peter 3:18

UNDERSTANDING THE DOCTRINE

Major Affirmations

As a mighty divine act in saving sinful people, justification is God's work to declare them not guilty but righteous instead. It is a different aspect of salvation from regeneration, adoption, and other mighty divine works. Justification is the legal ground of standing before God as forgiven and fully righteous people.

The backdrop for justification is God's perfect righteousness and his fallen image-bearers' guilt and liability to suffer condemnation because of their sinfulness. Christ's atoning sacrifice removes their guilt and condemnation.

An application of God's atoning work in Christ is justification. This is the mighty act by which God declares sinful, condemned people "not guilty" but "righteous instead." It is a legal pronouncement, a declaration that changes the status of sinful people before God but does not change their character (regeneration and sanctification deal with this transformative reality).

Justification has two aspects. The first is the forgiveness of sins. On the basis of Christ's substitutionary death, God declares people "not guilty." Christ has borne the punishment for them, so they are no longer under condemnation. The second aspect is imputation. On the basis of Christ's perfect righteousness, God declares people completely righteous. He imputes, or credits, Christ's righteousness to them. Thus, while they are not actually righteous, God views them as being so because of Christ's righteousness attributed to them.

According to Martin Luther, justification is a "sweet exchange" between Christ and a sinful person, whom Luther encouraged to pray, "You, Lord

Jesus, are my righteousness and I am your sin. You have taken on yourself what you were not, and have given to me what I am not." Sin is exchanged for righteousness.

Importantly, Luther distinguished between two kinds of righteousness: The first is alien righteousness, or the righteousness of another—in this case, the righteousness of Jesus Christ. It is external to people, coming to them from the outside, through the gospel. It is this alien righteousness that is imputed in justification. The second is actual righteousness, that which is proper to believers as they engage in good works on the basis of the alien righteousness that is theirs by faith. The order is key: first, alien righteousness; second, actual righteousness. Thus, good works make no contribution whatsoever to justification. But they flow from, and are evidence of, justification by faith alone, as those who are justified engage in good works out of thankfulness to God and his grace.

It is important to distinguish between the ground of justification and its appropriation. Its ground is the grace of God, specifically the provision of the work of Christ to remove guilt and condemnation. Its appropriation is faith in Christ and his work of salvation. Thus, faith itself does not save; rather, God, through his gracious provision of Christ's substitutionary death, saves. This gracious salvation is appropriated through faith. Faith is the reception of the gift of salvation. Importantly, justification *by grace* received *through faith* stands opposed to justification *by works/merit*.

At the time of the Reformation, a major point of division between Roman Catholic theology and the new Protestant theology was the doctrine of justification. Indeed, justification by God's grace alone through faith alone by the work of Christ alone was the *material principle* (the main doctrinal content) of Protestantism. It is opposed to the Catholic doctrine that justification "is not remission [forgiveness] of sins merely, but also the sanctification and renewal of the inward man."[24] This Catholic idea blends justification with regeneration and sanctification and makes it something that is not in accordance with Scripture.

An important distinction is between imputation and infusion. Imputation is the divine work of crediting Christ's righteousness to people who believe in him. Imputation stands in contrast with infusion, the divine work of introducing or adding grace to people who believe. According to Roman Catholic theology, infusion is especially accomplished by means of the seven sacraments. Through infusion the faithful's character is transformed.

Protestant theology embraces the imputation of righteousness and disagrees with Catholic theology's infusion of grace.

Biblical Support

Scripture underscores the precarious state of sinful people before God. They are unrighteous, as emphasized in Paul's litany of Old Testament citations beginning with "None is righteous, no, not one" (Rom. 3:10). Their dreadful state necessitates the work of Christ, who "suffered once for sins, the righteous for the unrighteous, that he might bring us to God" (1 Pet. 3:18).

This sweet exchange means that the judgment leading to condemnation that flows from Adam's sin is replaced by justification through Christ's righteousness: "For the judgment following one trespass brought condemnation, but the free gift following many trespasses brought justification" (Rom. 5:16; cf. v. 18). By his substitutionary atonement, Christ bore the penalty of sin so there is "now no condemnation for those who are in Christ Jesus" (8:1). Instead of condemnation, there is justification.

This contrast between justification and condemnation underscores that justification, like condemnation, is a legal declaration regarding guilt. The Old Testament presents justification as a pronouncement that a person is in harmony with the demands of the law and thus declared righteous (Deut. 25:1; Prov. 17:15). Similarly, the New Testament affirms justification is a declarative act that contrasts with condemnation (Rom. 8:33–34). Indeed, the unrighteousness of sinful humanity is overcome by the righteousness of God through the atoning sacrifice of Christ (3:20–28), "so that he might be just and the justifier of the one who has faith in Jesus" (3:26).

Accordingly, faith is the way of appropriating justification. A sinful person believes in Christ, and she is counted as righteous. This stands in contrast with justification by works. A sinful person attempts to merit God's favor through engagement in good deeds or keeping the law, and fails to achieve the righteousness that saves (Rom. 3:20; Titus 3:7; Eph. 2:8–9). Importantly, those who are justified by faith apart from works engage in good works as the fruit and evidence of their justification (James 2:18–26).

God's work of imputing righteousness by faith is exemplified by Abraham. Before engaging in good works and apart from the law (which did not yet exist), Abraham believed God's promise by faith, and God counted him righteous (Rom. 4). Abraham was a pagan who stood on the verge of trusting in Eliezer to be the fulfillment of God's promise of a son (Gen. 15:1–6), and then he trusted in God's promise of provision. Thus, "God justifies the ungodly" (Rom. 4:5) by imputing to them Christ's righteousness appropriated by faith.

Accordingly, God's work is one of imputation, crediting righteousness to those who believe, rather than one of infusion, imparting grace through the sacraments, the position of the Catholic Church. Justification is declarative, not transformative (though God also changes human nature). To mix the declarative justification with transformative regeneration and sanctification (which God also performs) results in salvation being a lifelong process of gaining greater and greater righteousness through the grace of the sacraments and thereby meriting eternal life. This idea does not have biblical foundation.

Major Errors

1. *An unbiblical understanding of justification.* Catholic theology commits several errors: One is the joining of the forgiveness of sins with regeneration and sanctification, rendering justification a transformative process rather than a declaration. A second error is a minimization or denial of imputation. Thus, salvation for Catholicism is the never-ending transformation of character, without any assurance that one is sufficiently righteous to be justified before God. But justification is a declaration, meaning that one's status before God is that of being counted fully righteous. A third error is the claim that Protestantism separates justification and sanctification, meaning that one can claim to be saved yet live an unrighteous life. But Protestantism, while distinguishing between these two mighty divine acts, insists that whomever God justifies, he also sanctifies. God intends to continue his work of salvation with those whom he justifies, so they will indeed continue in the faith and engage in good works.

2. *A redefinition of justification with the charge that the Reformers got it wrong (the "new perspective").* According to this view, the righteousness of God is not about the imputation of Christ's righteousness to sinners but about God's own covenant faithfulness to his promises. The doctrine of justification, then, is not about sinners being accepted by God but about identifying the true members of the covenant community. This "new perspective" fails in its understanding of the biblical ideas of

justification, imputation, faith, and works. Moreover, it misunderstands the Reformation debate on justification.

3. *Ecumenical initiatives that seek to minimize the great difference between the Catholic and Protestant doctrines of justification.* The Joint Declaration on the Doctrine of Justification (between the Lutheran World Fellowship and the Roman Catholic Church) rehearses the commonalities between the two traditions while acknowledging the divergences. It unhelpfully emphasizes the former and minimizes the latter.

ENACTING THE DOCTRINE

Justification by grace through faith gives us forgiveness of all our sins, a righteous standing before God, release from ever hearing the divine verdict of condemnation, and assurance of salvation. Imagine what it would be like if our salvation depended on us cooperating with God's grace to do good works with the goal of meriting eternal life. We could never be sure that we had adequately relied on grace and sufficiently engaged in good works in order to be justified. We could hope. But we could not have assurance of salvation.

> **Perennial Questions and Problematic Issues**
>
> - My Catholic friend assures me that his church agrees with my understanding of justification.
> - It's hard for me to imagine that this doctrine prompted such a monumental revolution as the Reformation.
> - My Baptist friend assures me that because God justified him when he understood the gospel and got baptized at the age of seven, he will be saved even though he doesn't care about or live for Christ at all.
> - How do good works factor into justification?

What's at stake in this doctrine? The nature of our standing before God. The way in which God rescues us. The reality of the divine verdict "not guilty, but righteous instead" being already pronounced over us. In short, our salvation is at stake.

TEACHING THE DOCTRINE

An important goal in teaching is to emphasize how crucial justification is for salvation. It is important historically, as this doctrine is the material principle of Protestantism, of which evangelicals are heirs. Justification was at the heart of the division of the Western church into Catholic and

Protestant. It continues to be important today, as this doctrine still distinguishes these two traditions. While strides have been taken to affirm agreement on some aspects (for example, Catholic theology and Protestant theology affirm that justification is the work of the Triune God, grounded on the death and resurrection of Christ, announced through the gospel), significant differences remain and must not be ignored.

A good starting point for teaching this doctrine, then, is to compare the Catholic understanding of justification with the Protestant understanding. Highlight the key contrasts of imputation versus infusion, a declarative act versus a transformative act, faith alone versus faith that cooperates with grace to engage in good works to merit eternal life, and more.

In line with Scripture, present Abraham as the embodiment of justification by grace alone through faith alone. Be sure to emphasize his pagan background, his readiness to trust in Eliezer as his heir, his faith in the divine promise, and God's declaration of his righteousness—a vivid illustration that God justifies the ungodly. At that moment, apart from any good works, Abraham was justified before God. The good works in which he later engaged (for example, obeying God in the sacrifice of Isaac [Gen. 22]) demonstrated that he had been justified by faith (as James 2:18–26 presents).

TEACHING OUTLINE

1. The summary
2. Justification in Catholic theology and Protestant theology
3. Major affirmations (with biblical support)
    A. Sin, guilt, and liability to suffer condemnation as background for justification
    B. Justification defined, and its two aspects
    C. The material principle of Protestantism
4. Major errors to avoid
    A. Holding to an unbiblical understanding of justification
    B. Redefining justification, together with the charge that the Reformers got it wrong
    C. Embracing ecumenical initiatives that seek to minimize the great difference between the Catholic and Protestant doctrines of justification

5. Enacting the doctrine
   A. Embracing the assurance of salvation that flows from God's mighty act of justification
   B. Refusing to compromise on this doctrine

RESOURCES

Allison, *Theological Terms*, s.vv. "imputation," "infusion," "justification"

Elwell, *Evangelical Dictionary of Theology*, s.v. "Justification"

Erickson, *Christian Theology*, 891–95

Grenz, *Theology for the Community of God*, chaps. 16–17

Grudem, *Systematic Theology*, chap. 37

Horton, *Pilgrim Theology*, chap. 12

Thoennes, *Life's Biggest Questions*, chap. 14

31

ADOPTION

SUMMARY

Adoption is the mighty act of God to take sinful people—enemies who are alienated and separated from him—and incorporate them as beloved children into his family forever.

MAIN THEMES

- The enmity and alienation of sinful people from God is the reason why reconciliation is necessary.
- Reconciliation results in sinful people's adoption as sons and daughters, together with the reception of the Spirit of adoption.
- Adoption brings with it an inheritance, and Christians are fellow heirs with their brother, Jesus Christ.
- Adoption as children into the family of God means further that Christians are brothers and sisters, united with one another.

KEY SCRIPTURE

John 1:12; Romans 8:15–17, 21, 29; Galatians 3:26–28; 4:4–7; Ephesians 1:5; 2:13–22; Colossians 1:20–22

UNDERSTANDING THE DOCTRINE

Major Affirmations

As a mighty divine act in saving sinful people, adoption is God's work to take those former rebels into his family. It is a different aspect of salvation from justification, regeneration, and other mighty divine works. Adoption also brings additional benefits to those who are adopted.

The backdrop for adoption is God's perfect holiness and his fallen image-bearers' thoroughgoing sinfulness. Being "sons of disobedience" and "children of wrath" (Eph. 2:2, 3), they are in a precarious position before God. This chasm may be described as enmity, hostility, alienation, and separation between God and sinful people. Such estrangement must be overcome for the two to be in relationship. Reconciliation, as one aspect of the atonement, is the divine removal of the antagonism and the restoration of peace between these two warring parties (Col. 1:20–22; 2 Cor. 5:17–21).

An application of God's reconciling work in Christ is adoption. This is the mighty act by which God embraces his formerly wayward creatures, bringing them as his beloved children into his family forever. Adoption has two aspects. It is a legal act: God incorporates them into his family, changing their status. And it is a relational reality by which God embraces them as their heavenly Father, and they respond to him as his sons and daughters.

As adopted children of God, Christians enjoy the presence of the Holy Spirit. By this "Spirit of adoption," they recognize and relate to God as their Father. Another benefit of adoption is the reception of an inheritance: along with their fellow heir, Christ, Christians possess a sure future of blessing. Adoption as children into the family of God means further that Christians are brothers and sisters, united with one another.

Biblical Support

The roots of adoption extend into eternity past. In the Triune God, the Second Person is eternally the Son of God. This relationship is not one of adoption but of eternal generation: the Father eternally grants to the Second Person of the Trinity his person-of-the-Son (John 5:26; 1 John 5:18). Thus, sonship eternally exists in the Godhead.

When the Triune God created the world, he included the creation of his first image bearer: Adam is the son of God in the sense of creation (Luke 3:38). Ideally, Adam would have remained God's upright son and, together with Eve, produced a vast line of godly offspring to rule the created world as royal sons and daughters. Tragically, Adam and Eve rebelled against their Creator and Father, resulting in alienation and expulsion from the presence of God (Gen. 3:8–13, 22–24).

The fall did not catch God by surprise. Indeed, his eternal purpose included the predestination of Christians "to be conformed to the image of his Son, in order that he [the Son] might be the firstborn among many brothers" (Rom. 8:29). The eternal plan was to redeem a large number of fallen human beings through the redeeming work of Christ and reestablish them into the family of God. The ultimate result of such salvation would be their total renewal into their Savior's image. They would be eminent "sons," with the preeminent (firstborn) Son receiving eternal worship from his "brothers." This purpose was not grounded in any inherent goodness or good works of those elect. Rather, God "predestined us for adoption to himself as sons through Jesus Christ, according to the purpose of his will" (Eph. 1:5).

To enact this eternal purpose, the eternal Son of God became incarnate (John 1:1, 14; 3:16). This incarnate sonship was effected through the Holy Spirit in the virgin Mary such that the son whom she would bear and name Jesus would be called "the Son of the Most High" (Luke 1:32). This incarnate sonship of the eternal Son was essential for Christ's mission to rescue lost humanity: "But when the fullness of time had come, God sent forth his Son, born of woman, born under the law, to redeem those who were under the law" (Gal. 4:4–5). This saving work of Christ took place "so that we might receive adoption as sons" (4:5). Through the divine work of adoption, Christians become sons of God: sonship takes place on a human level, on earth as it is in heaven (in a limited sense).

Importantly, this sonship pertains to both men and women saved through Christ. But the term "sonship" must be retained to emphasize the connection with the sonship of God the Son eternal and incarnate. In a way similar to the Second Person of the Trinity being the Son of God, so formerly alienated human beings are "sons" of God.

Furthermore, "because you are sons, God has sent the Spirit of his Son into our hearts, crying 'Abba! Father!'" (Gal. 4:6). The trinitarian work of adoption is evident: The Father sends "the Spirit of adoption" (Rom. 8:15) to dwell in his sons. This Spirit is the Spirit of the Father's Son. And the Spirit prompts recognition of, and relationship with, the Father, the one who adopts sons into his family. Thus, they address God in prayer as "our Father" (Matt. 6:9), experience his love (Rom. 5:5), and mature as children through his fatherly discipline (Heb. 12:5–11).

The former status of a sinful person before God is described as being a "slave." Wonderfully, this status changes with adoption: "So you are no longer a slave, but a son, and if a son, then an heir through God" (Gal. 4:7). As children rather than slaves, Christians enjoy a glorious freedom from their former way of life (Rom. 8:21).

Sonship brings with it another benefit: the inheritance with their fellow heir, Christ (Rom. 8:17). This future inheritance of glorious eternal life, which the children will enjoy, is the heritage that belongs first and foremost to their brother, Jesus Christ. He in turn shares it with his fellow heirs.

An additional benefit of adoption is the family relationship: all adopted children are brothers and sisters, united with one another (Gal. 3:26–28). Though all human beings have one Father in the sense of creation (Eph. 3:15; Acts 17:26), Christians additionally have the same Father in the sense of redemption. Thus, they are children of God and siblings in the same family, made so by faith in Christ (John 1:12). This unity is even more remarkable when one considers that the former enmity between Jews and Gentiles has been overcome by the reconciling work of Christ (Eph. 2:13–22).

Major Errors

1. *A confusion between being children of God in the sense of creation and being his children in the sense of redemption.* This is the error of Protestant liberalism. It is certainly true that all human beings have the same Father as their Creator. This view, however, extends that truth into universalism: all human beings also have God as their Savior. This view errs in conflating the one fatherhood (in terms of creation) with another fatherhood (in terms of redemption). The latter fatherhood only becomes a reality through embracing the gospel about God's Son, Jesus Christ, and experiencing God's mighty work of adoption.

2. *An exaggeration of the privileges of adoption to include many present material blessings.* This is the error of the prosperity gospel. It is certainly true that God may bless his adopted children with wealth, health, success, and more. However, to demand such blessings is wrong of obedient and dependent children, who are also called to suffer for Christ's sake. Moreover, this view fails to understand that the inheritance that comes with adoption consists of innumerable blessings in the future, not in the present.

ENACTING THE DOCTRINE

The presence of the Holy Spirit—the "Spirit of adoption"—brings assurance of salvation. His inner witness engages deeply with us and assures us that we belong to Christ now and forever (Rom. 8:16). As this is the privilege of all Christians, we should be attentive to those who are wrestling with doubts and uncertainties. Chapter 34 on perseverance and assurance of salvation will be helpful.

Adoption brings the benefit of an inheritance. We must live in hope: we do not and cannot see our eternal birthright, but we nurture a living hope in anticipation that one day in the future that heritage will be ours. Walking with God daily, worshiping him with the church, living this hope in community with other brothers and sisters, exhorting and admonishing one another to press ahead, and believing God's promises of future blessing fan the flames of hope.

Living out another benefit of adoption—the family relationships—means being genuine brothers and sisters in close, loving relationships. There is little opposition to brother-to-brother relationships and sister-to-sister relationships. Still, care should be taken that those relationships are grounded on the unity that all believers share in Christ and not on educational, economic, social, political, ethnic, racial, gender, and age similarities. We must be aware of and avoid classism, ageism, sexism, and racism. And we should encourage brothers and sisters to draw near to others quite different ("other") than they are. This is the privilege of adoption.

Because of potential dangers—sexual immorality, improper emotional attachment, fomenting jealousy—the tendency is for men and women not married to one another to erect barriers between each other and thus not engage in any kind of brother-sister relationships. While being very aware of the pitfalls, we cannot allow these hazards to chill the command to love one another. Brothers and sisters cannot avoid caring for, teaching, rejoicing and crying with, ministering to, and serving with one another. The appropriate precautions should be put in place to avoid the potential dangers from turning into actual failures. Then brothers and sisters are to love each other in all purity because they are adopted children in the family of God.

TEACHING THE DOCTRINE

Adoption of children into human families is a beautiful, concrete picture of God's adoption of Christians into his family. Motivated by compassion for the fatherless and motherless, human beings embrace complete strangers and take them into their family to care for, provide, raise, and love. This adoption is both a legal matter—adopted children become legal members of a family—and an ongoing relationship with many benefits.

Perennial Questions and Problematic Issues

- How is adoption different from justification and regeneration?
- It's hard for me to imagine Christ as my brother and being a fellow heir with him.
- How can we concretely live the reality that we are presently brothers and sisters and will be so for all eternity?

A good starting point, then, for teaching this doctrine is for participants to share their experience of adoption: those who have been adopted, those who have adopted children into their family, and those who know adoption through the experience of friends and family members. Parallels between adoption within the human realm and adoption within the saving realm should be drawn and provide concreteness to this mighty act of God.

The biblical texts that present adoption are limited, which encourages in-depth Bible study. Be sure to emphasize the specific benefits that flow from being adopted into God's family, having Christ as brother, being fellow heirs of him and of one another, and being united as sons and daughters. Also, though a bit difficult, connecting our adoption, with its privileges of sonship, to the eternal sonship of Christ in relation to the Father properly grounds this mighty work in the Triune God.

TEACHING OUTLINE

1. The summary
2. Adoption in the human realm and adoption in the saving realm

3. Major affirmations (with biblical support)

A. Alienation and reconciliation as background for adoption

B. Adoption defined, and its legal and relational aspects

C. The Spirit of adoption

D. Adoption and the inheritance

E. Adoption and being brothers and sisters in the same eternal family

4. Major errors to avoid

A. Confusing being children of God in the sense of creation and being his children in the sense of redemption

B. Exaggerating the privileges of adoption to include many present material blessings

5. Enacting the doctrine

A. Embracing the assurance of salvation that flows from God's mighty act of adoption

B. Walking in hope of our eternal inheritance

C. Enjoying close, personal relationships with our fellow brothers and sisters

RESOURCES

Allison, *Theological Terms*, s.v. "adoption"

Elwell, *Evangelical Dictionary of Theology*, s.v. "Adoption"

Erickson, *Christian Theology*, 891–95

Grudem, *Systematic Theology*, chap. 37

Horton, *Pilgrim Theology*, chap. 12

32

BAPTISM WITH THE HOLY SPIRIT

SUMMARY

When God saves a person through Jesus Christ, one of Christ's mighty saving acts is to baptize this new Christian with the Holy Spirit, thereby incorporating her into Christ's body, the church.

MAIN THEMES

- Baptism with the Holy Spirit is part of God's saving activity along with justification, regeneration, and more.
- Baptism with the Spirit was prophesied in the Old Testament, was promised by John the Baptist and Jesus Christ, and took place initially on the day of Pentecost.
- In keeping with his eternal procession from the Father and the Son, the Holy Spirit was sent by the Father and the Son on the day of Pentecost.
- There are four elements in this act: Christ is the baptizer, the new believer is the one baptized, the element of the

baptism is the Holy Spirit, and the purpose of the baptism is incorporation into the body of Christ, the church.

- Though all three actions involve the Holy Spirit, baptism with the Spirit is distinguishable from regeneration by the Spirit and repeated fillings of the Spirit.

- Many Pentecostals and charismatics hold that baptism with the Spirit, rather than taking place at the moment of salvation, occurs subsequent to salvation with the purpose of empowering Christians for dynamic, fruitful ministry.

KEY SCRIPTURE

Numbers 11:26–30; Isaiah 61:1–2; Ezekiel 36:25–27; Joel 2:28–32; Luke 3:15–17; 24:49; John 1:33; 7:37–39; 14:16, 26; 15:26; 16:7; Acts 1:4–5, 8; 2:1–4, 33; 1 Corinthians 12:13

UNDERSTANDING THE DOCTRINE

Major Affirmations

An often-overlooked aspect of salvation is baptism with the Holy Spirit. Whereas the church typically emphasizes the mighty divine acts of union with Christ, regeneration, justification, and adoption, another element of salvation is Christ's work to baptize new believers with the Holy Spirit. Though not an outwardly detectable experience, it does place new Christians in the body of Christ, the church.

Baptism with the Holy Spirit is most often associated with the descent of the Spirit on the day of Pentecost (Acts 2). That important event, however, was preceded by prophecies and promises about it. The Old Testament looked forward to a fresh, unprecedented outpouring of the Holy Spirit. John the Baptist continued and heightened this expectation by associating this outpouring of the Spirit with the Messiah, who was in the midst of the people of Israel. As the Messiah, Jesus himself continued and heightened this anticipation by promising his disciples that they would experience a greater intimacy and potency of the Spirit. Indeed, prior to his ascension and their embarking on mission as his witnesses, Jesus commanded them to wait in Jerusalem for the descent of the promised Holy Spirit.

Ten days after his ascension, Jesus the Son, together with the Father, sent the Holy Spirit on the day of Pentecost. This outpouring of the Spirit by both the Father and the Son reflects the Spirit's eternal procession from both of them: the Spirit proceeds from the Father and the Son. Appropriately, then, they together pour out the Spirit to inaugurate his new ministry and give birth to the new covenant church. This fresh, unprecedented outpouring does not mean the Spirit was inactive beforehand. On the contrary, he was at work among the people of Israel, especially its judges, kings, and prophets. As prophesied, the Spirit's new ministry would be more extensive and intensive.

As Christ baptized his disciples with the Holy Spirit on that Pentecost, so he continues to baptize new believers with the Spirit as part of their salvation. Jesus Christ does the baptizing. The new Christians are the ones who are baptized. The element with which Christ baptizes these new disciples is the Holy Spirit. And the purpose for this baptism is to incorporate them into Christ's body, the church.

Though involving the Holy Spirit, this mighty act is distinguishable from both regeneration by the Spirit and repeated fillings with the Spirit. Regeneration is the mighty act by which the Holy Spirit removes a sinful person's old nature and implants a new nature in its place. This is the work of the Spirit to cause a person to be born again. Baptism with the Spirit is the mighty act by which the Spirit is poured out on a person, thus being the initial filling with the Spirit. As that Christian walks in new life, she should be continuously filled with—controlled and guided by—the Spirit. Moreover, the filling with the Spirit provides power for the church as it engages in mission.

For the last century, Pentecostal churches and the charismatic movement have challenged this traditional understanding of Spirit baptism. Points of difference include the following: (1) Baptism with the Holy Spirit takes place as a second blessing subsequent to one's initial salvation experience. (2) This outpouring is characterized by speaking in tongues—that is, praying and praising God in unknown languages or utterances. (3) The purpose for this Spirit baptism is to empower Christians for effective ministry, often accompanied by signs, miracles, and wonders.

Two effects of this Pentecostal/charismatic perspective are evident: Positively, a mighty force for evangelism, church planting, and mission is sweeping the world. Negatively, a distinction between Christians who have experienced this second blessing of baptism with the Spirit and those who have not has divided the church worldwide.

Biblical Support

The Old Testament anticipated a fresh, unprecedented outpouring of the Holy Spirit. Moses wished that God would put his Spirit on all his people (Num. 11:26–30). Ezekiel prophesied a future day in which God would put his Spirit within his people so they would be obedient (Ezek. 36:25–27). Joel spoke of God pouring out his Spirit on all people: men and women, old and young, slave and free (Joel 2:28–32; cited in Acts 2:16–21). This new work of the Holy Spirit was particularly associated with the Suffering Servant/Messiah (Isa. 61:1–2; cited in Luke 4:18–19) and a new covenant to replace the old covenant (Jer. 31:31–34; cited in Heb. 8:8–12).

In the New Testament, John the Baptist continued and heightened this anticipation of a new, unprecedented outpouring when he described the Messiah as the one who would baptize with the Holy Spirit (Luke 3:15–17; John 1:33). As the Messiah, Jesus himself continued and heightened this expectation: Though the Spirit is indeed with Jesus's disciples, he will soon be in them (John 14:17). The life-giving Spirit will be like rivers of living water flowing out of them (7:37–39). In his instructions to his disciples prior to his ascension, Jesus commanded them to wait in Jerusalem until they would be "clothed with power from on high," as he would send "the promise of the Father" upon them (Luke 24:49; Acts 1:4–5).

The day of Pentecost marked the sending of the Spirit in a fresh, unprecedented way—an outpouring in fulfillment of the earlier promises. The Father and the Son sent the Spirit (John 14:16, 26; 15:26; 16:7; Acts 2:33), who descended on the 120 disciples. Empowered by the Spirit, the church began to expand into the world through the preaching of the gospel (Acts 1:8).

Not only a historical event on the day of Pentecost, baptism with the Spirit is also part of the initial experience of salvation for all Christians. Paul indicates that every believer has been baptized by Christ with the Holy Spirit (1 Cor. 12:13). Thus, this experience is initiatory, universal, and permanent. Indeed, as John Stott explained: "Baptism of the Holy Spirit is a *universal* Christian experience because it is the *initial* Christian experience."[25]

As they are filled and guided by the Spirit, Christians refuse to live according to their sinful nature and mature in Christlike character (Gal. 5:16–26). With its members being consistently Spirit-filled, the church experiences deep community, genuine worship, constant thanksgiving, and mutual submission (Eph. 5:18–21). Its leaders in particular should be characterized by the fullness of the Spirit (Acts 6:3, 5; 11:24), and it should engage in ministry relying on the filling of the Spirit (4:8, 31; 7:55; 13:9, 52).

The Pentecostal/charismatic position that baptism with the Spirit is subsequent to salvation focuses on several biblical passages in which the reception of the Spirit comes sometime after that saving experience. These include the following: (1) Jesus commanded his disciples, who were already believers, to wait for the Holy Spirit to come upon them (Luke 24:48–49; Acts 1:4–5). (2) The Samaritans, who embraced salvation and were baptized, had to wait for the baptism with the Spirit (Acts 8:4–25). (3) The experience of Cornelius and his family demonstrates that first come faith and repentance, resulting in salvation (10:43; 11:18), then comes baptism with the Spirit (10:44, 47). (4) The twelve disciples whom Paul encountered had not yet received the Spirit, so he conferred the Spirit on them (19:1–7).

The traditional perspective on baptism with the Spirit responds: (1) The passages themselves note the unusual nature of the narrated events (the Samaritans, Acts 8:16; the disciples of John the Baptist, Acts 19:2). Moreover, (2) the passages closely link salvation and baptism with the Spirit.

Major Errors

1. *Neglect of baptism with the Spirit.* This shameful oversight, true of the church throughout much of its history, fails to consider this experience that unites all Christians to the body of Christ.

2. *Tying baptism with the Spirit to a sacrament.* This position (characteristic of Roman Catholicism, Eastern Orthodoxy, and some Protestant churches) flattens the dynamic experiences of the Spirit's work as portrayed by Scripture, attempting to restrict it to a direct connection with a particular sacrament (often baptism or confirmation).

3. *The elevation of the experience of Spirit baptism subsequent to salvation in a way that promotes a feeling of pride in comparison with those who have not had such an experience.* No such sense of superiority may be permitted between Christians.

4. *The dismissal of people with such an experience as not being saved or even as being demon possessed.* This baseless judgment is misguided and dangerous.

ENACTING THE DOCTRINE

Baptism with the Holy Spirit, as one of the mighty acts of God in salvation, is a reason for praise and thanksgiving to Christ for his incorporation of new believers into his body. This commonality unites all Christians, who are members of Christ's universal church and thereby incorporated into a local church in which they worship, grow, serve, and multiply. As the church is thankful for the divine works of regeneration, justification, adoption, and the like, it gives thanks for Christ's baptism with the Spirit as well.

Rather than passively accepting the division between the two perspectives on this doctrine, Pentecostals and charismatics and non-Pentecostals and noncharismatics should come together to make progress toward greater agreement.

Perennial Questions and Problematic Issues

- Why have we heard so little about baptism with the Holy Spirit?
- I thought baptism with the Holy Spirit was something for Pentecostals and charismatics only.
- A while ago I attended a Pentecostal church (or a charismatic conference), and the leaders tried to get me to be baptized with the Spirit and speak in tongues.
- I wish my non-Pentecostal/charismatic friends would experience the intensity of worship, the dynamic prayer life, the boldness to share the gospel, and the large steps of maturity that I have experienced since being baptized with the Spirit.

TEACHING THE DOCTRINE

Because this doctrine has been largely overlooked, there should be no surprise that Christians who are not from a Pentecostal or charismatic background are unfamiliar with it. Ask if any of the participants come from this background and have had an experience of baptism with the Spirit after salvation. Alternatively, ask participants if they know people who have had this experience. This introductory tension will heighten interest in the topic and underscore why it is such an important matter.

Oppositely, if this doctrine is being presented among Pentecostal or charismatic Christians, ask them to compare and contrast their experience before and after their baptism with the Holy Spirit. Be sure they particularly focus on their worship, prayer life, ministry involvement, and sanctification before and afterward. Ask them to discuss how they view other Christians who have not had that same experience.

Given this controversy and the importance of the doctrine, teaching and discussing the various passages of Scripture that address it are of paramount importance. While advocating the church's position on this topic, be careful to fairly represent opposing interpretations of these texts. Additionally, care should be taken not to fall into the excesses noted above.

TEACHING OUTLINE

1. The summary of baptism with the Holy Spirit
2. A discussion that underscores the divergence of views
3. Major affirmations (with biblical support)
   A. One of the mighty acts of God
   B. The biblical anticipation of baptism with the Spirit
   C. The Father and the Son in relation to the sending of the Spirit
   D. The four elements in baptism with the Spirit
   E. The comparison of regeneration, baptism with the Spirit, and filling
   F. The Pentecostal/charismatic perspective
4. Major errors to avoid
   A. Neglecting baptism with the Spirit
   B. Tying baptism with the Spirit to a sacrament
   C. Elevating the experience of Spirit baptism subsequent to salvation in a way that promotes a feeling of pride in comparison with those who have not had such an experience
   D. Dismissing people with such an experience as not being saved or even as being demon possessed
5. Enacting the doctrine
   A. Thanking Jesus Christ for incorporating us into his body through baptism with the Spirit
   B. Progressing in understanding and agreement between Pentecostals and charismatics and non-Pentecostals and noncharismatics on this doctrine

RESOURCES

Allison, *Theological Terms*, s.vv. "baptism with/in/by the Holy Spirit," "filled with the Holy Spirit"

Elwell, *Evangelical Dictionary of Theology*, s.v. "Baptism of the Spirit"

Grenz, *Theology for the Community of God*, chap. 15

Grudem, *Systematic Theology*, chap. 39

33

SANCTIFICATION

SUMMARY

Sanctification—specifically progressive sanctification—is the cooperative work of God and Christians by which ongoing transformation into greater Christlikeness occurs.

MAIN THEMES

- Unlike monergistic works, sanctification is a synergistic work in which God and Christians cooperate.
- While some divine works, like justification and adoption, change one's status before God, sanctification, like regeneration, changes one's nature.
- It consists of three aspects: positional, progressive, and perfected sanctification.
- God works in ways that are appropriate for his divine agency.
- Christians work in ways that are appropriate for their human agency.
- Sanctification transpires especially through the Holy Spirit and the Word of God in the context of community.

KEY SCRIPTURE

John 17:17; Romans 6:1–14; 1 Corinthians 1:2; 6:11; 2 Corinthians 3:18; Ephesians 5:25–27; Philippians 2:12–13; 1 Thessalonians 5:23; Hebrews 10:24–25; 12:14, 23; 13:21; 1 Peter 1:1–2; 2:2

UNDERSTANDING THE DOCTRINE

Major Affirmations

The mighty acts of God in applying the work of Christ to one's life— union with Christ, regeneration, justification, adoption, and baptism with the Spirit—take place at the beginning of salvation. Sanctification, by contrast, is an ongoing work that continues throughout one's life.

Additionally, unlike those other works, which are monergistic, sanctification is synergistic. *Monergism* (from the Greek *monos*, "sole"; *ergon*, "work") refers to *a sole source* that works. God is the single agent that operates regeneration, justification, and so on. *Synergism* (from the Greek *syn*, "with"; *ergon*, "work") refers to two (or more) sources that *work together* in salvation. God and believers together operate in sanctification.

One more difference is important: Some mighty acts of God are legal in nature. They change one's status before him. For example, justification is a forensic work, affecting one's standing before God. Through justification, one is no longer guilty but righteous instead. Other mighty divine acts are transformative in nature. They change one's very being. For example, regeneration removes one's old nature and imparts a new nature. Sanctification, like regeneration, is a transformative work. It changes one's very being.

Specifically, sanctification consists of three aspects.

Positional sanctification refers to God's work of setting apart believers from sin and for his purposes. In this sense, even the newest Christian is sanctified: separated from her old life and consecrated to her new life in Christ. Positional sanctification takes place at the beginning of salvation and is equally true of all believers.

Progressive sanctification is what is usually meant by "sanctification" in both Scripture and theology. It is the cooperative work of God and Christians by which ongoing transformation into greater Christlikeness occurs. It entails an increasing break from sin and a growing conformity to the image of Christ. Progressive sanctification occurs from the beginning to the end of salvation and is greater in some believers and lesser in others. Such diversity of development depends on many factors.

Perfected sanctification refers to God's final work of completing salvation. When believers die, they are perfectly sanctified for their disembodied life in heaven. They become like Christ, but without their physical element. When Christ returns, believers will receive their resurrection bodies and will be fully sanctified for their embodied life to come. They will become completely like Christ, including their glorified body. Perfected sanctification will take place at the end of salvation and will be equally true of all believers.

Focusing on progressive sanctification, as a synergistic work, God works to sanctify his people in ways that are proper for his divine agency. He empowers them to overcome temptations and face trials, wills and works so that they accomplish his good pleasure, and much more. Together with this divine work, believers sanctify themselves in ways that are proper for their human agency. They read Scripture, pray, confess their sins, submit to the Spirit's guidance, resist temptation, and much more. Importantly, believers are not to attempt to do God's work for him, and God does not do their work for them.

In this process of sanctification, three points come into focus: The Holy Spirit is highlighted as the person of the Triune God especially responsible for sanctification. The Word of God is emphasized as the instrument through which sanctification occurs. And the community of faith is the context in which sanctification flourishes.

Biblical Support

From the beginning, God's intent has been to have a people who are holy like he is and consecrated for his purpose. In the Old Testament, God charged Pharaoh, "Let my people go, that they may serve me in the wilderness" (Exod. 7:16). As God established his liberated people, he ordered them to consecrate specific days (Sabbath; Exod. 20:8–11), places (tabernacle, Exod. 29:43–46; temple, 2 Chron. 6–7), people (Levites; Exod. 28:41), and more. And God commanded them, "You shall be holy, for I the LORD your God am holy" (Lev. 19:2). Though he continued to draw near to his rebellious people, they disobeyed his law and fell short of his holiness.

In his decisive action to rectify human sinfulness, "Christ loved the church and gave himself up for her, that he might sanctify her, . . . that she might be holy and without blemish" (Eph. 5:25–27). The theme of holiness is especially associated with sanctification as a position, an ongoing process, and a future promise.

Positional sanctification is seen in the fact that even the worldly Christians of Corinth are described as "sanctified in Christ Jesus" (1 Cor. 1:2; 6:11). Indeed, all believers are described as "those who are sanctified" (Acts 20:32).

Scripture most commonly presents this doctrine in terms of progressive sanctification. This divine-human cooperation is vividly expressed in Paul's command, "Work out your own salvation with fear and trembling, for it is God who works in you, both to will and to work for his good pleasure" (Phil. 2:12–13). In terms of divine agency, God noncoercively works in believers such that they desire and act to accomplish his purpose. In terms of human agency, believers willingly commit to and engage in achieving his plan.

Perfected sanctification is the divinely intended end for all believers. In heaven, "the spirits of the righteous made perfect" (Heb. 12:23) worship God. These are the deceased, disembodied saints who have been fully sanctified for their heavenly existence. They are like Christ, but lack an important component: their body. When he comes again, they will receive their glorified body and be fully sanctified for their embodied, future life (1 Cor. 15).

More specifically in progressive sanctification, the divine role involves the conviction of sin (John 16:8–11), the provision of resources to resist temptation and bear up under trial (2 Pet. 1:3–4), the illumination of Scripture (1 Cor. 2:14–16), aid through prayer (Rom. 8:26–27), empowerment for service (1 Cor. 12:6), and more. On the basis of this divine activity, believers have great confidence that God will sanctify them completely (1 Thess. 5:23).

The human role specifically entails two aspects, one passive, the other active. Passively, believers yield to God's work in and through their life. They present themselves to God "as a living sacrifice" (Rom. 12:1) and all aspects of their lives "to God as instruments for righteousness" (6:13). Such yielding is not an activity in which they engage but a continuous posture they adopt, submitting themselves to God's plan.

The second aspect consists of active engagement with the means God gives believers for their sanctification: obeying Scripture (2 Pet. 1:19), praying (Phil. 4:6–7), confessing sin (1 John 1:9), resisting Satan (James 4:7), fleeing temptation (1 Cor. 10:13), and putting to death sinful tendencies (Rom. 6:1–14).

Accordingly, sanctification is a synergistic reality. God does his role, and believers both yield to him and actively do their role.

Three themes resound in sanctification. One is the essential work of the Third Person of the Trinity, with whom sanctification is particularly associated (1 Pet. 1:2; 2 Thess. 2:13; 2 Cor. 3:18). The second emphasis is the instrumentality of Scripture, through which believers "grow up into salvation" (1 Pet. 2:2). As Jesus prayed, "Sanctify them in the truth; your word is truth" (John 17:17).

The third theme underscores the context in which sanctification flourishes, the church: "And let us consider how to stir up one another to love and good works, not neglecting to meet together, as is the habit of some, but encouraging one another" (Heb. 10:24–25). Continuous Christian community fosters sanctification as it provides corporate worship, preaching, the sacraments/ordinances, exhortation, discipleship, accountability, and much more.

God calls and nourishes his people to be holy as he is holy and to be devoted to his purpose. As he sanctifies them, he provides sufficient resources for their ongoing progress toward increasing Christlikeness. The exhortation, then, is to strive "for the holiness without which no one will see the Lord" (Heb. 12:14).

Major Errors

1. *An overemphasis on the divine role.* "Let go and let God" may rightly express the posture of yielding to his role in sanctification, but it overlooks human responsibility.

2. *Oppositely, an exaggerated emphasis on the human role.* In a frenetic overreach not to backslide but to outdo their latest efforts, believers shoulder the burden of making progress and collapse under its weight. This error is often associated with the next.

3. *Any view that insists that, whereas justification and the beginning of salvation is according to the Spirit, by grace, and through faith, sanctification is according to the law, by good works, and through human effort.* Paul condemns this notion (Gal. 3:3).

4. *Any view that dismisses progress in Christlikeness as an essential component of salvation.* "Once saved, always saved" may rightly express the truth of perseverance in the case of genuine believers. But when it is used to justify engaging in all manner of sin with no evidence of a changed

life after one "accepts Christ," it seriously misrepresents sanctification and threatens to give a false sense of assurance to those who are not Christians at all.

ENACTING THE DOCTRINE

Unlike his other mighty (monergistic) acts, God enlists our cooperation in (synergistic) sanctification. He is always at work "both to will and to work for his good pleasure" (Phil. 2:13) so that we have all the resources we need to please God fully. Individually, then, day by day, with reliance on him, we strive forward in holiness.

The biblical vision is that, from the moment of conversion, God's people make steady progress toward greater Christlikeness. The reality is that some believers start strong and reflect the pattern. Others begin well, fall into a temporary state of worldliness, and then emerge and move ahead. Still others make slow progress from the outset, struggling to forge ahead and beset by fears, worries, and doubts. The mature among us are urged to "admonish the idle, encourage the fainthearted, help the weak, be patient with them all" (1 Thess. 5:14). The church must be a safe haven where its members, all of whom are in need of sanctification, are cared for well and appropriately in order to become holy.

We pray that God may "equip you with everything good that you may do his will, working in us that which is pleasing in his sight, through Jesus Christ" (Heb. 13:21).

TEACHING THE DOCTRINE

Scripture has much to say about sanctification, so teaching it is straightforward.

Perennial Questions and Problematic Issues

- At times it feels like I'm making good progress in sanctification, while at other times it feels like two steps forward and three steps back.

- Some of my friends say they are Christians, but I've never seen any evidence of them living for Christ.

- Isn't it true, "Once saved, always saved"?

- I wish I could be as joyful and active as I was when I first became a Christian.

- I'm not getting anything out of reading the Bible and praying, so I'm stopping for now.

- What is our church going to do about all these unholy people in it who are smoking, drinking, sending their children to public schools, celebrating Halloween, and so on?

Because participants are familiar with this doctrine, they can contribute much in terms of discussion. Have them talk about the means of sanctification that are most helpful to them. Engage them in assessing their progress and their shortcomings. Encourage them to take concrete next steps to mature.

Watch out for unbalanced approaches to sanctification. Some participants may overemphasize the divine role. Be sure they grasp their responsibility to read Scripture, pray, and more. Other participants may exaggerate their human responsibility, carrying the weight of sanctification as evidenced by legalism, moralism, and/or behaviorism. Be sure they grasp the divine role and begin to yield to God's work. Be particularly attentive for participants who couldn't care less about sanctification. They are probably unbelievers who need to understand the gospel.

TEACHING OUTLINE

1. The summary
2. Contrasts: monergism versus synergism; legal versus transformative
3. Major affirmations (with biblical support)
   A. Positional sanctification
   B. Progressive sanctification
   C. Perfected sanctification
   D. The divine role in sanctification
   E. The human role in sanctification
   F. The special place of the Holy Spirit, the Bible, and the church
4. Major errors to avoid
   A. Overemphasizing the divine role
   B. Overemphasizing the human role
   C. Insisting that, whereas justification and the beginning of salvation is according to the Spirit, by grace, and through faith, sanctification is according to the law, by good works, and through human effort
   D. Dismissing progress in Christlikeness as an essential component of salvation

5. Enacting the doctrine
   A. Cooperating with God in sanctification
   B. Making steady progress toward greater Christlikeness, while accounting for divergences from this general pattern
   C. Creating a safe environment in which all church members are cared for well and appropriately to become holy

RESOURCES

Allison, *Theological Terms*, s.vv. "monergism," "perfectionism," "sanctification," "synergism"

Elwell, *Evangelical Dictionary of Theology*, s.vv. "Perfection, Perfectionism," "Sanctification"

Erickson, *Christian Theology*, chap. 46

Grenz, *Theology for the Community of God*, chap. 16

Grudem, *Systematic Theology*, chap. 38

Horton, *Pilgrim Theology*, chap. 13

Thoennes, *Life's Biggest Questions*, chap. 14

34

PERSEVERANCE (WITH ASSURANCE OF SALVATION)

SUMMARY

Perseverance is the mighty act of God to preserve Christians by his power through their ongoing faith, until their salvation is complete. Assurance of salvation is the subjective confidence that is the privilege of all genuine believers that they will remain Christians throughout their life.

MAIN THEMES

- Two divergent theological positions lead to different doctrines of perseverance and assurance.
- The Reformed/Calvinist view embraces perseverance in the case of each individual believer.
- The Arminian position embraces perseverance for believers generally.
- The two divergent doctrines of perseverance lead to two different doctrines of assurance of salvation.

- The Arminian position focuses on present faithfulness and obedience and the assurance that they engender, but does not embrace future assurance.

- The Reformed/Calvinist view adds that present assurance includes the confidence that believers will continue in Christ throughout their life.

KEY SCRIPTURE

John 6:37–40; 10:27–30; Romans 8:16, 28–39; Colossians 1:21–23; Hebrews 2:1–3; 3:12–15; 6:4–9; 7:23–25; 10:26–31; 1 Peter 1:3–9; 2 Peter 2:1–2; 1 John 5:11–13

UNDERSTANDING THE DOCTRINE

Major Affirmations

A key question is, Will the operation of divine grace begun in a true believer's life certainly continue and be brought to completion such that a genuine Christian can never fall away from Christ and fail to obtain eternal salvation? Two different answers—one positive, one negative—have historically been offered.[26]

The Reformed/Calvinist doctrine considers perseverance to be a mighty work by which God preserves believers in Christ forever. Divine power unfailingly protects Christians from temptation, trial, demonic attack, and overwhelming sin. Thus, they cannot ultimately fall away from Christ and lose their salvation. However, this protective power does not operate apart from the Christians' ongoing faith. The faithful and powerful God who saves also guards his people as they walk with him by faith, ultimately awarding them the fullness of salvation.

This doctrine does not apply to everyone who professes faith in Christ; it applies only to genuine believers whom God has elected and saved. Though they may temporarily fall into sin, these true believers will certainly persist in exercising faith and engaging in good works. This position refutes a common caricature of this doctrine that presents it as "once saved, always saved" in the sense that Christians will be redeemed no matter how they live. People who profess faith in Christ but do not walk with him by faith are not authentic believers. Perseverance does not apply to them.

Moreover, perseverance is a continuing divine work, and hence the future salvation of genuine Christians does not ultimately depend on their ability to resist temptation, withstand assaults, and hold themselves in Christ. And this divine power engages their continuing faith, which includes perseverance as a constitutive element: genuine faith perseveres, and when people do not persevere, they do not (and did not) have saving faith.

The Arminian doctrine emphasizes that God has made provision of persevering grace for the church, but this grace is conditional with respect to each individual Christian. A believer is protected by divine power, but she can resist this grace, apostatize, and lose her salvation. Ultimate salvation, then, depends on the believer persevering in the faith. Therefore, it is not possible to know if a particular Christian will persevere to the end. Although some Arminians consider apostasy by true believers only a possibility, others maintain that falling away does occur.

Key to this Arminian position is its notion of human free will: no causal condition can decisively incline a person's will in one direction or another. In choosing or acting, the person could always do otherwise. This view means that though a person cooperated with divine grace and was saved, that person can exercise that same free will to deny Christ and resist the divine grace once experienced.

These two divergent doctrines of perseverance lead to two different doctrines of assurance of salvation. This assurance is the subjective confidence of belonging to Christ and thus being heirs of eternal life.

The Arminian doctrine focuses on the reality of the present state of grace of Christians and the assurance that it engenders. As believers express faith and live obediently, they experience the confidence of belonging to Christ now, but not necessarily in the future. They can refuse the grace they are currently experiencing and fall away, thus losing their salvation.

The Reformed/Calvinist doctrine adds that present assurance of salvation includes the confidence that genuine Christians will continue as believers throughout their life and, when they die, they will certainly go to be with Christ in heaven, looking forward to the fullness of salvation when Christ returns. Because saving faith includes perseverance as an essential element, believers have confidence that they will remain Christians forever.

Biblical Support

Scriptural support for the Reformed/Calvinist doctrine of perseverance includes the following: God is faithful and sufficiently powerful to protect and preserve believers for ultimate salvation (1 Pet. 1:3–9; Phil. 1:6; 1 Cor. 1:8–9; 1 Thess. 5:23–24). Additionally, Christ pledges to unfailingly grasp his followers, never lose them, and give them eternal, resurrection life (John 6:37–40; 10:27–30), as he unceasingly prays for their salvation (Heb. 7:23–25; John 17:24). Moreover, the Holy Spirit has done his work of regeneration (John 3:3–8) and sealing (Eph. 1:13–14; 4:30), bears witness that they are indeed children of God (Rom. 8:16), and is in the process of transforming believers into the image of Christ (2 Cor. 3:18; Gal. 5:16–25).

Furthermore, the Word of God promises eternal life, and assurance of it, to all those who embrace the Son by faith (John 3:36; 5:24; 1 John 5:11–13). Finally, God's purposes—foreknowledge, predestination, calling, justification, and glorification—are all of a piece; they all apply together to the elect, and absolutely nothing can separate God's people from his love (Rom. 8:28–39). Indeed, their persistent faith and determined obedience, along with an increase in other virtues (2 Pet. 1:3–11), vividly confirm their genuine salvation.

Scriptural support for the Arminian doctrine of the conditionality of salvation includes the following: Scripture warns against apostasy (Heb. 2:1–3; 3:12; 10:26–31; 2 Pet. 3:17) and exhorts believers to remain firm in the faith (Col. 1:21–23; Heb. 3:14–15; John 15:1–7; Matt. 10:22). Such instructions would be superfluous if true believers could not fall away but are guaranteed eternal salvation. Additionally, Scripture presents actual cases of apostasy, evidence that genuine Christians do indeed fall away (Heb. 6:4–6; 1 John 2:18–19; 2 Pet. 2:1–2; Judas; Ananias and Sapphira [Acts 5:1–11]; Hymenaeus, Alexander, and Philetus [1 Tim. 1:19–20; 2 Tim. 2:16–18]). Moreover, objecting to the Reformed doctrine from a philosophical perspective, the Arminian view finds perseverance to be inconsistent with human free will, and claims that it leads to complacency and moral laxity.

Any approach to the doctrine of perseverance should seek to hold together passages that emphasize God's continuing work of preservation and those that underscore the responsibility of believers to persevere in the faith. This compatibilistic approach also frankly acknowledges the difficulty of knowing in some cases whether people are genuine Christians or not. Indeed, it admits that some nonbelievers give startling evidence of conversion. For example, Jesus warns about people who call him Lord and who prophesy, cast out demons, and do miracles in his name, yet his judgment is that he *never* knew them (Matt. 7:21–23). This approach also has a category for people who appear to be Christians yet turn away, not from saving faith, but from the religious experience or position they once held (Heb. 6:4–9).

Major Errors

1. *Abuse of the motto "Once saved, always saved."* Although from a Reformed perspective this motto contains some truth, it is often tragically misused to give assurance to unbelievers who make some kind of religious commitment yet never evidence a changed life, faithfulness and obedience, service for Christ, and more. This view overlooks the biblical portrait of salvation as including a Christlike life (1 John 2:6). Moreover, historically, both the Reformed and Arminian positions have denounced this notion.

2. *Shaking the proper confidence of genuine Christians who love, trust, and obey God by warning them about losing their salvation.* What earthly father, when his children are pleasing him consistently, shakes a chiding finger and threatens, "But if you ever . . ."? Neither does our heavenly Father intend the warning passages in his Word to upset his children who are abiding in him. Spiritual abuse of this kind in the church is reprehensible.

3. *A view of assurance that leads to presumptuousness, pride, laxity, and complacency.* These attitudes and habits are condemned throughout Scripture. Moreover, historically the church has cautioned against these two doctrines for the very reason that their abuse can result in such errors. A proper view of perseverance and assurance, from both the Reformed and Arminian positions, avoids and condemns this error.

ENACTING THE DOCTRINE

From a Reformed/Calvinist perspective, perseverance is of great comfort—the pressure is off Christians to maintain themselves in the faith—while encouraging ongoing faith and obedience. Out of thankfulness to God for his great salvation, they walk with him and continually engage in good works. Assurance of salvation, then, is a great privilege not for some elite group but for all believers. Doubts may arise as a result of satanic attack, inability to trust the biblical promises, personal anxiety, ignorance of biblical teaching, depression, and more. All these troubles can be effectively addressed.

The Arminian position emphasizes the divine provision of persevering grace for the church. Thus, individual Christians should avail themselves of this resource and, as they trust and obey, should hope in continuing faithfulness and obedience because of God's grace. Anxiety and worry are improper, so these feelings should be replaced with trust and hope in God's provision. They acknowledge that God has provided all the necessary resources for them to continue in Christ.

Perennial Questions and Problematic Issues

- I know outstanding Christians who were very faithful and obedient but are no longer walking with Christ and now say they were never believers.

- What is the purpose of biblical warnings about falling away from the faith and exhortations to continue in the faith?

- I'm really struggling with doubts about my salvation.

- If the Reformed/Calvinist position is correct, and our salvation is guaranteed, what happens to our free will and responsibility to persevere in salvation?

- If the Arminian position is correct and there is no guarantee of salvation, can there be any assurance of salvation?

TEACHING THE DOCTRINE

Given the debate over these doctrines, a key aspect of teaching is to compare and contrast the opposing views. While advocating the church's position, be careful to fairly represent the other side. As both perspectives appeal to Scripture, the most important considerations are the proper interpretation of the passages to which appeal is made and the most valid integration of them.

One of the most debated texts for this doctrine is Hebrews 6:4–12. The issue is this: Are the people described (vv. 4–6) genuine believers or not? If they are, then apostasy is possible, without any hope of restoration to salvation. If they are not genuine Christians, then they must resemble true believers yet not have actually embraced salvation. Is this the point that "better things—things that belong to salvation" (v. 9)—pertain to the readers of this letter, the genuine believers addressed by the author? Be ready to tackle this tough passage!

The tendency in teaching assurance of salvation is to focus doubting people's attention on their conversion experience. Often, questions like the following are thought to be helpful: Did you pray the prayer to accept Christ? When and where were you saved? What was your experience like?

278

(These are sometimes followed by sharing one's own conversion story and implying that unless the other person's experience of salvation was similar, it probably was defective.)

The problem is that grounding the assurance of salvation on one's experience is like building one's house on shifting sand. What if one can't remember the details? What if one's experience wasn't as radical as the conversions of others? What if one regularly walked the aisle, went forward at evangelistic meetings, and/or prayed a salvation prayer? Rather than this experientially oriented approach, teach the biblical support for perseverance as the foundation for the subjective assurance of salvation.

Be prepared to discuss a common experience: an acquaintance who was a strong Christian abandoned the faith. Questions like these will arise: Was she a genuine believer in the first place? If not, why did she appear so strongly to be a Christian? If she was such a vibrant believer yet fell away, shouldn't I fear that the same thing will happen to me? Both sides of the debate will address this matter differently, but they should be well prepared to do so.

TEACHING OUTLINE

1. The summary
2. The two divergent positions
3. Major affirmations (with biblical support)
   A. Perseverance according to the Reformed/Calvinist perspective
   B. Perseverance according to the Arminian position
   C. Assurance of salvation according to the Arminian view
   D. Assurance of salvation according to the Reformed/Calvinist view
   E. The comparison of the two views, and advocacy for the church's own position
4. Major errors to avoid
   A. Abusing the motto "Once saved, always saved"
   B. Shaking the proper confidence of genuine Christians who love, trust, and obey God by warning them about losing their salvation
   C. Developing a view of assurance that leads to presumptuousness, pride, laxity, and complacency

5. Enacting the doctrine
   A. Embracing the great comfort of perseverance and assurance of salvation
   B. Relying on the divine provision of persevering grace

RESOURCES

Allison, *Theological Terms*, s.vv. "apostasy," "assurance of salvation," "perseverance"

Elwell, *Evangelical Dictionary of Theology*, s.vv. "Apostasy," "Assurance," "Perseverance"

Erickson, *Christian Theology*, chap. 47

Grenz, *Theology for the Community of God*, chap. 16

Grudem, *Systematic Theology*, chap. 40

Horton, *Pilgrim Theology*, chap. 13

Thoennes, *Life's Biggest Questions*, chap. 14

PART 7

DOCTRINE

—— OF THE ——

CHURCH

35

THE CHURCH: NATURE AND MARKS

SUMMARY

The church is the people of God who have been saved by his grace and incorporated as the community of faith.

MAIN THEMES

- There are two diverse definitions of the church: the people of God throughout all time, and the people of God after the coming of Jesus Christ.
- These definitions reflects a key issue regarding the relationship between the old and new covenants.
- The church consists of two interrelated elements: the universal church and local churches.
- The nature of the church consists of several elements: doxological, Word centered, Spirit empowered, covenantal, confessional, missional, and already but not yet.

- Four traditional attributes characterize the church: one, holy, catholic, and apostolic.
- The marks of the church were developed by the Reformers.

KEY SCRIPTURE

Matthew 16:13–20; Acts 2:1–47; 8:4–25; 9:31; 10:1–11:30; 12:12; 13:1–3; 14:23; Ephesians 1:19–23; 4:1–16; 5:25–29; 1 Peter 2:9–10

UNDERSTANDING THE DOCTRINE

Major Affirmations

Study of this doctrine immediately plunges us into a major difference concerning the definition of the church. One position holds that the church is the people of God who have been saved by his grace through faith in God and his promises and incorporated as the community of faith throughout all time. The church began with Abraham (or Adam) and thus includes all believers from that starting point up to the present. Accordingly, the old covenant people of Israel and the new covenant Christians together compose the church.

The other position defines the church as the people of God who have been saved by his grace through faith in Jesus Christ and his work and incorporated into his body through baptism with the Holy Spirit. The church began with Christ's coming, specifically his suffering, death, resurrection, and ascension, together with the descent of the Spirit on Pentecost. The church consists of certain elements—explicit faith in Jesus the Messiah, Gentiles and Jews together in one body, baptism with the Spirit—that were not present before Christ's coming. Thus, the church did not exist before then.

These diverse definitions reflect different understandings of the relationship between the old covenant and the new covenant. Specifically, is there more continuity or more discontinuity between these covenants? The first definition reflects a position that finds more continuity. Thus, the experiences associated with salvation are very similar between the people of God before and after Christ. For example, all God's people experience regeneration by the Spirit. Also, the old covenant law is in many ways binding for the new covenant church. For example, directions regarding circumcision carry over to regulate (infant) baptism.

284

The second definition reflects a position that finds more discontinuity between the covenants. Accordingly, the experiences associated with salvation are significantly different between the people of God before and after Christ. For example, only Christians experience regeneration by, and baptism with, the Spirit. Also, the old covenant law is not binding for the new covenant church. For example, instructions about circumcision do not pertain to (believer's) baptism.

Thus, there is a major difference regarding the definition of the church.

Generally, both positions agree that the church consists of two interrelated elements: the universal church and local churches. The universal church is composed of all believers stretching from its inception (the two positions situate this point differently) to the present. It thus incorporates both deceased believers in heaven and living believers everywhere on earth. The former aspect of the universal church is gathered together as the "heavenly" church. The latter aspect does not gather together, nor does it organize under human leaders.

Local churches manifest this universal church in actual gatherings. A presentation of the nature, attributes, and marks of these local churches follows.

The nature of the church consists of the following. In terms of its origin and orientation, the church is *doxological*, or oriented to the glory of God. It is *Word centered*—that is, centered on the incarnate Word, Jesus Christ, and the inspired Word, Scripture. It is *Spirit empowered*, or created, gathered, gifted, and directed by the Holy Spirit. In terms of its gathering and sending, the church is *covenantal*, or gathered as members in covenantal relationship with God and with one another. It is *confessional*, with all its members having a personal confession of faith in Christ and together making a common confession of the Christian faith. The church is *missional*, consisting of messengers of the gospel who are divinely sent into the world as Christ's ambassadors. And it is *already but not yet*, already assembled in space and time as a church but not yet what it will be when Christ returns.

Furthermore, the church has historically described itself by means of four attributes. The church is *one* in that it is united. There is only one body, or church, of Christ, though it experiences this oneness incompletely. The church is *holy* in that it is already sanctified, though imperfectly. It is set apart for God's purposes, yet still sinful. The church is *catholic* (not the Roman Catholic Church) in that it is universal, committed to the Great

Commission and thus advancing into the entire world. Finally, the church is *apostolic* in that it is founded on the apostles, with specific reference to the apostolic writings, Scripture.

Moreover, the church is characterized by certain marks, the visible elements that distinguish a true church from a false church. The two marks are the preaching and hearing of the Word of God, and the administration of the sacraments/ordinances of baptism and the Lord's Supper. Some add a third mark: church discipline.

Biblical Support

Scripture refers often to the gathering of God's people. In the Old Testament, the people of Israel assembled together to hear the Word of God (Deut. 4:10; 31:9–13), to offer sacrifices (Exod. 12:6; Lev. 4:13–21), to express its commitment to keep the covenant (Josh. 8:30–35), and more.

In the New Testament, Christians assembled together in members' homes as part of the church in a particular city. For example, the house of Prisca and Aquila (Rom. 16:3, 5; 1 Cor. 16:19), the house of Nympha (Col. 4:15), Philemon's house (Philem. 2), and Mary's house (Acts 12:12) were locations in which Christians met. These individual assemblies were called churches. The same was true of gatherings of the whole church in a city ("when you come together as a church," 1 Cor. 11:18; cf. vv. 17, 20, 33), as exemplified by the "whole church" that Gaius hosted (Rom. 16:23) and "the church of the Thessalonians" (1 Thess. 1:1; 2 Thess. 1:1). The narratives of Acts portray the explosion of the church on Pentecost (2:1–47), its expansion into Samaria (8:4–25), its inclusion of the Gentiles (10:1–11:30), and its extension to "the end of the earth" (1:8; 28:17–31).

The New Testament also presents the universal church. It is this church for which Jesus died (Eph. 5:25). It is this church that Jesus is building (Matt. 16:18) and sanctifying (Eph. 5:26, 29) as its head (1:21–23) so that one day it will be completely holy (5:27). Moreover, "the church throughout all Judea and Galilee and Samaria" (Acts 9:31) was a regional entity, one that did not assemble all together. Additionally, Paul warns against giving offense "to Jews or to Greeks or to the church of God" (1 Cor. 10:32), three categories of people. Thus, "the church of God" in this verse does not refer to any particular local church but to the universal church—all believers throughout the world. The universal church also includes those who are already in heaven (Heb. 12:23).

Whereas many metaphors and images are used in reference to the church (for example, plant, letter, one loaf of bread, vineyard, flock, and bride), three stand out. The church is *the people of God*. After presenting Christians as "a chosen race, a royal priesthood, a holy nation, a people for his own possession," Peter reminds them, "Once you were not a people, but now you are God's people" (1 Pet. 2:9–10).

The church is *the body of Christ*. In exalting his Son, the Father "gave him as head over all things to the church, which is his body" (Eph. 1:22–23). Christ baptizes new believers with the Spirit, thereby incorporating them into his body (1 Cor. 12:13). Moreover, he gives them gifted people, whose purpose is "to equip the saints for the work of ministry" (Eph. 4:12) so that the whole body matures (4:8–16).

The church is *the temple of the Holy Spirit*. As Paul sternly warns church leaders: "Do you not know that you are God's temple and that God's Spirit dwells in you? If anyone destroys God's temple, God will destroy him. For God's temple is holy, and you are that temple" (1 Cor. 3:16–17).

At the time of the Reformation, the fledgling Protestant movement articulated the marks of the true church to distinguish its congregations from the false Roman Catholic Church. The Augsburg Confession (article 7) detailed two marks: "It is sufficient to agree concerning the doctrine of the gospel and the administration of the sacraments [baptism and the Lord's Supper]." The gospel is at the heart of the apostolic message (1 Cor. 15:1–8) and essential for salvation (Rom. 1:16). Baptism and the Lord's Supper were ordained by Christ for observance by his church (Matt. 28:18–20; 26:26–29). Some Reformers added a third mark of church discipline as an aspect of the church's keys of the kingdom (16:13–20; 18:15–20).

Major Errors

1. *Exclusivistic claims by churches that they alone are the true, pure church*. One example is the assertion that "the one Church of Christ . . . subsists in the Catholic Church." The corollary is that Protestant groups are "ecclesial communities" but not true churches. The claim is bolstered by appeals to apostolic succession—only the Catholic Church can trace its hierarchy to Peter and the other apostles—and a true Eucharist by means of transubstantiation.

2. *Inclusivistic claims that people can be saved without embracing the gospel*. While inclusivism affirms that salvation is possible only on the basis

of Christ's death and resurrection, it denies the necessity of hearing the gospel and believing it for salvation.

ENACTING THE DOCTRINE

While there is much to criticize about the church, God redeems sinful people and incorporates them into Christ's body so they are part of a community of faith. Christians should be thankful recipients of this grace. Additionally, God has given to the church everything it needs to mature and multiply, and it is his agent in this world for salvation and saturation with the gospel. The increasing number of people who claim to love Jesus but hate his church and refuse to participate in it are in a precarious position and should be soundly challenged to repent.

Perennial Questions and Problematic Issues

- Why are there so many different churches?
- Why is our church the way it is?
- If God is blessing churches of all types, maybe the doctrine of the church isn't very important.
- How can the church claim to be "one" and "holy" when it is so divided and sinful?
- How should parachurch movements like Cru, InterVarsity, and Navigators relate to local churches?

TEACHING THE DOCTRINE

A good place to start is with questions such as "What is your definition of the church?" and "What biblical passages address the nature and marks of the church?" As most participants simply assume these points, asking good questions will cause them to think consciously about the church.

From the outset, teaching on the church's nature and marks alerts participants to the different definitions. The church's own position should be taught and discussed first, followed by a fair treatment of the other positions. Discussion of the issue of continuity and discontinuity will help participants see the genesis of divergent definitions of the church.

Teaching about the two interrelated aspects of the church helps participants grasp that they belong to a movement that stretches across time and space. A focus on the universal church places them in solidarity with all believers before them and that now exist around the world. An emphasis on local churches as manifestations of the universal church reminds

288

participants that they cannot claim to be part of the universal church without also being members of a local church.

Teaching this doctrine is rendered concrete by reflection on the experience of a particular church's nature and marks. For example, after presenting the nature of the church, ask participants to discuss how well their church is doing in terms of the seven elements. The same assessment can be done in regard to the four traditional attributes and the two (or three) historical marks of the church.

TEACHING OUTLINE

1. The summary
2. Questions to explore the nature of the church and its biblical treatment
3. Major affirmations (with biblical support)
   A. Two different definitions
   B. The issue of continuity and discontinuity
   C. The universal church and its manifestation in local churches
   D. The nature of the church
   E. The traditional attributes of the church
   F. The historical marks of the church
4. Major errors to avoid
   A. Exclusivistically claiming that one's church is the only true, pure church
   B. Inclusivistically claiming that people can be saved without embracing the gospel
5. Enacting the doctrine
   A. Being thankful for God's gracious gift of Christian community
   B. Repenting of disrespect for, or rejection of, the church of Jesus Christ

RESOURCES

Allison, *Theological Terms*, s.vv. "body of Christ," "church," "marks of the church"
Elwell, *Evangelical Dictionary of Theology*, s.v. "Church"

Erickson, *Christian Theology*, chap. 49
Grenz, *Theology for the Community of God*, chap. 17
Grudem, *Systematic Theology*, chap. 44
Horton, *Pilgrim Theology*, chap. 17
Thoennes, *Life's Biggest Questions*, chap. 15

36

PURITY AND UNITY OF THE CHURCH

SUMMARY

The purity of the church is its attribute of holiness, or conformity to God's will. The unity of the church is its attribute of oneness and absence of divisions.

MAIN THEMES

- Two traditional attributes of the church are its purity, or holiness, and its unity, or oneness.
- The church is pure in a positional sense, a purposive sense, and an instrumental sense.
- The church is united in a positional sense, a purposive sense, and an instrumental sense.

KEY SCRIPTURE

John 17; Romans 12:16; 2 Corinthians 11:2–3; Ephesians 2:18–22; 4:1–16; 5:25–29; Philippians 2:2

UNDERSTANDING THE DOCTRINE

Major Affirmations

Two of the four traditional attributes of the church are its holiness and unity. (All four characteristics are treated together in chapter 35; the church's catholicity/universality, or mission, is also addressed further in chapter 43, and the church's apostolicity is addressed further as a criterion for canonicity in chapter 7.) Both purity and unity can be understood in three ways: (1) positionally, both are realities for the church because of God's work of setting it apart for his purposes and granting it oneness; (2) purposively, both are essential aims for the church as it matures; (3) instrumentally, both are essential processes fostering the church's growth.

The purity of the church is "its degree of freedom from wrong doctrine and conduct, and its degree of conformity to God's revealed will for the church."[27] In a positional sense, the church is already holy, being set apart and consecrated by God. By definition, then, the church is pure. In a purposive sense, purity is an essential aim: the church orients itself toward perfect holiness as its divinely established goal. In an instrumental sense, the church pursues greater and greater purity so that it grows. This pursuit of holiness is a means for the church to mature.

Some churches are more pure, while others are less pure. For example, the churches in Philippi and Thessalonica exhibited few if any disturbances to their purity. By contrast, the churches of Corinth and Galatia, beset by doctrinal and moral problems, were less pure. Empirically, some churches stand out today as more pure churches. They are characterized by faithful preaching, genuine worship, strong community, fruitful mission, and more. Oppositely, other churches are noted as less pure, characterized by shallow preaching, superficial worship, weak relationality, lack of missional engagement, and more.

Additionally, a church may be characterized by more pure aspects and less pure aspects. For example, a church may strongly reflect God's will in terms of its preaching and teaching but be less conformed to God's will in terms of prayer and missional engagement. Returning to the purposeful sense of purity, the church should aim at greater holiness in all areas, not just some.

In the instrumental sense of purity, a church should identify the areas of both more purity and less purity. It should work hard to maintain and even increase the holiness of its more pure aspects, giving thanks to God for those areas that please him. Furthermore, the church should develop ways forward to bring its less pure aspects into conformity with God's will. Focusing on people and processes that can work to bring greater purity in those areas is a wise approach to employ.

The unity of the church is its attribute of oneness, a sense and practice of harmony that extends to its doctrine, life, community identity, and mission, along with its absence of divisions. In a positional sense, the church is already united, endowed by the Spirit with the gift of oneness. By definition, then, the church is united. In a purposive sense, unity is an essential aim: the church orients itself toward perfect oneness as its divinely established goal. In an instrumental sense, the church works hard to maintain the unity with which it has been endowed. This upholding of oneness is a means for the church to mature.

The source of the church's unity is the Triune God, who eternally exists as three persons in perfect unity. This eternal trinitarian unity is not uniformity but unity in diversity. The three are distinct persons, but not three different gods. There is only one God, and the three distinct persons are perfectly united in oneness.

Though the church can never experience the same kind of oneness as the Father, Son, and Holy Spirit, its members are united by means of the Spirit and thus form one body. Following the pattern of trinitarian unity, the church is called to embrace unity in diversity. The church does not demand that every member be the same, thus denying their individuality and uniqueness of personality, gifting, and calling.

Endowed with the gift of unity, the church does not have to create this reality. Rather, it must work hard to maintain this conferred oneness. It does so by focusing on its many commonalities, expressing the requisite attributes like humility and gentleness, being eager to preserve this gift, and more. In seeking to maintain its unity, the church is helped by the Spirit of unity.

Biblical Support

Scripture underscores both the purity and unity of the church in three ways: (1) Positionally, the church is already holy (1 Cor. 1:1–2) and united (Eph. 4:3). (2) Purposively, both are essential aims for the church as it matures, with the church urged to be "holy and without blemish" (5:27) and to "attain to the unity of the faith" (4:13). (3) Instrumentally, both are essential processes fostering the growth of the church, which is exhorted to "strive for peace with everyone [unity], and for the holiness without which no one will see the Lord" (Heb. 12:14). Biblical support for the church's purity will be presented first, followed by support for the church's unity.

We begin with biblical support for the church's purity. Remarkably, the members of the Corinthian church are described as "those sanctified in Christ Jesus, called to be saints" (1 Cor. 1:2). This positional idea of purity is God's work of setting the church apart for his purposes such that even the worldly Corinthian church was holy.

Moreover, the holiness of the church is the purpose for which Christ sacrificed himself: "Christ loved the church and gave himself up for her, that he might sanctify her, . . . that she might be holy and without blemish" (Eph. 5:25–27). The image of a beautiful and chaste bride adorned for her husband is the biblical vision for the church's perfect future purity (2 Cor. 11:2–3). The actualization of this vision becomes the church's aim.

In the instrumental sense of purity, the church separates itself from whatever is not pure, cleansing itself "from every defilement of body and spirit, bringing holiness to completion in the fear of God" (2 Cor. 6:14–7:1). As it aims at perfect purity, the church, which is already positionally pure, purifies itself and pursues greater purity.

Biblical support for the church's unity is next. The template for the church's unity is the unity of the Triune God, expressed in Jesus's prayer to the Father, "Keep them [Christ's disciples] in your name, . . . that they may be one, even as we are one" (John 17:11; see also 17:21, 22). Such unity specifically encompasses a never-before-seen oneness between Jews and Gentiles, reflected in Jesus's mission to unite the two: "So there will be one flock, one shepherd" (10:16). This mission is being accomplished: "In him [Christ] you also [Jews and Gentiles] are being built together into a dwelling place for God by the Spirit" (Eph. 2:18–22).

Indeed, it is the Holy Spirit who grants unity to the church, which is then called not to create unity but to be "eager to maintain the unity of the Spirit in the bond of peace" (Eph. 4:3). Positionally, therefore, the church is united. Purposively, the church's aim is to "attain to the unity of the faith" (4:13). Instrumentally, the church must "strive for peace with everyone" (Heb. 12:14). Practically speaking, the church encourages its members to "live in harmony with one another" (Rom. 12:16), "being of the same mind, having the same love, being in full accord and of one mind" (Phil. 2:2). Factions that develop because of quarrels over spiritual leaders (1 Cor. 1:10–17), socioeconomic differences (11:17–34), disagreements among members (Phil. 4:2–3), and critical judgment due to differences in personal preferences (Rom. 14) are not allowed in the church.

Paul surrounds the Spirit's gift of oneness with seven commonalities that further unite the church: "There is one body and one Spirit—just as you were called to the one hope that belongs to your call—one Lord, one faith, one baptism, one God and Father of all, who is over all and through all and in all" (Eph. 4:4–6). Because all Christians share these seven commonalities, the unity of the church is fostered. Still other factors unify the church or express its unity: one loaf of bread shared during the Lord's Supper (1 Cor. 10:17), "one voice" directed to the glory of God in worship (Rom. 15:6), a common confession of faith (for example, 1 Tim. 3:16), unity-fostering attitudes of humility, gentleness, patience, and bearing with one another in love (Eph. 4:2), and eagerness and hard work to maintain unity (4:3).

Major Errors

1. *Exclusivistic claims by certain groups that they are the only pure church.* Historically, there has been a steady stream of such fringe movements, which often denounce established churches as being unbiblical, compromised, worldly institutions. Such groups fail to consider the pervasiveness of sin within their own midst.

2. *Attempts at formal church (re)union that amount to little more than agreement on some lowest common denominators.* In such cases, truth is often sacrificed for the sake of unity. While the recognition of commonalities is important, covering over divergences is unhelpful and will fail to achieve a lasting unity.

ENACTING THE DOCTRINE

It is easy to criticize the church for its hypocrisy and divisiveness. It is far more difficult to champion its purity by preaching, discipling, disciplining, praying, and working hard to maintain its unity. However, armed with a vision for greater purity and conserved unity, and aided by the Spirit, we can join with the Triune God in moving our church toward being more conformed to his will and joyfully united even as he—Father, Son, and Spirit—is.

TEACHING THE DOCTRINE

Because the purity and unity of the church often remain theoretical discussions, the teaching should be oriented to concrete applications of these two attributes. After presenting them and providing their biblical basis, direct the participants to assess how the church is progressing in terms of its purity and unity. Questions to propose include the following: As a church, are we more or less pure? Are we more free from error, and more fully conformed to God's will, or are we less free from error, and less conformed to God's will, in regard to our worship, preaching and teaching the Word of God, celebration of baptism and the Lord's Supper, prayer, community life, discipleship, leadership training, pastoral care, missional engagement, mercy, . . . (the list should be adapted to the church's specific situation)?

Perennial Questions and Problematic Issues

- Why are there so many hypocrites in the church?
- The church claims to be holy, but it is far from being so.
- Don't the many denominations and different theologies belie the church's claim to unity?
- In what areas is our church more pure, in which is it less pure, and what can I do about it?

After the frank assessment, lead the participants in giving thanks to God for the church's more pure aspects. Additionally, encourage them to identify one (or, at the most, two) less pure aspect(s) for which they feel particularly burdened. Challenge them to pray about how they may get involved in bringing greater purity in this area, and urge them to talk to the appropriate leaders about how to get involved.

As for the unity of the church, an initial application is to measure the participants' level of concern for this attribute. Today, leaving a church has become so commonplace that members do not even recognize such departure as breaking the church's unity. Until participants grasp the seriousness with which Scripture treats this matter, their application will remain vague.

Ask participants what can be done to stem the tide of people leaving the church and thus disturbing its unity. When someone leaves, does anyone in the church reach out to ascertain the reason for leaving and then seek to rectify the problem? A pursuing love, not stalking or arm-twisting, that does not let people go easily communicates that the church as a family is not like many human families that split apart far too commonly and easily.

TEACHING OUTLINE

1. The summary
2. Questions to assess the purity and unity of the church
3. Major affirmations (with biblical support)
   A. Purity and unity in positional, purposive, and instrumental senses
   B. The purity of the church
   C. The unity of the church
4. Major errors to avoid
   A. Exclusivistically claiming that one's church is the only true, pure church
   B. Attempting formal church (re)union that amounts to little more than agreement on some lowest common denominators
5. Enacting the doctrine
   A. Halting the common tendency to criticize the church
   B. Championing the church's purity and working hard to maintain its unity

RESOURCES

Allison, *Theological Terms*, s.vv. "holiness of the church," "unity"
Grudem, *Systematic Theology*, chap. 45
Horton, *Pilgrim Theology*, chap. 17

37

CHURCH DISCIPLINE

SUMMARY

Church discipline is the process of rebuking and correcting sinful members for the purpose of restoring them.

MAIN THEMES

- Church discipline is an anticipation of the future judgment that awaits sinful members if they persist in their sin.
- It is a process of rebuking and correcting them, with an escalating level of intervention and severity.
- It consists of four steps.
- Its goal is always restoration, but it also serves to rid the church of sinful examples and to protect the honor of Christ and the church.
- If the process persists, the last stage is excommunication.
- The church is to exercise discipline in various cases.

KEY SCRIPTURE

Matthew 18:15–20; Romans 16:17–18; 1 Corinthians 5; 2 Corinthians 2:6–11; Galatians 6:1; 1 Timothy 1:3–4; 5:19–21; Titus 1:9–14; 3:10–11; 1 John 2:18–19; 2 John 9–11

UNDERSTANDING THE DOCTRINE

Major Affirmations

Church discipline is a means that Christ gives to his church to promote its purity and to limit the havoc caused by persistent sin. The church exercises it in anticipation of the future judgment of Christ. At that eschatological event, Christ will mete out judgment against sinful people. So that its members will not face a bad sentence, the church engages in discipline to rebuke and correct its members who persist in sin.

Accordingly, church discipline is an anticipatory sign: the church forecasts the anticipated future divine judgment, and its discipline reflects the seriousness of that foreboding sentence. And church discipline is a declarative sign: the church believes its action reflects the divine judgment to come, but it recognizes that it does not render an infallible pronouncement. That definitive announcement belongs to Christ alone. In anticipation of that verdict, the church declares discipline against its persistently sinful members.

Church discipline is a process of rebuke and correction. It consists of four steps, with an escalating level of intervention and severity. The first stage is a personal confrontation. A Christian who has been sinned against by another Christian has a one-on-one conversation with the offender. If the offender acknowledges his sin, the matter is settled. The two are reconciled, and the process ends. If there is no admission of sin, the process escalates.

The second stage involves the offended person and one or two others, who rebuke the Christian who has sinned. The purpose of the other witness(es) is to ensure that the one who stands accused is properly confronted. If the offender confesses his sin, the matter is settled. The two are reconciled, and the process ends. If there is no acknowledgment of sin, the witness(es) confirms this refusal. The process escalates in severity.

The third stage involves the whole church. By an announcement of the entrenched problem, the church is made aware of the initial sin that provoked the situation and the failure of the first two steps to produce the desired repentance. Now the members admonish the sinful member, calling for confession and reconciliation. If the offender confesses his sin, the matter is settled. The two are reconciled, and the process ends. If the offender refuses to listen to the church's admonition, the process escalates to its most severe level.

The fourth stage again involves the entire church, which enacts excommunication. This action entails removal from church membership and ministry, exclusion from the Lord's Supper, and rupture of relationship with the church and with God.

The goal of this disciplinary process is always restoration. The church hopes and prays for confession of sin, which leads to reinstatement of the excommunicated person. Indeed, when that person repents, the church's responsibility is to warmly welcome him back into the community. Wisdom and prudence urge that the church provide specific measures to help the reinstated member make progress in holiness, as well as to guard against a relapse. A return to ministry must be carefully assessed as to if and when.

Two other purposes are served: Excommunication aids the church by ridding it of sinful examples that tend to prompt more sin. Removal of the persistently sinful member has a prophylactic effect, preventing the spread of sin. Additionally, excommunication protects the honor of Christ and the church. This drastic step underscores that Christ is holy and does not tolerate persistent, unconfessed sin (though he will forgive it when it is confessed). And it shows that Christ's body, being holy like him, does not put up with such stubborn sinning (though its members remain sinful).

The scenario just rehearsed is the common one in which one Christian sins against another. Other matters that require church discipline include (1) egregious/public moral failure, like blatant sexual immorality; (2) heretical teaching, so as to stop the dissemination of false doctrine; (3) divisiveness, which if uncontained will disrupt the church's unity; (4) idleness, a refusal to work though able to do so; (5) leadership failures, which exert a widespread influence on church members; and (6) other persistent, unconfessed, and public sins that can do irreparable damage to Christians and the church.

The church follows several rules of engagement as it exercises discipline. It determines the sins for which it exercises discipline by giving heed to Scripture. Scripture's sufficiency means that the evil attitudes and actions prohibited by Scripture, and those only, are sin. The church may not add to this list, inventing "sins" for which it exercises discipline. Rather, it disciplines only those sins proscribed by Scripture. Moreover, Spirit-filled Christians are to gently lead the process, watching carefully so they themselves don't fall into sin.

Biblical Support

Church discipline is one use of "the keys of the kingdom," according to which "whatever you [in the original context, Peter in conjunction with the apostles; and now, by extension, the church] bind on earth shall be bound in heaven, and whatever you loose on earth shall be loosed in heaven" (Matt. 16:19). Such binding and loosing is specifically applied to the process of church discipline (18:18). Jesus's statements relate church discipline to his eschatological judgment seat. It is the church's declaration that is intended to reflect Christ's own judicial sentence. For the persistently sinning member, the church's excommunication declares she is bound in her sin. For the repentant member, the church's restoration to membership declares she is loosed from her sin. Church discipline is carried out in the present while done in relation to the future divine judgment.

Jesus lays out the four-stage process in Matthew 18:15–20. As its last step, the church excommunicates the persistently sinful member who throughout the process has refused to listen to admonition—individual, small group, and church-wide. Excommunication involves considering him "as a Gentile and a tax collector"—that is, as an outsider to the community of faith. Jesus provides encouragement to the church engaged in disciplinary action: He promises to answer its prayers, which, in context, are those related to church discipline (for example, wisdom, discernment, unity, and stamina). And Jesus promises his special presence, which, in context, is particularly needed as the church carries out this time-, labor-, and energy-intensive responsibility.

Some sins are so egregious and public that the church must act immediately to excommunicate. Paul addresses this situation in the case of a Corinthian man who was engaged in sexual immorality with his father's wife (1 Cor. 5:1–7). Beyond doing nothing to halt this sin, the Corinthian church boasted in its tolerant attitude. Paul called for immediate excommunication: the man is to be removed from the church.

Paul presents a judicial atmosphere by means of a courtroom scene: Possessing apostolic authority, he has already rendered judgment in this case.

He promises to be present as the Corinthians are assembled in the name of Jesus and with the power of Jesus. It is a very serious matter the church is to undertake. They are to "deliver this man to Satan for the destruction of the flesh" (1 Cor. 5:5). The church's action of removing him from the community—the realm of grace, comfort, and protection—would expose him to satanic onslaught, temptation, and torment. Such misery would hopefully provoke this man to cease and desist from sexual immorality, the product of his "flesh," or sinful nature.

This excommunication also had a salvific purpose, related again to the future judgment: "so that his spirit may be saved in the day of the Lord" (1 Cor. 5:5). By the drastic action of excommunication, the church would expose the man to satanic attack, he would repent and stop sinning, and he would be saved from the coming divine judgment. Another benefit of such strong discipline is that it protects the church from the spread of sin. In accordance with the aphorism "a little leaven leavens the whole lump" (v. 6), removal of the persistently sinning member acts as a prophylactic, protecting the church from ever-expanding sin.

The church did what Paul asked: the majority of members enacted the punishment. The man was excommunicated. Moreover, the disciplinary action worked as hoped: experiencing intense sorrow for sin, the man repented. Accordingly, Paul called for the church to forgive the man and lovingly welcome him back into the community (2 Cor. 2:6–11).[28]

Church discipline is also demanded for other matters: people who spread heretical teaching (1 Tim. 1:3–4; Titus 1:9–14; 2 John 9–11), provoke divisions (Rom. 16:17–18; Titus 3:10–11; 1 John 2:18–19), and refuse to work though able to do so (2 Thess. 3:6, 11–12) are to be disciplined. Because of their influential and public roles, leaders who sin are in a special category (1 Tim. 5:19–21). Certainly, the church should be attentive to other situations of persistent, unconfessed, and public sins, and exercise discipline.

Finally, mature Christians who are walking in the Spirit are to undertake the process of discipline. They seek to restore the persistently sinful members with gentleness, while taking care that they are not seduced by the sin with which they are dealing in the others (Gal. 6:1).

Major Errors

1. *The neglect of, or refusal to engage in, church discipline.* Paul's rebuke of the lackadaisical attitude of the Corinthian church toward the incestuous

man stands as a reprimand to churches that have abandoned or dismissed this practice.

2. *Any exercise of discipline against church members that violates biblical instruction.* These cases include accusing members of "sin" that Scripture does not consider to be sin, engaging in the process with a spirit of harshness or vindictiveness rather than one of gentleness, and disciplining for the purpose of vengeance rather than repentance and restoration.

ENACTING THE DOCTRINE

While a very sobering matter, church discipline is a divinely sanctioned means for advancing the purity of the church and protecting it from the spread of sin. No church that wants to be all that Christ intends for it to be can neglect or dismiss this means.

Church discipline goes beyond the drastic help that it provides for persistently sinful members to escape from their entrenched sinfulness. It goes beyond the benefit it offers for members by removing a source of sin so as to prevent sin from spreading. Church discipline protects the honor of Christ himself. How would the church be viewed if charges that it is full of hypocrites would fail because of its high degree of holiness and its intolerance of sin? Moreover, what level of respect would the church enjoy if it could not be associated with dreadful sin? At the same time, Christ and his church would be known for the gospel of a salvation that provides not only the forgiveness of sin but the power to live a life of joyful freedom from sin.

TEACHING THE DOCTRINE

If the church regularly and properly exercises discipline, participants will already be familiar with the process. If this is not the case, a measured

Perennial Questions and Problematic Issues

- Because all of us are sinful, it doesn't seem right for the church to exercise discipline against any particular member.
- I've heard of so many abuses of church discipline that I don't want our church to do it.
- What should I do if I see an excommunicated member at the grocery store or at a sporting event?
- When one of our pastors suddenly disappeared from church, was that because of church discipline, and why weren't we members informed?
- Does our church believe that elders who have committed sexual immorality or embezzled money can be restored to ministry?

illustration of how the church has in the past exercised discipline will serve to render the teaching concrete.

In the case of a church plant, teaching about discipline fairly early on in its existence will prepare it well for the inevitable reality to come. In the case of an established church, teaching will either confirm that its exercise of discipline is in accordance with Scripture or expose its errors and hopefully lead to correction.

Importantly, the teaching cannot remain on a theoretical level. The last two stages of the process outlined by Jesus (Matt. 18:15–20) include the participation of the church. Thus, members must understand the nature, process, purposes, and atmosphere of church discipline and their specific responsibilities in it. They should be encouraged to submit to church discipline if they persist in sin, knowing that it will be an expression of the church's pursuing love for their ultimate benefit.

TEACHING OUTLINE

1. The summary
2. An illustration of church discipline
3. Major affirmations (with biblical support)
   A. The relationship of church discipline to Christ's future judgment
   B. The four-stage process
   C. The purposes and rules of engagement for church discipline
   D. Excommunication
   E. Sinful situations that call for church discipline
4. Major errors to avoid
   A. Neglecting or refusing to engage in church discipline
   B. Exercising discipline against church members that violates biblical instruction
5. Enacting the doctrine
   A. Advancing the purity of the church and protecting it from the spread of sin through church discipline
   B. Protecting the honor of Christ and the proper respect for the church through church discipline

RESOURCES

Allison, *Theological Terms*, s.vv. "church discipline," "excommunication"
Elwell, *Evangelical Dictionary of Theology*, s.v. "Church Discipline"
Grudem, *Systematic Theology*, chap. 46
Horton, *Pilgrim Theology*, 408–10

38

CHURCH OFFICES

SUMMARY

Church offices are the authoritative structures for the church's leadership and service: apostleship, bishopric, eldership, and diaconate.

MAIN THEMES

- Offices are church structures, and officers are the leaders who serve in those offices, taking on various responsibilities and being endowed with the authority that is fitting for those duties.
- Apostleship is the authoritative office exercised by the original apostles.
- Bishopric is the authoritative office exercised by bishops.
- Eldership is the authoritative office exercised by elders.
- Diaconate is the office of service.
- The church publicly recognizes these officers for the leadership and ministerial roles in which they engage.

KEY SCRIPTURE

Mark 3:13–15; Acts 1:12–26; 6:1–6; 14:23; Romans 16:1–2; 1 Corinthians 16:15–16; 1 Thessalonians 5:12–13; 1 Timothy 3:1–13; 5:17; Titus 1:5–9; Hebrews 13:17; James 5:13–15; 1 Peter 5:1–5

UNDERSTANDING THE DOCTRINE

Major Affirmations

Church offices are the authoritative structures for the church's leadership and service. Corresponding to these offices are the officers, or leaders, who serve in them, taking on various responsibilities (for example, preaching, administering the sacraments). With the offices comes the authority that is both fitting and necessary for the exercise of those duties.

Most churches have at least two of these offices in some combination, but at some point in its history all four offices have operated in the church. They are apostleship, bishopric, eldership, and diaconate.

Apostleship is the authoritative office exercised by the *apostles* and designed to provide the church's foundation. Foremost were the original apostles—"the Twelve"—whom Jesus called to follow him. They were Spirit-empowered eyewitnesses of his life, death, and resurrection. Other apostles were Paul, Barnabas, and James the Lord's brother. The apostles were the first to preach the gospel, and they led the church in Jerusalem, from which they established churches in other places. They performed signs and wonders, which confirmed their message. They established authoritative doctrine and practice for the church. Some wrote Scripture.

Bishopric is the authoritative office of oversight exercised by *bishops*. Possessing the ultimate authority in the church, they consecrate other bishops and ordain priests/elders and deacons. Their other responsibilities include teaching (preaching and catechizing), ruling (exercising ultimate oversight), and sanctifying (administering the sacraments).

Eldership (or *pastorate*, *presbyterate*, or *priesthood*) is the authoritative office exercised by *elders* (or *pastors* or *priests*) who have four responsibilities: They teach, or communicate sound doctrine. They lead, or provide overall direction. They pray, especially for the sick. And they shepherd, or guide, nourish, and protect the church.

Diaconate is the office exercised by those who serve in various ministries. This term (from the Greek *diakonia*, "service;" *diakonos*, "servant") and its derivatives are used generically to refer to anyone who engages in service, and are used technically for a person who is a publicly recognized officer serving in a church. The diaconate, as the office of service, is to be distinguished from the bishopric and/or the eldership, the office(s) of leadership.

As these leaders and servants meet the qualifications for their offices and engage in their responsibilities, the church publicly recognizes them for the leadership and ministerial roles in which they engage.

Biblical Support

Scripture urges the church to obey its leaders (Heb. 13:17; 1 Thess. 5:12–13; 1 Cor. 16:15–16). These general instructions presuppose the authority of certain people to whom the church's members are to submit. In his letter to "all the saints" in Philippi, Paul added "with the overseers [*episkopoi*] and deacons [*diakonoi*]" (Phil. 1:1). Thus, the bishopric and diaconate were early church offices.

Even as Jesus was establishing the foundation for his church, he chose twelve men (Mark 3:13–15), called the "apostles of Jesus Christ" or simply "the twelve" (Matt. 26:20; Mark 4:10; Luke 18:31; John 6:67, 71). Following the demise of Judas Iscariot (Matt. 26:14–25, 47–56; 27:3–10; Acts 1:18–19), Matthias was chosen, "and he was numbered with the eleven apostles" (Acts 1:26). The names of these twelve men are written on the foundation of the New Jerusalem (Rev. 21:14).

These disciples met the two qualifications for apostleship: (1) called by Jesus, they were with him from the beginning of his ministry; and (2) they were eyewitnesses of at least one of his postresurrection appearances (Acts 1:21–22). In addition to the twelve, a few other disciples were called apostles: Paul (9:1–9; 26:12–18), Barnabas (14:14; 1 Cor. 9:6; Gal. 2:9), and James the Lord's brother (Gal. 1:19; 2:9).

As for their apostolic ministry, they were the first messengers of the gospel (Acts 2:14–41; 3:11–26). They established the church in Jerusalem, providing authoritative teaching (2:42–47). They planted churches in other places (13:1–4; 16:11–40). They performed signs and wonders, which confirmed their message (Heb. 2:1–4; 2 Cor. 12:12). They set down sound doctrine and practice for the churches (1 Cor. 7:17–24; 14:29–35; 1 Thess. 4:1–8). Some—Matthew, John, Paul, James, and Peter—wrote Scripture.

Whereas the church has historically considered apostleship to have ceased as an office, some churches consider the gift of apostleship to continue today.

In Scripture, the words for *bishop/overseer* (*episkopos*), *elder/priest* (*presbyteros*), and *pastor* (*poimēn*) are interchangeable: they refer to one and the same leader. For example, Paul charges the *elders* (*presbyteroi*) of the church of Ephesus to *shepherd* (a derivative of *poimēn*) the flock in which the Spirit established them as *overseers* (*episkopoi*). Also, Paul addresses the qualifications for *bishop/overseer* (*episkopos*; 1 Tim. 3:1, 2) and later calls these officers *elders* (*presbyteroi*; 1 Tim. 5:17; cf. Titus 1:5, 7). Moreover, Peter exhorts the *elders* (*presbyteroi*) to *shepherd* (a derivative of *poimēn*; 1 Pet. 5:1–2) the church.

Thus, the office held by these leaders may be called *bishopric, eldership, presbyterate, priesthood,* or *pastorate*. It has four responsibilities: First, elders engage in teaching, which is the communication of sound doctrine and the Christlike practice that flows from it. Specifically, all elders must be able to teach (1 Tim. 3:2) and refute those who contradict sound doctrine (Titus 1:9). Some elders dedicate much of their effort to "preaching and teaching" (1 Tim. 5:17).

Second, bishops are responsible for leading, as they "care for God's church" (1 Tim. 3:5). Together, the elders lead (5:17), and the members are to submit to them (Heb. 13:17) and respect their leadership (1 Thess. 5:12).

Third, priests are to pray. Whereas prayer is the duty of all Christians, elders bear a special responsibility for prayer, especially for the sick (James 5:13–15).

Fourth, pastors engage in "shepherding the flock of God" (1 Pet. 5:2). This "pastoral" duty (a word related to "shepherding") entails teaching (as "shepherds [pastors] and teachers"; Eph. 4:11), exercising oversight (1 Pet. 5:2), and exemplifying Christlikeness (5:3).

The qualifications for elders are listed in 1 Timothy 3:1–7, Titus 1:5–9, and 1 Peter 5:1–5. They include a *call* from God (aspiring to the office; 1 Tim. 3:1), having an upright *character* (for example, sober-mindedness and self-control), exercising well-developed *competencies* (leading, teaching, and hospitality), and enjoying good *chemistry* with the other elders (that is, working in unity with them).

Scripture always presents a church being led by a plurality of elders ("council of elders"; 1 Tim. 4:14), never a solo leader. For example, at the end of their missionary journey, Paul and Barnabas appointed elders (plural) in each of the newly planted churches (Acts 14:23). Other examples of a plurality of elders include the churches of Jerusalem (Acts 15:2, 4, 6, 22, 23), Antioch (11:30), Ephesus (20:17, 28; 1 Tim. 5:17), Crete (Titus 1:5), and "the Dispersion" (James 1:1; 5:14).

The diaconate is the office of service, the qualifications for which are listed in 1 Timothy 3:8–13. This passage presents characteristics and qualifications for all servants (vv. 8–10), women (either deaconesses or the wives of deacons; v. 11), and male deacons (v. 12; the standards for women in the home are already covered in 2:15). It concludes with a commendation for all servants (3:13).

Some of these qualifications are similar to those for elders (for example, being dignified and not double tongued), while others are different (for example, the abilities to teach and to take care of [lead] the church are listed only for elders). Two examples of deacons are the table waiters in the Jerusalem church (Acts 6:1–6) and the patron Phoebe of the church of Cenchreae (Rom. 16:1–2).

It is important that the church publicly recognize the people holding these offices. The New Testament presents this public acknowledgment as the laying on of hands (for elders, 1 Tim. 5:22; for deacons, Acts 6:6).

Early on, the church made a distinction between a bishop and an elder, elevating the bishopric above the eldership/priesthood. This topic will be treated in the next chapter, "Church Government."

Major Errors

Church offices are one area in which it is hard to identify major errors, so the following two have more to do with abusive developments with the offices.

1. *The contemporary elevation of apostleship to the same level that the office had at the time of the original apostles.* Any church claiming that its highest leader is an apostle with absolute authority and without accountability to anyone else fails to understand the uniqueness of the original office and runs a great risk of abusing its members.

2. *Failure to follow biblical instructions about the qualifications and responsibilities of church officers.* Such failure runs the gamut from blatant disobedience to these directives to illegitimately restricting qualified and capable people from holding the offices.

ENACTING THE DOCTRINE

The application of the biblical qualifications and responsibilities for these offices is very important if churches desire to mature and multiply. Those who have intentionally disregarded or ignorantly overlooked these biblical directives should repent. Such repentance is needed if churches have selected their officers on the basis of characteristics—for example, popularity, money, business acumen—other than those presented in Scripture. Repentance is also called for if church officers have failed to carry out their biblically mandated responsibilities (for example, failure to pray for the sick) or carried them out in improper ways (for example, in a disgruntled, domineering manner).

Churches should also make sure that their officers have the authority to exercise properly their responsibilities. On the one hand, protection against the exercise of overbearing authority carried out in unbiblical ways is needed. On the other hand, protection against usurping the officers' legitimate authority is also needed.

To ensure that they have qualified people to lead and serve, churches should engage in intentional discipleship and mentoring of their members who manifest the biblical qualifications and demonstrate the biblical competencies for church offices. For example, churches should have structures in place for elders-in-training and deacons-in-training, always developing new leaders and servants to meet their growing need for greater maturity and expanding multiplication.

> ### Perennial Questions and Problematic Issues
>
> - I don't even know who the officers of our church are.
> - I don't think some of our officers meet the qualifications for their office.
> - What do our bishops do?
> - What do our pastors/elders/priests do?
> - What do our deacons and deaconesses do?
> - If Scripture presents churches as having a plurality of pastors, why does our church have only one?
> - If I'm interested in becoming a church officer, what do I need to do?

TEACHING THE DOCTRINE

In teaching this doctrine, reference should be made to actual officers who minister in the church's offices. So, depending on which offices exist, be ready to present the bishops, pastors, elders, priests, deacons, and deaconesses.

Better still, invite those leaders and servants to participate in the discussion. If the church has other leaders—for example, staff (who are not officers), directors, trustees, and ministry heads—be prepared to explain how they fit into the discussion.

Participants may be interested in the debate about the continuation or cessation of apostleship, but don't let that topic dominate the time. Another ongoing disagreement exists between complementarians, who restrict the office of bishop/elder/pastor/priest to qualified men and exclude women from it, and egalitarians, who permit both qualified men and women to hold it. Be aware that this debate can become very heated, and don't allow it to take over the discussion. A milder debate is whether the diaconate consists of only (male) deacons, or if deaconesses may hold that office.

When the qualifications for the different offices are being rehearsed, several are more difficult to address: (1) Does the requirement "the husband of one wife" (1 Tim. 3:2, 12; Titus 1:6) exclude a single man and disqualify a divorced man? (2) Does the qualification regarding the management of one's household and children (1 Tim. 3:5, 12; Titus 1:6) disqualify a man if his children are rebellious or unbelievers? (3) Do these qualifications mean that a person who regularly committed sexual immorality and got drunk before becoming a Christian is disqualified from church office?

TEACHING OUTLINE

1. The summary of church offices
2. Interaction with the leaders and servants functioning in these church offices
3. Major affirmations (with biblical support)
   A. The church's need for leaders and servants
   B. Apostleship and its qualifications and responsibilities
   C. Bishopric/eldership and its qualifications and responsibilities
   D. Diaconate and its qualifications and responsibilities
   E. Public recognition of church officers
4. Major errors to avoid
   A. Elevating apostleship to the same level that the office had at the time of the original apostles

B. Failing to follow biblical instructions about the qualifications and responsibilities of church officers

5. Enacting the doctrine

A. Repenting for intentionally disregarding or ignorantly overlooking the biblical directives for church offices

B. Ensuring that the officers have the authority needed to carry out their responsibilities

C. Raising up the next generation of church officers

RESOURCES

Allison, *Theological Terms*, s.vv. "apostle," "bishop," "deacon/deaconess/diaconate," "elder"

Elwell, *Evangelical Dictionary of Theology*, s.vv. "Apostle, Apostleship," "Bishop," "Church Officers," "Elder"

Erickson, *Christian Theology*, chap. 51

Grenz, *Theology for the Community of God*, chap. 20

Grudem, *Systematic Theology*, chap. 47

Horton, *Pilgrim Theology*, chap. 17

Thoennes, *Life's Biggest Questions*, chap. 15

39

CHURCH GOVERNMENT

SUMMARY

Church government is the way authority is structured in and among the offices (and possibly the congregation) of the church.

MAIN THEMES

- Government, or a structured authority, of some sort is necessary for the church.
- The head of the church is Jesus Christ.
- Historically, there are three forms of church government: episcopalianism, presbyterianism, and congregationalism.
- Several new forms of church government have been developed recently.

KEY SCRIPTURE

Matthew 16:13–20; Acts 15; 1 Corinthians 14:33, 40; Ephesians 1:19–23; 2:20; 1 Timothy 5:17

UNDERSTANDING THE DOCTRINE

Major Affirmations

Church government is the way authority is structured in and among the offices (and, in some cases, the congregation) of the church. As presented in the preceding chapter, "Church Offices," these offices are apostleship, an office that most churches consider to have ceased with the death of the apostles (and thus won't be discussed in this chapter); the episcopate, or office of bishop; the pastorate or eldership, or office of pastor or elder; and the diaconate, or office of deacon and deaconess. Though not an office, the congregation, consisting of the members of the church, plays a role in a certain form of church government.

Some sort of government or structured authority is necessary for the church. A key reason is that in saving human beings, God incorporates them as his people into the church. Reflecting the nature of the one who called it into existence, the church is an ordered community. Furthermore, God the Father, in exalting his Son, appointed him as the Lord of the church; thus, it is ruled by divine authority. Moreover, Scripture presents the church as being led by authoritative structures, and gives instructions about these offices. Accordingly, government is necessary for the church.

The head of the church is Jesus Christ. His lordship means that he is sovereign over the church, which is to submit to him in all things. Knowledge of and obedience to his will are the ultimate concern of the church's human leaders. Though he ordains that his church is governed by these human authorities, Christ never yields his ruling office to them. Still, Christ's headship does not eliminate human leadership in the church, and it is this authoritative responsibility that is the subject at hand. Historically, there are three forms of church government.

Episcopalianism is government in which ultimate authority resides in the bishop (Gk. *episkopos*). In this three-tiered governing structure, bishops are distinguished from presbyters (priests, elders) and deacons. As the first order of clergy, bishops exercise ultimate authority. This includes the act of maintaining the three offices by consecrating other bishops and ordaining priests/elders and deacons. As the second order of clergy, priests/elders are ordained ministers of local churches. Deacons, the third order, are ordained servants who help the bishops and priests. Some examples of episcopalian church government are the Roman Catholic Church, the Episcopal Church, and the United Methodist Church.

Presbyterianism is government by elders as representatives of the church. These elders (Gk. *presbyteroi*) govern in ranked authoritative structures and are of two types: Teaching elders are ordained, often seminary-trained clergy who are responsible for preaching the Word of God, administering the sacraments, and leading. Ruling elders, as (usually) nonordained laypeople, are responsible for leading with the teaching elder.

Presbyterianism has ranked authoritative structures: In a local church (for example, Calvin Presbyterian Church or Grace Reformed Church), the elders form a session or consistory. The elders in a geographical area form a presbytery or classis (for example, the presbytery of Philadelphia). The members of a presbytery or classis in a region form a synod (for example, the Synod of the Northeast). At the national level is a general assembly (for example, the General Assembly of the PCUSA). Examples of presbyterian churches are the Christian Reformed Church, the Presbyterian Church of America, and the Evangelical Presbyterian Church.

Congregationalism is government by the local congregation, in whose members ultimate authority resides. Each church is an autonomous entity, with no person (for example, a bishop, as in episcopalianism) or structure (for example, a presbytery or synod, as in presbyterianism) above it. Christ himself is its sole head.

Congregationalism is based on two principles: The first is autonomy, meaning that each church is independent and self-governing. It is responsible for its own leadership, finances, buildings, and ministries. The second is democracy, meaning that authority resides in its members, who together participate in congregational decisions through some process of affirmation or denial. Examples of congregational church government are Baptist churches, Evangelical Free churches, and Bible churches.

Recently, several new forms of church government have developed. Borrowing from leadership structures of businesses, some churches retooled their pastors' role along the lines of a chief operating officer of a company. Megachurches developed boards of directors mirroring corporate models of governance. Multisite churches developed governments with episcopalian, presbyterian, and congregational structures.

Biblical Support

Biblical support for the necessity of church government consists of several points. A key point is that the church, which has been called into existence by God, reflects the divine nature. Specifically, the church is an ordered community, not an unruly mob, "for God is not a God of confusion but of peace" (1 Cor. 14:33). Accordingly, Paul insists that "all things should be done decently and in order" (14:40; cf. Col. 2:5). Church government aids in sustaining this arranged community.

Other points regard the headship of Jesus Christ and divine revelation. By virtue of his ascension and exaltation, the Son was given as head of all creation to the church. The church is his (Matt. 16:18). Metaphorically, he is its cornerstone (Eph. 2:20) and foundation (1 Cor. 3:11), its Chief Shepherd (1 Pet. 5:4). Clearly, the church is to submit to his divine authority. As Lord of the church, Christ gave directives through the Holy Spirit and the apostles to the church for how it is to be governed. This divine revelation presents these leaders as undershepherds (5:1–5), elders or bishops/overseers (1 Tim. 3:1–7; Titus 1:5–9), and gifted equippers of the church's members (Eph. 4:11–16).

Thus, church government of some kind is necessary for the church.

But what kind of government is the church to have? Each of the three historical positions claims biblical support, and each relies on the account of the Jerusalem Council (Acts 15) for its justification.

Episcopalianism interprets Acts 15 as highlighting the bishop-like role of James at the Jerusalem Council. His foremost responsibility is confirmed as James is presented as the head of the church of Jerusalem (Acts 21:18). Additional support includes the authoritative role of Timothy (1 Tim. 1:3; 3:14–15; 2 Tim. 2:2) and Titus (Titus 1:5), emissaries of the apostle Paul to local churches with the responsibility of appointing elders. Episcopalianism points also to the development of the three-tiered ministry (bishop, presbyter/elder, deacon) in the early church (for example, Ignatius's advocacy of monoepiscopacy in the second century) and its development over the first five centuries.

Presbyterianism appeals to 1 Timothy 5:17 in support of its distinction between teaching elders and ruling elders. Paul presents two groups of leaders: "the elders who rule well" and "those who labor in preaching and teaching." The first group are the ruling elders; the second, teaching elders.

Justification for church government by elders in ranked authoritative structures includes biblical passages in which the word "church" refers to a concrete entity beyond a local congregation (Acts 9:31). Moreover, it is argued that early churches did not consist of single congregations. For example, the thousands of believers in Jerusalem gathered in multiple congregations (2:46; 12:12). Elsewhere, many small congregations gathered separately in homes (Rom. 16:5; 1 Cor. 16:19; Col. 4:15; Philem. 2), yet these assemblies were still considered to be one church (of Antioch, Acts 13:1–3; of Ephesus, Acts 20:17, 28).

The presbyterian interpretation of Acts 15 centers on the congregations of several churches—those "in Antioch and Syria and Cilicia" (Acts 15:23)—deciding to call a synod at the Jerusalem church to act as an authoritative church body. These proceedings resemble a typical presbyterian synod.

Congregationalism likewise appeals to biblical support. One line of evidence consists of the responsibilities assigned to the congregation. Church discipline engages the whole church (Matt. 18:15–20). An example of the majority of church members enacting such discipline is the case of the incestuous man in Corinth (1 Cor. 5; 2 Cor. 2:5–11). Additionally, the selection of the deacons (Acts 6:1–6) was delegated to its members. Even the Jerusalem Council's decision "seemed good to the apostles and the elders, with the whole church" (15:22). Without minimizing the overseeing role played by the apostles and elders, the important involvement of the whole church cannot be denied.

A second line of support for congregationalism consists of the church's role in setting apart certain people for specific responsibilities. The Jerusalem church sent Barnabas to Antioch (Acts 11:19–24). In turn, the Antioch church commissioned Barnabas and Paul for missionary service (13:1–3; 14:24–28), a commissioning that was repeated for Paul and Silas (15:36–41). The Corinthian church accredited its envoys who carried the congregation's financial help (1 Cor. 16:1–4; 2 Cor. 8:16–24).

Major Errors

1. *The papacy of the Roman Catholic Church.* All Protestant churches reject the papacy and its claim to universal authority over all churches.

2. *Domineering church governments that abuse their divinely given authority and mistreat their members.* This error extends to denominations that seek to compel their congregations to embrace false doctrines and unbiblical practices.

3. *Churches that reject all forms of church government.* Both biblically and practically, this antiauthoritarian model is wrong and unworkable.

ENACTING THE DOCTRINE

God has provided all the resources for the church to mature and multiply according to his will. Church government is one of those resources, so we can be thankful for this provision. If we are leaders in the church, we should always remind ourselves that the head of our church is Jesus Christ and not us. Thus, we should constantly seek the will of the Lord for our church and be ready to yield our own personal agendas and preferences. Additionally, one of our responsibilities is to be alert for church members whom God may be calling to become leaders.

> ### Perennial Questions and Problematic Issues
>
> • Why are there three different forms of church government?
>
> • Why is our church governed the way it is?
>
> • If God is blessing churches led in these different ways, maybe church government isn't very important.
>
> • I'm fearful of our church leadership because I distrust authority in general, so how can I grow in this area?

If we are members, we should learn how we can best support our leaders. We should always remind ourselves that they are not hired hands expected to do all the work. Rather, their primary purpose is to equip us for engaging in ministry, which we will carry out with joyful submission to their leadership. In congregational churches, we should take our responsibilities as members seriously. When our leaders present us with issues for our affirmation or denial (for example, the budget, a change in the bylaws, the purchase of property), we should voice our decision in line with the Lord's guidance of our church and its leaders.

TEACHING THE DOCTRINE

Let's be frank: the subject of church government often elicits yawns among some, while generating heated debate among others. Thus, a case must be made for teaching on this topic. Assure the first group that church government is important for the church to flourish and carry out its responsibilities. And remind the second group that churches governed according to all three forms have existed and continue to thrive today.

In teaching this doctrine, one should refer to the concrete form of government of one's church. In the case of an episcopalian-governed church, be sure to provide details like the name of the presiding bishop and initiatives that are coming from his or her office. In the case of a presbyterian-structured church, give details like the identities of the teaching elder and the ruling elders and the names of the presbytery and synod. Similarly, with congregational churches, present the names and responsibilities of the pastors/elders and deacons, and review the responsibilities of the members (for example, approving the budget, vetting new elders, and accepting new members).

Lead a discussion of the strengths and weaknesses of each of the three forms. Be alert to any misconceptions that may be voiced, and seek to clarify them. A Bible study on Acts 15, examined to see which (if any) of the three structures finds most support for itself in the narrative, prompts participants to carefully evaluate them.

TEACHING OUTLINE

1. The summary
2. Concrete discussion of the church's government
3. Major affirmations (with biblical support)
   A. The headship of Christ
   B. Episcopalianism
   C. Presbyterianism
   D. Congregationalism
4. Major errors to avoid
   A. Submitting to the papacy of the Roman Catholic Church
   B. Abusing a church's divinely given authority and mistreating its members
   C. Rejecting all forms of church government
5. Enacting the doctrine
   A. Submitting to the lordship of Jesus Christ, the head of the church
   B. Being on the alert for members whom God may be raising up to become future leaders
   C. Supporting our church's leaders

RESOURCES

Allison, *Theological Terms*, s.vv. "congregationalism," "episcopalianism," "presbyterianism"

Elwell, *Evangelical Dictionary of Theology*, s.vv. "Church, Authority in the," "Church Government"

Erickson, *Christian Theology*, chap. 51
Grenz, *Theology for the Community of God*, chap. 20
Grudem, *Systematic Theology*, chap. 47
Horton, *Pilgrim Theology*, chap. 17
Thoennes, *Life's Biggest Questions*, chap. 15

40

BAPTISM

SUMMARY

One of two sacraments or ordinances of the church, baptism is the initiatory rite or celebration of entering into the new covenant people of God.

MAIN THEMES

- The word "baptize" is a transliteration of the Greek word βαπτίζω (*baptizō*), to dip or plunge.
- Jesus ordained baptism as one of two sacraments or ordinances for his church.
- Baptism has several meanings.
- Disagreement exists among churches regarding who is to be baptized: infants or believers.
- Disagreement exists among churches regarding the proper mode of baptism: sprinkling, pouring, or immersion.

KEY SCRIPTURE

Matthew 3:1-17; 28:19; John 1:24-28; 3:23; 4:1-2; Acts 2:38, 41; 8:12, 36, 38; 9:18 (with 22:16); 10:47-48; 11:16-17; 16:15, 33; 18:8; 19:3-7; Romans 6:1-11; 1 Corinthians 1:16-17; Colossians 2:12; 1 Peter 3:20-21

UNDERSTANDING THE DOCTRINE

Major Affirmations

Baptism and the Lord's Supper are the two sacraments or ordinances that Jesus instituted for his church. In his Great Commission, Jesus commanded his disciple-making church to baptize "in the name of the Father and of the Son and of the Holy Spirit" (Matt. 28:19). The tangible element of this sacrament or ordinance is water. Obediently, churches have historically administered water baptism, viewing it as having various meanings: association with the Triune God; identification with the death, burial, and resurrection of Christ; cleansing from sin; escape from divine judgment; and an act leading to inclusion in the church.

Several fundamental differences exist among churches regarding this rite. One is the proper recipients of baptism: Should baptism be administered to infants (*paedobaptism*) or to believers (*credobaptism*)? A second issue is about mode: Should baptism be administered by *sprinkling* (dispensing a small amount of water over the head of a person), *pouring* (dispensing a large amount of water over her head), or *immersion* (lowering a person completely under water and bringing him out of the water)?

These divergences are the result of historical developments. Jesus's words to Nicodemus, "Unless one is born of water and the Spirit, he cannot enter the kingdom of God" (John 3:5), became the key support for the early church's belief in baptismal regeneration: through the water of baptism, one was born again to a new life. The church insisted that baptism is necessary for salvation.

Though the New Testament presents baptism as being administered to people who have heard the gospel and embraced salvation, this practice gradually gave way to infant baptism. Tertullian complained about what he considered novel development, objecting that innocent infants don't need baptism. Rather, they should be baptized when they become believers in Christ. Despite this protest, Origen explained the church's growing conviction: baptism cleanses from the filth of original sin, and everyone, including infants, needs the washing of baptism. Indeed, Cyprian objected to the practice of delaying infant baptism until the eighth day (note the link to the practice of circumcision), fearing for those babies who would die before being baptized. Augustine appealed approvingly to Cyprian to defend infant baptism. He reasoned that if baptism brings the forgiveness of sins, and if infants are born with the guilt and corruption of original sin, then infants should be baptized soon after they are born.

By the fifth century, infant baptism became the official church practice. It continued unhindered for about a thousand years.

The leading Reformers—Martin Luther, Huldrych Zwingli, and John Calvin—continued the traditional practice of infant baptism but developed it in different ways. Luther closely linked baptism with the Word of God and faith. Zwingli developed the analogy between circumcision in the old covenant and infant baptism in the new covenant. Biblical support for infant baptism included Jesus's welcoming of children (Luke 18:15–17) and household baptisms (Acts 16:13–15, 25–34). Like Zwingli, Calvin justified infant baptism by appealing to the parallel between the old covenant sign of circumcision and the new covenant sign of baptism. Baptism, which is a symbol of adoption of infants into the church, marks them as holy. Additionally, their parents see God's mercy being extended to their baptized children.

The Anabaptists broke from this centuries-old practice of infant baptism: only people who could consciously repent and believe in Christ should be baptized. They pointed to the biblical pattern of baptism following faith in the gospel. Furthermore, Christ commanded his church to baptize disciples, not infants. Following the Anabaptist tradition, Baptists denounced infant baptism and emphasized believer's baptism.

Despite these important differences, the church of Jesus Christ practices baptism as the initial rite or celebration of the Christian faith, a commonality that unites the church.

Biblical Support

Jesus was baptized at the outset of his ministry. The background for this practice was Jewish proselyte baptism or Jewish purification rituals, both of which involved immersion in water. Moreover, Jesus's forerunner was called John the *Baptist*, as he engaged in a ministry of baptism while calling people to repent in anticipation of the coming Messiah (Matt. 3:1–12; Mark 1:4–8; Luke 3:1–17; John 1:24–28; 3:23).

It was John who baptized Jesus, a fitting move to fulfill all righteousness: "And when Jesus was baptized, immediately he went up from the water, and behold, the heavens were opened to him, and he saw the Spirit of God descending like a dove and coming to rest on him; and behold, a voice from heaven said, 'This is my beloved Son, with whom I am well pleased'" (Matt. 3:13–17). In turn, Jesus engaged in baptizing people (John 4:1–2). After his resurrection, Jesus gave his disciples the Great Commission, with a key element being the baptism of new disciples in the name of the Triune God (Matt. 28:18–20).

The pages of Acts are peppered with stories of baptism. At the conclusion of his message on the day of Pentecost, Peter urged his listeners, "Repent and be baptized every one of you in the name of Jesus Christ for the forgiveness of your sins, and you will receive the gift of the Holy Spirit" (Acts 2:38). In obedience to his command, three thousand people repented, believed in Christ, and were baptized (v. 41). This pattern is repeated in subsequent narratives: The Samaritans "believed Philip as he preached good news about the kingdom of God and the name of Jesus Christ, [and] they were baptized, both men and women" (8:12). The Ethiopian eunuch "commanded the chariot to stop, and they both went down into the water, Philip and the eunuch, and he baptized him" (8:36, 38). Saul (9:18; 22:16), Cornelius and his family (10:47–48; 11:16–17), Lydia and her household (16:15), a jailer and his family (16:33), a large number of Corinthians (18:8), and a dozen disciples of John the Baptist (19:3–7) become baptized followers of Christ.

The significance of baptism is also presented elsewhere in the New Testament. Baptism associates people with the Triune God (Matt. 28:18–20). It vividly portrays a believer's identification with the death, burial, and resurrection of Christ (Rom. 6:1–11; cf. Col. 2:12). The act of baptism corresponds to the salvation of Noah and his family in the ark as they escaped the waters of divine judgment (1 Pet. 3:20–21). It beautifully portrays cleansing from sin (Acts 22:16). Additionally, baptism is an act of obedience, carried out publicly by a local church (there is no such thing as self-baptism) into which the newly baptized person is incorporated (Acts 2:38–47).

Major Errors

1. *Baptism is effective* ex opere operato *(literally, "by the work worked"): simply by applying water, the one being baptized is saved.* This is the common conception of the Catholic view, even among some of the Catholic faithful. In its extreme form, this view disengages baptism from the gospel, the church, faith, and the work of God. Even many Catholics would disavow this magical view of baptism, insisting instead that baptism, like the other sacraments, does not work in a mechanical way, apart from divine power.

2. *Because baptism is not necessary for salvation, it is therefore unimportant.* Many contemporary evangelicals adopt this idea. This position contradicts Jesus's Great Commission, which commands the church to baptize new disciples (Matt. 28:19), as the early church did on Pentecost (Acts 2:38, 41).

ENACTING THE DOCTRINE

Baptism is a sacrament or ordinance given by Jesus Christ to his church as it engages in making disciples throughout the world. Whether it practices infant baptism or believer's baptism, the church should be frequently and obediently baptizing people. This occasion is a celebration that encourages both the church that administers baptism and those who are baptized.

Churches in the West are coming more and more into contact with other religions. As churches lead Muslims, Buddhists, Hindus, and others to Christ, converts' baptism takes on an importance that is often overlooked, as they are baptized in the name of the Father and of the Son and of the Holy Spirit. Entailed in this association with the Triune God is a renunciation of their allegiance to other gods (Allah, Vishnu, Shiva, Devi). That is, baptism in the name of the one true God signifies that these other deities are false gods. Often, this radical step places these new Christians in danger, even to the point of being killed for their faith. Churches must prepare themselves for this reality.

TEACHING THE DOCTRINE

Teaching this doctrine is rendered concrete by observation of an actual baptism, whether in the case of infants or believers. If the teaching precedes the baptism, it should make reference to what will take place in that ceremony. Prompt the participants to observe the people, actions, confession of faith, promises, and solemnity of the event. A helpful exercise is to debrief after the baptism to discuss questions about and impressions of it. This discussion is also important if the teaching follows the baptism. If observation is not possible, participants in the class should be encouraged to share the story of their baptism.

Because participants will be most familiar with their church's practice of baptism, that view should be taught and discussed first, followed by a fair treatment of the other positions. In the case of infant baptism, the biblical support and historical development of the church's practice should be set forth. The evaluation of infant baptism by proponents of believer's baptism comes next, followed by the responses of proponents of infant baptism to that assessment. In the case of believer's baptism, the biblical support and historical development of the church's practice should be set forth. The evaluation of believer's baptism by supporters of infant baptism comes next, followed by the responses of supporters of believer's baptism to that assessment. Be truthful, fair, and respectful of other views while advocating for the

Perennial Questions and Problematic Issues

- I was baptized as an infant, which was meaningless to me, but when I heard the gospel and trusted Christ for salvation, I was baptized as his disciple, one of the most meaningful experiences of my life.
- I was baptized as a believer, which was very meaningful to me, but as I study infant baptism, I'm convinced that when we have kids, we will have them baptized because they belong in the covenant community with us.
- What happens to unbaptized infants?
- Though I was baptized as a believer, I was not walking with Christ for some time until I recently rededicated my life to him, and I would like to be rebaptized to commemorate this new experience.
- What do you think of parachurch movements like Cru, InterVarsity, and Navigators baptizing people who come to Christ through their ministry?
- I was baptized at eight because my parents encouraged me to be baptized, but now I'm not sure that I was a Christian then. Now that I believe the gospel and am sure of being Christ's disciple, should I be baptized or rebaptized or do nothing?
- How can churches that practice infant baptism consider it to be effective when so many of those who were baptized as infants have nothing to do with Christ now that they are adults?
- Why do churches that practice believer's baptism not understand that infant baptism is a pledge of God's future work in those babies who are baptized?

church's position. Again, encouraging the participants to share their experiences of one or both of these practices is helpful.

Remember, baptism is presented in Scripture as one of seven commonalities that unite the church of Jesus Christ. The divide that exists between churches because of divergent practices of baptism should thus be a cause of lament, disappointment, and concern. Be careful of triumphalist attitudes—both in teachers and learners!

TEACHING OUTLINE

1. The word "baptism" and the summary
2. Participation in a baptismal service and/or sharing stories of baptism
3. Major affirmations (with biblical support)
   A. Baptism: ordained by Christ and practiced in the church from its outset
   B. The various meanings of baptism
   C. Disagreements about baptism
   D. The early church, various meanings of baptism, and the turn to infant baptism and baptismal regeneration (the Catholic view)
4. Reformation developments: the Lutheran, Reformed, and Anabaptist/Baptist views
5. Major errors to avoid
   A. Believing that baptism is effective *ex opere operato* (literally, "by the work worked")
   B. Dismissing baptism as unimportant
6. Enacting the doctrine
   A. Administering baptism frequently, obediently, and joyfully
   B. Baptizing people in the name of the Triune God and recognizing that it is a radical and (potentially) costly step

---

RESOURCES

Allison, *Theological Terms*, s.v. "baptism"
Elwell, *Evangelical Dictionary of Theology*, s.vv. "Baptism," "Baptism, Believers'," "Baptism, Infant"

Erickson, *Christian Theology*, chap. 52
Grenz, *Theology for the Community of God*, chaps. 19–20
Grudem, *Systematic Theology*, chap. 49
Horton, *Pilgrim Theology*, chap. 16
Thoennes, *Life's Biggest Questions*, chap. 15

41

THE LORD'S SUPPER

SUMMARY

One of two sacraments or ordinances of the church, the Lord's Supper is the continuing rite or celebration of being in new covenant relationship with God.

MAIN THEMES

- Jesus established the Lord's Supper when he was celebrating the Passover feast (his last supper) with his disciples shortly before his crucifixion.

- Jesus ordained baptism as one of two sacraments or ordinances for his church.

- Other names for the Lord's Supper include Communion, the Eucharist, and breaking of bread.

- The Lord's Supper, intended as a unifying celebration, is a point of great division, focused on different views of the presence of Christ (transubstantiation, consubstantiation, memorial, spiritual presence, and Anabaptist/Baptist views).

- Churches have different views of what the Lord's Supper does.

KEY SCRIPTURE

Matthew 26:26–29; Mark 14:22–25; Luke 22:14–23; John 6:22–71; 1 Corinthians 10:14–22; 11:17–34

UNDERSTANDING THE DOCTRINE

Major Affirmations

The Lord's Supper and baptism are the two sacraments or ordinances that Jesus instituted for his church. At his last supper shortly before his death, Jesus celebrated the Passover feast. Changing that meal significantly, he added the three elements of the Lord's Supper: a broken loaf of bread for his body that would be broken on the cross; a cup of wine for his blood that would be shed on the cross; and, in response to his command to observe this meal until his return, his disciples' participation in this new commemoration.

Obediently, churches have historically administered the Lord's Supper, which is known by several other names. It is called *Communion* because Paul affirmed that partaking of the cup and bread is communion (*koinōnia*) with the blood and body of Christ (1 Cor. 10:16). The word *Eucharist* is associated with it because of Jesus's action of giving thanks (*eucharistia*) when he inaugurated this celebration (Mark 14:23; cf. 1 Cor. 11:24). It is referred to as *breaking of bread* because of the description of the early church's practice (Acts 2:42).

Though Jesus intended the Lord's Supper to be a regular observance that unifies his church, it has become a point of great division. The five major positions focus on the presence of Christ in the celebration. These divergences are the result of historical developments.

Transubstantiation. In 1215 the Roman Catholic Church officially proclaimed the doctrine of *transubstantiation*: during the celebration of the sacrament of the Eucharist, the bread is transubstantiated, or changed, into the body of Christ, and the wine is changed into the blood of Christ, by the power of God. Thomas Aquinas provided the philosophical explanation

331

for transubstantiation: the *substance* (that which makes something what it is) of the bread and wine is changed into the body and blood of Christ. However, the *accidents* (characteristics that can be perceived by the senses) remain the same: the bread and wine still look like, smell like, feel like, and taste like bread and wine.

Consubstantiation. Martin Luther understood the Eucharist as a sacramental union of Christ and believers. The view, commonly called *consubstantiation*, holds that Christ is truly present in both his deity and humanity "in, with, and under" the substance of the bread and wine. It is based on Jesus's words, "This is my body," which are taken literally. Consubstantiation is possible because Christ's body is everywhere present, not only located in heaven.

Memorial. Huldrych Zwingli developed the view that the Lord's Supper is a *memorial* of Christ's death. Christ's body is located in heaven and thus cannot be present in the Lord's Supper. Jesus's words, "This is my body," should be rendered, "This [bread] signifies my body." And Jesus commanded, "Do this in remembrance of me." Thus, the Lord's Supper is a memorial, by which the church calls to mind what Christ did on the cross on its behalf.

Spiritual presence. John Calvin moved beyond the memorial view. The bread and wine are certainly symbols, but they are not empty symbols. By his *spiritual presence*, Christ presents himself and his saving benefits through the elements. How Christ is spiritually present is a mystery, but Calvin appealed to the Holy Spirit's power to unite Christ in heaven with the church on earth. The church participates with Christ and is nourished by him.

Anabaptist/Baptist views. The Anabaptists broke from these Protestant positions, focusing on the Lord's Supper as a commemoration that could only be administered to those who had been baptized as believers, not as children. The Baptists embraced this order as well—first, baptism as a new believer, then the Lord's Supper—while developing two traditions, one that held Calvin's view and the other that held a memorial view.

Despite these important differences, the church regularly celebrates the Lord's Supper. Churches have different views of what the Lord's Supper does: it proclaims the gospel, fosters remembrance of Christ's death, signals the new covenant, benefits Christians as they participate in the body and blood of Christ, expresses commitment to Christ, and/or symbolizes and strengthens unity in the church.

Biblical Support

Jesus inaugurated the Lord's Supper at the Passover eaten with his disciples on the eve of his crucifixion (Matt. 26:26–29; Mark 14:22–25; Luke 22:14–23; some traditions include John 6:22–71). Though this meal began like all past observances of this Jewish festival, Jesus added elements that would change his last supper into the ongoing rite of the Lord's Supper.

Specifically, Jesus's instructions, "Take, eat; this is my body," transformed the meal from a remembrance of the Israelites' hasty departure from Egypt (Exod. 12:17; Deut. 16:3) to a commemoration of his upcoming sacrificial death on the cross. His further instructions, appended to the taking of the cup—"Drink of it, all of you, for this is my blood of the covenant, which is poured out for many for the forgiveness of sins" (Matt. 26:27–28)—annulled the old covenant and inaugurated the new covenant. No longer would God relate to his people on the basis of the former covenant, ratified by the blood of sacrificial animals. Instead, God initiated a new covenant, ratified by the blood of Jesus, to be shed on the cross for the forgiveness of his people.

Following Jesus's instructions, the disciples ate the bread and drank the wine, thereby participating in the first Lord's Supper. Moreover, these ritual actions were to be repeated as the church gathered together until Jesus would return. In its celebration, the church would remember Jesus and the vicarious nature of his sacrificial death.

Outside of the Synoptic Gospels, Paul treats the Lord's Supper in 1 Corinthians. Paul emphasizes that it is participation in the blood and body of Christ, as well as a symbol of unity (10:14–22). Rebuking the church for its abuse of the Lord's Supper, the apostle recounts the tradition he has received. Though it took place on the night of Judas's diabolical betrayal of Jesus, Jesus still gave thanks at the start of the celebration. He linked the bread that he broke with his body given for his disciples, and he linked the cup with the inauguration of the new covenant in his blood. Then he charged his disciples with the duty of frequently carrying out this same celebration in commemoration of him. The action of breaking and eating the bread and drinking the cup would be a visual proclamation of his death until his return. The weightiness of the Lord's Supper demands a proper manner for observing it: eschewing divisions among church members so as to participate in a worthy manner (11:17–34).

In summary, the Lord's Supper was instituted by Jesus as a continuing rite to be observed by the church between his first and second comings. It involves symbolic elements—a loaf of bread that is broken, a cup of wine, and the distribution of these elements to the church. These ritual actions strikingly picture the broken body of Jesus and his poured-out blood, together with the church's appropriation of his saving work. The church commemorates, and participates in, Jesus's sacrificial death and his blood, which ratified the new covenant in anticipation of his return.

Major Errors

A major divide exists between Catholics and Protestants: The Roman Catholic Church maintains that all Protestant views and celebrations of the Lord's Supper are defective because of their denial of transubstantiation and their lack of a priesthood that can properly administer the sacrament. All Protestant churches denounce transubstantiation because of its lack of biblical support, its incorrect philosophical foundation, and its late historical development. Transubstantiation is clearly a major error, and it is at the heart of the Catholic-Protestant division.

1. *It is effective* ex opere operato *(literally, "by the work worked"): by eating the consecrated bread and drinking the wine, one receives its benefits.* This is the common conception of the Catholic view, even among some of the Catholic faithful. In its extreme form, this view disengages the Lord's Supper from the gospel, the church, faith, and the work of God. But the Catholic Church would disavow this magical view, insisting instead that the Eucharist, like the other sacraments, does not work in a mechanical way, apart from divine power and the participant's disposition of faith and love.[29]

2. *Because the Lord's Supper is symbolic and a memorial, it is therefore unimportant.* Many contemporary evangelicals adopt this idea. This position contradicts Jesus's instructions to his disciples to celebrate it (Matt. 26:26–29), as the early church did regularly (Acts 2:42, 46). It also overlooks the many benefits that flow from the Lord's Supper.

ENACTING THE DOCTRINE

The Lord's Supper is a sacrament or ordinance given by Jesus Christ to his church as a sign of its new covenant relationship with God. Whatever its view of the presence of Christ in the celebration, the church should be regularly and obediently administering it. Its benefits are many (and differ from church to church) and should be duly noted. We see Christ's broken body and shed blood vividly and visually portrayed—this action proclaims the gospel! We are prompted to remember his work on our behalf—we are saved through him! We celebrate our incorporation into the new covenant—we are in relationship with God and others! We participate in the body and blood of Christ—we embrace Christ and his saving benefits! We express our commitment to Christ—we publicly swear allegiance to him! We are joined with our brothers and sisters in Christ—this rite symbolizes and strengthens unity in the church!

As churches that irregularly administer the Lord's Supper reflect on its many benefits, the challenge is for them to engage in more regular observance. For churches that frequently (weekly) administer it, the challenge is to celebrate it in ways that stop it from becoming a mere ritual, devoid of meaning.

TEACHING THE DOCTRINE

Teaching this doctrine is rendered concrete by observation of and (if appropriate) participation in an actual celebration of the Lord's Supper. If the teaching precedes the event, it should make reference to what will take place. A helpful exercise is to debrief after the celebration to discuss questions about and impressions of that event. This discussion is also important if the teaching follows the event. If observation or participating is not possible, class participants should be encouraged to share their stories of the Lord's Supper.

> ## Perennial Questions and Problematic Issues
>
> - Our church observes the Lord's Supper far too infrequently; it seems unimportant to us.
> - Our church celebrates the Lord's Supper far too often; it has become a meaningless ritual.
> - At what age does our church allow children / young people to start taking the Lord's Supper?
> - Does our church allow all Christians who are with us to take the Lord's Supper, or is it reserved for our church members only?
> - Why is it that some people don't take the Lord's Supper when our church serves it?
> - What should we do before we take the Lord's Supper so that we are worthy to participate?

Because participants will be most familiar with their church's practice of the Lord's Supper, that view should be taught and discussed first, followed by a fair treatment of the other positions. For each of the views (for example, memorial), its biblical support and historical development should be set forth. The evaluation of that position according to the other views (transubstantiation, consubstantiation, spiritual presence, and Anabaptist/Baptist) comes next, followed by the responses of that position.

Be truthful, fair, and respectful of other views while advocating for the church's position.

Remember, the Lord's Supper is presented in Scripture (1 Cor. 10:17) as symbolizing and fostering the unity of the church of Jesus Christ. The divide that exists between churches because of divergent practices of this sacrament/ordinance should thus be a cause of lament, disappointment, and concern.

TEACHING OUTLINE

1. The other names for the "Lord's Supper" and the summary
2. Participation in the Lord's Supper and/or sharing stories of participating
3. Major affirmations (with biblical support)
   A. The Lord's Supper: ordained by Christ and practiced in the church from its outset
   B. The Gospels
   C. Paul's tradition
   D. Transubstantiation
   E. Consubstantiation
   F. Memorial
   G. Spiritual presence
   H. Anabaptist/Baptist views
4. Major errors to avoid
   A. Believing that the Lord's Supper is effective *ex opere operato* (literally, "by the work worked")
   B. Dismissing the Lord's Supper as unimportant
5. Enacting the doctrine
   A. Administering the Lord's Supper frequently and obediently
   B. Celebrating the many benefits of the Lord's Supper

RESOURCES

Allison, *Theological Terms*, s.v. "Lord's Supper"

Elwell, *Evangelical Dictionary of Theology*, s.vv. "Lord's Supper," "Lord's Supper, Views of"

Erickson, *Christian Theology*, chap. 53

Grenz, *Theology for the Community of God*, chap. 19

Grudem, *Systematic Theology*, chap. 50

Horton, *Pilgrim Theology*, chap. 16

Thoennes, *Life's Biggest Questions*, chap. 15

42

WORSHIP

SUMMARY

Worship is an act of acknowledging and acclaiming the majestic greatness of God in ways that he prescribes.

MAIN THEMES

- In one sense, worship is the purpose for which all things exist.
- In this sense, then, everything in which Christians and churches engage, if done in faith and obedience to God, is worship.
- In another sense, worship is the specific and regular activity in which Christians engage corporately.
- Liturgy is an ordered structure of public worship.
- Such corporate worship of God consists in several specific elements.
- Different approaches to public worship reflect two different principles: the regulative principle and the normative principle.
- The church engages in worship to glorify God.

KEY SCRIPTURE

1 Kings 5–8; Ezra; Nehemiah; Psalms; Luke 4:16–30; John 4:23–24; Acts 2:41–47; 20:7; 1 Corinthians 11:17–34; 12:1–14:40; 16:2; 2 Corinthians 8–9; Colossians 3:16; 1 Timothy 2:1–2; 4:13

UNDERSTANDING THE DOCTRINE

Major Affirmations

In one sense, all that God has created is oriented to the glory of God: the heavens and the earth, the mountains and the forests, the angels, and human beings. Thus, worship—acknowledging and acclaiming the majestic greatness of God—is the purpose for which all things exist.

In the human realm, then, worship is any act done in faith and obedience with the goal of glorifying God: engagement in one's vocation, raising a family, and expressions of faith, hope, and love. Also, reading and meditating on Scripture, praying, and singing songs of praise and thanksgiving during personal devotions constitute individual worship. Moreover, anything in which the church engages with the orientation of faith and obedience is worship: prayer meetings, Sunday school, evangelism, feeding the poor, and community groups all constitute worship.

In another sense, worship is the particular activity in which Christians engage corporately on Sunday. This is usually called the *worship service*. It follows an ordered structure of activities, or *liturgy*. In a so-called high church, this liturgy is tightly structured and follows a historical pattern. In a so-called low church, this liturgy may be more relaxed and even appear to be spontaneous, but in most instances the service follows some order.

A common liturgy consists of the following elements: A call to worship. Praise and thanksgiving to God for his attributes and mighty acts through singing, praying, and responsive readings. Confession of sin and assurance of absolution (the announcement of forgiveness). Reading, preaching, and hearing the Word of God. Instruction and exhortation to respond to God with faithfulness and obedience. Giving of one's financial resources. Recitation of a creed or a confession of faith. Administration of the sacraments/ordinances of baptism and the Lord's Supper. A departing benediction.

Importantly, God prescribes the proper way in which he is to be worshiped. Scripture presents cases of illegitimate worship (for example, Nadab and Abihu; Lev. 10:1–2) and condemns false worship (for example, Isa. 1:10–15). The church is warned about falling into idolatry, implying that it is possible for it to orient its worship toward someone or something other than God (for example, societal recognition, numbers and buildings, a certain political agenda). Additionally, Scripture prohibits certain attitudes and actions from being expressed during worship (1 Cor. 14).

Two principles operate in response to the question, what elements may the church rightly incorporate into its worship service? The *regulative principle* states that only those elements that have biblical warrant—for example, reading Scripture, praying, singing praise—are permitted. The *normative principle* states that the church is free to incorporate any element—such as liturgical dance and "special music" (singing by an individual rather than everyone)—unless Scripture prohibits them.

Whatever the liturgical principle and approach, the church engages in worship because God is worthy of the glory ascribed to him. Moreover, he does not need the church's worship because he lacks glory, or needs to be appeased, or to merit his favor. Finally, the key to authentic worship is being a genuine worshiper, one who worships God "in spirit and truth" (John 4:21–24).

For most of its existence, the church has sought to worship God in standard ways. Justin Martyr provided a snapshot of an early church worship service: on Sunday, believers gathered for the reading of Scripture (our Old Testament) and the Gospels, teaching and exhortation by leaders, congregational prayer, the Lord's Supper, and financial giving. Later, other elements were added: reading of the rest of the New Testament writings, singing of the Psalms, and preaching by the elders and bishop.

Eventually, the highly structured Roman Mass became the pattern for the church's worship services. This gave way to the Roman-Gallican liturgy from which the modern Roman Catholic liturgy arose. These liturgies centered on the Eucharist and included formalized opening and closing moments, scripted prayers (with a trinitarian structure), and recitation of a creed.

In the Reformation, Martin Luther composed a liturgy that was conducted in German rather than Latin and emphasized the preaching of the Word of God. John Calvin developed a liturgy that featured the public confession of sin followed by a pastoral absolution (pronouncement of forgiveness) and the reading and exposition of Scripture.

New approaches to worship were developed in the modern era. Churches that were focused on revival oriented their Sunday services toward evangelism and personal renewal. These services often concluded with an invitation for nonbelievers to convert to Christ and for believers to join the church. Corporate gatherings that were historically focused on the worship of God became preoccupied with the individual participants' salvation and sanctification. The Pentecostal and charismatic revivals introduced new elements to worship services: sensitivity to the leading of the Holy Spirit, speaking or singing in tongues, and spontaneity rather than structure in worship.

Biblical Support

The Old Testament associates the worship of God with the patriarchs building altars (Noah, Gen. 8:20; Abraham, Gen. 12:7–8; 13:4, 18; Jacob, Gen. 35:1–7), the wandering people of Israel meeting God in the tabernacle (Exodus, Leviticus), the settled people of Israel coming to the Solomonic temple (1 Kings 5–8), and the postexilic people frequenting the second temple (Ezra, Nehemiah). The songbook of Israelite worship was the Psalms, with over a third of the psalms giving specific instructions for their use in corporate worship services.

Following the exile and the return to the land of Israel, those who were not near the restored temple worshiped in synagogues. Though sacrifices could not be offered, synagogue worship included reading and instruction from Scripture, prayer, singing, and ceremonial rites. By the time of Jesus, synagogue worship was common in Israel. Indeed, the Gospels narrate Jesus's participation in synagogues (for example, Luke 4:16–30).

Battling against the mistaken views that worship must take place on Mount Gerizim (Samaritan worship) or in the temple in Jerusalem (Jewish worship), Jesus revolutionized the notion of worship: "But the hour is coming, and is now here, when the true worshipers will worship the Father in spirit and truth, for the Father is seeking such people to worship him. God is spirit, and those who worship him must worship in spirit and truth" (John 4:23–24). It is not the location but the spiritually transformed people themselves that are at the heart of genuine worship.

Beyond this promise, Jesus did not give specific instructions about worship. In keeping with Jesus's promise, the Holy Spirit's descent on Pentecost inaugurated a new reality: worship in the new covenant church. Elements of that worship included apostolic teaching, community life with sacrificial giving, baptism and the Lord's Supper, prayer, and praising God (Acts 2:41–47). Other elements were the public reading of Scripture, exhortation, and teaching (1 Tim. 4:13); financial giving (2 Cor. 8–9); church discipline (Matt. 18:15–20; 1 Cor. 5; 2 Cor. 2:1–11); the corporate use of spiritual gifts for the church's edification (1 Cor. 12–14); and more (Eph. 5:19; Col. 3:16). These services took place on the first day of each week (Acts 20:7; 1 Cor. 16:2).

Major Errors

1. *The worship service is a misguided ritual in which people participate to appease God and/or to attempt to gain his favor.* This approach fails to discern the difference between religion (the human attempt to reach God) and genuine worship (acknowledging and acclaiming the majestic greatness of God with one's entire being; Rom. 12:1–2).

2. *The worship service is a Mass centered on the re-presentation of the sacrifice of Jesus Christ.* This Roman Catholic approach to worship is mistaken because of its incorrect view of the Lord's Supper (transubstantiation is critiqued in the preceding chapter) and because worship is to be centered on the gospel: the word about Christ, not the re-presented work of Christ.

3. *Novel elements are incorporated into the worship service in an unprincipled way.* Historically, the church has sought biblical warrant for the various aspects of its worship. Alternatively, it has at least determined that the elements of its worship bear some resemblance to biblical patterns and are not forbidden by Scripture. Such considerations are abandoned in some contemporary churches as they introduce willy-nilly practices such as painting during preaching, fogging the auditorium to create a mysterious environment, handling venomous snakes, and slaying in the Spirit.

4. *The so-called worship wars have divided the church.* While the division is often over the style of music, the issue is to whom the worship service should be directed. Many contemporary churches have changed from directing their services toward God (with benefits also accruing to the people worshiping) to directing them to the audience. This view fails to note the proper purpose of worship.

ENACTING THE DOCTRINE

As individual Christians, we properly consider that any act done in faith and obedience with the goal of glorifying God is an act of worship. When we work hard, love our spouse and/or friends, and help others, we glorify God. Also, when we read the Bible, pray, and sing songs of praise and thanksgiving during our devotional times, we glorify God. As church members, we rightly regard the various activities in which we engage—teaching Sunday school, singing in the choir, praying for the sick, and giving financially—as worshiping God. And as genuine worshipers, we gladly gather with other worshipers to sing praise and voice thanksgiving to God, hear Scripture read and expounded, and celebrate the Lord's Supper. In other words, our life should be characterized by a wholehearted and constant commitment to acknowledging and acclaiming the majestic greatness of God.

What's at stake in this doctrine and practice? It is not as though God lacks glory and thus needs our worship to make up a deficit. But God has created everything to be oriented to his glory. Thus, when we worship, we fulfill the purpose for which we exist.

TEACHING THE DOCTRINE

Teaching this doctrine is rendered concrete by participation in an actual worship service. If the teaching precedes the event, it should make reference to what will take place, explaining the various elements of the liturgy (whether explicit or implicit) and their purpose. A helpful exercise is to debrief after the service to discuss questions about and impressions of that event. This discussion is also important if the teaching follows the event. If observance is not possible, participants should be encouraged to share their stories of worship services.

A key element of teaching is demonstrating the biblical basis for the various liturgical elements (for example, preaching, praying, singing, and

> ### Perennial Questions and Problematic Issues
>
> - Our church always follows a certain order in its worship service, and it feels ritualistic to me.
> - Why does our church include the various aspects in its worship service?
> - I don't like it when we sing those loud contemporary songs—I don't know the words and it hurts my ears.
> - I don't like it when we sing those old stodgy hymns—the music is so outdated and the lyrics are too hard to follow.
> - What does Jesus mean when he says we worship "in spirit and truth"?
> - I've been in some Catholic churches, and I like the spaciousness of the sanctuary, the somberness of the worship, and the mystery of the Mass.

giving). Current books showing how liturgies aid the formation of gospel-centeredness and the inculcation of biblical virtues can be both helpful and eye opening.[30] If possible, interaction with the church's worship pastor or director of music should be arranged.

TEACHING OUTLINE

1. The summary
2. Participation in a worship service and/or sharing stories of participating
3. Major affirmations (with biblical support)
   A. Three different senses of worship
   B. The idea of liturgy
   C. The elements of worship
   D. The two principles of worship
   E. Worship for the glory of God
   F. How the church worships
4. Major errors to avoid
   A. Viewing a worship service as a misguided ritual, seeking to appease God and/or to gain his favor
   B. Viewing a Mass centered as the re-presentation of the sacrifice of Jesus Christ
   C. Incorporating novel elements into a worship service in a unprincipled way
   D. Joining in "worship wars," thereby dividing the church
5. Enacting the doctrine
   A. Living lives that are characterized by a wholehearted and constant commitment to acknowledging and acclaiming the majestic greatness of God
   B. Worshiping God in fulfillment of the purpose for which we exist

RESOURCES

Allison, *Theological Terms*, s.vv. "liturgy," "normative principle," "regulative principle," "worship"

Elwell, *Evangelical Dictionary of Theology*, s.vv. "Worship," "Worship in the Church"

Grenz, *Theology for the Community of God*, chap. 18

Grudem, *Systematic Theology*, chap. 51

Thoennes, *Life's Biggest Questions*, chap. 15

43

MISSION AND MINISTRY

SUMMARY

The mission and ministry of the church consist of its purposes and concrete services focused on the gospel as the center.

MAIN THEMES

- The church's mission and ministry are different from its nature, attributes, marks, and offices.
- At the heart of this mission and ministry is the gospel.
- The church's mission is its purposes or aims in relation to God, its members, and those outside the church.
- Its ministries are the concrete services in which the church engages in carrying out its purposes.
- Though there is much diversity among churches in regard to their ministries, common ones include worship, proclamation, evangelism, discipleship, caring for people, and cultural engagement.

KEY SCRIPTURE

Matthew 5:13–16; 28:18–20; Luke 24:44–47; John 4:23–24; 20:19–23; Acts 2:42–47; 1 Corinthians 9:6–18; 2 Corinthians 5:18–21; 8:1–9:14; Galatians 6:6, 9–10; Ephesians 3:21; 4:11–16; Colossians 3:16; 1 Timothy 2:1–2; 5:3–16, 17–18; 2 Timothy 4:2–4; James 1:27

UNDERSTANDING THE DOCTRINE

Major Affirmations

Previous chapters have treated topics related to the current one: (1) the nature of the church (doxological, Word centered, Spirit empowered, covenantal, confessional, missional, and already but not yet), (2) its attributes (one, holy, catholic, and apostolic), (3) the Reformation marks (preaching, the sacraments/ordinances, and [for some] church discipline), and (4) its offices (bishopric, eldership/pastorate, and diaconate). These matters are different from the church's mission and ministry.

The church's mission and ministry are centered on the gospel, the good news of Christ for the salvation of sinful people. It is a twofold announcement: (1) The Son of God became incarnate, lived a sinless life, suffered, was crucified and buried, rose again, and ascended into heaven. This is the accomplishment of salvation. (2) Sinful human beings who hear this good news are instructed to repent of their sins and believe in Christ. This is the appropriation of salvation. This gospel is at the heart of the church.

The mission and ministry of the church consist of its gospel-centered purposes and concrete services in relation to three "audiences": God, the church's members, and people outside the church. Reflecting this threefold orientation, the church's purposes are to glorify God, promote the growth of its members, and engage in the fulfillment of the Great Commission.

The church seeks to glorify God. In all its ministries, the church aims to spread God's fame by making him and his ways known. As new Christians begin to engage in praising him, as suffering believers give him honor in the midst of their pain, as children sing songs exalting him, God is glorified. Such adoration is what is meant by "giving God glory." It is one of the church's purposes.

A second purpose is the growth of the church. In relation to its members, the church aims to develop them into fully mature disciples of Christ. More than a purpose limited to individual progress, it emphasizes corporate growth: in all its relationships, in all its ministries, in all its beliefs and practices, the church seeks to grow together as one body in Christ.

God is from the beginning a missional God, evidenced most clearly in the Father's sending of the Son to accomplish salvation. To the church he gives the Great Commission, its third purpose: as it constantly reaches beyond itself, the church bears the responsibility to make disciples of Christ in every corner of the globe.

With this threefold purpose clearly in mind, the church engages in ministry, or concrete acts of service. Common ministries are worship, proclamation, evangelism, discipleship, caring for people, and cultural engagement.

The worship service is the particular activity in which Christians engage corporately on Sunday (treated in the preceding chapter, "Worship").

Proclamation of the Word of God, while part of the worship service, is not limited to that event. God is from the beginning a speaking God, which means that his people is a hearing and speaking people. Specifically, Scripture is the means by which God speaks to the church, which is "'worded' all the way down."[31] Thus, preaching and teaching the Word are essential in the church's worship services, discipleship, expressions of mercy, education, and more.

Evangelism is the activity of engaging nonbelievers with the gospel. Though its worship service may be primarily oriented toward God's glory, and though its community groups may be primarily oriented toward its members' growth, the church may also evangelize non-Christians through these ministries. Specific activities—door-to-door evangelism, evangelistic Bible studies, apologetics conferences on topics of interest to nonbelievers—seek to engage people who do not yet know Christ.

Discipleship is the intentional, lifelong, and multipronged process of developing the church's members to become fully devoted followers of Christ. This all-encompassing purpose is carried out through worship, proclamation, baptism, the Lord's Supper, and other activities associated with the worship service. Additionally, the church provides community groups, Christian education, counseling/pastoral care, and more for discipleship.

Caring for people is a multifaceted ministry to those both inside and outside the church. Prayer, while always directed to God, can focus on the needs of people. The church prays for its members, specifically for their progress in sanctification, knowledge of God and his ways, growth in love, and more. The church prays for those outside, including government officials, its enemies, and unbelievers. Moreover, the church cares for people by giving financially to support its pastors and ministries and to assist its members who are in need. Furthermore, the church educates its members and provides counseling for them.

Finally, cultural engagement is the church's service to the world at large. It has particular application in terms of extending mercy to the poor and disenfranchised. It helps concretely through financial support, medical clinics, job training, community development, and more. At the heart of this engagement is the church's stance both *for* and *against* the world. It is *for* the world as it equips its members to carry out the cultural mandate to build society. The church stands *against* the world in denouncing its culture of death and promoting vocations that relieve misery, poverty, injustice, crime, and more.

Biblical Support

The gospel finds its precursors in the Old Testament. Following the fall, God himself promised redemption through the seed of the woman (Gen. 3:15). The fulfillment of this prophecy was Jesus of Nazareth, who came "proclaiming the gospel of God, and saying, 'The time is fulfilled, and the kingdom of God is at hand; repent and believe in the gospel'" (Mark 1:14–15). He began to build his church-on-mission, which would be centered on the gospel.

The church's first purpose is to glorify God. All things are to be oriented to God's glory, and that includes the church: "To him be glory in the church and in Christ Jesus throughout all generations" (Eph. 3:21). The second purpose is summarized by Paul's vision of the church's growth "until we all attain to the unity of the faith and of the knowledge of the Son of God, to mature manhood, to the measure of the stature of the fullness of Christ" (4:13–16). The third purpose, the Great Commission, was established by Jesus in his mandate to his disciples: "Go therefore and make disciples of all nations" (Matt. 28:18–20).

Biblical support for the ministries of the church is extensive. Jesus underscored the type of worshipers whom God seeks (John 4:23–24), and Luke provides a snapshot of the first church's worship (Acts 2:42–47).

Proclamation of the Word was the hallmark of the Old Testament prophets who announced, "Thus says the LORD" (for example, Isa. 66:1).

Jesus proclaimed the gospel, as did his disciples (Acts 2:14–41; 3:11–26; 4:5–12; 5:27–42; etc.). Faith in Christ is ignited by proclaiming "the word of Christ" (Rom. 10:14–17), a constant ministry that is enjoined on the church (2 Tim. 4:2–4).

Evangelism is part of the Great Commission, discussed above. To the church God gives "the ministry of reconciliation; that is, in Christ God was reconciling the world to himself, not counting their trespasses against them." Specifically, this ministry is "the message [literally, *word*] of reconciliation" announced by "ambassadors for Christ" through whom God makes his appeal (2 Cor. 5:18–20). It leads to discipleship, which is also part of the Great Commission. The church proclaims Christ, "warning everyone and teaching everyone with all wisdom, that we may present everyone mature in Christ" (Col. 1:28).

Caring for people is rooted in the Old Testament's portrayal of God as "father of the fatherless and protector of widows" (Ps. 68:5; cf. Deut. 10:18). Much of Jesus's ministry was directed at the poor and marginalized (Matt. 9:10–13), earning him the reputation of being "a friend of tax collectors and sinners" (11:19). James urges, "Religion that is pure and undefiled before God the Father is this: to visit orphans and widows in their affliction" (James 1:27).

Concrete acts of care include praying for church members (Eph. 1:16–19; 3:14–19; Phil. 1:9–11; Col. 1:9–14; James 5:13–15), government leaders (1 Tim. 2:1–2), and enemies (Luke 6:28). Giving financially (2 Cor. 8–9) is another care ministry, specifically to support the church's pastors (1 Cor. 9:6–18; Gal. 6:6; 1 Tim. 5:17–18) and to assist its members who are in need, especially widows (1 Tim. 5:3–16).

The church's stand both for and against the world is grounded in its members' call "to do good to everyone" (Gal. 6:9–10) and to "love your neighbor as yourself" (Matt. 22:39). As "the salt of the earth" and "the light of the world," the church does not cower in fear and hide in the shadows, but obeys its Lord: "Let your light shine before others, so that they may see your good works and give glory to your Father who is in heaven" (5:13–16). Thus, the mission of the church, which begins with glory, ends with glory.

Major Errors

1. *The church defining its mission and ministry by something other than Scripture (for example, political involvement, concern for relevancy, and*

numbers and money). This illegitimate substitution for biblical priorities and directives often reflects a church's surrender to contemporary cultural pressures, an inordinate desire for society's approval, a loss of or confusion about the gospel, and more.

2. *The church reducing its mission and ministry to only some of these purposes and services.* This illegitimate reductionism often reflects the gifts and strengths of a lead/solo pastor. It is also encouraged by the movement to simplify the church in accordance with contemporary business philosophy.

ENACTING THE DOCTRINE

The church is not like other human communities. It is not a club (like the Girl Scouts), a social network (like Facebook), an association (like AARP), a league (like fantasy football), or a political organization (like a political action committee). Rather, it is the body of Christ, a community of faith that is centered on the gospel and has a divinely given mission and ministry. We don't invent the church's mission. We don't engage in concrete services that reflect those of the surrounding society. Though there may be overlap, the church engages missionally for other purposes. Faced with many pressures to conform and appear relevant to the world, the church does well to live out its mission and ministry based on Scripture.

> ### Perennial Questions and Problematic Issues
>
> - If our church has a mission statement, it seems too much like a business.
> - Why does our church engage in its various ministries?
> - I don't see any purpose for our ministry of blessing the animals (or some other ministry).
> - I think our church should engage in ministry to orphans and widows (or some other ministry).
> - All this talk about mercy ministry and cultural engagement sounds like the social gospel and threatens to replace evangelism.

TEACHING THE DOCTRINE

If participants are serving in the church, teaching about its mission and ministry should engage them in sharing about their ministries. Stories of God's grace displayed in teaching the Bible, leading someone to Christ, discipling a new believer, praying for persecutors, being merciful to a homeless person, and more will render this topic concrete and lead to thanksgiving to God.

Quite often the church takes for granted its mission and ministry. This topic provides an opportunity for a fresh assessment of the church's purposes (What are they? How are they being fulfilled? Do they need clarification?) and its concrete services (What are its ministries? What purpose[s] are they fulfilling? Do they need strengthening?). Participants will enjoy evaluating the church, but make sure they offer constructive criticism and not condemnation.

The church often struggles to formulate and communicate its mission. Perhaps the church doesn't know its mission or has never written it out. An exercise, then, is to engage participants in articulating in statement form what the church's purposes should be. If the church has a mission statement, encourage participants to see how its various ministries connect to one or more of its purposes. What if a certain ministry is not related to a purpose of the church? A discussion about what to do with tangential ministries may lead to some needed changes. What if the church lacks a certain ministry to fulfill its purposes? Again, discussion may lead to some participants starting a ministry.

TEACHING OUTLINE

1. The summary
2. Sharing about God's grace expressed through participants' ministries
3. Major affirmations (with biblical support)
   A. The centrality of the gospel
   B. The threefold mission of the church
   C. The ministries of the church
4. Major errors to avoid
   A. Defining the church's mission and ministry by something other than Scripture
   B. Reducing the church's mission and ministry to only a few purposes and services
5. Enacting the doctrine
   A. Respecting the church as the body of Christ, a community of faith unlike other human communities
   B. Living out the church's ministry and mission according to Scripture

RESOURCES

Allison, *Theological Terms*, s.vv. "disciple/discipleship," "evangelism," "gospel," "Great Commission," "ministry"

Elwell, *Evangelical Dictionary of Theology*, s.vv. "Great Commission," "Ministry"

Erickson, *Christian Theology*, chap. 50

Grenz, *Theology for the Community of God*, chap. 18

Grudem, *Systematic Theology*, chap. 48

Horton, *Pilgrim Theology*, chap. 17

PART 8

DOCTRINE

—————— OF ——————

FUTURE THINGS

44

DEATH AND THE
INTERMEDIATE STATE

SUMMARY

Death, which is a penalty for sin, is the cessation of the functioning of the body and its temporary separation from the soul. Death is not the end of all existence, as the disembodied person continues to exist in the intermediate state until the resurrection.

MAIN THEMES

- Death is the cessation of the functioning of a person's material element (body).
- It is also the temporary separation of the material aspect (body) and the immaterial aspect (soul/spirit).
- Death is a penalty for sin.
- The intermediate state is the condition of people between their death and the resurrection.

- At their death, Christians enter immediately into the presence of Christ in heaven and exist there as disembodied believers.
- At their death, non-Christians are plunged immediately into the torment of hell and exist there as disembodied unbelievers.
- Both disembodied believers and disembodied unbelievers await the resurrection of their bodies.

KEY SCRIPTURE

Genesis 3:19; Psalm 90; Ecclesiastes 3:1–2; 7:2, 4; 9:2–3; Luke 16:19–31; Romans 6:23; 1 Corinthians 15:21–22; 2 Corinthians 5:1–9; Philippians 1:23; Hebrews 12:23; Revelation 20

UNDERSTANDING THE DOCTRINE

Major Affirmations

Personal eschatology treats the topics of death and the intermediate state, or human existence between the end of embodied earthly life and the resurrection of the body. It is the future for all human beings, as death is one of the great inevitabilities of human existence.

The background for these doctrines is the makeup of human beings. Human nature is a complex essence consisting of a material aspect (body) and an immaterial aspect (soul/spirit), united into one. Human earthly existence, which begins at conception, features an inextricable union of the material and immaterial elements: a body-soul unity.

Death puts an end to earthly existence and begins a new stage of existence called the intermediate state. Death features two changes: First, it is the cessation of the functioning of a person's material aspect (body). In surrendering to cancer or being involved in a fatal car crash, for example, a person's physiological functioning ceases and her body dies. Second, death is the temporary separation of a person's material element and immaterial element. The body-soul unity is interrupted for a time. The lifeless body is sloughed off, and the two elements are separated.

Death is a penalty for sin. God, who created people in his image as complex beings, punishes them for their sinfulness. One part of this punishment is the dissolution of human existence as it was divinely designed. The state of disembodiment is abnormal, not the way it is supposed to be.

The intermediate state, then, is the condition of people between their death and the resurrection. People continue to exist as disembodied beings, which is irregular. At their death, Christians enter immediately into the presence of Christ in heaven and exist there as disembodied believers. Oppositely, non-Christians are plunged immediately into the torment of hell and exist there as disembodied unbelievers.

Both disembodied believers and disembodied unbelievers await the resurrection of their bodies. Accordingly, the intermediate state begins at death and ends at the resurrection. The intermediate state is distinguished from the final state, which is the new heaven and new earth.

Biblical Support

Death is first mentioned in Scripture as a divine threat for disobedience. God warned Adam, who was formed "of dust from the ground" (Gen. 2:7): "Of the tree of the knowledge of good and evil you shall not eat, for in the day that you eat of it you shall surely die" (2:17). After Adam and Eve violated this prohibition, God announced his punishment: "You are dust, and to dust you shall return" (3:19). Life, which was existence from and of the dust, would come to an end, a return to the dust. Physical death is the cessation of the physiological functioning of the body.

Death, then, is a penalty for sin (Rom. 6:23). It is one of the inevitabilities of human existence: there is "a time to be born, and a time to die" (Eccles. 3:1–2). Indeed, "it is appointed for man to die once, and after that comes judgment" (Heb. 9:27). Moreover, there is an inseparable connection between the death of all people and the death of Adam (Rom. 5:12–21; 1 Cor. 15:21–22).

Death is the end of all human beings: "You return man to dust. . . . The years of our life are seventy, or even by reason of strength eighty; . . . they are soon gone, and we fly away" (Ps. 90:3, 10). Reflection on death, without morbid introspection, gives wisdom for living (Eccles. 7:2, 4).

Death also involves the temporary separation of the material element (body) and the immaterial element (soul/spirit). The two, which have been inextricably united, are unzipped. Scripture makes a distinction between the two (body and soul, Matt. 10:28; body and spirit, James 2:26). Paul describes a deceased person in the intermediate state as being "naked" and "unclothed" (2 Cor. 5:3–4)—that is, without his earthly body ("the tent that is our earthly home," v. 1) and living in anticipation of his glorified, resurrected body ("not . . . unclothed, . . . but . . . further clothed, . . . swallowed up by life," v. 4). Paul shudders in horror as he describes this reality, underscoring the strangeness of the intermediate state.

Though both believers and unbelievers die (Eccles. 9:2–3), their destinies as disembodied people are very different. At their death, Christians enter immediately into the presence of Christ in heaven. They are "away from the body and at home with the Lord" (2 Cor. 5:8). This heavenly existence is "far better" than their earthly existence (Phil. 1:23). Though a disembodied existence and thus not one of completed salvation, it is a reality in which "the spirits of the righteous [have been] made perfect" (Heb. 12:23).

At their death, unbelievers are plunged immediately into misery in hell (Luke 16:19–31). Scripture frighteningly pictures their suffering with expressions like "weeping and gnashing of teeth" (Matt. 8:12; 25:30) and "the smoke of their torment goes up forever and ever, and they have no rest, day or night" (Rev. 14:11).

As this disembodied state is abnormal, both believers and unbelievers in the intermediate state await the resurrection of their bodies. Amillennialism and postmillennialism hold that the resurrection of both groups takes place at the final judgment, which occurs at the return of Christ (Rev. 20 presents events at Christ's return). Premillennialism maintains that the resurrection of believers takes place when Christ returns. Thus, believers receive their resurrection bodies and reign with Christ for the thousand-year millennium. The resurrection of unbelievers, however, awaits the final judgment of Christ, which occurs after the millennium (20:1–6 presents events at Christ's return, while 20:7–15 presents events after the millennium).

Major Errors

1. *A view of death as natural, some good thing to be embraced.* This view fails to understand that death is not the way it is supposed to be, because it is a penalty for sin. It is an enemy that robs human beings of life.

2. *Soul sleep.* Seventh-day Adventists and Jehovah's Witnesses believe that people exist in an unconscious condition in the intermediate state. Supposed biblical support includes the biblical descriptions of death as "sleep" (1 Kings 2:10; John 11:11; Acts 7:60; 13:36; 1 Thess. 4:13), which

is characterized by the absence of memory, praise, and hope (Pss. 6:5; 115:17; Isa. 38:18). This view misunderstands that Scripture uses "sleep" as a euphemism for death itself. It is not a description of what happens after death. Moreover, the biblical presentation of inactivity after death refers to the condition of people in Sheol, part of Old Testament eschatology that has been clarified in the further revelation of the New Testament. Finally, this position cannot account for the biblical passages that present believers being in the presence of Christ after their death.

3. *Purgatory.* According to Roman Catholicism, purgatory is the temporary state of purification of the Catholic faithful who were not fully obedient during their earthly existence. Bearing the stain of sin, these faithful experience the temporal punishment for sin in purgatory. When their purification is completed, they will go to heaven. A key support is 2 Maccabees 12:38–45, which is not considered canonical by Protestants. Biblical support includes Paul's descriptive statement, "If anyone's work is burned up, he will suffer loss, though he himself will be saved, but only as through fire" (1 Cor. 3:15). However, Paul is not describing purgatory but the final judgment of believers with regard to their poor work in the church. Finally, Jesus's words are invoked: "Whoever speaks against the Holy Spirit will not be forgiven, either in this age or in the age to come" (Matt. 12:32). The (mis)interpretation is that, whereas blasphemy against the Spirit can never be forgiven, other sins, if they are not forgiven in this age, can be forgiven in the age to come. But Jesus is emphasizing the unforgivable seriousness of blasphemy against the Spirit without implying anything about other, less serious sins.

4. *The denial of existence after death.* Neurophysiology is producing evidence that human existence is completely physical. Rationality, free will, moral consciousness, and faith are intimately tied to neurological processes. Such evidence of a solely material reality for human existence calls into question what happens after death, or the ceasing of the body's functioning. This development faces important challenges, such as explaining human consciousness and the universal notion of life after death. Moreover, Scripture's presentation of the intermediate state directly contradicts this view.

ENACTING THE DOCTRINE

Scripture urges us to learn how to live by going to "the house of mourning" (Eccles. 7:2, 4)—that is, by contemplating the inevitability of death.

While we should avoid morbid introspection, a measured consideration of our mortality can help us break the destructive patterns of overwork, misplaced priorities, and neglect of family and friends.

As opposed to contemporary discussions of "death with dignity," a biblical understanding helps us understand that death is no friend, but an enemy instead. It is not a natural part of life, but a penalty for sin. We should not long for death, anticipating it with eagerness. We should never downplay the tragedy, horror, and evil of death. Rather, as believers, we long for our merciful homecoming, our "gain" of being "with Christ" (Phil. 1:21, 23), which awaits us in the intermediate state. Thus, we face our own death and the death of other Christians with hope and joy, without fear. Such hope is not incompatible with tears and sorrow as we grieve.

Perennial Questions and Problematic Issues

- My father died last year—where is he now?
- Can people in heaven see us and help us?
- At my friend's Catholic church, the priest celebrates a mass once a year for my friend's mom, who died a few years ago.
- How can we worship God and fellowship with other believers in heaven without our body?

It is a different matter with the death of unbelievers. Our grief is not intermingled with joy, for we know the misery of their intermediate state. If their impending death prompted serious reflection about the gospel, we may have hope that they repented of their sins and believed in Christ. Still, we must avoid offering false assurance of salvation.

TEACHING THE DOCTRINE

Death is not a pleasant topic to discuss. From the outset, be aware that some participants will be uncomfortable with, or even saddened by, this teaching. Be sure to care well for those who find this difficult. Remind participants that Christ will conquer death as the last enemy (1 Cor. 15:50–57).

A positive outcome of this doctrine is contemplating death so as to gain wisdom for living. Ask participants if they have had a "near death" experience. Ask them how that brush with death affected their life, and emphasize for everyone the benefit of thinking about the inevitability of our death.

Participants from a Catholic background will ask questions about purgatory. After showing that biblical support doesn't exist for this belief, emphasize that God's mighty work of justification eliminates the need for purgatory. God has declared us not guilty but righteous instead, so we don't need to experience temporary punishment and purification for our sins.

Avoid speculation about the intermediate state. In light of limited biblical revelation about this matter, admitting that we just don't know the details is both true and avoids dangerous speculation. Watch out for participants who bring in descriptions of heaven from contemporary books by people who claim to have died, experienced heavenly existence, and then returned to this life. Many of these descriptions contradict Scripture.

TEACHING OUTLINE

1. The summary
2. Sharing "near death" experiences and lessons learned
3. Major affirmations (with biblical support)
   A. Death as cessation of physiological functioning
   B. Death as separation of material and immaterial aspects
   C. Death as a penalty for sin
   D. The intermediate state for believers and unbelievers
   E. The resurrection as the end of the intermediate state
4. Major errors to avoid
   A. Viewing death as natural—some good thing to be embraced
   B. Believing in soul sleep
   C. Believing in purgatory
   D. Denying existence after death
5. Enacting the doctrine
   A. Contemplating the inevitability of death
   B. Facing our own death and the death of other Christians
   C. Facing the death of non-Christians

RESOURCES

Allison, *Theological Terms*, s.vv. "death," "intermediate state"

Elwell, *Evangelical Dictionary of Theology*, s.vv. "Death," "Intermediate State"

Erickson, *Christian Theology*, chap. 55

Grenz, *Theology for the Community of God*, chap. 21

Grudem, *Systematic Theology*, chap. 41

Horton, *Pilgrim Theology*, 422–25

45

THE RETURN OF JESUS CHRIST

SUMMARY

The return of Jesus Christ is his future, or second, coming to earth, to bring fullness of salvation to his disciples.

MAIN THEMES

- At his first coming, Jesus Christ dealt with sin.
- At his second coming, Christ will bring ultimate salvation.
- Christ will return personally, bodily, suddenly, and triumphantly.
- Though God has determined the time of the second coming, human beings cannot know it.
- A key debate is whether the second coming will be preceded by the rapture of the church before the great tribulation.
- Another debate regards the relationship of Christ's return to the millennium (treated in the next chapter, "The Millennium").

KEY SCRIPTURE

Matthew 24; Mark 13; Luke 21; Acts 1:9–11; 1 Corinthians 1:7; 1 Thessalonians 3:13; 4:13–18; 2 Thessalonians 1:6–7; 2:8; 1 Timothy 6:14; 2 Timothy 4:8; Titus 2:13; Hebrews 9:28; 1 Peter 4:13

UNDERSTANDING THE DOCTRINE

Major Affirmations

At his first coming, the Son of God left the realm of glory and became incarnate as Jesus Christ. In his state of humiliation, he submitted himself to the law, experienced trials and temptations, endured suffering, and was crucified and buried. In his state of exaltation, he was raised from the dead, ascended into heaven, and sat down at the right hand of God the Father. The ultimate purpose of this first coming was to accomplish salvation.

At his second coming sometime in the future, the God-man will return to earth in glorious triumph, not to deal with sin but to fully save all those who believe in him. This return will be personal: Christ himself—not his influence, or his teaching, or his Spirit-mediated presence—will come to earth. He will return bodily, just as he left this earth when he ascended to heaven. His return will be sudden, taking by surprise unbelievers who are not expecting his second coming. Christ will return triumphantly, with glory and might.

As part of God's eternal plan, the return of Christ is established. It is not contingent on external factors, and God will certainly bring about its fulfillment. Though known by God, the timing of the second coming cannot be known by human beings.

The relationship of the second coming to the rapture of the church and the great tribulation is an ongoing debate. The rapture (from the Latin *rapere*, "to catch up") is a catching up of the church on earth preceding Christ's return. The great tribulation is the global, intense period of suffering associated with his return.

Dispensationalism holds that the rapture will occur prior to the seven-year period of tribulation. The purpose of this event is to remove the church and bring it to heaven so that it will be spared the evil and punishment of the great tribulation. Nondispensationalist views maintain that the church will continue on earth and experience at least in part the suffering and persecution of the great tribulation. The rapture will occur immediately before Christ's return for the purpose of catching up the church to meet Christ as he descends from heaven on his return to earth.[32]

In terms of the debate regarding the relationship of Christ's return to the millennium, the various positions are presented in the next chapter, "The Millennium."

Biblical Support

Scripture presents Christ's return in various ways. As the *parousia*, it is his coming or arrival (1 Thess. 3:13; 4:15; 2 Thess. 2:8). As an *apocalypse*, it is the revelation of Christ (1 Cor. 1:7; 2 Thess. 1:6–7; 1 Pet. 4:13). As an *epiphany*, it is his second appearing (1 Tim. 6:14; 2 Tim. 4:8; Titus 2:13). The contrast between his first coming and second coming is stark: "Christ, having been offered once to bear the sins of many, will appear a second time, not to deal with sin but to save those who are eagerly waiting for him" (Heb. 9:28). What Christ initiated at this first appearance—the accomplishment of salvation—will be completed at his second appearance, with the fullness of salvation for his disciples. Accordingly, we are "waiting for our blessed hope, the appearing of the glory of our great God and Savior Jesus Christ" (Titus 2:13).

Jesus prophesied his return. On the eve of his crucifixion, he spoke of his upcoming departure: "And if I go and prepare a place for you, I will come again and will take you to myself, that where I am you may be also" (John 14:3). At his trial, Jesus warned, "From now on you will see the Son of Man seated at the right hand of Power and coming on the clouds of heaven" (Matt. 26:63–64). Forty days after his resurrection, "as they [his disciples] were looking on, he was lifted up, and a cloud took him out of their sight." Then, two angels promised, "This Jesus, who was taken up from you into heaven, will come in the same way as you saw him go into heaven" (Acts 1:9, 11).

The purpose of his "long journey" away from earth is in accordance with the divine plan. Indeed, at the right time, God will "send the Christ appointed for you, Jesus, whom heaven must receive until the time" of restoration (Acts 3:20–21). Such restoration includes granting relief to Christ's persecuted followers (2 Thess. 1:7), delivering them "from the wrath to come" (1 Thess. 1:10), giving resurrection bodies (Phil. 3:21), awarding believers "the crown of righteousness" (2 Tim. 4:8), and conforming them fully to his image (Rom. 8:29) "in glory" (Col. 3:4).

Paul provides a vivid description of Christ's return: "We who are alive, who are left until the coming of the Lord, will not precede those who have fallen asleep. For the Lord himself will descend from heaven with a cry of command, with the voice of an archangel, and with the sound of the trumpet of God. And the dead in Christ will rise first. Then we who are alive, who are left, will be caught up together with them in the clouds to meet the Lord in the air, and so we will always be with the Lord" (1 Thess. 4:15–17).

Accordingly, as for the nature of the second coming, it will be a personal return, as "the Lord himself will descend from heaven" (4:16). It will be a physical return: just as he ascended bodily, Christ will "come in the same way" (Acts 1:11). Christ's return will be sudden, as "the day of the Lord will come like a thief in the night" (1 Thess. 5:2–3). And it will be triumphant, "with a cry of command, with the voice of an archangel, and with the sound of the trumpet of God" (4:16), and "with power and great glory" (Matt. 24:30).

Dispensationalism interprets the above passage not as a description of Christ's second coming but as a depiction of the rapture of the church prior to the great tribulation. At the outset of that seven-year period, Christ "himself will descend from heaven," and Christians living on the earth "will be caught up [Latin *rapere*] together with them [deceased believers in heaven] in the clouds to meet the Lord in the air" (1 Thess. 4:16–17). Thus, the rapture is the event of Christians being "caught up" with Christ in the air and accompanying him back to heaven. Such escape from divine tribulation has been promised to the church (1:10; 5:9; Rev. 3:10).

Nondispensationalist views interpret this passage as a description of the second coming. The rapture will occur immediately before Christ's return for the purpose of catching up the church to meet Christ as he descends from heaven on his return to earth.

Major Errors

1. *A denial of the personal, physical return of Christ.* Liberalism is prone to affirm some type of return, but understands it to be gradual extension of Christ's teaching and/or moral influence in the world. This view dismisses the biblical descriptions of the second coming.

2. *Any attempt at declaring or prophesying the exact date of Christ's return.* Rarely, yet tragically, this error arises and wreaks havoc in the church. Harold Camping set May 21, 2011, as the time of the rapture, and October

21, 2011, as the end of the world. This position clearly contradicts Scripture's own statement that human beings cannot know the time of Christ's return.

3. *Rampant speculation as to what will take place at the rapture.* Given the sparse treatment that Scripture gives to nature of this event, it is always dangerous to engage in speculation, then present this guesswork as biblical truth. This misleads some people, frightens others, and wrongly encourages still others.

ENACTING THE DOCTRINE

This doctrine should stir the church toward greater maturity and mission. For example, Paul addresses the suddenness of Christ's return—"The day of the Lord will come like a thief in the night"—and the destruction that will come upon those "in darkness." Immediately, he calms our fears, reminding us, "For you are all children of light, children of the day. We are not of the night or of the darkness. So then let us not sleep, as others do, but let us keep awake and be sober." As those of the day and who are sober minded, we are to "put on the breastplate of faith and love, and for a helmet the hope of salvation" (1 Thess. 5:2–8). Anticipation of the second coming prompts us to live the virtues of faith, hope, and love.

Moreover, we are to work hard now, serving the Lord who is to come: "Henceforth there is laid up for me the crown of righteousness, which the Lord, the righteous judge, will award to me on that day, and not only to me but also to all who have loved his appearing" (2 Tim. 4:8). Thus, "all who have loved his [first] appearing" should look eagerly forward to his second appearing, anticipating that their labor in and for the Lord will be richly rewarded (Gal. 6:9). Moreover, we wait patiently for Christ's return, whenever it will occur, knowing, "The Lord is not slow to fulfill his promise as some count slowness, but is patient toward you, not wishing that any should perish, but that all should reach repentance" (2 Pet. 3:9). We take advantage of the "delay" of this event, using it to communicate the gospel so that others will be saved.

TEACHING THE DOCTRINE

For some, teaching about the return of Jesus Christ conjures up wide-eyed prophets and mad prognosticators who have predicted his second coming, been proven wrong, and brought disgrace upon the church. For others,

Perennial Questions and Problematic Issues

- When do you think Christ will return?

- If the Bible says that we can't know the time of Christ's return, why do people still predict when it will happen?

- What are the similarities and differences between the first and second comings of Christ?

- If Christ returns to a specific location on earth—Jerusalem—how will it be possible for the whole world to see his return?

- I have read many books on the second coming, and, frankly, I'm disgusted by the matter.

- I have read many books on the second coming, and I am so encouraged that I can't wait for it to happen.

- How does this hope for Christ's return affect our lives and church now?

books like *The Late Great Planet Earth* and the Left Behind series have fueled an eager expectation of the second coming or, at least, the rapture of the church. Presenting this doctrine, then, offers some interesting challenges.

First off, what is needed is a call to clear thinking and careful (re)consideration of biblical teaching on this topic. Emerging from the biblical material are many points of agreement that can form a general consensus: Jesus Christ will return, at a time known only to God, in a manner that is personal, bodily, sudden, and triumphantly glorious, bringing great blessings to Christians. The church embraces and rejoices in these common beliefs.

Second, then, the differences should be fairly and concisely discussed. To avoid the tendency toward speculation on this doctrine, teaching it should focus on biblical texts and provide a model of appropriate reservation and humility about this matter. The purpose for this doctrine is to stir the church toward greater maturity and mission. So make sure that the material is presented with that goal as foremost in mind and structure.

TEACHING OUTLINE

1. The summary
2. Measuring participants' reaction to this doctrine
3. Major affirmations (with biblical support)
   A. Contrasting the first and second comings of Christ
   B. The nature of Christ's return: personal, bodily, sudden, and triumphant
   C. The blessings of the second coming for Christians

D. The issue of the rapture—pretribulation or posttribulation?

E. How Christians should live in light of the hope of the second coming

4. Major errors to avoid

A. Denying the personal, physical return of Christ

B. Attempting to declare or prophesy the exact date of Christ's return

C. Engaging in rampant speculation as to what will take place at the rapture

5. Enacting the doctrine

A. Anticipating the return of Christ in a way that stirs the church toward greater maturity and mission

B. Working hard now by serving the Lord who is to come

C. Taking advantage of the "delay" of this event by using it to communicate the gospel so that others will be saved

RESOURCES

Allison, *Theological Terms*, s.vv. "Great Tribulation," "rapture," "second coming"

Elwell, *Evangelical Dictionary of Theology*, s.vv. "Rapture of the Church," "Second Coming of Christ," "Tribulation"

Erickson, *Christian Theology*, chap. 56

Grenz, *Theology for the Community of God*, chap. 22

Grudem, *Systematic Theology*, chap. 54

Horton, *Pilgrim Theology*, chap. 18

Thoennes, *Life's Biggest Questions*, chap. 16

46

THE MILLENNIUM

SUMMARY

The millennium is either another name for the current church age or a future period in relation to the second coming of Jesus Christ.

MAIN THEMES

- "Millennium" is from the Latin *mille*, "thousand," and *annum*, "year."

- "Millennium" finds expression as "a thousand years" in Revelation 20:1–6.

- The nature of the millennium and its relationship to the return of Christ and the tribulation are debated, with four primary views.

- *Amillennialism* identifies the millennium with the current church age.

- *Postmillennialism* considers the millennium to be a golden age, after which Christ will return.

- *Historic premillennialism* locates the return of Christ before the millennium, which is a one-thousand-year reign of Christ on the earth; additionally, Christ's return is after the great tribulation.

- *Pretribulational,* or *dispensational, premillennialism* places the return of Christ before the millennium as a one-thousand-year reign of Christ on the earth; additionally, the rapture of the church takes place before the great tribulation.

KEY SCRIPTURE

Revelation 20

UNDERSTANDING THE DOCTRINE

Major Affirmations

With respect to eschatology, or the doctrine of last things, the church has historically shared widespread agreement on the return of Christ, the resurrection, the final judgment, eternal life for the righteous and eternal death for the unrighteous, and the new heaven and new earth. Disagreement, however, surrounds the relationship of Christ's return to two other eschatological matters: the great tribulation and the millennium.

The word "millennium" is from the Latin *mille,* "thousand," and *annum,* "year," so literally, *a thousand years.* It finds expression in Revelation 20:1–6 (emphasis added):

Then I saw an angel coming down from heaven, holding in his hand the key to the bottomless pit and a great chain. And he seized the dragon, that ancient serpent, who is the devil and Satan, and bound him for *a thousand years* and threw him into the pit, and shut it and sealed it over him, so that he might not deceive the nations any longer, until *the thousand years* were ended. After that he must be released for a little while.

Then I saw thrones, and seated on them were those to whom the authority to judge was committed. Also I saw the souls of those who had been beheaded for the testimony of Jesus and for the word of God, and those who had not worshiped the beast or its image and had not received its mark on their foreheads or their hands. They came to life and reigned with Christ for *a thousand years*. The rest of the dead did not come to life until *the thousand years* were ended. This is the first resurrection. Blessed and holy is the one who shares in the first resurrection! Over such the second death has no power, but they will be priests of God and of Christ, and they will reign with him for *a thousand years*.

Christ's return was the topic of the last chapter. The great tribulation is the global, intense period of suffering associated with his return. This doctrine, then, concerns the nature of the millennium and its relationship to Christ's return and the great tribulation. There are four primary views.

Amillennialism is the position that there is no (thus, *a-*) millennium, or no future thousand-year period of Christ's reign on the earth. Rather, it identifies the millennium with the current church age. At the end of this present era, Christ will return and defeat Satan, thus ushering in the last judgment, the resurrection, and the new heaven and new earth.

Postmillennialism is the position that Christ's return will occur after (thus, *post-*) the millennium, which will be an age of peace and prosperity on earth. The impact of the gospel will be powerful and very extensive, with much of the world's population becoming Christian. As a result, the world will be Christianized, or dominated by Christian principles. While not a literal one-thousand-year period, the millennium will be an age of righteousness, harmony, and flourishing. Following it, Christ will return, execute the last judgment and the resurrection, and establish the new heaven and new earth.

Historic premillennialism is the position that Christ's return will occur before (thus, *pre-*) the millennium, which is a (literal) thousand-year reign of Christ on the earth. Prior to Christ's return, the great tribulation will occur on the earth, with the church experiencing at least in part this seven-year period of intense suffering. Thus, Christ's return will be *after* the tribulation (*post*tribulational) and *before* the millennium (*pre*millennial).

Pretribulational, or dispensational, premillennialism is the position that Christ's return will occur before (thus, *pre-*) the millennium, which is a (literal) thousand-year reign of Christ on the earth. Prior to Christ's return, the great tribulation will occur on the earth, but Christ will rapture, or remove, the church so that it does not experience this seven-year period of intense suffering. Thus, the rapture will be *before* the tribulation (*pre*tribulational) and Christ's return will be *before* the millennium (*pre*-millennial). Because of its association with dispensationalism, this position is also called dispensational premillennialism.

Biblical Support

Each of the four positions interprets Revelation 20:1–6 differently and thus uses this passage in support. *Amillennialism* takes a nonliteral approach: Satan's binding is God's current restraint of him, enabling the gospel to advance everywhere. Saints who rule are Christians who have died and are now with Christ in heaven. Their first resurrection is a spiritual reality (they become Christians), while the second resurrection will be a bodily reality. At the end of this present era, Christ will defeat a loosed Satan. Thus, the millennium is the current church age.

Postmillennialism also interprets Revelation 20:1–6 in a nonliteral way. The millennium is not the present church age, nor is it a future period of Christ's earthly reign. Rather, it will be a golden age emerging out of the current period as the gospel exerts its mighty impact. Satan's binding paves the way for the expansion of the gospel throughout the entire world. Several of Jesus's parables portray the gradual development of the kingdom of God: It is like a mustard seed, "the smallest of all seeds," which, as it grows, eventually "becomes a tree so that the birds of the air come and makes nests in its branches" (Matt. 13:31–32). Similarly, it "is like leaven that a woman took and hid in three measures of flour, till it was all leavened" (13:33). These parables emphasize the gradual growth of the gospel until it impacts the entire world. Thus, the millennium is this future age of peace and prosperity, after which Christ will return.

Both versions of *premillennialism* interpret Revelation 20:1–6 literally. The millennium will be preceded by the great tribulation, which will begin with the appearance of "the abomination of desolation," also called "the man of lawlessness" (Matt. 24:15; 2 Thess. 2:3–4), who will wreak havoc. This unprecedented time of trouble, which seems to last seven years (Dan. 9:27), will feature unmatched satanic attack, unparalleled human evil, and furious divine wrath (Rev. 6–19). After this great tribulation punishes the earth, Christ will return to rule over it (while Satan is bound) for a thousand years. At its conclusion, Satan will be loosed and then defeated in his futile effort to oppose Christ (Rev. 20).

The two versions of premillennialism differ over a key point: *Historic premillennialism* believes that the church will go through the great tribulation, experiencing its horrors at least in part. This suffering is in keeping with the church's expected suffering (Phil. 1:29; Acts 14:22; 1 Thess. 3:3–4; 2 Tim. 3:12). *Pretribulational premillennialism* holds that the church will be removed from the earth before the onset of the great tribulation. This rapture is described as Christians being "caught up" with Christ in the air and accompanying him back to heaven (1 Thess. 4:13–18). Such escape from divine tribulation has been promised to the church, which Jesus delivers "from the wrath to come" (1:10; 5:9). Indeed, the church will be kept from "the hour of trial that is coming on the whole world, to try those who dwell on the earth" (Rev. 3:10). Because the tribulation targets nonbelievers, it has no purpose for the church, which escapes from it.

Premillennialism often appeals to other biblical passages in support. For example, Isaiah's prophecy of "new heavens and a new earth" contains language that is not easily squared with an eternal state: "No more shall there be in it [Jerusalem] an infant who lives but a few days, or an old man who does not fill out his days, for the young man shall die a hundred years old, and the sinner a hundred years old shall be accursed" (Isa. 65:17, 20). Premillennialism understands this description to refer to the thousand-year reign of Christ on the earth, which still features death. Moreover, the position believes that the divine promises of a future restoration of the people of Israel to the promised land will be fulfilled in this millennial period. And it will be during this time that Christ's promise to his disciples as he instituted the Lord's Supper—"I tell you I will not drink again of this fruit of the vine until that day when I drink it new with you in my Father's kingdom"—will be fulfilled (Matt. 26:29).

Major Errors

1. *Dogmatically pretending to know too much about the nature of the millennium.* For example, in the early church, some leaders wrote elaborate descriptions of the abundant fertility of the millennium. The speculative emphasis on the opulent productivity of that earthly existence soured other leaders on premillennialism. They had difficulty reconciling such material blessings with the New Testament's focus on spiritual blessings. Engaging in such fanciful imagination fails to acknowledge

that Scripture has very little to say about this matter, and speculation is not helpful.

2. *An exaggerated confidence in the gospel to penetrate the world so as to Christianize it.* This position does not deal adequately with the entrenched reality of human and systemic sin, along with satanic evil. Moreover, it risks embracing an overrealized eschatology that is at odds with the biblical worldview.

ENACTING THE DOCTRINE

From an amillennial perspective, Christ's return will usher in the last judgment, the resurrection, and the new heaven and new earth. It stimulates hope in his second coming as the next cataclysmic divine event, which will mark the dividing point between this present age and the eternal state.

> ### Perennial Questions and Problematic Issues
>
> - Is our church amillennial, postmillennial, historic premillennial, or pretribulational premillennial, and why?
> - Why is there a need for a millennial reign of Christ on earth?
> - What does our church believe about the future of Israel?

From a postmillennial perspective, the gospel is a leavening agent that is slowly but certainly penetrating the human race and this earthly existence. This growing presence of Christ's kingdom stimulates hope in a future golden age of peace and human flourishing. Beyond that lies the hope of the last judgment, the resurrection, and the new heaven and new earth.

From a premillennial perspective, Christ's return will usher in his earthly thousand-year reign. He will rule as a benevolent king, powerfully and publicly demonstrating his righteousness, goodness, and justice. Beyond that lies the hope of the last judgment, the resurrection, and the new heaven and new earth.

All of the positions provide reasons for hope in God's future activity on behalf of his people and his creation.

TEACHING THE DOCTRINE

Eschatology fascinates many people, and debate about the millennium engenders a high degree of interest in this doctrine. It is far too easy to lose sight of the commonalities shared by all sides of the debate. A good starting point, then, is to remind the participants of those matters that unite us: the return of Christ, the resurrection, the last judgment, eternal life for the righteous and eternal death for the unrighteous, and the new heaven and new earth.

Following this presentation, the four positions should be fairly and concisely set out. Diagrams that simply present the four views side by side can be quite helpful to highlight the differences. Be sure to explain your church's millennial view. If it does not take a stance, encourage participants to develop their own view while they are respectful of other positions. As all the views appeal to Revelation 20 for support, study this passage carefully. Noting its different interpretations by the four positions will underscore the fact that all of them seek to be biblically well grounded.

TEACHING OUTLINE

1. *Mille annum*, Revelation 20:1–6, and the summary
2. Major affirmations (with biblical support)
   A. Amillennialism
   B. Postmillennialism
   C. Historic premillennialism
   D. Pretribulational, or dispensational, premillennialism
3. Major errors to avoid
   A. Pretending to know too much about the nature of the millennium
   B. Exhibiting an exaggerated confidence in the gospel to penetrate the world so as to Christianize it
4. Enacting the doctrine
   A. Deciding which view of the millennium one holds
   B. Hoping in God's future activity on behalf of his people and his creation

RESOURCES

Allison, *Theological Terms*, s.vv. "amillennialism," "dispensational premillennialism," "Great Tribulation," "historic premillennialism," "postmillennialism"
Elwell, *Evangelical Dictionary of Theology*, s.v. "Millennium, Views of the"

Erickson, *Christian Theology*, chap. 57

Grenz, *Theology for the Community of God*, chap. 22

Grudem, *Systematic Theology*, chap. 55

Horton, *Pilgrim Theology*, chap. 18

Thoennes, *Life's Biggest Questions*, chap. 16

47

THE RESURRECTION

SUMMARY

Resurrection is rising again, with reembodiment, after death. The resurrection of believers is their glorification, the final mighty act of God in their salvation.

MAIN THEMES

- As the final mighty act of salvation, the bodily resurrection of believers completes the divine work of redemption and is their glorification.
- Glorification will occur when Christ returns.
- It is both the reembodiment of deceased believers in heaven and the change of embodied states for living believers on earth.
- The resurrection bodies will be imperishable, glorious, powerful, and spiritual.
- Unbelievers will also experience bodily resurrection.

UNDERSTANDING THE DOCTRINE

Major Affirmations

Following the mighty divine acts of union with Christ, regeneration, justification, adoption, baptism with the Holy Spirit, sanctification, and perseverance, the final saving act is glorification. It completes the preceding divine works and has particular reference to the resurrection of the bodies of believers.

Glorification will occur at Christ's return and will be both (1) the re-embodiment of believers who have died and exist without their bodies in heaven and (2) the instantaneous change in the bodies of believers on earth. In the first case, their bodies will be raised from the dead and transformed. They will once again, and forever, be embodied. In the second case, their current bodies will be immediately transformed. They will not have to die, but will experience a change in their embodied states from earthly body to glorified body.

In both cases, resurrection bodies will be different from earthly bodies. Bodies in their earthly existence are perishable (susceptible to wearing out and becoming ill), shameful (thus covered by clothes), weak (impotent), and natural (dominated by fallenness). Bodies in their resurrection state will be imperishable (never wearing out or becoming sick), glorious (beautiful, perhaps radiant), powerful (not superhuman but full strength), and spiritual (dominated by the Holy Spirit).

The resurrection body of Jesus Christ is the prototype of the resurrection bodies of believers. As his body is in his resurrected and ascended state, so will be the bodies of believers. They will live forever as gloriously embodied people, fully conformed to the image of Christ, in the new heaven and new earth.

Unbelievers will also experience the resurrection of their bodies. As to when this event will take place, amillennialism and postmillennialism link it with the return of Christ, the final judgment, and the inauguration of the new heaven and new earth. That is, both believers and unbelievers will experience bodily resurrection at the same time. Premillennialism holds that at Christ's second coming, believers will receive their resurrection bodies and join him for his thousand-year earthly kingdom. Only at the completion of the millennium will unbelievers experience their bodily resurrection.

Biblical Support

Seeds of the hope of bodily resurrection are found in the Old Testament. Job expressed his hope: "After my skin has been thus destroyed, yet in my flesh I shall see God" (Job 19:26). With great expectation, Isaiah exclaimed, "Your dead shall live; their bodies shall rise. You who dwell in the dust, awake and sing for joy! For your dew is a dew of light, and the earth will give birth to the dead" (Isa. 26:19; cf. Dan. 12:2).

Jesus continued and heightened this resurrection hope. When Lazarus died, and Martha expressed confidence "that he will rise again in the resurrection on the last day," Jesus pointed to himself, promising, "I am the resurrection and the life. Whoever believes in me, though he die, yet shall he live, and everyone who lives and believes in me shall never die" (John 11:23–26). Indeed, it was for the purpose of resurrection that Jesus engaged in his saving mission: "For this is the will of my Father, that everyone who looks on the Son and believes in him should have eternal life, and I will raise him up on the last day" (6:38–40).

In order to accomplish this mission, Jesus first had to die and be raised from the dead. He predicted both his crucifixion and his resurrection (Matt. 16:21). Thus, Jesus is "the firstborn from the dead" (Col. 1:18; Rev. 1:5), the prototype of his followers: "Christ has been raised from the dead, the firstfruits of those who have fallen asleep. For as by a man came death, by a man has come also the resurrection of the dead" (1 Cor. 15:20–21).

This hope in the resurrection became a major point of the apostles' message, illustrated by Paul: "I stand here testifying . . . that the Christ must suffer and that, by being the first to rise from the dead, he would proclaim light both to our people and to the Gentiles" (Acts 26:22–23). Indeed, the gospel summarized is "that Christ died for our sins in accordance with the Scriptures, that he was buried, that he was raised on the third day in accordance with the Scriptures" (1 Cor. 15:3–4).

Believers have been promised, and thus look forward to, the glorification of their entire person, when Christ returns. As John notes, "We know that when he appears we shall be like him, because we shall see him as he is" (1 John 3:2). Progression in salvation during this life prepares believers to be "pure and blameless for the day of Christ, filled with the fruit of righteousness" (Phil. 1:10–11), "holy and blameless and above reproach before him" (Col. 1:22), and "guiltless in the day of our Lord Jesus Christ" (1 Cor. 1:8). This glorification is the completion of their salvation, the climax of all the mighty acts of God leading up to, and anticipating, it.

Importantly, such perfection includes physical wholeness as well. Believers await the return of Christ, "who will transform our lowly body to be like his glorious body, by the power that enables him even to subject all things to himself" (Phil. 3:21). This resurrection body contrasts strikingly with one's current earthly body: "What is sown is perishable; what is raised is imperishable. It is sown in dishonor; it is raised in glory. It is sown in weakness; it is raised in power. It is sown a natural body; it is raised a spiritual body" (1 Cor. 15:42–44). Longing for the glorious completion of their salvation, believers "groan inwardly as [they] wait eagerly for adoption as sons, the redemption of [their] bodies" (Rom. 8:23). The fullness of salvation clearly includes bodily resurrection.

At Christ's return, there will be disembodied believers in heaven with him and embodied believers on the earth. The dead will be raised first, receiving their resurrection bodies (1 Thess. 4:15–17). They will be followed by living believers, who will not die but will have their resurrection bodies slipped over their current bodies (2 Cor. 5:1–5).

As for the resurrection of unbelievers, amillennialism and postmillennialism point to biblical passages that affirm one resurrection. Addressing eternal punishment, the Old Testament presents a division between those in the resurrection who will experience "everlasting life" and others who will experience "shame and everlasting contempt" (Dan. 12:2). Though the two groups will have different destinies, they will experience bodily resurrection at the same time. Similarly, Jesus promised a coming event "when all who are in the tombs will hear his [Jesus's] voice and come out, those who have done good to the resurrection of life, and those who have done evil to the resurrection of judgment" (John 5:28–29; cf. Acts 24:15).

Premillennialism separates the resurrection of believers, which will occur at Christ's return, and the resurrection of unbelievers, which will occur at the end of the millennium. This position appeals to the distinction between two groups in Revelation 20: "They [Christ's followers] came to life and reigned with Christ for *a thousand years*. The rest of the dead did not come to life until *the thousand years* were ended. This is the first resurrection. Blessed and holy is the one who shares in the first resurrection!" (vv. 4–6). Thus, the first resurrection is that of believers at Christ's return, which reembodies them for their millennial existence. The second resurrection is that of "the rest of the dead," or unbelievers, which will occur at the conclusion of the millennium.

Major Errors

1. *As the resurrection of Christ has been dismissed, the resurrection of believers has been set aside as being mythical and physically impossible.* This view is tied to the rejection of miracles. They are considered to be impossible, because they violate physical laws. It is also associated with a view of salvation that is purely spiritual in nature and does not at all pertain to the body. Thus, ultimate salvation is the escape of the soul from the body at death, with eternal life having no physical component at all.

2. *Physical resurrection and reembodiment of believers have been rejected because human existence is only physical.* This increasingly common view is fueled by neuroscience. Its identification of human life with human embodiment means that when one's physical organism—the body—ceases to function, human existence terminates. There is no disembodied existence of believers in heaven after death, and there cannot be. This view contradicts the biblical and traditional doctrine of the intermediate state, as well as the doctrine of the resurrection.

ENACTING THE DOCTRINE

Living in light of Christ's return, the completion of our salvation with glorification, and our bodily resurrection have implications for how we live our earthly existence as believers. As John explains, "Beloved, we are God's children now, and what we will be has not yet appeared; but we know that when he appears we shall be like him, because we shall see him as he is. And everyone who thus hopes in him purifies himself as he is pure" (1 John 3:2–3). As disciples of Christ, into whose image one day we will be fully conformed, we now strive to be blameless, righteous, holy, guiltless, and beyond reproach. Thankfully, we do not have to rely on ourselves for ongoing sanctification. Let us avail ourselves, therefore, of the adequate resources God provides for progressing in maturity: the Word of God, the

Spirit of God, fellowship with other believers, the spiritual disciplines, and more. And let the hope of our glorification push us to live in light of our eternal existence.

TEACHING THE DOCTRINE

After treating the many divine works of salvation—union with Christ, regeneration, justification, adoption, baptism with the Holy Spirit, sanctification, and perseverance—a good starting point in teaching this doctrine is to ask, where are all these mighty saving acts leading? That is, the application of salvation is purposeful, aiming at an ultimate goal, which is glorification with bodily resurrection.

Because of much confusion regarding this point, an important clarification to make is that the ultimate hope of salvation is not that believers die and live with Christ forever as disembodied souls in heaven. Rather, the ultimate hope is physical resurrection, the reembodiment of believers, who will then live eternally in the new heaven and new earth (a physical future).

As the only authoritative source of true knowledge about glorification is divine revelation, teaching this doctrine should focus

Perennial Questions and Problematic Issues

- How will God bring about the resurrection of believers?
- What exactly will our resurrection bodies be like?
- If we are nothing but our body, when our body ceases to function, death means the end of our existence such that there cannot be life beyond this one.
- I've always heard that our greatest hope is to die so our soul can be with Jesus forever in heaven.

on biblical texts and provide a model of appropriate reservation and humility about this matter. People may wonder, How will God bring about the resurrection of believers? and What exactly will our resurrection bodies be like? But there are no definitive answers to questions like these, beyond what Scripture presents, and there cannot be. So guard against getting carried away with speculation.

At the same time, imagining one's resurrection body can be very helpful to participants who are suffering debilitating physical problems and/or who have family members and friends who are suffering such handicaps. Those who live now with chronic pain, disabling fatigue, malfunctioning or missing limbs, and more can imagine a coming day when Christ makes all things new and gives them a new body that is completely whole, free from all suffering.

TEACHING OUTLINE

1. The summary
2. Where are all the mighty saving acts of God leading?
3. Major affirmations (with biblical support)
   A. Glorification: the final act of salvation
   B. The hope of the resurrection
   C. Jesus as the first to be resurrected and the prototype of believers' resurrection
   D. The nature of the resurrection body
4. Major errors to avoid
   A. Dismissing the resurrection of believers as being mythical and physically impossible
   B. Rejecting the physical resurrection and reembodiment of believers by believing that human existence is only physical
5. Enacting the doctrine
   A. Striving now to be blameless, righteous, holy, guiltless, and beyond reproach as we hope in our future resurrection and eternal existence
   B. Relying on divine resources for progressing in maturity

---

RESOURCES

Allison, *Theological Terms*, s.vv. "glorification," "resurrection of people"

Elwell, *Evangelical Dictionary of Theology*, s.vv. "Glorification," "Resurrection of the Dead"

Erickson, *Christian Theology*, 924–29

Grenz, *Theology for the Community of God*, chap. 21

Grudem, *Systematic Theology*, chap. 42

Horton, *Pilgrim Theology*, chap. 14

Thoennes, *Life's Biggest Questions*, chap. 16

48

THE FINAL JUDGMENT

SUMMARY

The final judgment is the future, universal, public verdict rendered by Christ in which he will evaluate all human beings and angelic beings.

MAIN THEMES

- This climactic event is called the "great white throne judgment."
- Unlike the personal judgment that occurs at death, the final judgment will be a world-encompassing and public verdict.
- While some locate this judgment at Christ's return, others believe it will take place at the end of the millennium.
- Christ himself will execute the judgment, but his followers will also join in.
- All human beings will be judged.
- Degrees of rewards will be meted out to believers, and degrees of punishments will be meted out to unbelievers.
- Angelic beings will be judged.

- Christ will be just and impartial in his judgment.
- The judgment will be final and eternal.

KEY SCRIPTURE

Matthew 25:31–46; John 5:19–29; Acts 10:42; 17:30–31; Romans 2:1–11; 1 Corinthians 3:10–15; 6:1–8; 2 Corinthians 5:10; 2 Timothy 4:1; 1 Peter 4:5; Revelation 20

UNDERSTANDING THE DOCTRINE

Major Affirmations

The final judgment, or great white throne judgment (Rev. 20:11–15), is the future, universal, public verdict rendered by Christ in which he will evaluate all human beings and angelic beings. All human beings are judged at their death, but that judgment is personal, not public. It determines their temporary destiny as disembodied people, with believers going to be with Christ in heaven and unbelievers going into torment in hell. The final judgment, by contrast, is a public display in which Christ will evaluate all human beings and angelic beings for their final and eternal destiny.

Amillennialism and postmillennialism hold that the great white throne judgment will take place at the second coming of Christ. Premillennialism of both types (historic and dispensational/pretribulational) maintains that this judgment will take place at the end of the millennium. After Satan wages one last-ditch battle and is decisively defeated, Christ will execute the final judgment.

At the great white throne judgment, Christ himself will be the judge. This is his prerogative, as delegated to him by God the Father. In some way, Christ will engage his followers in this final judgment, a task for which they will be competent.

All human beings will be judged, and Christ will mete out two sentences: The righteous will experience divine remunerative justice. They will be recompensed with eternal life, as well as degrees of rewards according to their works. The unrighteous will experience divine retributive justice. They will be sentenced to eternal conscious punishment, as well as degrees of chastisement according to their works.

388

Angelic beings will be judged, and Christ will engage his followers in his assessment. This judgment may encompass both good angels, to reward them for their service, and bad angels, or demons, to punish them for their wickedness. Or it may be directed at the evil angels only.

Christ the judge will be just, impartial, and fair. He will not show favoritism in his judgment, and he will not be deceived by appearance or performance so as to assess wrongly. Moreover, his authoritative judgment will be final and eternal. It will stand forever and will ultimately be manifested in the final state.

Biblical Support

The Old Testament introduces the reality of final judgment, often associated with the "day of the LORD" (Joel 2:1, 11, 31; Zeph. 1:14). It involves both divine destruction (Isa. 13:6, 9; Ezek. 30:3; Joel 1:15; 2:31) and divine vengeance (Jer. 46:10; Obad. 15). Despite this theme of doom, a measure of hope is also associated with the "latter days" (Isa. 2:20; 9:1; Jer. 48:47; 49:39).

The New Testament picks up on this theme. Beginning with Christ's first coming, the "last/latter days" have begun (Heb. 1:1–2). The descent of the Holy Spirit on Pentecost initiated this period (Acts 2:17–21; citing Joel 2:28–32), which is full of trouble (1 Tim. 4:1; 2 Tim. 3:1). Still, the day of the Lord has future reference, in regard to both salvation (1 Cor. 5:5) and destruction (1 Thess. 5:1–11; 2 Thess. 2:1–12).

Judgment with respect to both salvation and destruction belongs to Jesus Christ. Though God the Father is the judge, he has delegated authority to his Son to execute judgment (John 5:22, 27). Indeed, the Lord "has fixed a day on which he will judge the world in righteousness by a man whom he has appointed" (Acts 17:31).

Both believers and unbelievers experience some divine judgment during their earthly life. As believers experience justification, God declares them "not guilty" but "righteous instead." He renders a future verdict ahead of time, before the final judgment (Rom. 3:21–4:25). Thus, believers will never face condemnation (8:1).

Unbelievers, meanwhile, are in dire straits. They already live under a divine sentence of condemnation (John 3:18). At times, they experience a foretaste of the destruction to come in the sufferings and heartaches they endure. Even when their life is easy, however, Paul's warning applies to them: "But because of your hard and impenitent heart you are storing up wrath for yourself on the day of wrath when God's righteous judgment will be revealed" (Rom. 2:5). There is a wrathful judgment to come on the day of the Lord.

As a climactic event, the day of the Lord culminates in Christ's great white throne judgment:

> Then I saw a great white throne and him who was seated on it. From his presence earth and sky fled away, and no place was found for them. And I saw the dead, great and small, standing before the throne, and books were opened. Then another book was opened, which is the book of life. And the dead were judged by what was written in the books, according to what they had done. And the sea gave up the dead who were in it, Death and Hades gave up the dead who were in them, and they were judged, each one of them, according to what they had done. Then Death and Hades were thrown into the lake of fire. This is the second death, the lake of fire. And if anyone's name was not found written in the book of life, he was thrown into the lake of fire. (Rev. 20:11–15)

Christ himself is "the one appointed by God to be judge of the living and the dead" (Acts 10:42; see also 2 Tim. 4:1). He will judge all human beings, "render[ing] to each one according to his works" (Rom. 2:6–8). Christ's judgment will be meted out on the living and the dead, on believers and unbelievers.

In the case of believers, the divine verdict of justification has already been rendered. They will inherit eternal life and "not come into judgment" (John 5:24). As part of the divine remunerative justice, they will be recompensed with degrees of rewards (2 Cor. 5:10). Good works done for the glory of God and out of love for him and other people will be richly rewarded. Evil deeds done in the flesh and for self-promotion will result in a forfeit of reward (1 Cor. 3:12–15).

In the case of unbelievers, their lack of belief in Christ leads to condemnation (John 3:36). They will be sentenced to eternal conscious punishment. As part of divine retributive justice, they will experience degrees of chastisement according to their works, "a greater condemnation" (Luke 20:47) for some unbelievers, and a "more bearable/tolerable" day of judgment for others (Matt. 11:22, 24).

Christ will also be the judge of angelic beings. Certainly, Christ will judge Satan and the demons in "the judgment of the great day" (Jude 6;

see also 2 Pet. 2:4). He may also judge the good angels (assuming the referent of "angels" in 1 Cor. 6:3 is to both the bad and good angels). In some way, Christ's followers will join him in this final judgment: "The saints will judge the world" and will "judge angels" (vv. 1–8).

As to the time of this event, amillennialism and postmillennialism hold that the great white throne judgment will take place at Christ's second coming. Biblical support depends on an interpretation of the millennium (Rev. 20:1–6) as either the current church age or a golden age that will arise out of this present period. After this era, Christ will come again, defeat Satan, and execute the final judgment (20:7–15).

Premillennialism maintains that this final judgment will take place at the end of the millennium. It depends on an interpretation of the millennium (Rev. 20:1–6) as a future thousand-year period. Christ will come again and reign on earth during the millennium. At its close, Satan will wage one last-ditch battle but will be decisively defeated (20:7–10). Christ will then execute the final judgment (20:11–15).

God "judges impartially according to each one's deeds" (1 Pet. 1:17; cf. Rom. 2:11). Accordingly, at his great white throne judgment, Jesus's judgments will be "true and just" (Rev. 16:7; 19:2). He will not judge based on appearance (John 7:24), nor will he be deceived by mere show (Matt. 6:1, 5, 16, 18).

The great white throne judgment is both final and eternal. It will be the last, climactic divine judgment. And the verdict rendered will stand forever: The wicked "will go away into eternal punishment, but the righteous into eternal life" (Matt. 25:46). The eternal nature of the final judgment of the wicked will be the topic of the next chapter ("Eternal Punishment").

Major Errors

1. *A denial of the final judgment.* A key reason for liberalism's denial is the rejection of God's retributive justice. This view fails to acknowledge that Scripture has much to say about both divine retribution and Christ's final judgment.

2. *A tendency to speculate about the details of this event.* This "end times" extremism fails to recognize that Scripture treats the final judgment with great reserve, and speculation is often incorrect and even dangerous.

3. *Confusion over the judgment that Christians will face.* Some misunderstand this doctrine as setting forth two grounds for justification: God's pronouncement of initial justification, which is rendered on the basis of faith alone, and his verdict of final justification, which will be rendered on the basis of one's works. This position fails to see that justification is by faith alone. Good works, which flow from and manifest justification, are the necessary fruit of faith and will also be assessed, not for salvation, but for reward.

ENACTING THE DOCTRINE

From the fact that "we will all stand before the judgment seat of God," Paul urges us to stop passing judgment and despising our brothers and sisters. Each Christian "will give an account of himself to God," so we should stop being obstacles to others and destroying them by our judgments (Rom. 14:10–13).

Christ commands us, "Do not lay up for yourselves treasures on earth, . . . but lay up for yourselves treasures in heaven" (Matt. 6:19–20). Though personal gain is not our primary motivation (magnifying the glory of God is), it is a proper motivation for us to do good. Beyond eternal life in the presence of God, enjoying the rewards of our labor is a hope to which we should look forward (Gal. 6:9–10).

TEACHING THE DOCTRINE

This doctrine resonates with the common human desire for the good to be rewarded and the bad to be punished. Importantly, Christianity's approach to this universal longing has some important differences from the common notion (for example, the gospel's emphasis on faith in Christ to rescue evil people sets it apart from the desire that everyone get their due). Still, it can be a point of contact with unbelievers who have a strong sense of justice. The great white throne judgment will be that climactic event in which the righteous in Christ will be rewarded while the unrighteous will be judged. The tables will be turned, all wrongs will be made right, and divine justice will be vindicated. So try to connect with the participants' sense of fairness and justice.

Be sure to distinguish between personal judgment that occurs at death and the public final judgment. Watch for participants who dislike the idea of rewards for believers. A popular notion is that we should only be concerned for the glory of God and have no regard for personal blessing and gain. Be sure to emphasize that Scripture itself sets forth rewards for faithful service as a good motivation for Christians.

The dreadful destiny of the unrighteous should spur on the church to share the gospel with nonbelievers (Rom. 10:5–17).

TEACHING OUTLINE

1. The summary
2. Discussion on the universal sense of fairness and justice
3. Major affirmations (with biblical support)
   A. The time of the final judgment
   B. Christ the judge
   C. The judgment of believers
   D. The judgment of unbelievers
   E. The judgment of angels
   F. The fairness and justice of the final judgment
   G. The finality and eternality of the final judgment
4. Major errors to avoid
   A. Denying the final judgment
   B. Speculating about the details of this event
   C. Being confused about the judgment that Christians will face
5. Enacting the doctrine
   A. Avoiding being obstacles to others and destroying them by our judgments
   B. Being motivated by the promise of future rewards at the judgment seat of Christ

RESOURCES

Allison, *Theological Terms*, s.v. "great white throne judgment"

Elwell, *Evangelical Dictionary of Theology*, s.vv. "Judgment Seat," "Last Judgment"

Erickson, *Christian Theology*, chap. 56

Grenz, *Theology for the Community of God*, chap. 23

Grudem, *Systematic Theology*, chap. 56

Horton, *Pilgrim Theology*, chap. 19

Thoennes, *Life's Biggest Questions*, chap. 16

49

ETERNAL PUNISHMENT

SUMMARY

One of two results of Christ's final judgment of people (the other being eternal life), this sentence against the unrighteous consists of conscious retribution in hell forever.

MAIN THEMES

- The final judgment will be a world-encompassing, public verdict rendered by Christ.
- The righteous will be rewarded with eternal life, but the unrighteous will be sentenced to eternal conscious punishment in hell / the lake of fire.
- While some locate this judgment at Christ's return, others believe it will take place at the end of the millennium.
- While eternal conscious punishment of the wicked is the historical position of the church, it is challenged by three heresies.
- *Universalism* believes that everyone will be saved.

- *Conditional immortality* maintains that believers will exist forever, but unbelievers will cease to exist at death.
- *Annihilationism* holds that after a period of punishment, the wicked will be destroyed and thus not experience eternal punishment.

KEY SCRIPTURE

Daniel 12:2; Matthew 25:31–46; Mark 9:43–48; 2 Thessalonians 1:9; Revelation 14:14–20; 20:11–15

UNDERSTANDING THE DOCTRINE

Major Affirmations

The previous chapter addressed the final judgment, or great white throne judgment, of Jesus Christ. This world-encompassing, public verdict pronounced by Christ will consist of two sentences: The righteous will experience divine remunerative justice and be rewarded with eternal life. They will live forever with the Triune God in the new heaven and new earth. The unrighteous will experience divine retributive justice and be sentenced to eternal conscious punishment in hell. They will live forever apart from the presence of God, suffering divine vengeance.

Amillennialism and *postmillennialism* locate this judgment at Christ's return, as the precursor to the eternal state of either blessedness in the new heaven and new earth or retribution in hell / the lake of fire. Accordingly, eternal conscious punishment for the wicked follows the return of Christ. *Historic premillennialism* and *pretribulational*, or *dispensational*, *premillennialism* place this judgment after the millennium, as the precursor to the eternal state. Accordingly, eternal conscious punishment for the wicked in hell / the lake of fire follows Christ's defeat of Satan as the millennium concludes.

This historic church position has rarely been challenged, but the twentieth century witnessed the rise of more virulent attacks against it. These wrong views are of three types:

Universalism is the position that if not in life, then after death, all people will ultimately embrace salvation. It fails to respect death as the point at which human destiny, based on faith in Christ during one's lifetime, is fixed. It also imagines some type of postmortem evangelism by which people who rejected the gospel during their earthly existence will receive another opportunity to believe in Christ and be saved.

Conditional immortality is the position that God alone possesses immortality; he is intrinsically immortal. Believers by God's grace receive eternal life—immortality—by becoming partakers of his nature. Unbelievers, who do not possess or receive immortality, naturally die. Conditional immortality differs from universalism because it denies that everyone will be saved. It differs from the church's historic position because it considers that view to be based on the immortality of the soul, a belief that it deems not a biblical teaching. Rather, believers receive immortality and unbelievers cease to exist.

Annihilationism is the position that after death, the wicked will be destroyed as punishment for their sin. It differs from conditional immortality because it holds that, after death, unbelievers will suffer punishment for their sin for a time and then they will be annihilated. This position points to the biblical expression "eternal destruction" (2 Thess. 1:9) as indicative of the destiny of the wicked: their punishment is cessation of existence. Moreover, the imagery of fire—a destructive element—in association with hell suggests annihilation rather than ongoing suffering. Furthermore, appealing to the legal principle that one's punishment must match one's crime, the position maintains that eternal punishment of the wicked would be cruel and unjust. Thus, the wicked will ultimately be destroyed after limited punishment.

The church has faced these challenges and consistently denounced them. It has always maintained that the wicked will experience eternal conscious punishment.

Biblical Support

The Old Testament introduces the reality of eternal punishment when it presents a division between those in the resurrection who will experience "everlasting life" and others who will experience "shame and everlasting contempt" (Dan. 12:2). Jesus picks up on this imagery as he describes the final judgment: "These [the unrighteous] will go away into eternal punishment, but the righteous into eternal life" (Matt. 25:46). Importantly, the two destinies are modified by the same adjective: both life and punishment are *eternal*. Similarly, Jesus contrasts the future of "those who have done good to the resurrection of life, and those who have done evil to the resurrection of judgment" (John 5:29).

Scripture presents hell as the place of misery and torment for the unrighteous. The expressions associated with it—"weeping and gnashing of teeth" (Matt. 8:12; 25:30), "the unquenchable fire" (Mark 9:43, 48), "their worm does not die" (v. 48), "the smoke of their torment goes up forever and ever, and they have no rest, day or night" (Rev. 14:11)—underscore the painful, castigating nature of hell. Indeed, hell is first and foremost the sphere of punishment for Satan and demons (2 Pet. 2:4). It then becomes the state and place of unbelievers who have died. Still, they do not experience the fullness of their punishment, which awaits their resurrection and the final judgment: "Then Death and Hades were thrown into the lake of fire. This is the second death, the lake of fire. And if anyone's name was not found written in the book of life, he was thrown into the lake of fire" (Rev. 20:14–15). The eternal conscious punishment of the wicked begins in hell and continues in the lake of fire.

The three major challenges to the traditional doctrine attempt to build a biblical case, but each one fails.

Universalism appeals to biblical affirmations that in and through Christ, all will be justified and live forever (Rom. 5:18; 1 Cor. 15:22). It also underscores the biblical teaching that one day all things will be subjected to Christ "that God may be all in all" (1 Cor. 15:28). However, Paul's comments apply specifically to believers—"those who receive the abundance of grace and the free gift of righteousness" (Rom. 5:17), those who have faith and hope in Christ (1 Cor. 15:14, 17, 19)—not to all people. As for the glory of God being "all in all," even in the divine punishment of the wicked forever, God will be glorified as holy, righteous, and just.

Conditional immortality is correct that God alone possesses immortality; he is intrinsically immortal (1 Tim. 6:16). Whether the traditional view is dependent on the Greek concept of the immortality of the soul is not important, for a biblical case for the everlasting existence of human beings can be made. Not in themselves, but because of God's providence, human beings will continue to exist forever, either as the righteous blessed with eternal life or as the unrighteous cursed with eternal destruction (Matt. 25:46).

Annihilationism takes the biblical expression "eternal destruction" (Phil. 3:19; 2 Thess. 1:9) to indicate that the destiny of the wicked is the cessation of existence. Additionally, it appeals to the imagery of fire—a symbol of destruction—to support annihilation rather than ongoing suffering. In response, "destruction" does not necessarily mean cessation of existence. Rather, it can refer to the retributive, damning nature of the eternal punishment. Also, Jesus drew the parallel between eternal life and eternal punishment (Matt. 25:46). If the former is everlasting (blessed) existence, then the latter must be everlasting (cursed) existence. As for the imagery of fire, when Jesus used it to describe hell, he modified the word with "unquenchable" (Mark 9:43–48), indicating that in regard to hell, fire does not destroy but will continually smoke.

Major Errors

In addition to the three heresies discussed above, two other errors arise in conjunction with this doctrine.

1. *The dismissal of eternal conscious punishment.* One reason for this is the rejection of divine retributive justice because this attribute does not present God in the way people want him to be. Another reason is the legal principle that the punishment must match the crime, with the conclusion drawn that because the sin of human beings is finite, so God's punishment of their sin must be finite. The church has responded to this argument in several ways: First, the view undervalues the enormity of the crime that human beings commit against God. Second, the view overlooks the fact that unbelievers in hell do not cease to sin, but continue to do so eternally. Third, the punishment for a crime is meted out according to the dignity of the person against whom the crime is committed. Because sin is committed against God, who is infinitely majestic, sin deserves infinite punishment.

2. *A gleeful anticipation of the eternal punishment of the wicked.* In one sense, this sentiment is correct: God is right and just in meting out eternal condemnation against entrenched sinners. Moreover, such divine punishment corresponds with the human sense of justice. Where it errs is when believers prefer that nonbelievers experience damnation rather than salvation. Like God, who does not wish "that any should perish, but that all should reach repentance" (2 Pet. 3:9), and "who desires all people to be saved and to come to the knowledge of the truth" (1 Tim. 2:4), Christians should share that same sentiment. No matter how much they have been mistreated, believers must long for the perpetrators of those

crimes to turn to Christ and be saved. If that does not occur due to the wrongdoers' rejection of the gospel, then believers will rest contentedly with the eternal conscious punishment that God will mete out against those evil ones.

ENACTING THE DOCTRINE

Knowing the fate of the wicked should push the church to engage missionally with non-believers. We should take the initiative to share the gospel with those around us. As a church, we should plant churches both in our city and around our country. Furthermore, as a church, we should send out missionaries into every part of the globe, especially to unreached people groups, so that people everywhere may hear the good news, believe in Christ, be incorporated into a church, and engage their neighbors, their nation, and the world with the gospel.

What's at stake in this doctrine? The prerogative of our holy God to exercise his retributive justice and punish his image bearers who refuse to honor his Son and avail themselves of the salvation that his Son accomplished.

TEACHING THE DOCTRINE

Whereas eschatology fascinates many people, a discussion of the eternal conscious punishment of the wicked often brings consternation. Like the doctrine of reprobation, this doctrine concerns the eternal destiny of our ancestors, parents, siblings, spouses, children, friends, coworkers, and multitudes of others. Accordingly, acknowledge the difficulties, and exercise care, in teaching it. Refuse to compromise the holiness and justice of God, especially the rightness of his retributive justice. Oppositely, refuse to allow participants to picture God as a sadistic tormentor. Those whom he justly consigns to eternal conscious punishment in hell are, after all, his image bearers who willfully refused to embrace his rescue scheme.

Participants will likely be surprised by the amount of biblical material that addresses this doctrine. It is Scripture, rather than our emotions or our preferences, which must form our belief on this matter. So be sure to spend adequate time studying what the Bible affirms about it. Reinforce this doctrine by explaining that the church has historically and unapologetically held to the eternal conscious punishment of the wicked. Indeed, it was not until the nineteenth century that the doctrine came under serious attack.

And attacked it has been! Work through the three major challenges—universalism, conditional immortality, and annihilationism—and demonstrate the misunderstanding of the biblical passages to which their proponents appeal. Underscore Jesus's description of the final judgment: "These [the unrighteous] will go away into eternal punishment, but the righteous into eternal life" (Matt. 25:46). The three major errors contradict, in one way or another, what our Lord affirmed on this matter.

TEACHING OUTLINE

1. The summary
2. Major affirmations (with biblical support)
   A. The nature of the final judgment
   B. The eternal conscious punishment of the wicked in hell / the lake of fire
   C. Three major challenges to the traditional doctrine
      i. Universalism
      ii. Conditional immortality
      iii. Annihilationism
3. Major errors to avoid
   A. Dismissing eternal conscious punishment
   B. Anticipating gleefully the eternal punishment of the wicked
4. Enacting the doctrine
   A. Taking the initiative to engage nonbelievers with the gospel
   B. Planting churches that plant other churches
   C. Sending out missionaries to unreached people groups

RESOURCES

Allison, *Theological Terms*, s.vv. "annihilationism," "conditional immortality," "eternal conscious punishment," "universalism"

Elwell, *Evangelical Dictionary of Theology*, s.vv. "Annihilationism," "Eternal Punishment," "Universalism"

Erickson, *Christian Theology*, chap. 58

Grenz, *Theology for the Community of God*, chap. 23

Grudem, *Systematic Theology*, chap. 56

Horton, *Pilgrim Theology*, chap. 19

Thoennes, *Life's Biggest Questions*, chap. 16

50

THE NEW HEAVEN AND NEW EARTH

SUMMARY

The new heaven and new earth is the final and eternal state of the universe resulting from the renewal of the current, fallen creation, for the glory of God.

MAIN THEMES

- The original heaven and the earth, as God created it, was very good.
- Because of the human fall into sin, God cursed the creation so that it too is fallen.
- The future of the creation is tied to the future of redeemed humanity.
- A total renewal of the entire creation, which is the hope toward which all exists, will take place.
- This may involve the destruction of the current cosmos, followed by its renewal.

- The timing of this renewal is a point of debate.
- God created everything for his glory, and the new heaven and new earth will perfectly display that glory.

KEY SCRIPTURE

Isaiah 65:17-25; Romans 8:18-25; 2 Peter 3:7-10; Revelation 21

UNDERSTANDING THE DOCTRINE

Major Affirmations

"In the beginning, God created the heavens and the earth" (Gen. 1:1). This original creation, fashioned according to the divine design, was "very good" (1:31). It was fruitful, lush, beautiful, and in harmony with the first human beings, to whom was given the responsibility to work and keep it (2:8–9, 15). It redounded flawlessly to the glory of God.

Tragically, Adam and Eve rebelled against God. As a punishment for their fall into sin, God cursed the creation: no longer would it be a hospitable place in which they would dwell, and its productivity would be severely compromised (Gen. 3:17–19, 23–24). From that woeful point and continuing today, the creation is not what it is supposed to be. And it yearns for renewal.

Though the creation was not willingly subjected to futility, God rendered it unproductive as a consequence of human sinfulness. This marred creation's future is closely linked to the ultimate salvation of sinful humanity. When the redeemed people of God are fully set free from sin and corruption, then the creation will also be restored to its pristine condition. It will once again be fruitful, lush, beautiful, and in harmony with human beings. It will once again redound immaculately to the glory of God.

This renewal of the heaven and the earth is the ultimate hope of all that exists. According to one view, this consummation will be the same cosmos as the present one, but transformed by purging and purification. According to another view, this new universe will emerge after the entire destruction of the current heaven and earth. In any case, the eternal state of the new heaven and new earth is the ultimate future hope and blessing, to the glory of God.

Biblical Support

To counteract the devastation of creation due to sin, the Old Testament presents a hope for God to do something new: He will renew his people. He will establish a new covenant. He even promises, "For behold, I create new heavens and a new earth, and the former things shall not be remembered or come into mind" (Isa. 65:17). The promise focuses on the renewal of human existence, which is purged of weeping, death, unproductive work, and pain in childbirth (65:18–24)—a reversal of the original curses (Gen. 3:14–19). Still, it portrays an about-face for the physical creation as well: "The wolf and the lamb shall graze together; the lion shall eat straw like the ox, and dust shall be the serpent's food. They shall not hurt or destroy in all my holy mountain" (Isa. 65:25). This hope, too, is a reversal of the curse that God placed on his creation (Gen. 3:17–19).

Paul addresses this curse on creation (Rom. 8:18–25). Though his discussion centers on the ultimate salvation of human beings, he parallels the creation's present yearning for freedom from corruption with redeemed humanity's current longing for release from sin and suffering. Paul underscores that it was not the creation that sinned and thus merited divine judgment. Rather, reflecting on Genesis 3:17–19, he explains that the creation was subjected to the divine curse as a punishment for human sin. Accordingly, the redemption of the creation is closely tied to the redemption of fallen human beings: when they will be fully redeemed, the creation will be fully renewed.

How this renewal of creation will occur is a matter of minor debate. In line with 2 Peter 3:7–13, some believe that this present universe will be completely destroyed by fire, then replaced by a brand-new cosmos. Peter speaks of the current heaven and earth being "stored up for fire" such that "the heavens will pass away with a roar, and the heavenly bodies will be burned up and dissolved, and the earth and the works that are done on it will be exposed." If "the heavens will be set on fire and dissolved, and the heavenly bodies will melt as they burn," the expectation is annihilation of the present universe. Thus, a fiery destruction of all that exists will be followed by the new heaven and the new earth.

In line with Psalm 102:25–27, others maintain that God will alter or change the existing universe, not destroy and replace it with a new one. Moreover, 2 Peter 3:7–10 parallels the future judgment of fire with the ancient judgment of water when God sent the flood. That watery judgment did not annihilate the existing world. Likewise, the fiery judgment will not totally destroy what currently exists. Indeed, the expectation is not *another* heaven and *another* earth, but a *new* heaven and a *new* earth.

When this renewal of creation will occur is also a matter of minor debate. Both amillennialism and postmillennialism maintain that following the return of Christ, the resurrection, and the last judgment, the eternal state will begin. That is, there will be no millennium between Christ's return and the new heaven and the new earth. Premillennialism, in both its historical and dispensational varieties, holds that Christ will return to earth and establish his kingdom for a thousand years. After this millennium, the eternal state will be established.

No matter how and when, the present state of the cursed creation will be reversed one day through the renewal of all that exists in the new heaven and new earth (Rev. 21:1). The people of God will experience ultimate salvation. God will once again reside in the midst of his people. His glory will be resplendent. Importantly, the new heaven and new earth will be a physical place, a renewed location in which God and his people will dwell forever.

Major Errors

1. *A spiritualizing of the new heaven and new earth such that its physicality is minimized or denied.* This gnostic view rejects the goodness of the present physical world and projects this rejection onto the future heaven and earth. But gnosticism is countered by God's creation of a good physical world. Thus, his re-creation of heaven and earth is consistent with his original design and work.

2. *The reigning secular worldview that the ultimate hope of this world is a more evolved form of it.* The biblical worldview is at great odds with the naturalistic worldview that is often associated with evolution (see chapter 12). The true ultimate hope is that God will justly put an end to this fallen world and graciously renew it.

3. *The common Christian view that the ultimate hope of believers is to die and go to be with Jesus Christ in heaven.* Some of this confusion results from the failure of the ecumenical creeds and the major Protestant confessions of faith to conclude with a statement of belief in the new heaven and new earth. Churches need to correct this oversight and present the proper object of the ultimate hope as the eternal state.

ENACTING THE DOCTRINE

Rather than stimulate speculation and unproductive "heavenly-mindedness," the hope of the new heaven and new earth should foster maturity and mission in this fallen world. Peter urges Christians to model lives of holiness and godliness and use the remaining time to call unbelievers to repentance. He further admonishes them to turn a deaf ear to scoffers who mock this hope, and to believe the divine promise while "waiting for new heavens and a new earth in which righteousness dwells" (2 Pet. 3:7–13).

What's at stake in this doctrine? The proper object of the Christian's/church's hope. Although existence in the intermediate state will be far better than our current existence, it pales in comparison with life in the new heaven and new earth. Indeed, salvation is far more than individual redemption from sin, escape from hell, and eternity in heaven. It is all-encompassing, with the redemption of the present fallen creation closely linked with the redemption of the people of God.

> ### Perennial Questions and Problematic Issues
>
> • Why don't we ever talk about this topic?
>
> • I thought that when we die, we go to heaven and live there with Christ forever.
>
> • What are the similarities and differences between the original heaven and earth and the new heaven and earth?
>
> • How does this hope for the new heaven and new earth affect our lives and church now?

As Gordon Lewis and Bruce Demarest affirm, "In glorified bodies we will enjoy a restored and improved Eden, a place of pristine beauty and unbroken fellowship. . . . The new heaven and earth will provide an environment conducive to the most precious values we now know—just and loving relationships, fellowship, beauty, and significant activity."[33]

TEACHING THE DOCTRINE

The overall goal of teaching this doctrine, the last to be treated, is to encourage people to orient properly their hope for what God will do in the future. A key element, therefore, is to elevate their vision beyond themselves as individuals, and even beyond their church, to consider the renewal of all things. A good place to start, therefore, is by posing a question for discussion: "What may we hope?"

Perhaps people have become soured to this discussion because of the weird ideas regarding end-time matters fostered by cults. Further hesitancy is spurred on by pop notions of the eternal state, with the redeemed playing harps while walking on streets of gold—activities that many consider to be boring. Help to overcome this evasion and reluctance is needed. Others may want to engage in speculation or become angered over the destruction-transformation debate. Such developments should be squelched.

Though Scripture rarely treats this topic, the only authoritative source of true knowledge about the new heaven and new earth is this revelation. Accordingly, teaching this doctrine should focus on biblical texts and provide a model of appropriate reservation and humility about this matter. By presenting the big picture, the teaching will helpfully unfold God's universal plan: to create the cosmos, permit the fall (with repercussions on the creation), redeem his people (with a close link to his creation), and ultimately consummate his will by renewing the creation.

TEACHING OUTLINE

1. The summary
2. Discussion on "What may we hope?"
3. Major affirmations (with biblical support)
   A. Creation, fall, redemption, and consummation as this story line relates to the current and future heaven and earth
   B. The debate between destruction and transformation
   C. How Christians should live in light of the hope for the new heaven and new earth
4. Major errors to avoid
   A. Spiritualizing the new heaven and new earth such that its physicality is minimized or denied
   B. Agreeing with the reigning secular worldview that the ultimate hope of this world is a more evolved form of it
   C. Believing that the ultimate hope of believers is to die and go to be with Jesus Christ in heaven
5. Enacting the doctrine
   A. Fostering maturity and mission in this fallen world because of the hope of the new heaven and new earth
   B. Having this eternal state as the proper object of hope

RESOURCES

Allison, *Theological Terms*, s.v. "new heaven and new earth"

Elwell, *Evangelical Dictionary of Theology*, s.vv. "New Creation, New Creature," "New Heavens and New Earth"

Erickson, *Christian Theology*, chap. 58

Grenz, *Theology for the Community of God*, chap. 23

Grudem, *Systematic Theology*, chap. 57

Horton, *Pilgrim Theology*, chap. 19

Thoennes, *Life's Biggest Questions*, chap. 16

NOTES

1. Gregg R. Allison, *The Baker Compact Dictionary of Theological Terms* (Grand Rapids: Baker Books, 2016).

2. Gregg R. Allison, *Historical Theology: An Introduction to Christian Doctrine* (Grand Rapids: Zondervan, 2011).

3. This list has been taken from Gregg R. Allison, "The *Corpus Theologicum* of the Church and Presumptive Authority," in *Revisioning, Renewing, Rediscovering the Triune Center: Essays in Honor of Stanley J. Grenz*, ed. Derek J. Tidball, Brian S. Harris, and Jason S. Sexton (Eugene, OR: Cascade, 2014), 324.

4. Paul Feinberg, "The Meaning of Inerrancy," in *Inerrancy*, ed. Norman L. Geisler (Grand Rapids: Zondervan, 1980), 294.

5. Timothy Ward, *Words of Life: Scripture as the Living and Active Word of God* (Downers Grove, IL: IVP Academic, 2009), 27 (italics in original).

6. John Killinger, *Ten Things I Learned Wrong from a Conservative Church* (New York: Crossroad, 2002), 20.

7. Allison, *Historical Theology*, 82.

8. Ward, *Words of Life*, 12.

9. J. L. Austin, *How to Do Things with Words* (Cambridge, MA: Harvard University Press, 1962); Kevin Vanhoozer, *First Theology: God, Scripture and Hermeneutics* (Downers Grove, IL: InterVarsity, 2002), chaps. 5–6; Ward, *Words of Life*, 56–60.

10. Ward, *Words of Life*, 27 (italics in original).

11. Augustine, *On the Trinity* 1.4.7, in *A Select Library of Nicene and Post-Nicene Fathers of the Christian Church*, 1st series, ed. Philip Schaff, vol. 3, *St. Augustin: On the Holy Trinity, Doctrinal Treatises, Moral Treatises*, trans. Arthur West Haddan (repr., Grand Rapids: Eerdmans, 1978), 20.

12. Gregory of Nazianzus, *Oration* 40.41, in *A Select Library of Nicene and Post-Nicene Fathers of the Christian Church*, 2nd series, ed. Philip Schaff and Henry Wace, vol. 7, *Cyril of Jerusalem, Gregory of Nazianzen*, trans. Charles G. Browne and James E. Swallow (repr., Grand Rapids: Eerdmans, 1983), 375.

13. Irenaeus, *Against Heresies* 5.28.3, in *The Ante-Nicene Fathers*, vol. 1, *The Apostolic Fathers with Justin Martyr and Irenaeus*, ed. and trans. Alexander Roberts and James Donaldson (1885; repr., Grand Rapids, Eerdmans, n.d.), 557.

14. One version of theistic evolution holds that God created matter and after that did not guide or intervene to cause any empirically detectable change in the natural behavior of matter until all living things had evolved by purely natural processes. Another variety believes that God acted at three junctures: to bring the universe into existence, to inaugurate biotic life (living creatures), and to form the first human being in the divine image (perhaps employing culturally advanced pre-Adamic hominids like *Homo erectus*). Another version maintains that God created all living things with the capability of evolving according to his design. Still another variety appeals to some general divine guidance of the process of natural selection. For further discussion, see J. P. Moreland, Stephen C. Meyer, Christopher Shaw, and Wayne Grudem, eds., *Theistic Evolution: A Scientific, Philosophical, and Theological Critique* (Wheaton: Crossway, 2017).

15. J. Richard Middleton, *The Liberating Image: The* Imago Dei *in Genesis 1* (Grand Rapids: Brazos, 2005).

16. John Calvin, *Institutes of the Christian Religion*, ed. John T. McNeill, trans. Ford Lewis Battles, Library of Christian Classics (Philadelphia: Westminster, 1960), 1.1.1 (1:35).

17. I have rendered the Chalcedonian Creed in clearer language for contemporary readers.

18. Gregory of Nazianzus, *Letters* 102, in *A Select Library of Nicene and Post-Nicene Fathers of the Christian Church*, 2nd series, ed. Philip Schaff and Henry Wace, vol. 7, *Cyril of Jerusalem, Gregory of Nazianzen*, trans. Charles G. Browne and James E. Swallow (repr., Grand Rapids: Eerdmans, 1983), 443–45; cf. Gregory of Nazianzus, *Orations* 29.19, in Schaff and Wace, *Cyril of Jerusalem*, 308.

19. Eusebius, *Ecclesiastical History* 1.3.8, in *A Select Library of Nicene and Post-Nicene Fathers of the Christian Church*, 2nd series, ed. Philip Schaff and Henry Wace, vol. 1, *Eusebius: Church History, Life of Constantine the Great, and Oration in Praise of Constantine*, trans. Arthur Cushman McGiffert (repr., Grand Rapids: Eerdmans, 1982), 86.

20. Calvin, *Institutes of the Christian Religion*, 2.15 (1:494–503).

21. Augustine, *On the Trinity* 1.4.7, in *A Select Library of Nicene and Post-Nicene Fathers of the Christian Church*, 1st series, ed. Philip Schaff, vol. 3, *St. Augustin: On the Holy Trinity, Doctrinal Treatises, Moral Treatises*, trans. Arthur West Haddan (repr., Grand Rapids: Eerdmans, 1978), 20.

22. John Murray, *Redemption: Accomplished and Applied* (Grand Rapids: Eerdmans, 1955), 161.

23. Augustine, *Enchiridion on Faith, Hope, and Love*, chap. 32, in *A Select Library of the Nicene and Post-Nicene Fathers of the Christian Church*, 1st series, ed. Philip Schaff, vol. 3, *St. Augustin: On the Holy Trinity, Doctrinal Treatises, Moral Treatises*, trans. Arthur West Haddan (repr., Grand Rapids: Eerdmans, 1978), 248.

24. Decree on Justification, chap. 7, Council of Trent, 6th session (January 13, 1547), in *The Canons and Decrees of the Sacred and Oecumenical Council of Trent*, trans. J. Waterworth (London: Dolman, 1848), https://history.hanover.edu/texts/trent/ct06.html.

25. John Stott, *The Baptism and Fullness of the Holy Spirit* (Downers Grove, IL: InterVarsity, 1969), 12 (italics in original).

26. Discussion of this doctrine is based on Gregg R. Allison, "Assurance of Salvation" and "Eternal Security," in *Evangelical Dictionary of World Missions*, ed. A. Scott Moreau (Grand Rapids: Baker Academic, 2000), 92, 318–19.

27. Wayne Grudem, *Systematic Theology: An Introduction to Biblical Doctrine* (Grand Rapids: Zondervan, 1994), 873 (italics in original have been omitted).

28. This interpretation assumes that the man whom Paul discusses in 2 Corinthians 2:6–11 is the incestuous man of 1 Corinthians 5:1–7. For support, see the comments on

2:6–11 in David E. Garland, *2 Corinthians*, New American Commentary 29 (Nashville: Broadman & Holman, 1999).

29. For example, see the *Catechism of the Catholic Church*, §§1127–28.

30. See, for example, James K. A. Smith, *Desiring the Kingdom: Worship, Worldview, and Cultural Formation*, Cultural Liturgies 1 (Grand Rapids: Baker Academic, 2009).

31. Michael Horton, *People and Place: A Covenant Ecclesiology* (Louisville: Westminster John Knox, 2008), 44.

32. Nondispensationalism rarely calls this event the "rapture," to distinguish its position from the "secret rapture" view of dispensationalism.

33. Gordon R. Lewis and Bruce A. Demarest, *Integrative Theology*, 3 vols. in 1 (Grand Rapids: Zondervan, 1996), 3:469.

FOR FURTHER READING

PART 1 DOCTRINE OF THE WORD OF GOD

DeYoung, Kevin. *Taking God at His Word: Why the Bible Is Knowable, Necessary, and Enough, and What That Means for You and Me*. Wheaton: Crossway, 2014.

Frame, John. *The Doctrine of the Word of God*. A Theology of Lordship 4. Phillipsburg, NJ: P&R, 2010.

Ward, Timothy. *Words of Life: Scripture as the Living and Active Word of God*. Downers Grove, IL: IVP Academic, 2009.

PART 2 DOCTRINE OF GOD

Frame, John. *The Doctrine of God*. A Theology of Lordship 2. Phillipsburg, NJ: P&R, 2002.

Packer, J. I. *Knowing God*. Downers Grove, IL: InterVarsity, 1993.

Reeves, Michael. *Delighting in the Trinity: An Introduction to the Christian Faith*. Downers Grove, IL: InterVarsity, 2012.

Sanders, Fred. *The Deep Things of God: How the Trinity Changes Everything*. 2nd ed. Wheaton: Crossway, 2017.

PART 3 DOCTRINE OF GOD'S CREATURES

Cooper, John W. *Body, Soul, and Life Everlasting: Biblical Anthropology and the Monism-Dualism Debate*. Grand Rapids: Eerdmans, 1989.

Hoekema, Anthony A. *Created in God's Image*. Grand Rapids: Eerdmans, 1986.

Plantinga, Cornelius, Jr. *Not the Way It's Supposed to Be: A Breviary of Sin*. Grand Rapids: Eerdmans, 1995.

PART 4 DOCTRINE OF GOD THE SON

Letham, Robert. *The Work of Christ*. Contours of Christian Theology. Downers Grove, IL: InterVarsity, 1993.

Macleod, Donald. *The Person of Christ*. Contours of Christian Theology. Downers Grove, IL: InterVarsity, 1998.

Reeves, Michael. *Rejoicing in Christ*. Downers Grove, IL: InterVarsity, 2015.

Stott, John. *The Cross of Christ*. 20th anniversary ed. Downers Grove, IL: InterVarsity, 2006.

Wellum, Stephen J. *God the Son Incarnate: The Doctrine of Christ*. Foundations of Evangelical Theology. Wheaton: Crossway, 2016.

PART 5 DOCTRINE OF GOD THE HOLY SPIRIT

Cole, Graham A. *He Who Gives Life: The Doctrine of the Holy Spirit*. Foundations of Evangelical Theology. Wheaton: Crossway, 2007.

Ferguson, Sinclair B. *Holy Spirit*. Contours of Christian Theology. Downers Grove, IL: InterVarsity, 1997.

Horton, Michael. *Rediscovering the Holy Spirit: God's Perfecting Presence in Creation, Redemption, and Everyday Life*. Grand Rapids: Zondervan, 2017.

PART 6 DOCTRINE OF SALVATION

Demarest, Bruce. *The Cross and Salvation: The Doctrine of the Church*. Foundations of Evangelical Theology. Wheaton: Crossway, 1997.

Murray, John. *Redemption Accomplished and Applied*. 1955. Reprint with foreword by Carl Trueman, Grand Rapids: Eerdmans, 2015.

Vickers, Brian. *Justification by Grace through Faith: Finding Freedom from Legalism, Lawlessness, Pride, and Despair*. Explorations in Biblical Theology. Phillipsburg, NJ: P&R, 2013.

PART 7 DOCTRINE OF THE CHURCH

Allison, Gregg R. *Sojourners and Strangers: The Doctrine of the Church*. Foundations of Evangelical Theology. Wheaton: Crossway, 2012.

Clowney, Edmund. *The Church*. Contours of Christian Theology. Downers Grove, IL: InterVarsity, 1995.

Hammet, John. *Biblical Foundations for Baptist Churches: A Contemporary Ecclesiology*. Grand Rapids: Kregel, 2005.

Horton, Michael. *People and Place: A Covenant Ecclesiology*. Louisville: Westminster John Knox, 2008.

PART 8 DOCTRINE OF FUTURE THINGS

Alcorn, Randy. *Heaven*. Carol Stream, IL: Tyndale, 2004.

Erickson, Millard J. *A Basic Guide to Eschatology: Making Sense of the Millennium*. Grand Rapids: Baker, 1998.

Peterson, Robert. *Hell on Trial: The Case for Eternal Punishment*. Phillipsburg, NJ: P&R, 1995.

SCRIPTURE INDEX

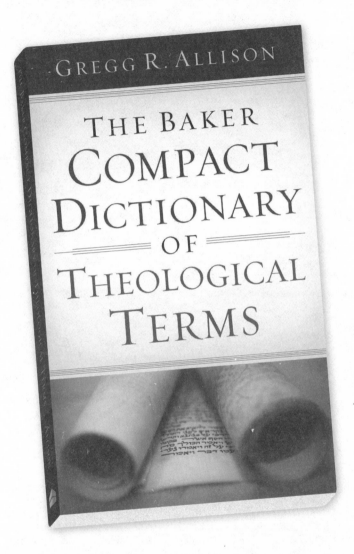